Is Oedipus Online?

Siting Freud after Freud

Jerry Aline Flieger

THE MIT PRESS   CAMBRIDGE, MASSACHUSETTS   LONDON, ENGLAND

This book was set in Copperplate 33bc and Joanna by Graphic Composition, Inc., and was printed and bound in the United States of America.

MIT Press books may be purchased at special quantity discounts for business or sales promotional use. For information, please email special_sales@mitpress.mit.edu or write to Special Sales Department, The MIT Press, 5 Cambridge Center, Cambridge, MA 02142.

Library of Congress Cataloging-in-Publication Data

Flieger, Jerry Aline, 1947–
    Is Oedipus online? siting Freud after Freud / Jerry Aline Flieger
        p. cm. — (Short circuits)
    Includes bibliographical references and index.
    ISBN 0-262-56207-3 (pbk. : alk. paper)
    1. Psychoanalysis and culture. 2. Freud, Sigmund, 1865–1939. 3. Lacan, Jacques, 1901–
I. Title. II. Series.

BF175.4.C84F65 2005
150.19′52—dc22

                                                                                    2004055170

10 9 8 7 6 5 4 3 2 1

For my mother, Betty Jane Flieger

CONTENTS

A short circuit occurs when there is a faulty connection in the network—faulty, of course, from the standpoint of the network's smooth functioning. Is not the shock of short-circuiting, therefore, one of the best metaphors for a critical reading? Is not one of the most effective critical procedures to cross wires that do not usually touch: to take a major classic (text, author, notion), and read it in a short-circuiting way, through the lens of a "minor" author, text, or conceptual apparatus ("minor" should be understood here in Deleuze's sense: not "of lesser quality," but marginalized, disavowed by the hegemonic ideology, or dealing with a "lower," less dignified topic)? If the minor reference is well chosen, such a procedure can lead to insights which completely shatter and undermine our common perceptions. This is what Marx, among others, did with philosophy and religion (short-circuiting philosophical speculation through the lens of political economy, that is to say, economic speculation); this is what Freud and Nietzsche did with morality (short-circuiting the highest ethical notions through the lens of the unconscious libidinal economy). What such a reading achieves is not a simple "desublimation," a reduction of the higher intellectual content to its lower economic or libidinal cause; the aim of such an approach is, rather, the inherent decentering of the interpreted text, which brings to light its "unthought," its disavowed presuppositions and consequences.

And this is what "Short Circuits" wants to do, again and again. The underlying premise of the series is that Lacanian psychoanalysis is a privileged instrument of such an approach, whose purpose is to illuminate a standard text or ideological formation, making it readable in a totally new way—the long history of Lacanian interventions in philosophy, religion, the arts (from the visual arts to the cinema, music, and literature), ideology, and politics justifies this premise. This, then, is not a new series of books on psychoanalysis, but a series of "connections in the Freudian field"—of short Lacanian interventions in art, philosophy, theology, and ideology.

"Short Circuits" intends to revive a practice of reading which confronts a classic text, author, or notion with its own hidden presuppositions, and thus reveals its disavowed truth. The basic criterion for the texts that will be published is that they effectuate such a theoretical short circuit. After reading a book in this series, the reader should not simply have learned something new: the point is, rather, to make him or her aware of another—disturbing—side of something he or she knew all the time.

Slavoj Žižek

Acknowledgments

An interdisciplinary project of this scope has required extensive research and travel, and I am grateful to several institutions for making this possible. I would like to thank Rutgers University for consistently encouraging interdisciplinary projects outside conventional fields of research. The Department of French and the Program in Comparative Literature have been particularly supportive, by providing funds for travel and opportunities to teach theory courses not limited to literary theory. The group of graduate students who have worked with me on topics related to this book—through five long years of seminars on Freud and culture—deserve special thanks. Their enthusiasm for this project has buoyed me throughout the long process of research and writing.

Many colleagues have been equally helpful. In particular, I wish to thank Fredric Jameson, Slavoj Žižek, John Higgins, Ian Buchanan, my friend and editor the late Elizabeth Wright, and Edmond Wright for encouraging this research and the publication of my work. This project has provided extensive contact with scholars worldwide, and I am grateful to the institutions and colleagues who have invited me to visit and to teach. Specifically, I wish to thank David Bennett and the Department of English at the University of Melbourne for sponsoring my research grant as visiting scholar in 2000; as well as Ian Buchanan for his invitations to speak in Tasmania and at the Deleuze conference in Western Australia. In the same year, Hisashi Muroi and Hiroshi Yoshioka arranged for me to meet scholars and researchers in Japan at Yokohama University, Konan University in Kyoto, Tokyo University, and the Japanese Institute for Media Arts and Science (IMAS). These visits provided fascinating opportunities to study media art and culture in Asia, and to exchange ideas with people in Japan who are engaged in related work. I also wish to thank Ranjit Nair and Shiva K. Srinivasan for arranging my visit to

India in 2000, where I met many interesting scientists and theorists at the India Institute of Technology and at the Institute for the Foundation of Science and Culture in Delhi. In the People's Republic of China, Wang Ning and his colleagues at the Universities of Beijing and Nanjing provided invaluable opportunities to exchange ideas at conferences on East-West cultural relations and cultural theory. I also wish to thank Antal Bokay and the Soros foundation for sponsoring my graduate seminar on "millennialism" at Janos Pannonius University in Hungary. Finally, I wish to thank the Slovenian art review *Maska*, and the Department of Philosophy at Ljubljana University, for sponsoring my 2003 visit to Slovenia.

The actual writing of this book began with a paper at the international 1996 Cyberconf in Spain, sponsored by the Telefonica corporation, so I am especially grateful to the organizers Susie Ramsey, Rosanne Stone, and Rafael Lorenzo-Hammer. Meeting the theorists and performance artists who participated in that weeklong event in Madrid was an unforgettable experience that has shaped my work ever since. My friends and colleagues in South Africa also deserve particular thanks—especially John Higgins, John Noyes, and Reingard Nethersole and the "hard-thinking gang" at Cape Town—for inviting me to visit and teach at the University of Cape Town, University of the Western Cape, University of the Witwatersrand, and Rhodes University. Finally, I am grateful for the many opportunities that Norman Holland's group IPSA has provided for contacts with people working on psychoanalysis and culture in Russia and Western Europe, including Robert Silhol's group in France. These intellectual opportunities abroad have contributed enormously to this work and have shaped my assessment of global culture in this "bimillennial" era.

I am equally indebted to friends and colleagues in this country for their help in the research and writing of this book, and to Roger Conover, Slavoj Žižek, and my editors at MIT for their patience and generosity in bringing the project to fruition. For their contribution to my knowledge of the clinical practice of psychoanalysis and its relation to culture, I wish to thank the organizers and participants of the ongoing seminar at the Cornell University Medical School's Department of the History of Psychiatry. I also need to express special thanks to Manuel De Landa, who was a peerless resource when I was thinking about the scientific aspects of this project. Special thanks also go to my friends Christopher Lane, Martha Noel Evans, and John Bloom for their useful intellectual and editorial feedback during the writing process.

I wish to thank the University of Minnesota geology website for permission to include and refer to their topological models. Rob Scharein—designer of the Knot Plot website—generously provided help to my illustrator with visual models in knot theory. I would also like to acknowledge the hard work of my computer illustrator, Roger Groce, who took on many difficult challenges.

Finally, I want to express heartfelt gratitude to my dear friends Sandi Fellman and Claudia Jadlocki, who provided their own artwork for this book and whose artistic vision helped shape its ideas. I am equally grateful for the emotional and intellectual support of my friends Linda Gillman, Christopher Lane, Martha Noel Evans, Josephine Diamond, Sandi Fellman, and my "second family" Mary Shaw and François Cornilliat, and their children Ben, Elizabeth, and Pierre, who have kept me going through the long process of completing Is Oedipus Online?

I am deeply grateful for the love and support of my own family: my mother, David and Juliana, Richard and Joyce, my nephews Joe, Ken, David, Rick and his new family Kelly and Mark, and my niece Lauren. I could not have completed this work without them.

Above all, I am thankful for my parents, who taught me to look and to wonder.

This book is dedicated to my mother, Betty Jane Flieger, and to the memory of my father, Verle J. Flieger.

IS OEDIPUS ONLINE?

INTRODUCTION

FORWARDING FREUD:
NODAL POINT AS HYPERTEXT

Like Freud's mythic antihero—itinerant and clever, but all-too-human—today's global citizens are good at deciphering enigmas, even at cracking the code of human life itself. But Freud's reading of Oedipus reminds us to be wary about mistaking transit for progress, and information for wisdom.

Like the king who knew too much and too little, we find ourselves at a crossroads where discoveries present new dilemmas. As in the tale of Oedipus—prefaced by the oracle's clear warning, with a hitch—events today often seem to be subject to a cosmic catch, caught in a time warp of looped cause and effect. Many emerging cultural phenomena no longer seem subject to linear chronology (as shown by the escalating conflict between ancient and modern belief systems in the post-9/11 world), and facts are not all that matter.

Yet, of course, nonlinear phenomena are not unique to our era. Over a century ago Freud was already describing psychic reality in nonlinear terms, as an effect of Nachträglichkeit (aftereffect), whereby causes sometimes emerge only after their symptoms are manifest.[1] In spite of the farsightedness of Freud's vision, however, the question now is whether his twentieth-century paradigm, describing human experience as an effect of desire, is still relevant to the techno-cultural tangles of the new millennium.

Like the legend of Oedipus, then, this book is about trials, ciphers, and drives—conscious and unconscious, hard and soft. It is also about intersections, staging an encounter between psychoanalysis and the new century. The four chapters of part I, "Resiting Oedipus," begin by engaging the work of a number of major millennial theorists—particularly Lyotard, Žižek, Deleuze, Virilio, Baudrillard, and Haraway—in order to refute the assumption that we are living in a "post-oedipal" world where Freud's founding paradigm no longer has purchase. The four chapters of part II, "Freud Sightings in Millennial Theory," go on to suggest that an upgraded oedipal paradigm may in fact coincide with and elucidate new paradigms in science and culture, such as fractality, emergence, and topological modeling. In other words, Is Oedipus Online? is intended to test the viability of "Freud" in light of the new realities of the twenty-first century, both by responding to prominent critics of psychoanalytic theory today, and by suggesting a Freudian take on the psychical impact of these seismic shifts.

Hence the question: Is Oedipus online?

Twenty-first Century as (Para-) Site

The issue of the relevance of Oedipus today is embedded in two larger questions: the status of the Freudian unconscious as determinant of the human, and the fate of "human being" in the new era. These questions intersect at our unique historical *site* (*sitos/seed*): we experience our moment in time as a locale, a juncture self-consciously situated at the end of one century and the beginning of another. Many of our current preoccupations—such as the global economy, the information network, the borderless war—are characterized by a rhetoric of shifting site and systemic linkage. In fact our era might qualify as a *para*-site, literally a "site beside itself," where modern and postmodern concerns are mutually refracted across the millennial divide.

But just as our age is para-sitic, it is also literally para-noiac, the era of the hyperconscious human *mind beside itself*. In this time of warp-speed advances in knowledge, the species anxiously contemplates itself, wondering just what human being is and where it is going. The current debate over the ethics of human cloning, for instance, bears out Freud's observation of the spooky effect of doubling, as something uncanny (*unheimlich*)—literally *unhomelike*, alien. The anxiety of our self-scrutiny is exacerbated by uncanny scientific discoveries, such as the multiple dimensions extending beyond (or coiled within) our meager four dimensions in space-time. Little wonder that human beings are increasingly on edge: just as we have begun to recognize ourselves as an infant species on a tiny parasite of one unimpressive middle-aged star, we have also had to confront the statistical near-certainty of a "para-noid" cosmos, where *minds besides ourselves* are probably out there looking back.

Meanwhile back on Earth, we are in the grip of acute anxiety about everything from corporate conspiracies, to international terror networks, to viruses lurking in our computers: today the most basic human activities—chatting, eating, breathing, lovemaking—put us at risk. Voyeurism and speculation often drive our hyperconscious culture of anxiety: commentators blame school carnage on video games; eavesdropping is hot entertainment as reality TV; and war has become a 24/7 spectacle on cable. We eye our computers with mistrust, as potential instruments of surveillance or carriers of viral contagion. (In France and England, a popular new program dubbed "Child Find" now allows parents to track their progeny's whereabouts on a screen, at any hour, as long as the child's cell phone is turned on.) And as the anthrax and unabomber attacks have demonstrated, in this grave new world even our real mail, delivered by unwitting carriers, may harbor a lethal message.

Given this pervasive climate of paranoia, it is perhaps worthwhile to revisit the Y2K crisis as a liminal event in the age of anxiety, even if it now seems remote. It was not after all so long ago that the entire wired world held its breath on New Year's Eve, as the midnight hour marched across twenty-four time zones. Yet in spite of live coverage, this countdown had a spectral quality, since the crisis consisted of *speculation* around a *projection* of *possible* problems that *might* be triggered by an *unreal* event, an arbitrary date determined centuries ago by Christian cosmology.

The fantasmatic character of this crisis, as ironic as any oracle, became evident as the event drew near: officials fretted about the effects of the public perception of the threat, more than the actual impact of real computer glitches. As we approached the moment of truth, the media buzzed with forecasts of shortages from hoarding, or predictions of an epidemic of shootings by a jumpy gunpacking citizenry, or warnings about financial collapse resulting from a larger-than-usual withdrawal of cash from ATMs on December 31.

The morning after, in spite of forecasts of TEOTWAWKI (cyberspeak for The End Of The World As We Know It), the human race was still here. But the Y2K bug proved resilient, mutating into the morning-after rumor that the whole business had been a plot to sell high-tech security software. The irony is rich: precisely because the crisis did not materialize, we can never know whether the threat was as dire as the oracles feared, or merely another way for computer-makers to make money selling Y2K-compliant hardware to all-too-compliant consumers. The same irony now marks the repeated official proclamations of a state of highest alert in the United States, when terrorist attacks do not in fact materialize.

In any case, conventional paradigms no longer seem to provide adequate psychic mooring in today's escape-velocity culture. One NASA physicist recently registered the magnitude of millennial shock in the sciences, when he responded to a question about the implications of the acceleration of particles beyond the speed of light: "This changes *Everything.*" The geopolitical scene is marked by another seismic divide (before and after 9/11), whose psychic impact first centered on a specific site—ground zero—but which now radiates in ever-expanding circles, serving as the rationale for an ever-escalating, if unlocalizable, "borderless war."

The sheer number of commentaries on "paranoid," "manic," and "panic" culture today suggests that we are living in an age where Freudian terms still have resonance. In *Technologies of the Gendered Body: Reading Cyborg Women*, Anne Balsamo has coined the term "panic postmodernism" to describe the pandemic of alarm, while Teresa Brennan (*History after Lacan*) has called our era "the age of anxiety."[2] The list of recommendations which an online bookseller recently supplied "just for me" are telling: *The Pyrotechnic Insanitarium: American Culture on the Brink; Hystories: Hysterical Epidemics and Modern Media; Flame Wars; Apocalypse Culture; The Plague of Fantasies; Art and Fear; Ground Zero; The Information Bomb; How We Became Posthuman; One World Ready or Not: The Manic Logic of Global Capitalism;* and last but not least, *"I Am Not Sick I Don't Need Help."* This recent list, updated every time I sign on, ends with a slew of works analyzing the increasing hostility between *The American Enemy* (Philippe Roger, from France) and just about everyone else. In a more whimsical if equally dystopian mode, the site publicizes a number of sensationalist works analyzing the erotics of robocopulation and the ascendancy of virtual sex. Not only is the apocalyptic tenor of this list alarming, but its mere appearance on my screen is paranoia-inducing: based on surveillance of my online buying habits, it reminds me not so subtly that I will never be caught up on the reading that "similar customers have purchased."

Judging from the sheer volume of references to anxiety and hysteria in contemporary discourse, it seems that if Freud did not exist we would have to invent him.

FREUD'S Y2K BUG

In spite of the currency of psychoanalytic terms in contemporary discourse, "Freud" as institution and icon is undeniably suffering from his own Y2K crisis. These days hardly a season goes by without the appearance of a bestseller on *Why Freud Was Wrong* (Richard Webster) or another account of *The Freud Wars* (John Forrester).[3] Although venerated on nearly every "greatest thinkers of the last millennium" list, Freud is nonetheless often dismissed as an intellectual dinosaur whose theory is governed by modern concepts that no longer fit a post-postmodern scheme.

Post-Freudian thought ranges from the benign classification of psychoanalysis as a step in the history of ideas, noteworthy but passé; to the characterization of psychoanalysis as a culturally bound production that invents its own objects and manipulates its own findings; to the rejection of the notion of the unconscious in favor of a strict biologism preferring brain to mind (Hobson, D'Souza).[4] Freud gets criticized not just by those eager to trade the analytic couch for the laboratory examining-table, but also by those nostalgic for the good old days of High Culture, who inculpate psychoanalysis in everything from the erosion of civilized mores to the lack of rigorous grading standards in the academy.

Nor do the Freud-bashers hesitate to question the ethical and intellectual legitimacy of the Father of Psychoanalysis himself. The title of an oft-cited article dating back some decades—"Was Freud a Liar?"—shows that this is not a new debate.[5] In fact, Gilles Deleuze spearheaded the attack in theory circles decades ago with *Anti-Oedipus* (1972), accusing Freud's own antihero—mythical Oedipus shows how *not* to "work through" human dilemmas—of collusion with capitalism, racism, and patriarchy.[6] Michel Foucault joined the onslaught with *The History of Sexuality* (1976), charging that Freud invented a prurient *scientia sexualis* that actually engenders the sexual symptoms it studies.[7] And almost since the inception of psychoanalysis, some feminists have labeled Father Freud a misogynist patriarch who invented, or induced, hysteria. Some even accuse him of being a mesmerizer, a sleazy drug-addled seducer, who polluted his female patients with implanted memories.[8] In our own day, Freud is the object of increasingly acrid ad hominem attacks, often from former disciples such as Frederick Crews, who depicts his one-time idol as a self-aggrandizing guru preaching a vatic "theosophy" of scant intellectual value.[9]

Several of the best-known anti-Freudians of late (Allen Esterson, Morton Schatzman, Elaine Showalter, Peter Swales) hold Freud responsible for the excesses of the recovered-memory movement—as well as the appearance of pandemic hysteria with symptoms ranging from fantasies of alien abduction to Satanism to chronic fatigue syndrome.[10] Conversely, some critics hold Freud responsible for *not* believing in the recovered memories of patients, and thus failing to honor the testimony of incest victims.

As the man many intellectuals love to hate, Freud is getting it from all sides.

Nor has "French Freud" proved immune to ethical objections: the work of Jacques Lacan—the *enfant terrible* of psychoanalysis—has been indicted for phallocentrism and religiosity by everyone from Derrida ("The Purveyor of Truth") to Irigaray (*This Sex Which Is Not One*).[11] More recently, Judith Butler (*Bodies That Matter*) has added charges of heterosexism to the litany of reproach.[12] As if this were not enough, psychoanalysis has been confronted of late by a rash of criticisms with a postcolonial/postmodern turn, often charging that Freud is inattentive to cultural difference. Since the appearance decades ago of the canonical works on postmodernism by Jean-François Lyotard and Fredric Jameson, it has been conventional to associate modernism with depth and postmodernism with surface, in terms of both the object of study and the methods deployed.[13] In this dichotomy, Freud is invariably sited as a modern, the inventor of a depth psychology that has been superseded by postmodern surface-oriented theories emphasizing contact and cognition, synapse and network. In the cross-sites between modernism and its afterlife, Freud is often cast as a visionary who plumbed the depths of the human psyche, but one whose notion of depth has gone as deep as it can go. Did psychoanalysis come stamped with an expired "use by" date, circa 2000?

In this book, I raise that question in light of three distinct tendencies in the field of critical theory today: the discrediting of Freudo-Lacanian thought in many intellectual circles; the ascendancy of the field of cultural studies in the university; and the prevalent paranoid tenor of much cultural commentary today. We do indeed seem to be living in a panic culture, with panic construed both literally (as global) and figuratively (as hysterical). To the list of millennial symptoms we may now add post-traumatic stress disorder, perpetuated electronically by endlessly looped images of "shock and awe," terrorist attack, war and carnage.

On the ideational front, Freud himself still seems to cause panic, eliciting attack from all sides. Yet since many of Freud's most virulent critics are former disciples, we might suspect that an "anxiety of influence" (Harold Bloom's term) is responsible for much of the anti-Freudian fervor.[14] Indeed, the vitriolic attacks may in fact be considered in terms that Freud himself contributed to cultural discourse— as examples of classic denial (Freud is *not* my intellectual father), paranoid generalization (Freud is to blame for *everything*), or intellectual hysteria (Freud reduces everything to *sex*). Oedipus himself never manifested such animus against the Father.

Yet even when his speculations are outlandish, Freud is never *simply* wrong: many of the cutting-edge works that purport to be anti- or post-Freud are in fact deeply indebted to Freud's insights. And the ethical objections to Freud tend to overlook the fact that the most controversial issues in psychoanalysis—such as the erotics of the analytic transference—are raised in Freud's own work. As for the challenge from neurobiology, we need to recall that Freud himself believed that there was a somatic correlate to every psychic symptom he described; he fully expected psychoanalysis to be revised in light of future medical findings. (Indeed, recent neurological research by Mark Solms and others—locating dream activity in the brain regions governing figural representation and latent memory, isolated from regions devoted to judgment—actually vindicates Freud's views about the qualitatively different work being performed by primary and secondary process.)

Whatever their motivation, attacks charging Freud with personal arrogance or scientific error miss the point. More important than the rightness or wrongness of any of Freud's theoretical speculations is the fact that his thought encourages us to question rigidly held truths as inherently suspect in their motivation, thus opening a field for debate and revision. It is in Freud's spirit, then, that we may temper the manifold critiques with a reconsideration of the pertinence of psychoanalysis to cultural theory in the new century.

Perhaps if Freud may be upgraded to Y2K compliance—an effort with which he would almost certainly sympathize—his work may yet provide valuable insight on the bewildering issues confronting us today. "Freud" is not simply a modern depth psychology, digging for answers; it is also a postmodern topology, searching for ramified links, *cathexes*. Psychoanalytic method complicates our assumptions not only by delving under the surface, but also by extending the search along many paths, hooking up depth psychology to a network of sites in cultural studies, philosophy, and science.

FROM SUBTEXT TO HYPERTEXT: IS OEDIPUS "COMPLEX"?

The figure of Oedipus has always evoked mythical archetypes of wanderer and sleuth, but he also resembles our twenty-first-century Internet avatars, the bots or search engines that allow us to maneuver around unfamiliar domains. "Oedipus" might even serve as an emblem of human being on trial, a species work-in-progress. Recasting Oedipus in the role of a cyberspace icon or screen identity—Oedipus Internaut—might also help reconceptualize psychoanalysis as a program of sorts, a navigation device for the twenty-first-century subject. In other words, the oedipal process of intersubjective linkage—Oedipus Interknot?—may serve as a hypertext link of sorts, embedded in any number of cultural sites. But the founding Freudian myth has another vector as well. Rather than remaining typecast as the action hero of family psychodrama, "Oedipus" may be recast as an "engineering diagram" (Gilles Deleuze's term), a paradigm for any number of socializing processes by which human beings become human. To be sure, Freudo-Lacanian theory considers the human subject as a node: a site linked by intersubjective desire to a network of human others, as indicated by the famous Lacanian aphorism "[Human] Desire is the desire of the Other."[15] Even in Freud's earliest work, the patient's symptom is called a *nodal point*, a dense knot of over-determined experiences and desires. This suggests that twenty-first-century oedipal theory need not be confined to family romance, but may be extended to other instances of interlinked desire, whether operating in an individual or in a population, online or off.

In a sense, Freud's nodal concept of symptom anticipates the concept of hypertext, the navigation device for our emerging techno-mythology. The blue lettering on our screens makes us all internauts, sending us hither and yon in cyberspace, *fort* and *da*, even while providing a string by which we can find our way back out of the labyrinth to a home page. And what is hypertext but the condensation (Freud's *Verdichtung*) of several sites into one node? What is an information string but a skein unwinding in many directions? Freud himself likens fantasy (*Wunsch*) to a threading that condenses chronologically dispersed events on a filament of psychic energy: "past, present, and future are threaded, as it were, on the string of the wish that runs through them all."[16] Nearly a century before the new physics, Freud's own string theory reconceptualized space-time, insisting on the capacity of desire to be both compacted and strung out, viscous and motile. Like Heisenberg's restless electron, which introduces uncertainty into our most carefully plotted experiments, Freudian desire is always in more than one place at a time.[17]

Freud's *Traumdeutung* also anticipates something like hypertext, since it focuses on the "umbilicus" of the dream (yet another significant knot linked to a cord). And the dream itself is characterized as a lead, "the royal road to the unconscious."[18] This umbilical node is ground zero for primary process, producing a dream scene with tentacular links to other sites. Freud also asserts that the dream imagery bypasses the rules of linear time and logic, making connections that ignore the triage of wakeful reason.

Decades before computer imaging dreamed up morphing as a technique, Freud insisted on the plasticity of the dream scene, comparing the dream to a picture puzzle, or rebus. He observed that this fluid scene displays the three telltale characteristics of unconscious processes: timelessness, absence of contradiction, and motility of cathexis. The nonchronological (timeless) dream scene that Freud describes, with its constantly shifting elements (thanks to the fluidity of unconscious desire), is impervious to judgment, absent from contradiction. The dream is also free of negation: "there is no 'no' in the unconscious." Since the dream mode stages a visual spectacle in concrete images, displayed as what is, it cannot picture what is not there. But of course the protean dream figures connect to any number of off-stage referents, including what Freud terms the "daily residue" of wakeful experience. In fact, the psychoanalytic term *cathexis* is suggestive of this netting of reference, since it means tying-on: a symptom is a knot in a web with links to multiple nodes.[19] In *The Ethics of Psychoanalysis*, Jacques Lacan devises his own term for the meshwork linking site to site within the psyche, as well as the individual psyche to multiple "others."[20] He proposes the paradigm of *Bahnungen* ("pathways," sometimes translated as "facilitation") to characterize this nodal webbing, replacing the classic mode of sequential linear reason that privileges cause and effect. Interestingly, the concept of *Bahnungen* also anticipates a prime focus of millennial science, since it figures the psyche as a *multidimensional* site. "A knot cannot make itself flat," Lacan asserts ("Un noeud ne saurait se mettre à plat"), punning on the sound of "egg" and "knot" in French to insist on the indigestible nature (the knottiness?) of human desire. (*Oeufs à plat* are eggs on a platter, sunnyside up; and because the final consonants are silent in French, the phrase rimes with *noeud à plat*, a flattened knot.) Lacan's knotty imagery is at once witty and discomfiting: like a knot in the gut, Lacanian desire refuses to lie still; it wriggles on the spot. (The unsettling image—derived from Freud's comparison of libido to an amoeba with pseudopodia—is taken up again in Lacan's comparison of *désir* to a slippery placenta that sneaks up and smothers us, not unlike a stringy alien pod of sci-fi.)[21] For Lacan, human subjects have too much on their plate to assimilate without remainder.

For all its whimsy, Lacan's notion of *Bahnungen* is also consistent with paradigms of networking in cybernetics, physics, and systems theory, as well as paradigms in poststructuralist philosophy and postmodern aesthetics. The term *Bahnungen* likewise evokes Deleuze's rhizome—a bristling system of entangled nodes. Far from constituting a linear Aristotelian narrative about a problem that may be outgrown or outwitted, the twists and trysts of the founding oedipal myth do in fact configure a rhizome in the Deleuzian sense, where "every point is connected to every other point, and must be."[22] The example of Oedipus at the crossroads also helps us to think of Lacan's *Bahnungen* as intersections: the term itself evokes an exchange, a jumping-off point, like a railway switchyard or a cloverleaf on the Autobahn. Nodes of redirection as well as juncture, *Bahnungen* may be considered sites of affordance (James Gibson's new-science term) that permit the voyager to continue along any number of potential paths.[23] Like Freud before him, Lacan often seems prescient, spinning an updated version of psychoanalytic theory that may "facilitate" the navigation of our own cultural maze. While I am not suggesting that psychoanalysis explains or even eases the posthuman condition, I think it may serve as a kind of home page for exploring the ramifications of the bimillennial mind.

The figure of Oedipus, itinerant and sleuth, seems an appropriate emblem for this "search" at the millennial cusp. After all, the oedipal tale itself emphasizes a *crucial* site, the crossroads between Thebes and Corinth, as the site of apparently random events with chaotic ramifications. In the language of twenty-first-century chaos theory, Oedipus' situation at the crossroads represents a bifurcation, and his random act is a tipping point in the destiny of embodied matter. Perhaps linking Freud's oedipal model to current epistemological paradigms may re-sight blind Oedipus, redeploying him on a mission in search of a *viable* humanity. For although "human being" is clearly plagued by its chronic shortsightedness, the species is also chronically inquisitive, out to see the (in)sights.

AT THE END OF OUR TROPE: "FIGURATION"

Following Freud's lead some three decades ago, Jean-François Lyotard (*Discours, figure*) pointed out that a dream figure has an eloquent and aesthetic plasticity. A dream image, like a poem, is subject to shaping, twisting, and rendering by the threefold effect of unconscious processes (condensation [thickening: *Verdichtung*]; displacement [shifting: *Verschiebung*]; and regression or representability the "behind-the-scenes" staging, selecting dream material that may be rendered as a visual scene [*Rucksicht auf Darstellungskeit*]).[24] In his work on jokes, Freud maintains that dream figuration is also a by-product of a regressive (as in primal or infantile) tendency of unconscious primary process to regard "words as things," opaque objects rather than transparent instruments of reference. Freud also suggests that the dream is literally regressive, because it is hallucinatory: it turns perception backward, physically *regressing* from its daytime engagement with the external world to produce images within the sleeper's psyche.

More recently, Donna Haraway has used the term "figuration" to designate actual objects as well as dream figments, giving Freud's term concrete mooring in matter, the real-life factor so often missing in the field of theory. Haraway's characterization of techno-science as a network of fetish objects (in *Modest Witness@*

Second Millennium) affords an intriguing link with Freud's stringy imagery: "Any interesting being in techno science, such as a textbook, molecule, equation, mouse pipette, bomb, fungus, technician, agitator or scientist can be teased open to show sticky economic, technical, political, mythic and textual threads."[25] Following Freud's lead, Haraway focuses on material/figural objects in popular culture, where the investment is at once ideological and economic, linking "progress" and profit. (She cites the ripe controversial figure of the genetically engineered tomato, featured in Heinz ketchup ads.) In her work, "figure" is itself a cross-sited term, its twenty-first-century use enriched by its twentieth-century intellectual history, rooted in psychoanalysis. ("Figurations are performative images that can be inhabited. Verbal or visual, figurations can be condensed maps of contestable worlds.")[26]

I draw upon Haraway's analysis of figuration, and Freud's own proclivity to wordplay, to orient this book around a homonymic pun (siting/sighting/citing). This figure of speech is an affordance, linking three activities: "siting" Freud in the emerging field of millennial theory, by "sighting" the often-invisible articulations between psychoanalysis and cultural theory, and thus "(re)citing/resighting" Oedipus in new contexts. The word "sighting" these days also has whimsical associations with dead rock stars and alien drop-ins; and no one loved a good joke more than Freud did.

Throughout this book, I figure the activity of siting/sighting/citing in a number of cultural icons that haunt millennial discourse, concrete objects that mark interconnected sites of fascination, anxiety, and fantasy: eye; gene; particle; black hole; globe; virus; screen; spacecraft; net; fractal. Such icons describe the phase space of the posthuman, sited at the permeable boundaries between human and animal, animal and machine, science and culture. The common site in which all of these fetish-figures are embedded is technology, the nodal know-how that links millennial science, philosophy, and culture. These essays are intended to facilitate the connection of these cultural knots with aspects of psychoanalytic thought. But these landing sites are springboards, docking stations rather than final destinations.

SEEING DOUBLE: FREUD'S BIMILLENNIAL SIGHT

One of the most persistent icons of the millennial era is the eye/lens, a figure that evokes knowledge as well as surveillance. This iconography is ancient, of course, dating back at least to the convention of Byzantine painting, and continuing all the way through to modern times in examples such as Magritte's famous surrealist image of a vacant eye, filled only by sky. And in today's media culture, the figure is everywhere: from the CBS trademark, to the dollar bill, to any number of film images and commercial logos. But of late the species is turning an eye back on the heavens that we have always suspected of training an eye on us, whether as the watchful deities of old or as today's bug-eyed visitors who survey us from eye-shaped craft.

We are after all living in an era where news is not only global but cosmic, and where knowledge is associated with extensions of sight. It is the era where forty billion new galaxies were discovered literally overnight by the Hubble telescope, in a single adjustment of focus by space-walking astronauts. This is the era where a scientific double-take—taking a chance second look at a modest rock (ALH8004), fifteen years after its discovery, with the aid of an electron microscope—has engendered speculation that we ourselves may have been seeded by Martian life, predating life on earth by a billion years. Of course, more recently our rovers have uncovered solid evidence of the once-humid environment on Mars, increasing the chances that the Red Planet once sustained life. These days, we humans have our eye trained on the cosmos.

Yet for more than a century now, Freud has had his eye on us. When he names "mental life" as the object of his new science, Freud invokes optical technology, describing the mind as a seeing machine, articulate and articulated: "we assume that mental life is the function of an *apparatus*, to which we ascribe the characteristics of being extended in space and of being made up of several portions—which we imagine, that is, of being a telescope or a microscope, or something of the sort."[27]

Freud is explicit: the psychoanalytic activity, unfolding the mind to study itself, is itself scopic in nature, looking inward and outward, forward and backward in time, focusing on the internal and the far-removed, mimicking the activities "of the microscope or telescope" . . . or "something of the sort." Freud's addition of "something of the sort" may justify the extension of his twentieth-century optics to the specular science of our century—space rovers, MRI machines, search engines, surveillance cameras, spy satellites, microsurgical probes, electron microscopes, reality television, nano cameras swallowed in a pill. We live in the age of the optical probe, where the human eye—its vision now sharpened by laser—is ceaselessly searching for brand-new thrills.

Significantly, Freud cites the optical prosthesis as a material *model* of knowledge, rather than a metaphor. Reflexive and reflective, his modern science proposes to contemplate the human mind through the looking glass, where the mind's projections are refracted in self-conscious analysis. After all, Freud subjected himself to the scrutiny of autoanalysis, while Lacan insisted on the importance of the gaze—considered not as metaphor but as a physical function of the embodied human eye—as the field in which every human subject is constituted.

Like Freud before him, Lacan emphasizes the specular aspect of the analytic process itself, insisting on the role of the analyst's own desire in the patient's transference.[28] This scopic desire means that the analyst's observations are not exempt from error; the analyst, by definition, wants to see, to penetrate the mystery. But Lacan insists that the expert is never more than a mirage-authority (whom he terms the "sujet supposé savoir," *the subject supposed to know*): in a sense, the analyst is merely a screen that reflects the multiple investments of the patient. Again, Freud himself was the first to evoke these multiple refractive dimensions of analysis, when he noted that there are always four people present in the consulting-room, the two principals and the patient's parents. (But of course this logic quickly overpopulates the room, like the proliferation of images in cross-reflecting mirrors. For the patient has parents who have parents who have parents . . . and so does the analyst.)

Psychoanalysis has thus opened a peculiar visual field, where an object looks back, but where it is also reflected at a carefully maintained distance, from the alien intimacy of the analytic couch. Psychoanalysis, unlike other sciences, deliberately confounds the object of scrutiny with the scrutinizer—this has ever been the drawback and the fascination of Freud's para-science, where the mind is deliberately positioned "beside itself." In the memoirs of Freud's most famous paranoid, the "Psychotic Dr. Schreber," even God is imagined as a prurient monitor linked to a subject in ecstasy: the deity is an overseeing eye, erotically invested in its creation.[29] Indeed, all of the tendencies of classical paranoia exhibited by Schreber insist in millennial discourse: scenarios of surveillance, construction of elaborate systems, projection of internal reality onto the external world. It seems that in disseminating a theory of paranoia, Freud did more than put the mind under the microscope; he also projected a highly figural self-scrutinizing text—Schreber's memoirs—onto an intersubjective screen, eliciting replies.

In any case, as Sherry Turkle remarks in her reflections on Internet culture (*Life on the Screen*), "psychoanalysis is a survivor discourse" still making itself heard in today's techno-culture.[30] And this survivor discourse implicitly asks about the survival of the species that it examines, linking the question of survival with a narrative of domestication of the wild by the will. "Where id was, ego shall be": this is Freud's oft-cited motto of rational conquest.

But Freud is no rationalist imperialist, and no sanguine humanist. In speculative essays such as *Civilization and Its Discontents*, "Instincts and Their Vicissitudes," and "Why War?," he wonders whether humanity will be done in by its own complexities.[31] Our anxiety has shifted somewhat these days—now there is less worry about humanity's repressed libidinal nature than about the passionate *expressed* fanaticism that endangers the species. We face a phantasm of retreat, in which hypercivilized technology, rather than the natural, threatens us with extinction. Will something essentially human continue to exist in a posthuman world, in the face of genome mapping, cloning, cybersex, cellular phones, corporate terror? Are new age devices—accoutrements that collapse public into private, natural into technological—augmentations of the human, or symptoms of its demise?

Reading Freud today reminds us of the complications of the Sphinx's riddle, the enigma that Oedipus only thought he solved: the question of what it is to be human. Psychoanalysis continues to pose that question at the crossroads between instincts and their vicissitudes.

PART I

RESITING OEDIPUS

CHAPTER 1

IS OEDIPUS ONLINE? SURFING THE PSYCHE

C. J. Jadlocki, *Synapse*, 1999.

In which light do mental images appear?
—Paul Virilio, *The Lost Dimension*

Descartes was perhaps the first to worry about virtual reality, as he sat musing in front of the fire, wondering if the hand before him were "his" hand, and if he himself might not be a figment of someone else's dream. He proceeded to cogitate himself into existence; but can we post-postmoderns follow his lead? After all, the rules have changed: today, when the first hand transplant recipient is sitting in front of his fire in suburban New Jersey, contemplating the hand at the end of his arm, he *knows* that it grew on someone else's arm, a convict executed for murder. And he knows that this very hand can now connect him to any number of screen identities via his palm pilot, in a new age version of the fireside chat. Not only do Descartes's questions—about identity, certainty, phantom limbs—still have legs today, but these questions have become more compelling in the virtual age.

In a lecture at Columbia University in 1998, Slavoj Žižek coined a millennial aphorism that foregrounds the equivocal status of human being in the information age: "We are what we want, in cyberspace." This neo-Cartesian provocation, which recasts ontological status as an effect of virtual desire, suggests why some bimillennials are still reading Freud: to discover if our "posthuman" society has succeeded in substituting interface for face-to-face.

That the public imagination is increasingly prone to virtual seduction is obvious from the proliferation of programs about cyberromance on the talk-show circuit (even in France, highbrow culture maven Bernard Pivot recently featured couples who are divorcing because of virtual adultery). Science fiction takes the erotic fascination with technology to its logical conclusion, inventing literal sex objects. (Is there a stunning replicant in your future—the Standard Pleasure Model of *Blade Runner*, or a muscled *Terminator*, programmed to please—or even to run for office?)

Popular publications such as *Wired* and *Online* warn the new cybermasses that it is rough out there in the virtual world, teeming with pornographers and con artists. In 1984, the cult film *Lawnmower Man* first raised the question of virtual violence: when the woman is raped in a virtual sex game, has a crime been committed? Today, as the number of potential virtual contacts grows exponentially, hyperspace is increasingly haunted by a free-floating angst about our own accessibility to Anyone, Out There.

The latest high-tech mischief by hackers involves setting up fake viruses, then putting out the word over the Internet that a vicious new strain is loose online, set to go off at midnight. Hypertension has even invaded romper space: on the children's cable network, a child psychologist warns kids about the dangers of the new frontier: "Above all, don't give out information about who you 'really' are. Use good sense, as you would in any public place."

"Any public place"—cyberspace seems to have acquired the density of matter in the public imagination. But the part of the body that inhabits the cranium seems very worried about the fate of the rest of it in the virtual age. Is gray matter itself in imminent danger of being outwitted by hardware? (The epic battle between chess master Kasparov and the steely intelligence of Big Blue is marked by human pathos: Big Blue is the reigning champion as of this writing, with Kasparov begging for a rematch.) Are we really witnessing the demise of social being, as suggested by dystopian thinkers like Jean Baudrillard and Paul Virilio? Even many former fans of the techno-revolution and the postmodern "decentered subject" (notably Jean-François Lyotard and the Baudrillard of the 1980s) now express concerns about the addictive immediacy of virtual gratification, suggesting that oedipal models of intersubjective interaction no longer speak to the narcissistic realities of the information age. To couch these issues in Lacanian terms, we could say that cultural theorists are commenting on an eclipse of Lacan's symbolic order by the imaginary order, even while predicting dire political consequences of the ascendancy of the image. This hyperbolic atmosphere of alarm suggests one good reason to continue to consult Freud in the age of paranoia, as the ur-theorist of angst.

Still, we have seen that Freud-bashing is a popular sport for millennial intellectuals. Surprisingly, we find even Slavoj Žižek ("We are what we want, in cyberspace") among the tragic chorus discrediting the oedipal drama as outmoded family romance. His card-carrying Lacanian credentials notwithstanding, Žižek has remarked (in the aforementioned seminar) that "what gets lost in virtual communication is the very opacity of the Other." But this assertion is worth contesting, for the opacity of the Other (the Other stands for all our "others" in their radical estrangement and impenetrability) founds both Freud's and Lacan's accounts of human being. Lacan even considers the "self" (or rather le moi, the illusory self-image) as its own Other, a mirage-identity that appears to be known only thanks to a delusion, a "misrecognition" (méconnaissance). For Lacan, the illusory nature of self-knowledge is already manifest in the primal scene of the mirror stage, when the young human first identities itself in its reflection, but only by comparing the image in the mirror to other human beings in its visual field. The child's original sense of identity, paradoxically, arises in a field of multiple Others, and crystallizes thanks only to an illusion, since the perception of the self is a mere image reflected at a distance. For Lacan, distance from and delusion about the "self" are actually constitutive of subjectivity (that is why Lacan's diagram of the process presents the subject as a barred figure [$] from whom the unconscious dimension is always hidden). The field of Others in which a human subject emerges is equally opaque, only ever provisionally understood by a self-alienating approximation, by mentally imagining "oneself" in the Other's place.

But Žižek and his fellow travelers have argued that in today's society, there is a loss of this opaque dimension between self and Other, an overexposure or flattening that has consequences in the social order. Žižek even maintains that the elision of mystery in the show-all culture of transparency may produce a totalitarian structure in which the Other may become, in his words, "fully contextualized" or transparent, laid bare. It follows that the totalitarian social field is by definition paranoia-inducing, since it aims to enforce the complete transparency of all subjects to a single monitoring point of view, a global disciplinary vantage point.

The currency of this version of postsociety suggests the compelling nature of the phantasms aroused by the virtual in our day, where drive as desire is replaced by drive as circuitry, and performativity is the new criterion of success unencumbered by ethics. This would seem to be consistent with the convention in theory equating today's "postmodern" zeitgeist with a modality of surface, as opposed to the emphasis on depth (including the "depth psychology" of Freud) that characterizes the bygone "modern" mode. But is it really true that the instant gratification offered by virtual reality contributes to a collapse of enabling distance between self and Other? Is real human interaction inevitably occluded in the glare of onscreen life?

The alarm being sounded by many cultural theorists today stresses the fragility of the human psyche vulnerable to programming by information networks. And the vulnerability of the mind is often considered a correlate to the frailty of the human body, subject to colonization by deadly viruses, invasive experiments, or techno-mechanization. This anxiety is manifest in myriad sci-fi films about epidemics, invasion by aliens, or a throng of creepy undead (in new age classics such as Outbreak, the Alien series—even Michael Jackson's 1980s Thriller video, itself rendering homage to the 1950s cult classic The Night of the Living Dead). Such cultural artifacts have become classics because they elaborate a thematic of incursion or penetration that speaks to us all in today's techno-environment. In the near-future setting of the classic Alien, the threat is gestated in the spaceship's circuitry, and subsequently infiltrates the innards of its crew; while in Jurassic Park and its progeny, the archaeological past—representing the literal "return of the repressed" as fossilized information—becomes a deadly threat to the present, thanks to manipulation of dinosaur DNA. Of course the technological threat to human convention is real as well as phantasmal, judging from the reaction to the first cloned human embryos. In 2001, the New York Times featured a spooky article on the possibilities of cloning a replacement for a lost child; while the cable Science Channel today routinely airs documentaries on cryogenics, the "science" of freezing corpses to be revived one day when a cure for death is available. A documentary on the Discovery Channel (*Weird Science*, 2000) has even chronicled experiments on primate head transplants, aimed at eventually giving quadriplegics a recycled body from a brain-dead donor. The new techno-science thus lends a whole new materiality to separation anxiety, and raises perplexing questions about where "one" is located in a body composed of mechanical, borrowed, and renewable parts.

To be sure, the "yuk factor" accompanying these developments contributes to the reactionary tenor of panic theory today. But perhaps these new technological symptoms, inspired by the search for immortality, are merely the newest reaction formations against loss, inspired by third-millennium versions of age-old separation anxiety. In any case, it is somewhat disheartening to see progressive psychoanalytic theorists like Žižek adopt gloomy "posthuman" diagnoses wholesale, lending credence to the notion of the inexorable eclipse of the Lacanian symbolic by the imaginary. According to such accounts of our hyperoptical era, there is no longer an oedipal resolution by which human subjects emerge into social being, as Freud described—just a sustained pre-oedipal absorption in self and screen, where the subject remains glued to the Mother Board. As compelling as this account may be, psychoanalytic theorists ought to know better. For this is giving up on the radical aspect of Freud's discovery of the unconscious, as well as Lacan's description of the symbolic order as an intersubjective social domain, the very predication of the human in and through language (with language broadly construed as all instances of cultural interchange).

No theorist has raised these issues in more spectacularly paranoid terms than Jean Baudrillard, whose work—from *Simulacra and Simulations* to *The Transparency of Evil*—has decried the post-oedipal era of information circulation, where the simulacrum (virtual image) is the new cultural currency.[1] For Baudrillard, the network of simulacra no longer conforms to the three Lacanian categories of human experience: the imaginary, the symbolic, and the real. Baudrillard argues, rather, that the "imaginary" and the "real" have now merged in the hyperreal. (This is a virtual image that no longer just represents an object, but actually replaces it. Baudrillard's example is the transparent grid computer drawings of automobiles in commercials, where the auto is never shown.) Baudrillard's first discussions of simulacra two decades ago now seem impressively ahead of their time, since today the whole World Wide Web could be considered an instance of Baudrillard's hyperreal domain. And Baudrillard, like Žižek, seems to think that the symbolic order, as a function of opacity or maintained difference between subjects, is threatened by a pandemic of hypervisibility, where the flat screen incessantly displays an "ob-scene" array of fetish objects providing instant gratification with a click of the mouse.

Baudrillard goes even further: he argues that not only are we seeing the obsolescence of oedipal theories of interaction, with bodies now "reduced to control screens" ("The Ecstasy of Communication"), but we are also witnessing the obsolescence of *all* psychoanalytic object theory. Taking issue with Barthes's characterization of the automobile as object of identification, Baudrillard notes the disappearance of "a subjective logic of possession and projection." There are no more fantasies of power, where speed and image are linked to the object itself, says Baudrillard. For in our age, "the subject is a computer at the wheel, the vehicle a kind of capsule," and the logic of possession has been replaced by "the logic of driving itself." This suggests that old-fashioned Freudian object-related desire has lost its symbolic dimension, and with it, its enabling capacity of differentiation. The driver is "a computer at the wheel," just as the astronaut is "a navigating device, a terminal screen."[2] It would seem that for Baudrillard, we are indeed becoming cyborgs of sorts: we no longer identify with our objects of desire, we *meld* with them.

For all his histrionics, Baudrillard has a point. In this age of the global village, the joy of encounter with difference often seems to be replaced by the comfort of homogenized global ambiance, serving up Big Macs on Tiananmen Square, Thai food in Tallahassee. Deploying one of his favorite images, Baudrillard suggests that the mindlessness of our age is concomitant with a certain bodilessness: "the centrifugal force of our technologies has stripped us of all weight . . . freed of all density, all gravity, we are being dragged into an orbital motion."[3] Perhaps this figure of the encapsulated astronaut is so captivating because of its thematic of monitored hypervisibility, which speaks to our own anxiety about surveillance: the astronaut's every function is watched and broadcast. This figure also evokes a vacuous mentality impinging on identity, an "unbearable lightness of being." Baudrillard argues that this absence of substance in today's culture produces a vapid, flattened subject, incapable of creative projection. In his new order, the loss of space required for the deployment of metaphor is associated with the loss in space of human agency: "This realization of a living satellite in quotidian space [causes] what was projected psychologically and mentally, what used to be lived out on earth as metaphor [to be] henceforth projected onto reality, without any metaphor at all, in an absolute space which is that of dissimulation."[4] Sleepwalker, spacewalker, computer nerd: whether we experience a collapse of space or a sense of boundless vacancy, we suffer an unmooring of self, without somatic coordinates.

Interestingly, this description of hyperreality, transcoded into Freudian terms, bears a resemblance to classic paranoid psychosis as described in Freud's famous case study of the memoirs of Daniel Paul Schreber. Schreber elaborates a fantastic masochistic cosmology where he is penetrated by the "rays" of an amorous but hostile deity, who turns him into a woman to serve His pleasure.[5] In his discussion of Schreber, Freud contends that the paranoid projects his own global vision of reality outward, constructing an absolute delusional system in place of the real world of others. Like Dr. Schreber a century ago, the space-age paranoid described by Baudrillard seems to live not so much in fantasy as in the hyperreal, substituted for the quotidian experience of "real life."

As Lacan puts it, the paranoid no longer believes in the Other, which, along with its role as emblem of the radical alterity of others, also often designates the grounding of the symbolic social order founded on consensual pact and common belief as to what counts as reality. The paranoid believes in the *Other of the Other*, the final Authority behind the scenes of the system, the know-it-all whose totalitarian vision explains everything, beyond the shadow of a doubt.[6] Žižek's twenty-first-century critique of hypervisible culture as *The Plague of Fantasies* follows Lacan in this regard. In Žižek's new age scenario of totalitarian surveillance, it is little comfort that virtual Marxists are monitoring the playground of cyberspace, the new opiate of the people. (Marilouise and Arthur Kroker, for instance, worry about the exploitation of "virtual flesh," and even discuss virtual surplus value, apparently soon to be measured in e-money.)[7] But does the emergent homogeneous global culture, transacted in bits and bytes, necessarily signal the advent of a totalitarian age?

Even theorists who have been relatively sanguine about postmodernity, such as Donna Haraway and Jean-François Lyotard, increasingly express anxiety about the loss of our mooring to material reality today. Lyotard's famous early work on postmodernity (*The Postmodern Condition*), describing the new social order as a challenge to totalizing systems (the lack of belief in "metanarrative"), has given way to the chillier world of *The Inhuman*, deeply critical of postmodernity in its dehumanizing social effects.[8] Similarly, Manuel De Landa points out the danger inherent in the "paranoid" reasoning of today's computers, when the Pentagon uses them to stage doomsday scenarios of virtual war games.[9] Donna Haraway's new age classic, the relatively upbeat "Manifesto for Cyborgs," has also been followed by a more sinister ideological critique of biotech in cahoots with capitalism (*Modest Witness@Second Millennium*).[10] Even in the earlier pro-cyborg manifesto, Haraway already concedes the monstrous aspects of the new somatics, suggesting that we are all postmodern Frankensteins: "By the late 20th century, we are all chimeras, theorized and fabricated hybrids of machine and organism; in that, we are cyborgs. The cyborg gives us our ontology, our politics." In the same essay, significantly—like Baudrillard, Žižek, Deleuze—she dismisses the oedipal paradigm, as representative of an outworn redemptive telos: "The cyborg incarnation is outside salvation history: the most promising monsters in cyborg worlds are embodied in non-oedipal narratives with a different logic of repression, which we need to understand for our survival."[11]

We could say that this "different logic of repression" invoked by Haraway is a matter not of depth but of surface—with a collapse of dimension—governed by the logic of the network, circuit, or single-surface Moebius loop. Her analysis owes a great deal to Michel Foucault's concept of "discipline" as something systemic, more complicated than top-down repression. For the new conduits of energy that Haraway invokes—which can no longer quite be called "power," since that term implies a struggle rather than a circuit—make their rounds along a looped itinerary, obedient only to the hydraulic logic of source and tributary.

Haraway taps into a more primal fear when she invokes the monstrosity of the cyborg, produced by a process of grafting which melds disparate elements into a piecemeal entity:

> This cyborg is a creature in a postgender world; it has no truck with preoedipal symbolica or other seductions to organic wholeness through appropriation of all the powers of the parts into a higher unity. In a sense, the cyborg has no original story in the Western sense, a final irony since the cyborg is also the artful apocalyptic telos of the West's escalating domination of abstract identification, a man in space.[12]

Like Baudrillard, Haraway launches us into orbit, and once again Oedipus does not have the right stuff to serve as astronaut.

No Body Sees Me

It is difficult simply to discount all this paranoid theorizing, however hyperbolic; for the human being has in fact been cut down to size in what scientists now call the visible universe, reflecting our scaled-down sense of capability. Our new age astronomy has even put Copernicus in his place: not only are suns more numerous than grains of sand, but our own little star is not even centrally located in the universe ("Location, location . . ."). This sense of diminished human importance may account for much of the phobic tone of popular cultural today. Consider, for instance, the ubiquitous trope of the astronaut lost in space. The lonely astronauts in classics such as Silent Running and 2001: A Space Odyssey find that their only surviving companions are cybernetic. Just as poignantly, an episode of the Eastern European Red Shoe Diaries stages a stylized ritual as doomed astronauts make love while dying in orbit; while in the 2003 film Solaris, the isolated astronaut falls in love with an alien entity disguised as his dead wife. And the very concept of cyberspace navigated by virtual astronauts, first popularized by William Gibson's 1984 Neuromancer, also echoes a primal dread of the vacuum.

Freud would probably have argued that this new age panic attests to an ancestral phylogenetic fear, already manifest in the myths of Odysseus and Jason; and of course Jason's argonauts are directly referenced in the term "astronaut." But in the new mythology, the voyager is fitted with techno-trappings, embarking on interstellar travels through time or even hallucinatory trips through inner space induced by brain implants. In another version of this motif, the scientist has been reduced to molecular scale in order to undertake a harrowing nanotech mission within the patient's body (the premise of the 1950s classic *Fantastic Voyage* and its many comic follow-ups, such as *Osmosis Jones* in 2002). The terrifying thematic of being lost in space turns up everywhere, and the space may be outer, inner, innard, or wayward. In the 2001 film *Mission to Mars*, for instance, the spacewalk veers into nightmare (Tim Robbins overshoots the space capsule and sails into orbit around the Red Planet . . . for eternity). Our cultural productions constantly remind us that every astronaut risks flying off into space, slipping out of electronic reach, or severing the umbilical tether to the Mother Ship. The chilling image in *Mission to Mars*, where the doomed astronaut floats away, receding from view (doubtless a tribute to the similarly unforgettable image in Kubrick's *2001: A Space Odyssey*), plugs into an age-old terror of sailing off into a void, and arouses primal human separation anxiety. Once the cord to the Mother Ship is cut, the familiar human axial symmetry of absence followed by presence is lost.

This is the very rhythm that Freud observes in an infant's play, in the peekaboo here-gone, present-absent, yes-no rhythm that grounds human communication.[13] In the famous scene from *Beyond the Pleasure Principle*, the toddler pronounces the words *fort!* and *da!* as he repeatedly casts away and retrieves a sort of yo-yo, reenacting the disappearance and reappearance of his mother. An intriguing parallel to the famous *fort-da* now occurs in cybernetics, where the same digital rhythm (absent-present, on-off) underwrites our informational code, comprised of 0's and 1's. In fact, the term "digital" itself is haunted by the specter of the biaxial body and its members, our "digits" now occluded and retrieved in light-speed binary alternation. All twenty-first-century internauts share a new version of the phobia of failed retrieval: the terror of data loss (and, of course, lost digits or members recall an older "oedipal" fear). Like an astronaut who has missed his window, our data risk oblivion if our too-human digits miss a key, deleting the record. While data loss is a real problem, the terror it evokes suggests a deeper fantasy, and one which the virus hoaxers exploit to the fullest by launching rumors of impending data doom. Certainly we never feel so helpless as when our computer interrupts our operations to scold us ("This program has performed an illegal operation and will be shut down"). Insult added to injury, we are without appeal: we are offered but one choice, to hit the "OK" button consenting to our punishment.

Perhaps harder to take than data disappearance is the paralysis of words, "hung" in our full view but beyond retrieval—as frozen and inaccessible as the astronaut's corpse in orbit. Witnessing this catastrophe, we have no choice but to cut our losses and return "home," rebooting the computer without the data; and the experience of this truncation is traumatic indeed. This trauma, however, is nothing compared to the shock of sudden data death in a hard-disk crash, every bit as scary as that other "hard-disk crash" at Roswell, which continues to trouble the collective memory half a century later.

Weightlessness, paralysis, invasion, dismemberment, exposure—these specters haunt the millennial body. Indeed, if so many theorists frame their analyses in optical imagery, it is perhaps because our postsociety is *more* than a *Society of the Spectacle* (Guy Debord), or even a community of *World Spectators* (Kaja Silverman):[14] What we encounter now is not just visibility, but *hypervisibility*. It is an epidemic of what Baudrillard terms the ob-scene, and Žižek calls pornography: the all-seeing view that captures, freezes, and objectifies the viewer.[15]

One of the best-known theorists of optic phobia is Paul Virilio: in *Open Sky*, he criticizes a "paraoptics" that flattens depth and difference, facilitating mind control. Virilio characterizes absorption in the computer or television screen as hypnotic psychosis, causing "the interpretive delirium of the observer."[16] It does seem that a mind-numbing flatness characterizes the scant intellectual (if heavily ideological) content broadcast these days "twenty-four/seven" as "live news." And this is the age of reality TV, which has now spread to Europe: entertainment that chastises, derides, or spies on guests. "The Weakest Link" features a dominatrix schoolmarm figure who humiliates the contestants; "Survivor" maroons the contestants on an island and, in a new age *Lord of the Flies*, exposes just how low they will go to win (in the French version, the contestants are forced to eat "*du rat*"). Meanwhile, the wildly popular court of Judge Judy—another stern Phallic Mother—exposes feuding parties to a public dressing-down, and a whole parade of Jerry Springer clones feature talk-show exhibitionists eager to air their dirty linen to howls of opprobrium from onlookers, in a media parody of the all-American witch hunt.

Virilio's work (*Open Sky, The Lost Dimension, The Information Bomb*), like the work of Baudrillard and Avital Ronell, compares the immediacy of visual gratification to a mind-numbing drug ("These quick fixes deprive us of the basis of reasoning").[17] And Virilio, like Baudrillard, seems racked by nostalgia, a longing for a return to depth perspective, a unified Renaissance worldview moored in a single vanishing point at the horizon. But even the logic of line and point is outmoded: it has been called into question by the new nonlinear geometry.

Yet before perspective was challenged by the new sciences, it was challenged by Freud. For Freud's discovery insists on the inevitable invisibility of some aspect of reality. Psychoanalysis shows that the classical Cartesian *cogito*—the base of enlightenment and knowledge—always occludes "something" unconscious. (In his work on Freud [*Discours, figure*], Lyotard likens this "invisibility" to the "opacity of the designated"; when an object is viewed from any perspective, some of its faces are necessarily obscured.)[18]

Anticipating the new science, Freud challenges the possibility of a complete self-image or transparent rational identity, which is always in part illusory. Perhaps, then, the millennial obsession with hypervisibility as complete transparency is itself a denial of Freud's discovery that no matter how much is shown, the full picture never emerges. The panic philosophers may just protest too much about the loss of opacity, denying the deeply troubling invisibilities postulated by the subject of psychoanalysis.

Nonetheless, something *has* happened culturally since Freud's day, "in light of" new millennial scientific paradigms. In the late 1980s, Arthur Kroker and David Cook were already describing the "postmodern scene" as a number of cultural symptoms accompanied by body angst, such as dismemberment of the broadcast body in advertising, as well as the hygienic practice of "sex without secretions."[19] It does seem that virtual sex has become popular precisely because it does not necessitate contact, as the ultimate safe sex. Paradoxically, however, sexual availability is increasing even as sexual contact is decreasing: sex is disseminated far and wide, with booming online dating and e-mail bride businesses, as well as hundreds of thousands of cyberporn sites. Online voyeurism has recently been further commercialized in a new version of the "reality" craze, in websites such as "Upskirting.com" designed to accommodate the virtual Peeping Tom (the cameramen lurk beneath urban street grates to photograph unsuspected miniskirted passersby, transmitting the images to paying cyberpeepers live, online).

Thus the body is increasingly offered up to unprecedented mass access, even as it is increasingly distanced from real contact. But we are also experiencing a symptomatic obsessive return of the real body, which refuses to be deleted: might this not account for popular trends like tattooing or body piercing, assuring the body's material mooring by visible marks? It is as though the pixelated body may be both reclaimed and weighed down by mortification, its owner securing a kind of copyright identity on the body itself. A proliferation of articles in the new age press (*Re-search, Found Object, Atlantica*) have in fact commented on the primitivism of body art as "techno-paganism." Moreover, theorists like Mark Dery (*Escape Velocity*) and Adam Parfrey (*Apocalypse Culture*) point out that the culture of "Cyberia" often foregrounds violence, as in the sadomasochistic performances of the hard-edged cyber culture continuing the 1980s punk aesthetic.[20] One performance artist of self-martyrdom (Stelarc) hangs suspended on meat hooks; the notorious video performance of Nine-Inch Nails ("Happiness," banned on MTV) displays the erotics of torture; and in the spectacular concerts of Marilyn Manson (before the carnage at Columbine), the rocker arrived suspended on a burning cross. Even if spectacle is the domain of fantasy, the urban hyperreality of video rock/hip-hop culture, like the phenomenal popularity of camp TV, seems to attest to an underlying thirst not for fantasy but for reality: we can't get enough of it, even on hundreds of cable channels. And voyeurism is only one side of the coin, since in the popular imagination millennial subjects are not just onlookers but also *objects* of surveillance, often with sacrificial resonance. (Witness the fascination with the abductees who report being probed under glaring lights with steely implements, wielded by opaque-eyed aliens.)

GENESIS Y2K: LET THERE BE LIGHT

A particularly compelling illustration of the coincidence of hypervisibility, sacrifice, techno-science, cyborg culture, and virtuality is found in the case of the virtual cadaver Adam, created to train surgeons on screen. The real subject, once a live convict with a name, became EveryCorpse after execution, frozen in blue jelly, his body parts cut into 18,000 cross sections, like a big deli sandwich. Adam's parts were photographed slice-by-slice on slides, then computer-arranged. He is now on perpetual view at *VisibleHumanProject*.edu., his once private parts now very public. His organs may be examined in any combination, from any angle, and sliced up again and again with a virtual scalpel. Adam was joined by Eve in 2000, thanks to the Texas execution of a female convict, and the dead couple has gone global. The many spin-off sites now listed, apparently without irony, include the "Visible Human Slice Server"; the "Visible Human Project Products" site, touting scans of fresh cadavers; and the "Visible Human Female Head and Pelvis Browser." Cyber-Adam's genesis is a fitting creation story in the age of the posthuman. Now Foucault's famous panopticon, where the prison warden oversees the slices of *space* inhabited by inmates, has been transposed onto the microscope of his disciplinary clinic, overseeing slices of the inmates themselves.

The modern complaint of Eliot's urban *Wasteland*—that "nobody sees me," engulfed by the crowd—has now shifted. The millennial complaint from Adam's point of view, so to speak, is that EveryBody sees me, even though I do not exist. (The "I," in fact, is dead.) In the age of the virtual, it would seem that even the *dead* Other has lost his imaginary clout, his spookiness, along with his privacy.

But even the dead, as Žižek points out, are not entirely accommodating: the vampires and Zombies who abound in popular film attest to the Freudian uncanny as the "return of the repressed," refusing to remain buried.[21] Like so many uncanny phantasms, the timeworn motif of the undead now has an objective cor-

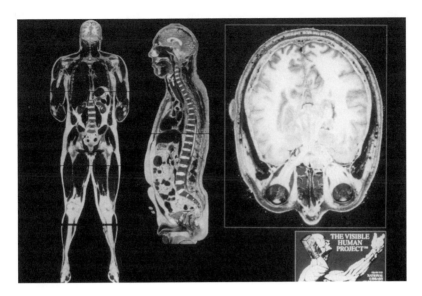

The Visible Human Project, *Adam*, 2001.

relative in real life: stockpiled bodies frozen in liquid nitrogen tanks—called "patients" by the Alcor Life Extension Foundation—are artifacts at the blurred boundary between nightmare and utopia, awaiting resurrection. ("Neuro-patients" are severed heads only, floating in picnic-cooler-size tanks.) The widely publicized custody fight about freezing Ted Williams's remains—which has turned an All-American sports hero into an icon of the creepy excesses of technology—demonstrates the public investment in techno-cultural practice.

In millennial culture, boundaries are newly permeable (live/dead; me/you; human/machine; man/woman). And since the fall of iconic twentieth-century borders such as the Iron Curtain and the Berlin Wall, geopolitical frontiers between "us" and "them" are increasingly violable. Now, try as we will, we can't seem to find the enemy at his home, or keep him out of ours. Al-Qaeda is the emblem of the invisible enemy who seems to be everywhere at once; its spokesmen are media superstars whose latest releases receive worldwide play.

In other words, humanity today is dogged by the suspicion that the body is in crisis or obsolescence (an obscene leftover, like the astronaut's orbiting corpse). Or we are troubled by the corollary fear that the body is a public domain, displayed by monitors (like Stanley Kubrick's iconic computer HAL, who keeps an eye on everyone onboard, killing them when he doesn't like what he sees). The fragile fetal astronaut floating at the end of his tether reflects the real-life nightmare of the space pioneer cut off from earth (*Apollo 13*), in full view of NASA's monitor. And as Linda Singer and other feminist theorists point out, these images of astronauts at risk intersect with real political life in the posters of the Right to Life movement. (The gigantic intrauterine fetus on freeway billboards bears more than a passing resemblance to the floating spacesuited astronaut, cathected at the waist to a placental lifeline.)[22]

In a cyberpunk variant of this nightmare, the human subject is *overcathected* to objects (Gibson's *Mona Lisa Overdrive*; Bruce Sterling's *Global Head*; Pat Cadigan's *Synners*; Neal Stephenson's *Snow Crash*). David Cronenberg's horrific remake of the 1950s classic *The Fly* merges scientist, insect, and teleport hardware, in a monstrosity that drags its wires and hairy limbs across the floor, while still-human eyes plead with the heroine to fire and end the creature's misery. (Again, there is a resonance of abortion gone wrong, as Jeff Goldblum emerges bloody and mutilated from the "telepod.") Like the many eyes of cyberspace, the multivision of *The Fly* reminds us of the new limits of human being in an evolutionary battle that we once considered already won by the survival of the smartest.

CYBERANALYSIS IN PSYCHOSPACE

A fascinating if weird reflection on the fate of the body, providing yet another take on human evolution, appears in Jean-François Lyotard's essay "Can Thought Go On without a Body?"[23] Here, boundary wars are framed in a gendered dialogue between "he" and "she," as the interlocutors ponder the feasibility of colonization of the universe by thinking machines, after the inevitable extinction of the human race. (Lyotard points out that this will occur in four billion years with the explosion of the sun, assuming some microbe or warhead or ecological disaster or asteroid doesn't get us first.) The question becomes philosophic—can computers think? The essay rehearses the argument first presented in 1979 by Hubert Dreyfus (*What Computers Can't Do*): the opacity of the world is experienced by a body with depth and substance, a corpus which puts us *there*, on the scene (Heidegger's *Dasein*), permitting us to anticipate unseen surfaces.[24] We position ourselves analogically, "as if" we could see from another angle, thanks to identification with the other's point of view. This projective vision exceeds the binary logic of here/there; on/off; either/or; the embodied vision is not limited by the square cadre of the pixel. Even when 3D computer imaging circumvents an object—says cyberfather Nicholas Negroponte (*Being Digital*), there is no "as if" to its logic: it sees sequentially, rather than by identification or intuition.[25]

In Lyotard's gendered dialogue, the interlocutor labeled "she" predictably argues for the incommensurability of binary logic with thought: "humanity" is an effect of all-too-human suffering ("The pain of thinking isn't a symptom coming from outside to inscribe itself on the mind instead of its true place"). What Lyotard calls "thought itself resolving to be irresolute" (the opposite of the Cartesian plan by which thought resolves to rid itself of error) is "[thought] deciding to be patient, wanting not to want, wanting, precisely, not to produce a meaning in place of what must be signified."[26] Human thought requires a patient and painful receptivity to the other's point of view.

In Lacanian terms, this argument reflects the *transitivism of the subject position*: listening itself may be considered a function of human mobility, in a conversation made possible by the shifting point of view of interconnected subjects.[27] As the conversation is bandied back and forth, the participants are obliged to project their vision to the place of the other, lending the other the pronoun "I," for a turn. The subject is thus obliged to see "self" as object, to see from another's site/sight, perceiving "where s/he is coming from."

In this volley, Lyotard underscores the radical Lacanian point that human thought has a gender, and that this is a productive stigma, an aspect of an incompleteness that motivates a reaching out to other subjects. Lyotard argues that thinking machines will not colonize the universe unless they can learn to suffer, to yearn, to submit to the condition of lack activated by difference. And this is not just sexual difference, but also the difference between self and other, between you and me—even the difference between I and me, subject and self-image.

Lacan's version of this concept insists that human beings dwell in the gaze of the Other, thanks to the space of difference that alienates but facilitates; and our bodies give us a position in that field, in the eye of the Other. This recognition of the shiftiness of the listening eye, site of a multiple gaze, counters the conventional Western aspiration to one correct overview, the position associated from the Renaissance onward (as Lyotard points out) with the unifying eye of the monarch, the triumph of one-point perspective. In our mobility and capacity for trying on other positions, we lose our near-sighted vainglory, our illusion of sovereignty.

The many visual fields of cyberspace may remind us of the contingency of our human being; but if we are online, are we at the end of the line? Perhaps we may cut ourselves some slack and suggest that all of this technophobic paranoid theorizing, even if it is descriptive, is not necessarily predictive. Oedipus is perhaps not quite dead, though vital signs may be flagging. Perhaps the psychoanalytic model of depth in the subject may suggest ways of retrieving our embodied minds from their hypersurfing, reeling them back into physicality. For every *fort* will have its *da*.

Lacan's work suggests a way to counter the paranoid zeitgeist by recasting the term "paranoid" itself. In his third seminar, he describes a paranoid modality governing the acquisition of human knowledge, rather than always resulting in psychosis.[28] Every time we structure our discourse in light of an anticipated response, we are fantasizing and constructing in a paranoid mode, acting "as if" we know what others might perceive.

But is not human knowledge always-already deflected through the Other, the "eye in the sky" over the cradle, the hovering giant visage at once alien and like us? Lacan asserts that the infant is caught in a whole web of objects—animate and inanimate—that seem to look back, so many faces enlivened by our attention and reflecting our desire. In psychoanalysis, object desire is contagion, contracted by the larval infant in interaction with other human beings and their objects. And though the world may respond to the infant's needs, it will never fully conform to its demands—for of course every baby, even when fed, warm, and dry, still cries implacably for something more. This is expressed succinctly in Lacan's famous formula: "desire is the excess of demand over need."[29] We never get what we want, even if we get what we need. (Interestingly enough, Lacanian doctrine, notoriously difficult, has now infiltrated pop culture: the entire first scene of the 2003 release *The Life of David Gale* consists of a professor's lecture [Kevin Spacey] to a packed auditorium on the philosophical implications of Lacan's *objet petit a*.)

In any case, a Lacanian perspective on cyberspace might help counter the panic aroused by the frontier of virtual reality—millennial culture's "hyperimaginary" mode. For in the region of hypertext, space is not necessarily a vacuous no-man's-land; it may be a crossroads, a site of communication in a maze of difference. If this sounds familiar, it is because I am invoking Freud's "resolution of the Oedipus complex," which he describes as a move from lethal incestuous short circuit to salutary social detour, thanks to the presence of the overseeing Other as prohibitory third, an enabling screen. This dimensionalization allows us to think what a postmodern subject might be, if not a soporific video consumer, stupefied by what Ray Barglow and others have termed the "preoedipal" computer, the addictive lure of the Mother Board to which one is connected for hours on end.[30]

Lacan's reading of Freud suggests that the posthuman subject may indeed be paranoid, but in a sanguine sense, engaged in anticipatory thinking and projection *vis-à-vis* the Other. Rather than a tool of surveillance—the one-sided screen mirror of the panopticon—the *intersubjective* gaze may adopt other subject positions, seeing "as if" through other eyes. Might we reconceptualize cyberspace as a field that may *enfranchise* human subjectivity, a net in which the Other is caught but not captured? As Sherry Turkle points out, the virtual permits us to try out other corporeal perspectives, other points of view, thanks to our symbolic capacity to visit the "other's" site.[31] Lacan, after Freud, insists that the symbolic is at the heart of the social; the gendered body is at the heart of the symbolic; and human difference (as gender) is at the heart of the body.

Somewhat more whimsically, we might conceive of communication in the information age as Lacan's "paranoid knowledge" in action. In cyberspace we gain information through projective identification, identifying with screen names, playing roles in chat groups, re-placing ourselves with visual icons or "avatars," as our representatives are termed online. We are self-nominated participants in intersubjective play, as well as in professional interest groups through which we identify with areas of expertise. (We can, of course, "lurk" online without participating, but that very possibility extended to all others creates the ambient paranoia of cyberspace, the sense that "someone is watching.")

What is a message path but a labyrinthine voyage in space, a peregrination traced in the header, enacting Lacan's axiom ("the signifier is a subject for another signifier"), where the address is a message for another address?[32] When Žižek quips that "We are what we want, in cyberspace," it does not have to mean that we are stuck in a narcissistic circuit: we are following a communicative filament, passing linked bits of paranoid knowledge from other to other. When we perform a search, our little spider-messengers crawl around in the cybermaze, following and spinning a "string." In fact, given the prevalence of cyber terms invoking the labyrinth—net, web, webcrawlers, strings and paths—the myth of Ariadne and Theseus rivals that of Oedipus as a millennial paradigm.

THE LABYRINTH AS SCHEMA L

As the link between myth and cyberculture suggests, even if the virtual is an imaginary structure in the Lacanian sense, it is a symbolic circuit as well, a "signifying chain" sending an always-rerouted message in search of an always-missing object. In the cyber version of Lacan's circuit, the missing object is the real letter of which e-mail is the simulacrum, and by extension, the simulacrum of the real person who sends it, staying in touch but out of reach.

The message path retraces the vicissitudes of the subject as constituted in Lacan's "Schema L," the first and clearest elaboration of the relation of the Lacanian subject to objects of desire.[33] The diagram traces the circuitous path of deflected desire by which what we *imagine* we want (*object petit a*, the other) is linked to who we *think* we are (our self-image [*a'*]; and also to the way we *desire to be seen by our objects and Others* [A for *Autre*]. What we desire is to be desired, to be reflected and magnified in the eye of the Other.

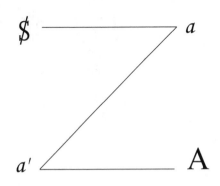

The Schema L.

In Lacan's pictogram of dynamic subjectivity, first elaborated in the 1950s, the subject is primordially split (since the unconscious is never fully known to us, no matter how long we are in analysis: Lacan figures a *barred* subject as $, invested in and moving among the "other" positions). The subject is constituted in relation to its object of desire (the *objet petit a*, in the schema above); as well as in relation to its own image (the ego/imago: "*moi*" or *a'* in Lacan's schema). The subject is also constituted as in relation to the Other (A; *Autre*), which may stand for several things, among them the classic oedipal father who figures prohibition of the subject's desire. Even in this early diagram of subjectivity as intersubjectivity, we can see that for Lacan the subject is alienated in and by its Others, in a relay where desire is refracted and circulated among the various positions in the field.

Perhaps today the Lacanian model finds an instance in (E)go-mail, bounced back and forwarded. Marked by its origins, always recursive, it is a "Purloined Letter" of sorts (Poe's famous detective story is the inspiration for Lacan's most famous seminar, where he plays on the French term for a letter suspended in circulation: *en souffrance/in suffering*).[34] To be sure, e-mail is a response to the Desire of the Other. We may think of the zigzagging pass of desire in the Schema L as an electronic path, where our own messages often return to us in inverted form. It is as though our own ego-mail is "forwarded" online, with a proliferation of screen names and headers, returning to us relabeled as a message from another site on the net, perhaps enclosed in an anonymous mailer, at once replying to and eliciting replies from a chain of screen interlocutors. To cite Lacan's famous aphorism in the commentary on Poe: "a letter always reaches its destination." Like a homing device, our own encoded message, a refraction of our own desiring gaze, may return to us, sometimes labeled with deadpan irony (like the message that recently appeared on my screen: "reply/forward/reply/re:no subject"). And our desire, expressed online by our purchases and haunts, also returns to us as spam from unseen others who pay to know what we want, and where they can find us. For if "a letter always reaches its destination," as Lacan concludes, it is perhaps because one's chickens come home to roost with the accuracy of a smart bomb. ("Why do *those people* hate us so much?")

The recursive path of ego-mail also recalls the Lacanian formula: "desire is the excess of demand over need." For do we in fact *need* all this information, on demand? Perhaps the information deluge—a welter of chat, usenets, search sites—is a symptom of the insatiability of the social as human desire, rather than of its demise. The virtual never provides complete gratification, by definition: its success is measured by how real the experience *seems*, as adjudicated by a real body. And that body receives the message almost in spite of itself (cyberromance can set the heart pounding like a face-to-face encounter). This may remind us that virtual games are premised on real desire, even if they are always perpetuated by the unavailability of the Real Thing—not only in cyberspace, but in any human space. In cyberspace, the virtual seduces by the promise of "real" access; but the inaccessibility of the Real is what the virtual delivers.

Thus the virtual is merely the techno-form of a psychic configuration as old as the species itself. Freud's imaginary, be it daydream or fantasy, is virtual reality minus the hardware. As Freud points out in his description of the desire of the writer, our imaginary narratives have always helped us to navigate life. Freud also insists, however, that the difference between creativity and onanistic fantasy is that the artist's desire does not end in private gratification; it is routed outward toward an audience. Lacan's Schema L thus schematizes Freud's desiring long circuit, that must visit the Other-as-audience.

In any case, our transactions in cyberspace give a new cast to the psychoanalytic notion of desire as web, or chain. Our (online) "desire is the desire of the Other": our Internet service providers exhort us to visit the hottest websites, and reward us with a cookie when we do so, banding the pigeon for retailers. As surely as in any Lacanian parable, "a subject is a subject for another signifier" online, in a chain disseminating the latest joke/hoax/rumor, or even bearing a call to political action (the online petition is the tool of the twenty-first-century organizer). Meanwhile, cyberdating reveals that virtual love is an effect of ambivalence, as always. The traditional lover's protest, "I need my space," may now be acted out by establishing one's own site, by changing e-mail addresses, or by hiding behind a screen name. Even the psychosis of paranoia has a cyberinstance: projected desire often comes back at us as a fantasmatic persecution, displaying all the aggressivity of mail bounced by the Mailer Daemon, maliciously labeled "no path to host" or "fatal error." (Ironically enough, when our own message is bounced back to us like a boomerang, the voice of a familiar stranger announces cheerily: "You have mail.")

Indeed, cyberspace is fairly humming with voices, and this buzz has created its own institutional paranoia among self-righteous officials, from Berlin to Washington, who are attempting to censor the emerging field of cyberspace. But these attempts to legislate behavior have given rise to electronic resistance, like the Blue Ribbon Internet crusade for free speech, complete with an electronic "march on Washington" in 2000 that flooded Congress with e-mails. On a more spontaneous level, the Internet encourages fantasies of revenge, such as the mass dissemination of the outrageously priced "secret" Nieman-Marcus cookie recipe by a furious consumer. (It seems that the incident itself is apocryphal, but the fact that it was so widely circulated shows our desire that greedy online vendors "get what is coming to them.")[35]

But a return is not always a rebuke, as the spacewalker knows when he touches ground, Odysseus come home. In his own homecoming to Father Freud, Lacan recasts the oedipal narrative as the symbolic pact with fellow beings. Perhaps it is this social net which will also bring us back from the ether, tangled up in real life, always owing what Lacan calls "the Symbolic Debt," the social desire caught from, then retransmitted to, our Others. Perhaps we should keep Oedipus around to cruise the Net: for millennial psychoanalysis, far from losing its purchase, offers us ways of thinking about space without endangering Otherness. Since psychoanalysis views the psyche as plural and social, it may help us to temper an antisocial and isolationist view of the future, giving us some say in the shape of things to come.

POST-OEDIPAL POSTSCRIPT

Oedipus is still accused of consorting with Descartes: two members of the old boys' network, they are accused of being vestiges of a positivist patriarchy. But whereas Descartes thinks to exist, Oedipus exists to think, and is thus post-Cartesian, even "postmodern," in spite of himself. And let us also give the Doubter his due: Descartes is as skeptical as any postmodern in his search for answers; even while intrepid Oedipus is in deep denial of the evidence that inculpates him. However, Oedipus and Descartes part company when it comes to the status of the "I" asking the questions. Descartes justifies himself by interpellating the Other as all-knowing God who guarantees existence ("*He* thinks, therefore I am," is the gist of Descartes's ontological cop-out). But Oedipus interrogates the Other as enigma, to discover that even when "I" solve the riddle through reason, "I" am precisely never who my reason thinks I am.

Lacan's account of intersubjectivity shows us that Oedipus must ultimately pay the Symbolic Debt for solving the riddle of the Sphinx concerning humanity. As

Lacan points out in his discussion of Descartes ("The Instance of the Letter in the Unconscious"), the "I think" of Oedipus is actually an anti-*cogito*. For his confident assertion underscores that "he is not" who he thinks he is, and that the eventual revelation of who he really is will only provoke wounding and wandering. Oedipus discovers that when language seems to make things clear, solving enigmas and securing our position, it may actually only obscure the truth in a potentially tragic misrecognition. In fact, Oedipus is never so off the mark, so deluded about his "identity," as when he solves the riddle of the human and is "recognized" as Jocasta's rightful husband. Lacan's version of Oedipus (the Schema L) is a diagram of the human condition, the domain of missed meanings and appointments, as well as a field of ever-renewed hope.

As a reminder of our mortality, Lacan insists on the notion of access to the symbolic order as dismemberment, reminding us of the fractal nature of "identity," which only *appears* to be whole. The mirage is predicated on a primal psychic wounding (emblematized by Lacan's "mirror stage"), a splitting of "oneself" into subject and object positions, body and mirror image.[36] This splitting is a function of depth—the recognition of "one's" reflection only *seems* to abolish distance and establish "identity." This mirage of unified identity paradoxically takes place only *thanks to* the maintained space from our self-perception, the space in which the image is reflected back.

Yet Lacan's reading of Freudian subjectivity as an effect of the symbolic order may open the way to a new assessment of social possibility in the information age. Perhaps the social is not dead, but has just changed its site. This is Freud's lesson in *Beyond the Pleasure Principle*, where the pleasure of the final resolution (death) is always deferred by the life drive compelling the organism to prolong its journey. To say that Oedipus is dead is to misread Sophocles' tale as ur-narrative, rather than paradigm, confusing the content of the message with its path. Cyberchat still reverberates with Oedipus' questions: Are my others who they appear to be? What is human, what is monstrous? But, more significantly, Oedipus' itinerary—the play of delusion and deferral as he approaches and avoids the knowledge of "who he is"—is also the circuit of cyberspace. Human doubt is now interactive, since we may hide behind the screen; but has it ever been otherwise, in the human web of roles, pretense, and misrecognition? More important than what millennial Oedipae ask is how and why they ask it, by what circumlocution. Cyberspace is an intersubjective maze where we grope to find our way in the field of the Other, "searching" a psychic URL where the Other may be addressed, but not found. The Other's perception of me is the "subject" in the chatroom of the symbolic.

Perhaps virtual reality deploys, electronically, the same intersubjective dynamic of guesswork and role-playing ("My screen name is . . .") that has always constituted human identity. For Freud's subject is a function of *space*, of shifting subject positions, shuttling between self and Alien Other. As Lacan suggests, identity is an effect of maintained space, a function of metaphor, where the paternal name is an illusory unifying *figure of speech*, standing in for the divided self it misrepresents.[37]

Just so, virtual reality simulates the real in the space of metaphor, "as if." Contrary to the assertions of Baudrillard concerning the impossibility of metaphor on a flattened screen, the virtual metaphor is alive and well, taking its point of reference in actions performed by the body, like a smile mimicked in the smiley face "emoticon"

:)

And a whole chat lexicon of emotions has joined this familiar sidelong grin, denoting everything from displeasure

: <

to desire (denoted by a furrowed brow with tongue hanging out)

} :p

to quixotic puzzlement

: \

It is as if the more virtual technology abstracts the Real, the more tenaciously the material world insists, with cyber trappings figured as pets (the mouse, the webcrawler, the gopher) and manual tools (the scissors, the paintbrush). Online, it is an hourglass that enjoins us to wait, a symbol more primitive and "material" than any clock, analogue or digital.

Nor have we completely escaped the Cartesian grid: in our worries about the Other who is pushing the buttons, Descartes haunts us still. He did, after all, voice the worry that the whole show might be staged by an "evil genius," the ultimate Internet hoaxer/host. For being online does not assuage desire; it engenders it. In our interpellations of the unknowable Other ("Who goes there?"), we continue to play out the oedipal drama of masquerade and query ("Who is out there? What do you want? Can you come out [or into my chat group] and play?"). In the search for answers, we might do well to suit up errant Oedipus for the third millennium, his website mapped at the crossroads between Thebes and Corinth.

Resiting Freud suggests that cyberspace is the latest playground for the Other (big O), who might just be Oedipus asking us to come online.

CHAPTER 2

HAS OEDIPUS STRUCK OUT?
ŽIŽEK ON THE CYBERFIELD

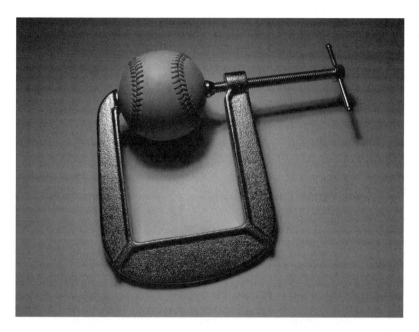

Stephen Everett, *Squeeze Play*, 2003.

> Chaos umpire sits,
> And by decision more embroils the fray
> By which he reigns

—John Milton, *Paradise Lost*

Costello: I'm only asking you. Who's the guy on first base?
Abbott: That's right.

—Abbott and Costello, *Who's on First?* (1936)

Perhaps in part because of his attention to cutting-edge millennial culture, Slavoj Žižek enjoys a unique celebrity status in cultural studies today. In fact, his reputation as both showman and intellectual is confirmed by a colorful moniker—the Giant of Ljubljana—that confers the charisma of a sports hero on this Lacanian philosopher.

But decades before Lacan's grandstand play diagrammed Žižek's future playing field—as the relay of intersubjective desire around four bases in the Schema L—popular culture had already produced a peerless demonstration of sliding subjectivity in a diamond-shaped field. For Abbott and Costello's classic routine on baseball, *Who's on First?* (1936), hilariously muddles meaning and position: the straight man Abbott pitches a slippery signifier ("Who") to his hopelessly confused partner Costello, who, unable to catch its meaning, nonetheless gives the pronoun merry chase as it rounds the bases.

Costello: Look Abbott, if you're the coach, you must know all the players.

Abbott: I certainly do.

Costello: So you'll have to tell me their names, and then I'll know who's playing on the team.

Abbott: . . . Well, let's see, we have on the bags . . . Who's on first, What's on second, I Don't Know's on third . . .

Costello: That's what I want to find out.

From the opening exchange, Costello misrecognizes the straight man's pitch as his own question bounced back to him. Lacanian theory would say that Abbott is invested by his interlocutor as symbolic authority, the *subject supposed to know* ("if you're the coach, you must know all the players").[1]

One could hardly ask for a livelier demonstration of the play of the Lacanian object, where the pronoun "who"—what Jakobson, significantly, calls the "shifter"—derives meaning from position. "Who" is both an other (the object of desire, Lacan's *objet petit a*) and an Other (a mysterious unknown). Even the comic impact of the routine is an effect of a positioning, causing a simple misunderstanding: the question "Who's on first?" can also be an answer, depending on whether "Who" is taken as a proper noun or a pronoun. Dependent on this mode of double meaning and transfer, the comic pitch demonstrates that any conversational play is an effect of a shifting subjective site, where one catches meaning only to toss it back into play.

Meanwhile back at the ball game, the crowd enjoys the wrangles between player and umpire—where meaning is always up for grabs, where the player's demand for satisfaction is unending, and where the "vested" authority, the *subject supposed to know*, is blind (according to the traditional insult hurled at the umpire from the stands).

This preliminary step onto the Lacanian field shows that baseball lingo redounds with images that are resonant with psychoanalysis. Both concern a positional play governed by arbitrary signals, relayed from a removed Other. In baseball, the Other is the coach in the dugout whose coded signals designate him as the hidden lawgiver calling the shots from afar. In Freud's theory, the outsider/ Other is the paternal lawgiver; and, at the level of society, the authority is the *dead father* of *Totem and Taboo*. In Lacan's version, the place of the Other may also be occupied by the analyst, or even the patient's own unconscious.

Interestingly, in the sort of happy coincidence that Lacan loved to exploit in his own parables, the shape of both playing fields is a diamond (*losange*). For, as we saw in the Schema L, the diamond takes pride of place in the doubled triangle, describing a relay of desire around four bases (subject, object, ego, Other), with the subject function parsed into two positions: barred subject and self-image. Connecting the four corners (rounding the bases) reveals the diamond shape of Lacan's oedipal elaboration. Note that in Freud's original *triangle*, $\mathcal{S}$ and a' share one position, the agent; a is the object, and the Father is thus the third term.

a) $\mathcal{S}$ (barred subject)
b) child (agent)
c) Oedipus the Criminal/Wounded
d) analysand
e) "Who?" (barred subject)

a) *objet petit a* (*autre*/other/object of desire)
b) mother
c) Jocasta the Mother/Wife
d) analyst as object of desire
e) "What?" (unattainable object of the chase)

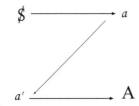

a) a' *moi* (ego, ego ideal)
b) child's self-image (agent)
c) Oedipus the Wise/King
d) analysand's self-conception/misrecognized "identity"/analyst conceived as Authority, as "subject supposed to know"
e) "I Don't Know" (an empty identity)

a) *Autre* (Other/radical alterity)
b) father as lawgiver
c) Laius the Father/Stranger
d) analyst/opaque Other/analyst conceived as the unconscious ("*ça parle*")
e) "Home plate" or dugout; coach or referee as lawgiver outside the game

The Schema L as Oedipus' field.

In later versions of the Schema L (see page 216), Lacan connects all four positions, emphasizing the implication of each term in the other three, creating a double *losange* by drawing new lines $\text{\textbf{\textsterling}} \rightarrow a$, $a \rightarrow A$, and $\text{\textbf{\textsterling}} \rightarrow A$.

In later work, Lacan also uses a *losange* for his algorithmic notation of the subject's fantasy relation to the "object," perpetually in flight: $\text{\textbf{\textsterling}} \lozenge a$. (This algorithm indicates that the barred *subject* $\text{\textbf{\textsterling}}$ is a function of the *objet petit a* about which it fantasizes, but never apprehends.)[2] And in *Seminar XVII*, on the "four discourses" (master, hysteric, analyst, university), Lacan again explicitly draws a diamond field, where the four players circulate among four bases, by rotating a quarter turn each time. From a Lacanian base, then, *Who's on First?* reads like an object lesson in learning to distinguish always contingent truth from seemingly firmly grounded fact: the most direct answer will be missed in our desire to apprehend it. (Costello gets the answer from the outset, but he doesn't hold on to it; he either drops the ball, or fires it back to his pitcher.) Lacan's own striking grandstand play—the Seminar delivered in a Paris auditorium, packed to the rafters—was a spectacle aimed at exposing the limitations of the *"sujet supposé savoir"* (the Authority, in this case Lacan himself) to an onlooking throng. In the pun on *supposer*, Lacan foregrounds an effect of positioning, as *super-posing*. In the same way, Abbott and Costello's performance plays out the Lacanian axiom that the "Other [at least as Ultimate Answer Man, Infallible Referee] does not exist."[3]

When the Giant of Ljubljana makes his entrance onto the Freudian field at the end of the twentieth century, his commentary emphasizes that Lacanian subjectivity is positional and agonistic, determined by slide and shift, feint and theft. Again, baseball may illustrate the point: the art of stealing bases, honored in an official statistic of the game, is first a contest between opposing subjects. While the runner tries to read the pitcher's feint, the pitcher's sidelong glance sizes up the runner's intent to steal a base between pitches.

Žižek describes Lacan's notion of the imaginary duel between subjects in strikingly similar terms. He adds that the imaginary game of feint progresses to "symbolic deception," feigning to the next power, as it were. This feigning takes place in the field of the intersubjective gaze, at once interactive and interpassive, objectified and objectifying. In symbolic feint, the subject does not simply lie, but tries to fake out his adversary by telling the truth: "human feigning is the feigning of feigning itself: in imaginary deception, I simply present a false image of myself, while in symbolic deception, I present a true image and count on its being taken for a lie."[4]

Appropriately enough, this example is itself situated in a chain of intertextual references, passed from player to player. For Žižek is staging a replay of Lacan's discussion on symbolic deception (spelled out in *Seminars III* and *XI*); while Lacan has nabbed his own example from Freud (*Jokes and their Relation to the Unconscious*), who in turn got his example from Jewish oral tradition. (Freud relays the timeworn Jewish joke about two old men on the road to Krakow, who seek to outwit each other by appearing to lie while telling the truth.)[5] The Jewish tradition is "up" first in this series (as purveyor of the traditional joke), with Freud and Lacan on deck and Žižek batting fourth in the lineup, poised to drive the point home to today's public. This same kind of circulation insists throughout Lacan's seminars, accounting for his reliance on parable, schema, or matheme as symbolic notations of transfer and interchange. And it is a strategy that the Giant of Ljubljana has learned well from the coach.

In *Looking Awry*, for instance, Žižek points out that while any theory is contingent on the position of the theorist, this is especially true of the position of the official who is "supposed to know" the answers. For the authority is in fact partially blind, thanks to the opaque spot in the intersubjective gaze itself, the fact that (as Lacan puts it) "you never look at me from the place where I see you."[6] Žižek refers to this spot as the opacity of the Other, whose "truth" we can guess only by projection, from trying to see from and in its place, or from an oblique angle, *Looking Awry*. Even the *subject supposed to know* can do no more than confer an always subjective meaning on a field of vision that is by definition skewed and partial, emanating from a circumscribed a point of view.

In fact, Žižek's most recent essay on cyberspace ("Is it Possible to Traverse the Fantasy in Cyberspace?") may be read as a play-by-play reflection on the consequences of position, in the new field of cyberrelations.[7] Or is it so new? Žižek's play of positions may reveal that the rules of the game have not changed all that much: who's on first is still an effect of "who" or "what" is on second and third, and how and why they got there. And the player's position is still contingent on the pitch of the sportscaster who is calling the plays as *he* sees them.

CHANGING THE LINEUP

Costello: All I'm trying to find out is . . . What's the guy's name on first base.
Abbott: Well, don't change the players around.

In his first essay on online interaction ("The Unbearable Closure of Being"), Žižek takes on two postmodern myths about virtual interaction: (1) cyberspace provides a kind of delirious aesthetic media experience, even possibly affording a more intense sensual experience than that of "RL" (real life); (2) cyberspace, as an effect of simulation, provokes a confusion of the domains of "RL" (real life) and "VR" (virtual reality).[8]

To these two "myths," Žižek adds a third common perception that he attributes to Sherry Turkle and Allucquére Rosanne Stone: the assumption that the experience of cyberspace is *liberating* for the postmodern "decentered" subject. While he is sympathetic to this third view, Žižek goes on to mount a convincing critique of all three assumptions, calling attention to the fact that the subject in cyberspace is, after all, an extension of the ego. Thus any search for identity in cyberspace must take into account the fundamental split that grounds all subjectivity, in a far more radical division than that emphasized by the "postmodern" experience of decentering/disorientation in simulated space.

Having voiced his objections to the three positions that he outlines, Žižek proposes a fourth position, as a sort of friendly correction of Turkle and Stone, positioned "on third." For he concedes that, even if cyberspace does not decenter an always-already split subject in any radical way, the ascendancy of the virtual may indeed harbor social potential, attenuating the hard knocks of real life. Žižek even suggests, apparently without irony, that we may someday see the settling of war in a virtual arena.

In the more recent essay on cyberspace ("Is it Possible to Traverse the Fantasy in Cyberspace?"), Žižek again proposes to adjudicate a *triad* of theoretical positions. But this time, the star opponent is Oedipus rather than postmodern theory. The structure of the first essay, however, is reproduced in this second piece, which again traces a field where three bases subsequently open up to a fourth base in the conclusion. Thus Žižek's own constructed playing-ground is a diamond, uncannily reminiscent of Lacan's *losange* relating subject and object ($ \mathcal{S} \lozenge a$). In any case, in both essays Žižek's four-base circuit ensures that it is he himself who will reach home base, scoring the winning point or at least batting the others in.

Significantly, Žižek's opening move is a *self-positioning* in the field:

> As a psychoanalytically oriented (Lacanian) philosopher, let me begin with the question one expects an analyst to raise: what are the consequences of cyberspace for Oedipus—that is , for the mode of subjectivization that psychoanalysis conceptualized as the Oedipus complex and its dissolution? ("Is it Possible," 111)

Thus Žižek announces that his topic is determined by the expectations of his readers: "let me begin with the question one expects an analyst to raise." This is entirely appropriate for a Lacanian, of course, because Lacan insists that our own subject position is always taken up in the preexisting field of the Other's desire, and our own stance is in part determined by our anticipation of the Other's move. So it is to be expected, when the Giant of Ljubljana steps up to the plate to comment on millennial culture, that he should acknowledge himself as a player.

A problem, however, is that Žižek also sets himself up as the umpire. He does attempt to insure fair play by professing neutrality in this first formulation. But a closer look reveals that even in this opening play, the game may already be up for

Oedipus: by putting the verb "conceptualize" in the past tense, Žižek has already subtly pitched the discussion from a post-oedipal angle, at the same time that he pitches Oedipus as a "complex," rather than as a paradigm of subject formation.

Like any theorist playing on the diamond of intersubjectivity, then, Žižek has an angle. Yet Žižek's position disqualifying Oedipus would seem to move twenty-first-century psychoanalytic theory somewhere outside the Freudian field—a move which, given Lacan's own insistence on "returning to Freud," is radical indeed. How and why does Žižek get from here to there?

First of all, he changes the lineup from essay one to essay two, with new players. In the second go-round, the focus has been shifted from the "postmodern" subject to Oedipus, the star player who seems to be on the verge of being thrown out of the game. But an even more aggressive change is Žižek's own preemptive strike, where he moves to pathologize all three of what he calls the "predominant" views on Oedipus and cyberspace, in a single ruling.

> Clinically it is easy to categorize these three versions as psychosis, perversion, and hysteria: the first version claims that cyberspace entails universalized psychosis; according to the second one, cyberspace opens up the liberating perspective of globalized multiple perversion; the third one claims that cyberspace remains within the confines of the enigmatic Other that hystericizes the subject. ("Is It Possible," 116)

This new strategy may perhaps be attributed to Žižek's heightened focus on oedipal subject-formation in the second essay, since the clinical diagnosis would seem to contribute stylistically and rhetorically to his psychoanalytic angle. Yet the question remains just what the stakes of this play may be. For in a sense, Oedipus is brought into the game only as a player who has already been thrown out of it: "The predominant doxa today is that cyberspace explodes, or at least potentially undermines the reign of Oedipus, announcing instead some new post-oedipal libidinal economy" (110). As we shall see, Žižek underscores Oedipus' "has-been" status by attributing this new post-oedipal economy to the players on both first and second base in his essay. But on third, he introduces a new argument into the lineup, which he calls "the assertion of the continuity of cyberspace with the oedipal mode of subjectivation" (113). This third base is given some importance in its positioning adjacent to home plate, since third is the base from which the runner is poised to score. But whereas the coach names names in filling bases one (Virilio, Vattimo, Baudrillard) and two (Stone and Turkle) in his new lineup, he leaves "third" empty, characterizing it elliptically as the position of "some rare, if none the less penetrating theorists."

I can go no further in this discussion without acknowledging the stakes of my own position here. For Žižek's analyses of culture figure prominently in my effort at resiting Oedipus in millennial culture, the topic of the entire first section of this book.[9] But I am "interested" in his article in a more direct way as well, since the only reference that Žižek's footnote cites as an example of the nameless theorist(s) "on third" is in fact an early version of "Is Oedipus Online?," the title chapter of this book. One motivation for my discussion here, then, is a reprisal of Žižek's reading, since I think he may get my argument wrong by displacing some of its terms. I am also, admittedly, staging an effort to get back in the game, since Žižek's discussion of the third position, among other things, responds to issues raised in this book.

ROTATING THE LINEUP

In any case, by appending his own view to the three views he evaluates, Žižek once again actually diagrams a field with four bases: a move that recalls Lacan's own iterations of a dimensionalized triangle, doubled/expanded to four bases. In fact, Lacan quite literally "opens up" the oedipal triangle in the Schema L (actually resembling a Greek lambda or Z) by unhinging and unfolding one of its three sides. In other words, the fourth base is created by splitting the locus of the subject into two positions at once—the barred subject and the self-image or ego. This unfolding of the oedipal triangle continues in his work in *Seminar XV*, this time characterizing the analytic transference as a process occurring around four bases. (Here, Lacan refers to the structure of the transference in therapy as a tetrahedron, remarking on a rotation of subject positions among the symbolic, imaginary, and real registers; and these registers are themselves depicted in a series of embedded triangular configurations in a number of diagrams of progressive complexity.) This reference to a four-sided process cannot fail to evoke Freud's famous remark that there are always four people present in any analytic session: the analyst, the patient, and the patient's parents. The details of Lacan's version of this tetrahedron, while intriguing, need not be rehearsed here—and indeed cannot be reproduced here, since the "authorized" translation has yet to appear.

Suffice it to say that the process of Lacanian "trans-ference" ultimately repositions the subject/patient in the position of the analyst, as "she" moves into a position to see that the *subject supposed to know* does not in fact possess superior knowledge of what ails her. The subject thus begins to analyze for herself, as the new subject of a more complete, if always unfinished, knowledge. This rotation recalls Freud's account of "The Dissolution of the Oedipus Complex" (1924), where the subject rotates to the position of authority or lawgiver, ultimately reenacting the process with a new generation, becoming in turn the parental "know-it-all."[10] And we have seen that yet another rotation of four players among bases—also an effect of shifting power and authority—structures Lacan's discussion of the four primary discourses, where each figure occupies four successive "places" in turn.[11]

But before these speculations take us too far afield, let us return to Žižek's face-off with Oedipus. By insisting on the three-to-four, triangle-to-diamond structure that subtends Lacan's subject-formation, as well as his version of the analytic situation, Žižek's essay finally has implications about positionality itself—and about "thirdness" as an attribute of fourthness. In fact, the essay may say more about the stakes of taking a base than it says about any player (including the subject Oedipus himself) who provisionally occupies a given base in the intersubjective circuit.

Thus, if I reargue the question of Oedipus Internaut here, it is not simply to declare Oedipus online or Žižek off-base. In fact Žižek's work provides a refreshing contrast to the doomsday tenor of much millennial theory (the social order is dead! the machines have already won!). Rather than acceding to the demand to pronounce a ready-made judgment about whether cyberspace is simply good or bad for the human subject, the Giant of theory quite rightly questions the premises of the question itself. But one can certainly challenge the umpire on his removal of Oedipus from this game, as an exclusion that may risk removing Freud himself from the thick of the action on the Psychoanalytic Field.

MAKING THE DOUBLE PLAY

Costello: What's the guy's name on first base?

Abbott: No. What is on second.

Costello: I'm not asking you who's on second.

Abbott: Who's on first.

Žižek begins his critique of cyber-Oedipus with a double play of sorts, combining the two scenarios (on first and second) that he says describe a version of "the end of Oedipus," but differentiating these two bases according to the stance of the theorist ("Of course, the mode of perception of this 'end' of Oedipus depends on the standpoint of the theoretician" ["Is It Possible," 111]).

About the theorists that he visits "at first," whom he names parenthetically (Baudrillard, Virilio, and Vattimo), Žižek writes:

First, there are those who see in this a dystopian prospect of individuals regressing to pre-symbolic psychotic immersion, of losing the symbolic distance that sustains the minimum of critical/ reflective attitude (the idea that the computer functions as a maternal Thing that swallows the subject, who entertains an attitude of incestuous fusion towards it). (111)

In other words, the ascendance of virtual simulacra is considered a dangerous lure by this dystopian contingent, associated with "the idea that the computer functions as a maternal Thing that swallows the subject." The opening section of the original essay, restated in chapter 1 above, makes a similar point, highlighting the "cyberchosis" of the panic philosophers (Baudrillard, Virilio, and others), and maintaining that their end-of-the-world scenarios have much in common with Freud's description of paranoia in the famous Schreber case. And Žižek's evocation of "the maternal Thing that swallows the subject" resonates with another passage in "Is Oedipus Online?," which alludes to Ray Barglow's image of the cybernaut "mesmerized and stymied by the addictive lure of the Mother Board to which one is connected for hours on end." But there are a number of differences between Zizek's assessments and my position, which I think contribute to Žižek's tendency to underrate the role of Oedipus in cyberspace.

Although Žižek limits himself to three players "on first" as representatives of the "psychotic" interpretation of cybersubjectivity, this dystopian view is in fact extremely widespread in millennial theory. The selection of three very well-known theorists (Baudrillard, Virilio, Vattimo), figures whose names may stand metonymically for the whole body of their work, lends this position a certain authority, and perhaps a certain virility as well, since Žižek does not invoke the many feminist theorists who share this "dystopian" reading. Recent books by Anne Balsamo and Claudia Springer, for instance, criticize cyberculture as masculinist, even misogynist—claiming that the discourse of Cyberia consigns women to the sci-fi trope of "cyber babe," even while it commodifies sexuality in the virtual sex business.[12]

A second potential problem with Žižek's position "on first" concerns the location of the psychotic tendency itself. For rather than insisting that the subject in cyberspace is somehow necessarily psychotic—which may plug into defeatist appraisals of human possibilities in the new age—one might consider this paranoid theory as an overestimation of the Lacanian imaginary that follows from the standpoint of the theorist. In chapter 1, we saw that panic philosophers like Virilio and Baudrillard claim to lament a loss of human mooring in real life. However, they really seem to be mourning a (mythical, illusory) transcendental human subject, the identity of the self in the good old days when boundaries were clear and rules of conduct were defined, including the rules of our "naturally" gendered positions.

Žižek's own discussion may show signs of this nostalgic temptation. For he asserts that the psychotic dystopian reading is "at its strongest when it insists on the difference between appearance and simulacrum." And he goes on to assert that what is really lost in Virilio and Vattimo's "postmodern Brave New World of universalized simulacra" is "appearance" in the Kantian sense: "appearance is thus the domain not simply of phenomena, but of those 'magic moments' in which another, noumenal dimension momentarily 'appears' in ('shines through') some empirical, contingent phenomena" ("Is It Possible," 111).

In this framing, it is no longer clear whether Žižek is simply explaining the position of the dystopians "at their strongest," criticizing that position (to which he refers in passing as a "sentimental platitude"), or actually advocating it. The lack of attribution permits Žižek to "slide" from the position of observer to that of advocate, as he seems to do with this assertion: "Therein lies the problem with cyberspace and virtual reality: what virtual reality threatens is not reality, which is dissolved in the multiplicity of its simulacra, but on the contrary, appearance itself" (111).

Žižek's sympathy with the first-base position becomes more apparent when he affirms that what is missing in cyberspace is not material reality itself, but a certain "symbolic efficacy" that depends on retaining a kind of mystery when designating reality.

The third problem with Žižek's affinity with the first-base position is his simultaneous qualification of this standpoint as post-oedipal (a "libidinal economy beyond Oedipus") and pre-oedipal ("the threat of fusion with the maternal Thing"). Even if this logical contradiction could be resolved, neither of these two states—pre-oedipal implosion or post-oedipal psychosis—may be considered beyond Oedipus, as Žižek asserts, since the first (implosion) regresses to before Oedipus, and the second (psychosis) is a defensive symptomatic reaction to the threat posed by the oedipal order itself.

Thus, in stealing onto first base alongside his players, Žižek seems to keep Oedipus in the game.

What's on Second?

Žižek's second example of "the end of Oedipus" is problematic for some of the same reasons. For both Stone and Turkle make arguments that are much more detailed and subtle than Žižek's brief reference acknowledges: these are no naive utopians, enchanted with every aspect of cyberculture. Turkle discusses the problem of online crime and its psychological impact; while Stone's work performs a provocative analysis of cultural phenomena—such as the attraction of the Gothic in "Cyberia" as an effect of millennial anxiety about miscegenation, blurred gender boundaries, and diseases of the blood.[13] The short shrift that Žižek gives to these arguments is also regrettable from a gender perspective, for the two theorists "on second" are named with the familiar forms of their feminine given names (Sandy Stone and Sherry Turkle), while the male theorists on first are referenced formally, with the patronymic. In other words, if the first base is unduly masculinized in Žižek's presentation, the postmodern position "on second" is unduly feminized in a move that unfortunately may appear to be related to his critical view of postmodern theories of the subject.

But the major problem with Žižek's alignment of Stone and Turkle is more fundamental. For in point of fact, neither Stone nor Turkle actually focuses on "the end of Oedipus," as he suggests. (Donna Haraway does refer to a post-oedipal, post-gender societal organization, but Žižek does not mention her work.) In fact, Stone does not really treat the status of psychoanalysis at all: her work is a cultural chronicle of the origins of the Internet at the juncture between two California cultures (Silicon Valley and new age counterculture), but Freud is not even cited in her index.

The fact that Žižek associates the patriarchal transcendental ego critiqued by feminists automatically with Oedipus may say more about a blind spot in his own position than it does about the position that he terms postmodern. Indeed, although Žižek aligns Stone and Turkle with a clinically perverse position, it is his own reading of them that seems to be quite literally *per-verse* (turned aside, diverted), since it reroutes their argument to support "the end of Oedipus." And the libidinal model they do espouse, even if it may be called perverse in a certain sense (since it describes the free circulation of the libido in a "polymorphous perverse" virtual domain), is a derepressive "perversity" that is all but unrecognizable as it is recast in Žižek's version (as a male masochist submitting to a female dominatrix, avid for Law and punishment).

Again, baseball lingo provides an apt term for the move that Žižek performs here: it is a double play, where two players are caught off-base and ruled "out." At the same time, there is a chiasmus in Žižek's move: he subtly (and no doubt unintentionally) elevates the first (masculinized) position, associating it with a "strong version" of the Kantian notion of appearance—even while he seems to want to refute this position; conversely, he seems to misrepresent the second feminized position—even while, as we shall see, he appears to be advocating a version of it, as the new improved "perversion" in his conclusion. So while this double play subtly steals first base by appropriating the position of the dystopians, it steals into second as well, by correcting the weakness of its argument in the name of rigor.

Finally, Žižek's double play promoting the end of Oedipus seems to underplay a crucial point: the original Oedipus to which Freud refers (Sophocles' *Oedipus Rex*) could itself be subtitled "The End of Oedipus," since it depicts the mythical tragic hero as exiled, done in by fate. Freud's infamous "family romance," laid onto the Sophoclean tragedy, describes a shift from *Oedipus Rex* to *oedipus complex*. Thus Freud's own theory is already a postscript, a repositioning of Oedipus beyond the myth-ical, literary Oedipus, asking how each new human subject manages to *avoid* the tragic model of incest and parricide.

Freud's own theory on oedipal subject-formation, in any case, already implies the first two positions that Žižek sketches, as the dystopian and utopian versions, respectively, of "the end of Oedipus." For Freud's own version of the post-oedipal subject, in his work on psychosis, deals with the consequences of a failure to re-solve the castration complex, resulting in a foreclosure of the primal scene (or of "castration"). Indeed, we could say that a dystopian oedipal consequence ("*Oedi-pus Wrecks*, the Tragedy") is enacted by Schreber, the Wolf Man, and other tragic heroes of psychosis. The second more felicitous scenario of a successful move be-yond Oedipus ("*Oedipus Wrecks, the Comedy*") is also elaborated in key Freudian texts which detail compelling human endeavors (joking, literature, play, mar-riage). The best example of Freud's cultural theory is perhaps still his account of the transgressive activity of joking (as I argue in my discussion of Deleuze in chapter 4). As Freud insists, joking breaks laws and reestablishes them simulta-neously, averting tragic conflict by rerouting hostile impulses along a route of substitutive conciliation.

Although Freud does not seem to perceive the convergence of the joking sce-nario that he describes in *Jokes and Their Relation to the Unconscious* with the oedipal sce-nario that he sketches elsewhere, the coincidence of terms is uncanny. (We recall that Freud posits a classic locker-room scenario: a male jokes about the female ob-ject of his desire with a third party, another male who acts as both obstacle to the original sexual seduction and facilitator of a substitutive process of enjoyment, based on identification and social bonding.) As in the classic Freudian oedipal sce-nario, a dyadic structure of conquest is opened to a triadic circuit of circumven-tion. Thanks to the intervention of an "overdetermined" outsider who acts as both obstacle and audience, the subject is ushered into a social interaction beyond tragic incestuous closure. The oedipal tragedy is replayed as comedy.

In *Seminar IV*, Lacan elaborates the joking phenomenon as an effect of *désir*, the very motor of the "signifying chain" (the Lacanian term for the net of language/culture). Thus commenting on only the first base of this position "beyond Oedi-pus" (the tragic version, ending in psychosis), without the mitigating possibility held out by Freud himself as the foundation of social being, may be not only be to "look awry" at Freud's account of subject-formation, but also to lose sight of the bigger picture—the role of the same dynamic in larger social formations.

In other words, since Freud's Oedipus is already beyond Oedipus, do we need the Žižekian move "traversing the fantasy"?

On Coming in Third

Abbott: Who's on first?

Costello: I don't know.

Abbott: He's on third, we're not talking about him.

Žižek introduces "Is Oedipus Online?" obliquely, in a formulation emphasizing its third position among the theories he cites: "However, opposed to both versions of 'cyberspace as the end of Oedipus' are some rare, if none the less penetrating, theoreticians who assert the continuity of cyberspace with the oedipal mode of subjectivation" ("Is It Possible," 113).

While Žižek's text refers to "theoreticians," in the plural, his footnote reference cites only the single example of "Is Oedipus Online?" (Incidentally, I would nominate Lyotard, Turkle, Haraway, and the Žižek of *Looking Awry* himself, to share third base.) My essay in fact uses Žižek's work as framework: "In a recent lecture at Columbia University, Slavoj Žižek coined a millennial aphorism that foregrounds the equivocal status of being in the information age: 'We are what we want, in cyberspace.'"[14]

Žižek responds explicitly to this opening pitch, citing my citation of him in the single quotation style: "Yes, in cyberspace, 'you can be whatever you want'; you are free to choose a symbolic identity (a screen persona), but you must choose one in a way which will always betray you, which will never be fully adequate" ("Is It Possible," 115). And there is a more explicit echo in this relay:

> *Flieger:* This provocation, which recasts ontological status as an effect of virtual desire, explains why some bimillennials are still reading Freud, to discover if our "postsociety" has in fact succeeded in replacing interface for face-to-face. ("Is Oedipus Online," 81)
>
> *Žižek:* In short, interface means that my relationship to the Other is never face-to-face. ("Is It Possible," 114)

Žižek goes on to mention another focus of "Is Oedipus Online?"—the convergence of the Schema L with the "configuration" of intersubjective cyberspace: "It thus seems that cyberspace materializes directly the so-called Schema L elaborated by Lacan in the early fifties" ("Is It Possible," 115). The conversational volley with "Is Oedipus Online?" culminates in a passage where the title serves as a metonymy for the entire third-base position: "There is, however, a sense in which 'Oedipus Online' no long functions as Oedipus proper" (114).

Indeed. My central point is that "Oedipus proper" is already an elaboration of a more radical subjectifying process, encountered throughout Freud's most challenging essays on culture. Freud's paradigm has implications that go far beyond the gender- and culture-bound casting of Oedipus as "castration *complex*."

Thus it is appropriate that Žižek has placed "Oedipus Online" third in his own lineup, since the argument there is about "thirdness" itself as a site introducing both complexity/context and exteriority/exile into the intersubjective relation. In fact, the oedipal diagram introduces the Other out in left field, as an obstacle trying to interfere with the subject's direct progress in a beeline to the next base. As such, the Outfielder/Other (as well as the shortstop, or any of the players on the field) stands for the alienation that subject-formation entails for all human subjects.

Žižek himself sums up the argument about "thirdness" as obstruction, deflection, or screen:

> Cyberspace retains the fundamental oedipal structure of an intervening Third Order which, in its very capacity as the agency of mediation, sustains the subject's desire, while simultaneously acting as the agent of prohibition that prevents its direct, full gratification. ("Is It Possible," 113)

In other words, Oedipus can be read as a screen name of sorts; he is a pinch hitter standing in for the human subject. In this sense, "Oedipus Internaut" denotes the overdetermined subject not only of cyberspace, but of any human space, as a field of dreams which is always an effect of position, played out as a long circuit of desire.

Return to Freud

This insistence on the importance of the third in the subjectifying configuration rests directly on Freud's work, including the founding myth of society that he proposes in *Totem and Taboo*.[15] (After killing the father, the rebellious upstart sons of the tribe finally renounce incestuous gratification and focus their sexual desires beyond the immediate community itself, instituting exogamy, in response to the Law that honors the Dead Father, the ultimate outsider, a ghostly legislator.) It is obviously not a question of taking this parable literally, but *Totem and Taboo* does suggest how the threat of tragic infighting resonates far beyond the conflict of sexual interest in the nuclear family (the "oedipus complex"), addressing the even more fundamental human tendency to appropriate the Other's base. Lacan picks up on this, when he locates the socializing function of the symbolic order as the domain of language: "What makes the human world a world covered with objects derives from the fact that the object of human interest is the object of the other's desire . . . speech overcomes this rivalry, arriving at agreement—this is yours, this is mine—a symbolic pact."[16]

As early as 1905, however, Freud's work on jokes had already entertainingly emphasized both of these cultural processes: the social configuration (elaborated later in *Totem and Taboo*) as a transactional circuit; and the symbolic function of language as pact. Significantly, both processes are associated explicitly with the function of thirdness in joking. (Freud: "The tendentious joke calls for three people . . . when the first person finds his libidinal impulse inhibited by the woman, he develops a hostile trend against the second person [the woman, here], and calls upon the original interfering third party as his ally.")[17] Not only is the third party the recipient of the joking pleasure, "he" is a collaborator with the teller. As Freud puts it: "I myself cannot laugh at a joke which has occurred to me without his help," and insists that the third party will go on to *perpetuate* the whole process by telling the joke to someone else.[18] The same sort of triangulation underlies the oedipal formation—interference deflects an original biological urge into a social circuit, a field of one or many others/Others, as observers or players. And the joking/oedipal triangle always functions as if it had four terms, since it is always begun anew from home base, in a reiterated circuit that is both compulsive and deflective in nature.[19] (The hearer, Freud insists, is *compelled* to pass the joke on.)

Fifteen years later, in *Beyond the Pleasure Principle*, Freud uses child's play to illustrate a new instance of repetition and transformation, effecting the transfer of a harrowing situation—the departure of the mother—into a creative solution (the famous *fort-da* game, where the toy stands in for the missing object of desire).[20] But again, the action is motivated by a third term (in this instance, the significant object—the child's mother—is presumably absent for the evening because she has been taken away by a "behind-the-scene" paternal Other [the boy's father, Freud's son-in-law]. Indeed, as onlooker, Grandpa Freud himself is a behind-the-screen Other, the fourth party in this play).

This modality (opening from an imploded dyad to a social triad to a four-base repetition in the diamond) insists throughout Freud's work, and in fact appears much earlier in his joking scenario than in his work on Oedipus. So the priority of what Žižek calls "Oedipus proper," or the Oedipus complex, as the fundamental structure in psychoanalysis, is open to question. Even if Oedipus as complex provides one particularly compelling narrative instance of a more fundamental intersubjective paradigm, it must be considered historically contingent and culturally bound as (as Lacan points out in his own critique of "Oedipus proper" in *Seminar XV*), pitched from the base of European patriarchal culture from which Freud himself was theorizing.

In my own relay of these ideas pitched back from the new century, I suggest that "Oedipus" is less about saving any particular position for the star player—as Žižek's focus suggests—than it is about rotational site or differential position. My reiterative reading of "Freud after Freud" is less about complex than complexity, in the twenty-first-century sense of that term. For current complexity theory examines the nonlinear dynamics of change at the "tipping point," by the addition of a term that changes the very nature of the process in which it intervenes, like a catalyst in a chemical reaction.

TOUCHING BASE, OR "TRAVERSING THE FANTASY"

Žižek does point out the importance of thirdness in Freud's configuration of subjectivity: "Owing to this intervening Third, every partial gratification/satisfaction is marked by a fundamental 'this is not that'" ("Is It Possible," 115). And I concur with his eloquent formulation of the view from third, minus the reduction of the dynamic process to purely formal structure: "In other words, what is 'beyond Oedipus' (as a certain historically specified narrative/myth) is Oedipus itself qua purely formal structure cosubstantial with the very fact of the symbolic order" (115).

Yet Žižek's essay finally objects to the pro-oedipal argument on (appropriately enough) three grounds:

1. He asserts that "Oedipus Online" inadequately explains the persistence of the myth that it claims to replace. ("However clear and elucidating it may appear, this difference between Oedipus qua mythical narrative and Oedipus qua formal structure leaves a crucial question unanswered: where does the need for the narrative supplement to the formal structure come from?" [115].)

2. He objects that a distillation of the oedipal structure eliminates the "little piece of the Real" upon which (as he maintains in Looking Awry) any symbolic transaction must be based, or it risks hardening into a hollow formalism that lacks mooring in reality. ("'The transference' must be supported by the peu du réel, by some remainder of the Real" [115].)

3. He concludes that the position of "Oedipus Online" hystericizes the subject, by the agency of a hyperrepressive symbolic that even risks provoking psychosis. ("Paradoxically, cyberspace thus designates a potential 'relapse' into psychosis, a breakdown of the symbolic mediation, precisely in so far as it actualizes the pure structure of symbolic prohibition/mediation without the 'little piece of the real' of a figure of the father that gives body to it" [115].)

Žižek suggests that evaluating "Oedipus" in the new information culture depends on "getting the break with 'Oedipus proper' clear" (114), so it is important to touch base with his three objections in order to keep Oedipus in the twenty-first-century lineup:

1. First, Žižek asks why we need the myth. My reading of Oedipus does not disqualify the mythic resonance of Oedipus in favor of an empty symbolic structure. It does deemphasize the Father as character rather than position, by suggesting that the family romance is not the only important aspect of the myth of Oedipus. For the myth of Oedipus is just as much about the vicissitudes of knowledge as about any rivalry or usurpation of erotic rights: as Oedipus solves the riddle of the Sphinx, he in turn becomes the *subject supposed to know* to his subjects. The marriage with Jocasta is his deadly reward for presuming to know all.

In *Seminar XV*, Lacan emphasizes the end of analysis as the fall of the *subject supposed to know*, a move that exposes the analyst as a mere mortal implicated in the countertransference. Just so, the tragic history of Oedipus is one of misrecognition: his knowledge is not so profound as it is clever (he is good at riddles); it is intrepid but empty (as he searches for the culprit), and blind in the crucial spot where the criminal himself looks back from his own mirror. The concept of Oedipus Online does not neglect the myth, but it seeks to dislocate the privilege and priority of Oedipus the King—a coronation that has contributed to so many reductions of Freud (as "only about sex"). In fact Žižek's own most compelling theorizations of the subject in culture, based on pointing out the blind spot in any field of vision, are strikingly demonstrated by the drama of misrecognition and discovery, blindness and insight, that mythic Oedipus enacts—first as Greek monarch and player, and in our day as Internaut navigating the field of digital play.

2. Rather than attempting to promote Oedipus as a strictly symbolic function, limited to pure structure without connection to the real, "Oedipus Online" emphasizes that the many cultural registers in which Freud and Lacan replay versions of the oedipal circuit actually enrich its connections with "real life." Indeed, putting "Oedipus Online" involves a psychoanalytic grounding of virtual experience in material ways. It necessarily addresses developments in the new media and techno-science, arguing that the Internet is real life, the site of interactions embedded in economics and culture—just as literature, television, drama, and religion are. If anything, cyberspace brings materiality into the symbolic/oedipal equation in a critical way, by making the computer itself an important player in the intersubjective process.

3. The automatic hystericization of the subject by primal repression—which Žižek claims is reinforced by the "continuation of Oedipus by other means"—is a Lacanian principle about which I in fact have reservations. Lacan equates the hysteric's discourse with that of the barred subject, without sufficiently distinguishing between the clinical pathology of neurosis and the ontological and epistemological status of the subject as "s/he" who will never know everything, from all positions, at once.

One answer to this question, however, would be that the symbolic can and does function in countless instances without being embodied by a flesh-and-blood father, as Freud's own examples concerning joking, creative writing, cultural inmixing, and the transference in analysis attest. (Even in the "real-life" oedipus complex, Freud points out that it is often the mother or nursemaid who threatens the male child with castration, in order to curtail masturbation.) But Žižek continues: "why can we not simply enter the symbolic order, and directly assume the loss involved in this entry?" The framing of this rhetorical query almost seems to manifest a longing for simplicity and directness ("Why can we not *simply* enter the symbolic order and *directly* assume the loss?") But directness is the antithesis of Freud's circuitous move. Indeed, the entry into the symbolic is essentially and inherently a process of complexification, necessitating a structural long- circuiting. You can't get home by "directly" traversing the field (or the fantasy), cutting the corners by "simply" skipping the bases. In Freud, jaywalking is against the Law.

Žižek goes on to link his query, however, with the enigma of the prohibition in psychoanalysis. His observation is framed in a rhetoric of assumption that is found throughout the essay, whereby performance pinch hits for demonstration, sliding into the place of certainty ("it is easy to see"; "it is needless to add"): "Needless to add, we thereby encounter the enigma of the prohibition of the impossible; if *jouissance* [the enjoyment of the object of desire] is impossible, why do we need the gesture of formally prohibiting it?" ("Is It Possible," 115). Again, Freud might answer that it is not a question here of a legal move, or of a voluntaristic gesture, or especially of what we *need*; but of primal repression, a structural prohibition inhering in the configuration of human desire itself.

But, more specifically, Žižek seems puzzled about what he sees as the central enigma: he says that the prohibition or law (the incest taboo laid down by the symbolic Father) seems superfluous, since enjoyment (*jouissance*) is "always already" impossible, by definition long-circuited and deflected. But this reasoning itself suffers from a short circuit: it too-simply conflates the symbolic register with the real world. For real incestuous enjoyment is by no means physically impossible or unheard of in the real world, as evinced by the countless cases of child seduction within the family. The very base of the psychoanalytic endeavor, however, is the discovery of the radical incommensurability of our psychic desire with its real-life objects: even when desire is consummated, our objects always give us chase, staying one step ahead of us. It is in the nature of human desire not to coincide adequately with its objects, always missing the appointment on base (we want what we don't have, and when we obtain something, we displace our desire to another object).

Perhaps Freud himself gives the only adequate explanation for this perversity of desire. In the *Three Essays on the Theory of Sexuality*, he suggests that human desire is always off-track and out of line, pursuing something that is always-already lost. It is thus always-already misplaced onto substitute objects with which it does not fully coincide (this is the doctrine of the *Anlehnung*, whereby sexuality "leans on," but does not coincide with, the biological need to feed).[21]

I cannot presume to speculate, from my own limited viewing-point, concerning Zizek's stake in his argument "beyond" Oedipus. But I can point out the effects of a blind spot on his theory—he ends up suggesting that a real flesh-and-blood father must be a player in the symbolic act of subject-formation. And why? To avoid the consequences of the symbolic act, allowing fantasy to persist ("So the only consistent answer to the question: 'Why does the superfluous prohibition emerge, which merely prohibits the impossible?' is: in order to obfuscate this inherent possibility—that is, in order to sustain the illusion that, were it not for the externally imposed prohibition, the full gratification would be possible" ["Is It Possible," 116]).

In other words, Žižek is positing fetishism and disavowal here as the fundamental operation in subject-formation, and as a fundamental alibi for foreclosing a devouring Father too terrible to be faced, a symbolic debt too heavy to be assumed. Or, in more general terms, he seems to be suggesting that it is perhaps the truth of death or inadequacy which the subject must elude at all costs, hope against hope. Maybe I can avoid the lesson of Oedipus, maybe I can have my cake and eat it too—or (in the masculinist language of fetishism) maybe Mother really does have my genitalia; so I myself am not subject to any kind of wounding . . . maybe, just maybe, the oracle does not really apply to *me*.

Žižek ends up criticizing the third-base position on the strange grounds that it does *not* postulate this escape—in other words, that it fails to provide an alibi, a denial or disavowal of the symbolic order itself, and that it fails to provide the illusory solace of regression to a pre-oedipal state of completeness: "The problem with 'Oedipus Online' is thus that what is missing in it is precisely this 'pacifying' function of the paternal figure which enables us to obfuscate the debilitating deadlock of desire" (115; emphasis added). Indeed. A Freudian perspective does decline to read not only cyberlife, but real life, as a potential Eden.

Another symptom of this phantasm in Žižek's own position is perhaps his equation of perversity with male masochism, which he thinks actually obfuscates a longing for discipline at the hands of the dominatrix (the phallic mother of "Slaves are Us," the New York agency cited in Žižek's own kinky double play [118]). Here Žižek plays doubly double—his private fantasy eliminating a terrible symbolic father is in fact reinforced by a "need" for the "pacifying" real father, who seems to have some conventional maternal qualities. On the other hand, the fantasy of an infantile reunion with the mother that subtends the formulation of parent-as-pacifier seems to be accompanied by a need for a chastising real mother (the dominatrix). This cross-dressing at the oedipal crossroads seems at once to mask, regender, and reconfigure the terrifying Symbolic Father as Phallic Mother, and the Nurturing Mother as Mr. Mom, in order to avoid the confrontation (at the oedipal intersection or website) with the other as . . . Other.

Coming Home Too Soon

In his closing argument, made after pathologizing all three positions he treats (as psychotic, perverse, and neurotic, respectively), Žižek performs a final sliding move, in a kind of "goldilocks play': "That is to say, both standard reactions to cyberspace are deficient: one is 'too strong' (cyberspace as involving a break with Oedipus); one is 'too weak' (cyberspace as a continuation of Oedipus by other means)" ("Is It Possible," 116–117).

This move collapses the original triad, citing only two positions (the first is too hard, the second is too soft), leaving his own position (which is "just right") to stand in at third. He allows that his position is actually a replay of Turkle and Stone's "perverse" position, "corrected" from his own point of view (adopted "on condition that one characterizes perversion in a much stricter way" [116]). Thus Žižek's final disciplinary action as referee adds the scenario of the male masochist and bitch goddess to this complex mix, conflating the position of object and Other ("the proverbial male masochist elevates his partner into a Lawgiver whose orders are to be obeyed . . ." thus "it is the object itself that makes the law" [117]. This locates "enjoyment in the very agency that prohibits access to enjoyment" [the player desires the umpire?]). The conflation of the position of object and Other is highly problematic from a Lacanian standpoint, since Lacan describes this kind of collapse as characteristic of the short circuit of hypnosis, where the "gaze of the Other" is also the desired object upon which the patient fixates.[22] For Lacan, the other and the Other are complicated, perhaps even mutually substitutable, but three positions are implied in (nonpsychotic) subjectivity. This collapse of object and Other is also problematic in Žižek's own system, where this same conflation of subject and object positions characterizes pornography. ("Pornography thus misses, reduces the point of the object gaze in the other.")[23]

Adding to the confusion, in the very next passage Žižek reinstates four positions (the original three, plus his own); but in this pass he reorders them, switching second and third. However, he does propose a conciliation: "What if it is wrong and misleading to ask directly which of the four versions of the libidinal/symbolic economy that we outlined is the 'correct' one?"

This play of proliferated/collapsed positions, involving acts of feint and appropriation, is baffling enough. But the referee has also performed a sleight of hand, sneaking the oedipus *complex*—referred to only as "Oedipus" on the previous page—back into the game.

But the bigger problem is perhaps that a "fantasy of the fantasy" subtends Žižek's conclusion. The "fundamental fantasy" that cyberspace attempts to traverse is conceived as a scene so terrible and ineffable that it can never be formulated or confronted, yet Žižek depicts it here, quite graphically, as a region where dislocated limbs float around—where the *disjecta membra* in the Latin phrase suggest a fantasy of castration. And how are we supposed to traverse this scene, which we can never actually confront? By "acting out" in cyberspace:

> And perhaps cyberspace, with its capacity to externalize our innermost fantasies in all their inconsistency, opens up to artistic practice a unique possibility to stage, to "act out," the fantasmatic support of our existence, up to the fundamental "sado-masochistic" fantasy that can never be subjectivized. ("Is It Possible," 122)

But as both Freud and Lacan were at pains to point out, acting out is the antithesis of "working through." And Žižek's "fundamental fantasy," inassimilable to the subject here, seems in fact to stage a veiled replay of his "perverse" scene (the male masochist suffering humiliation and dismemberment at the hands of the Lady of the House). Indeed, Žižek's prescription for traversing the fantasy, and thus working through its symptoms (possible only "if we follow [cyberspace] to the end, if we immerse ourselves in it without restraint" ["Is It Possible," 122–123]), sounds uncannily like the original "illness" itself, characterized earlier by Žižek as "the dystopian prospect of individuals regressing to pre-symbolic psychotic immersion" (111). Žižek's "post-oedipal" trajectory risks sending him back to first base, without scoring his point.

Perhaps it would be better to let Oedipus back in the game.

In any case, Žižek's conclusion, which proposes to reopen the question of the social and material contexts and consequences of cybersubjectivity, is well worth cheering on.

> What if, ultimately . . . the choice is ours, the stake in a politico-ideological struggle? How cyberspace will affect us is not directly inscribed into its technological properties, it hinges on the network of socio-symbolic relations (of power and domination, etc.) which always-already overdetermine the way cyberspace affects us. (123)

Words to play by. However, since it is precisely just such a network of socio-symbolic relations that Freud and Lacan configure as the oedipal/symbolic register, Žižek's very conclusion would seem to put Oedipus back in circulation.

Perhaps it is best to leave the post-game wrap-up to the poets and jokers, as Freud does, and to the players of popular culture, as is Žižek's wont. The good news is that in *Who's on First?* Costello does finally manage to understand Abbott's pitch. But even this position demonstrating knowledge, where Costello reels off information in the rapid-fire delivery of the sportscaster, is immediately resituated between between certainty and uncertainty, cut off by the intervention of the Other.

Costello: Who picks up the ball and throws it to What. What throws it to I Don't Know. I Don't Know throws it back to Tomorrow, triple play! Another guy gets up and hits a long fly ball to Because. Why? I Don't Know! He's on third and . . .
I DON'T GIVE A DARN!

Abbott: Oh . . . that's our shortstop.

As Oedipus knows, feigned indifference is but a screen for desire—it just stops us short, and puts us back in the lineup.

CHAPTER 3

THE LISTENING EYE: POST-OEDIPAL OPTICS AND PARANOID KNOWLEDGE

Roger Groce, *Puzzle*, 2004.

"To the insides of the ear belong those who have a sight of internal hearing." That is the nocturnal look. The listening eye.

—Emmanuel Swedenborg, cited by Jean-François Lyotard in *The Inhuman*

In this chapter, I take a cue from Slavoj Žižek's discussion of Lacanian anamorphosis or skewed perspective, in order to read three representative "millennial" works alongside one another, and from a "paranoid" slant.[1] The three works I discuss here—*The Transparency of Evil* (Jean Baudrillard), *Looking Awry* (Slavoj Žižek), and *The Inhuman* (Jean-François Lyotard)—all share a focus on optics, and they all emphasize the dehumanizing effects of technology.[2] Indeed, all three seem to adopt the near-paranoid perspective that appears to permeate so much theory in this transitional age. However, these theorists of "hypervisibility" and posthuman optics may also suggest ways to go beyond a simplistic panic perspective, with the help of psychoanalytic theory. For the idea of paranoia as mode of knowledge, first elaborated by Jacques Lacan in the 1950s, suggests that posthuman being may have a future after all.

Jean Baudrillard's doomsday vision in *The Transparency of Evil* is the prime example of full-blown posthuman panic: he depicts a weightless satellite man, cut loose from his moorings, "freed of all density, all gravity," "dragged into orbit" by "the centrifugal force of our proliferating technologies" (30–31). Similarly, in "The Ecstasy of Communication" (1983), Baudrillard describes a robotic subject mesmerized by an obscene hypervisibility, "more visible than the visible . . . the obscenity of what no longer has any secret, or what dissolves completely in information and communication."[3] For Baudrillard, our hypervisual culture is literally panic ("global"): it bombards us with images even while it exposes us to surveillant monitors, flattening human interaction to a screen existence.

Although he is more upbeat than Baudrillard, Lyotard also regrets the loss of dimensional intersubjectivity, suggesting that space is no longer an enabling interval between subjects, the scene of the exchanged gaze: contemporary cyberspace is the scene of communication without community, saturated with an excess of information that contributes to "the inhuman" tenor of life in our time. But while for Baudrillard we are already in a post-catastrophic aftermath, for Lyotard our fate is not yet cast. In fact, Lyotard suggests that the specter of disaster— the end of the species—may provide a telos for our existence.

Žižek is not nearly so metaphysical nor so glum as his fellow post-philosophers, but he is every bit as concerned with the optical, especially in *Looking Awry* and *The Plague of Fantasies*. In these works, he is a patient and even cheery exegete of Lacan, attempting to clarify Lacanian thought by looking at film, detective fiction, and other user-friendly instances of modern culture. Compared to his fellow travelers, Žižek is decidedly earthbound, focusing on the contemporary human subject as consumer-spectator, seated not in a satellite capsule or at a computer terminal, but at the movies, popcorn in hand.

Yet in spite of his goodwill, Žižek's take on postsociety is anything but sanguine: he, too, depicts a subject who is prey to the overexposed culture of image. For Žižek, the mesmerized subject is also threatened by the eruption of the Lacanian real into the web of the imaginary order, characterized by the fascination with image or illusion. The real also threatens the web of symbolic reality, that is, everything that counts as reality in consensual society. We could say that this disconcerting intrusion of the real disrupts imaginary fantasy (for the real is brute matter, unassimilated to meaning), even while it also upsets symbolic reality or narrative meaning. Like the sudden appearance of a hair on the projector lens that awakens the moviegoer from a complete absorption in the image on the screen, the real interrupts our illusions and conventions with a disturbing reminder of the precariousness of all that appears meaningful.

As an example of the menacing Lacanian real—"The Obscene Object of Postmodernity" described in *Looking Awry*—Žižek depicts a stain that sticks out, refusing assimilation to the spectator's gaze, eclipsing the meaning that holds our symbolic reality together. He argues that this all-too-visible object remains impenetrable, like the sinister objects upon which Hitchcock's camera often focuses (a bird on a wire, the Bates motel sign). Žižek describes these objects as uncanny intrusions of an ineffable blot: "[The blot of the real] produces a radical opacity and blocks every essay of interpretation" (*Looking Awry*, 151). Thus his notion of the obscene object as opacity suggests a counterweight to Baudrillard's characterization of the noxious trans-parency of a hyperexposed world.

In any case, all three of these works seem to be anti-posthuman in their perspective, pleading for a new-fashioned humanism as an effect of intersubjectivity, respecting difference. They suggest some intriguing connections along the way (the moviegoer meets Holbein and Kant). Still, the inherited litany of postmodernist discourse continues to permeate the work of all three "panic postmodernists" (Anne Balsamo's term, in *Technologies of the Gendered Body*). For they all emphasize the precarious nature of human identity and the parodic repetition of cultural residue; and they all pose a challenge to totalizing systems. Perhaps this seems all-too-familiar: from Habermas to Jameson, we have wrestled with these issues before. Yet even if these works remind us that postmodernism as a term is now overtaxed, they also attest to its continuing pull as a concept, however elusive. Citing Zeno's fable of the race between Achilles and the hare, Žižek (via Lacan) describes postmodern sensibility as the effect of the inaccessiblility of the pursued object. The postmodern object always seems to be ahead of or behind us: indeed, the concept of postmodernity itself seems to be missing its appointment with theory, refusing to be pinned down to the spot where we are.

Lyotard, Baudrillard, and Žižek all go beyond the aesthetics of postmodernism to address concrete millennial issues, enjoining the reader to resist the seduction of the global image network. In the new age a certain frantic energy feeds on itself, promoting a cancerous growth (Lyotard), putting everything on obscene display (Žižek), reducing human beings to stations in the cybernetic information circuit (Baudrillard). These post-theorists worry that the hidden face of our Others and our objects (what Lyotard, in *Discours, figure*, calls "the opacity of the designated") is now in danger of becoming hypervisible. They ask if there is any dimension left in a homogenized global world, always on media display. Reversing the perspective of Columbus, the post-philosophers seem to claim that the world is indeed flat, or is at least in danger of becoming completely transparent to itself: in the homogeneous global culture, there is little Otherness left in each other.

Yet all three works, from very different slants, enjoin the reader not just to look but to *see*, to engage something like a "listening eye" in an act of mindful encounter with the world. For if any dimension is left in our flattened, hypervisible world, it is perhaps to be found in the sphere of the human eye.

This reflects new possibilities for postmodern perspective itself, defined by Lyotard in *The Postmodern Condition*, citing Beckett, as "the presentation that the unpresentable exists." The reflections of this millennial threesome, for all their pessimism, suggest that "looking awry" may refresh the vision of the blasé visitor to the global museum of "unpresentable" artifacts.

BAUDRILLARD: THE EPIDEMIC OF TRANS-PARENCY

> Since the world is on a delusional course we must adopt a delusional standpoint towards the world.
> —Jean Baudrillard, *The Transparency of Evil*

Baudrillard, the most strident of the philosophers of hypervisibility, adopts a viral metaphor for what ails today's world. He argues that our social corpus has lost its natural immune powers—its salutary contact with radical otherness—and thus has been invaded by a pernicious evil: "Aids, terrorism, crack cocaine, or computer viruses . . . contain within them the whole logic of our system" (*Transparency of Evil*, 67). The corrosive effect "resides in the affinity between all these processes" (67). This assertion of *systemic* viral contagion is characteristic of Baudrillard's spectacularly paranoid tone, lamenting a cultural overload. By turns apocalyptic and arch, his warning resonates in a hyperbolic space odyssey mode laced with acid humor (Pynchon meets Kubrick), capturing the reader in its orbit.

But Baudrillard's oracular tone is wily: it ups the ante when we aren't looking, effecting a series of questionable equations by sleight of hand. His trans-theory not only lists various viral cultural phenomena—transsexuality, transeconomics, trans-aesthetics—but also simply *equates* them as "a kind of chain reaction [that] makes all valuation impossible" (5). Baudrillard speculates that a new particle of value, a *fractal* value (that is, a process that endlessly reproduces "the same" at different scales), has superseded the agonistic political and semiotic categories of exchange-value, use-value, sign-value.[4] The aftermath of the explosive orgy of modernism has deracinated social exchange, producing a mind-dulling homogeneity: "When things, signs or actions are freed from their respective ideas, concepts, essences, values, [they] embark upon an endless process of self-reproduction" (6). Nondifferentiated spheres overlap in a promiscuous circulation: "Everything is sexual. Everything is political. Everything is aesthetic. All at once" (9). And the metastasis is self-perpetuating: "energy [arises] from the expenditure of energy, thanks to the miracle of substitution" (102). In the global feeding frenzy, humanity is at risk less because of need than because of excess, threatened by "runaway energy flows, chain reactions, frenzied autonomous developments," breeding "indiscriminate trans-action, rather than critical interaction" (10).

In a particularly caustic vein, Baudrillard remarks: "[the world is so full of] naive sentimentality, self-important rectitude and sycophancy that irony, mockery, and the subjective energy of evil are always in the weaker position. At this rate every last negative sentiment will soon be forced into a clandestine existence" (107). Evil is thus less a moral category, for Baudrillard, than a principle of complexity. Yet his cynical rhetoric sometimes veers into a distinctly paranoid mode, evoking a transpolitical global plot:

> Subtly everything begins to operate as though some International Political Federation had suspended the public for an indeterminate period and expelled it from all stadiums to ensure the objective conduct of the match. Such is our present transpolitical arena: a transparent form of public space from which all the actors have been withdrawn. (33)

The new transcitizen implodes: "It is as though the two poles of our world had been brought into contact, *short-circuiting* in such a way that they simultaneously hyperstimulate and enervate potential energies" (33; emphasis added). And this short-circuiting has consequences: the rights of the individual "lose their meaning as soon as the individual is no longer engaged with others" (33).

In other words, Baudrillard complains that the information explosion has put us in communication, but not in touch. The posthuman subject is prey to a bombardment of superconductive events that affect "entire transversal structures: sex, money, information, communications" (34). Perhaps the most poignant moment of Baudrillard's argument is the depiction of the isolated subject, online with a virtual interlocutor, "terminally" absorbed in the screen. For Baudrillard, the monitor works like a mirror, sometimes producing an "image itself [that] is light years away—a special kind of distance which can only be described as unbridgeable by the body" (55). This screen-life, Baudrillard argues, results in a loss of contact, creating an alien dimension, no longer quite human, that depolarizes space in a short-circuited parody of communication. (Indeed, many psychologists have expressed alarm at the new virtual addiction: the new society peopled by adolescent males, linked only by hours of violent online video gaming, without ever meeting in person, and isolated from participation in real life.) Baudrillard claims that we are transfixed by instantaneous access to . . . everything. But the thrill of the exotic is replaced by the thrall of programmed thought, in a mechanical feedback loop.

Baudrillard also casts his critique in aesthetic terms: he argues that in today's "transaesthetic" world, dominated by simulacra, "art has been dissolved with a general aesthetization of everyday life, giving way to a pure circulation of images, a transaesthetics of banality, of market art, designed to sell, to 'perform'" (11). Again, he decries the leveling of depth and perspective, complaining that even "the possibility of metaphor is disappearing in every sphere [affecting] all disciplines as they lose their specificity and partake of a process of confusion and contagion" (7).

This also applies to fashion, to the hollow aesthetic of "the look," as we check out the other's image in a grotesque parody of desire. But this kind of narcissism provides no shield against the loneliness of the subject before the mirror, for (as has been noticed by thinkers from Ovid to Freud) the narcissistic double is also alien, Other: "The double, properly speaking, is not a prosthesis; [it is] an imaginary figure, like the soul, the shadow, or the mirror-image, which haunts the subject as his 'Other,' causing him to be himself while at the same time never seeming like himself" (121). But unlike Lacan (who discusses a kind of doubling in the mirror stage), Baudrillard fails to remark that when doubling interiorizes a haunting alien rather than a mirror reflection of the same, it also wrests the subject from narcissistic implosion, in a breach that permits intersubjective interaction.[5] Lacan's mirror stage is the precursor of symbolic engagement between subjects; while for Baudrillard, "doubling" simply effaces symbolic space or difference in a replication of the same. He complains that this also brings about an erasure of historical memory; it is a whitewashing, an "oddly enthusiastic mourning process" which sanitizes and trivializes real events like the Holocaust.

For Baudrillard, even violence is increasingly a question of image, for the violence produced by hypermodernity is terrorism, which depends on media to disseminate its effect. Terrorism is "a simulacrum of violence, emerging less from passion than from the screen. . . . Thus even violence exists potentially in the emptiness of the screen, in the hole the screen opens in the mental universe" (75). Because of the proximity of this sort of vacuous black hole, Baudrillard's new age astronaut-subject is in danger of being expelled from the safe intrauterine world of the communication capsule: "Everything is sucked violently out into the void as a result of the variation in pressure between inside and out. All that is needed is for a small rift or hole to be made in the ultra-thin envelope that separates two worlds" (75). (And this discourse is politically charged, equating the astronaut with the aborted fetus.)

Whether or not such deeply invested image-making is a conscious ideological strategy, Baudrillard's call for a return to historical consciousness does seem to be motivated by a nostalgia for Otherness: "Alienation is no more: the Other as gaze, the Other as mirror, the Other as opacity, all are gone. Henceforward it is the transparency of others that represents absolute danger . . . consciousness of self is threatened with irradiation in the void" (122). It would seem that Otherness has been assimilated by global homogeneity: "Childhood, lunacy, death, primitive societies—all have been categorized, integrated and absorbed as parts of a universal harmony" (127).

Baudrillard inveighs against touchy-feely bonding: "Enough with whitewashing and feeble pallid 'understanding' . . . where nothing can come from anywhere except from us" (145). In other words, he charges that this "universal harmony" cannibalizes and digests the Other, who ought to stick in our craw. (For true knowledge "is knowledge of exactly what we can never understand in the other": 148.) This, however, is no idealization of natural man—here "the primitive Aboriginal presence" that destabilizes Western rule is vampiric, a "viral, spectral presence in the synapses of our brains, in the circuitry of our rocket ship, as Alien. . . . Everything we once thought dead and buried, everything we thought left behind for ever by the ineluctable march of universal progress is not dead at all, but on the contrary is likely to return" (137–138). Thus Baudrillard cautions that we ignore Evil at our peril, for it will return as a life-sapping virus preying on selfsameness, the revenge of the foreclosed Other. (Again, the evocation of AIDS as a scourge of "sameness" is hardly politically neutral. Still, the wording almost seems prescient today: the idea of an insidious virus preying on too much openness permeates the public discourse of today's "borderless war" against the invasion of alien Evil.)

This alarming conclusion is somewhat mitigated by Baudrillard's injunction to critical thought, again cast in optical imagery: "The essential thing is to point the searchlight the right way. . . . We can only comb the sky" (110). So the function of the intellect is to train a searching eye on the world, seeking contradictions and exercising irony: "combing the sky" reactivates the role of a resisting subject in the search for answers. Rather than remaining a passive object of a panoptic monitor (the eye in the sky), or claiming the omniscience of a privileged over-view, the intellectual has to look several ways at once—inward, outward, up-ward—exercising insight rather than oversight. In a none-too-subtle allusion to political correctness, Baudrillard enjoins the cultural critic to be obstructive, re-sisting the temptation to become polite and consensual. In short, the intellectual should draw the line; Baudrillard craves the boundaries necessary for productive opposition.

The question, of course, is what is new about this approach. Isn't this a nos-talgia for the good old days when the bad guys wore black hats, as clearly visible and identifiable enemies? Such nostalgia haunts political discourse today, where the bad guys are "wanted dead or alive." And pop culture, especially sci-fi, tends to portray good and evil in "black and white," as Alien and Human: they are in-vaders, we are explorers; they are terrorists, we are liberators.

However hackneyed his nostalgia may be, Baudrillard does demand something new from the intellectual, borrowed from chaos theory—the notion of object as strange attractor. For "to capture such strange events, theory itself must be remade as something strange: as a perfect crime, or as a strange attractor" (110). (Strange attractors in the new physics are those forces that govern apparently chaotic pat-terns, determining, for instance, the erratic movement of "a pendulum on a pendulum.")

Although he sometimes engages in murky theory-speak, Baudrillard evokes something beyond the flat transparent function of communication—he wants to play with the alien and alienating capacities of language: "everything, that is, which causes language at its most radical level to be other than the subject (and also other to the subject)" (126–127). Like Lacan, who insists on "the materiality of the signifier," Baudrillard celebrates the opacity of language, its resistance to complete appropriation: "The existence of this level accounts for the play in lan-guage, for its appeal in its materiality, for its susceptibility to chance, and is what makes language not just a set of trivial differences, as it is in the eyes of structural analysis, but truly a matter, symbolically speaking, of life and death" (127).

Here Baudrillard approaches Lyotard, who sees *opaque* matter as the stubbornly sublime stuff of creativity, and Žižek, who sees "the object of postmodernity" as something that sticks out, refusing to be flattened. For Baudrillard, all that is left of our humane "ironical surplus" is a desire that resists appropriation, exceeding the closed reflexivity of mirrored visibility: "The Object is what theory can be for reality; [it is] not a reflection but a challenge, and a strange attractor" (174).

Matter in our effort performs its anamnesis.

—Jean-François Lyotard, *The Inhuman*

Paradoxically, *The Inhuman* is the most straightforwardly humanist of the works discussed here. For Lyotard's argument begins with a lyric emphasis on humanity: "What shall we call human in humans, the initial misery of their childhood: or their capacity to acquire a second nature, which, thanks to language, makes them fit to share in communal life?" (4).

Lyotard goes on to counterpoise two distinct manifestations of the inhuman: one social and economic (the "negative entropy" or unbridled growth in the global order), the other philosophical and genetic (something alien and insatiable in our very nature, which gnaws away at us). The first inhumanity characterizes technological globalism, a developmental system that feeds on itself, thanks in part to the universal access to information. For Lyotard, the communication network, which saturates us with data, is a mindless disembodied memory bank: "[This is] information belonging to everyone and to nobody, [for] the body supporting the memory is no longer an earth-bound body. This process produces a monad more complete than humanity itself could ever be" (64).

Thus Lyotard, like Baudrillard and other high-profile theorists such as Paul Virilio (*The Information Bomb*) and Gianni Vattimo (*The Transparent Society*), is deeply alarmed by the ramifications of the information explosion, which produces creative atrophy and political apathy:[6] "Experience shows . . . a new barbarism, illiteracy and impoverishment of language, new poverty, merciless remodeling of opinion by the media, immiseration of the mind, obsolescence of the soul, the necessity of witnessing globalization" (63).

Interestingly, this indictment of the contemporary global scene does not spare the concept of the postmodern, which Lyotard once championed as the vanguard of critical thought, spurred by incredulity toward totalizing "metanarratives."[7] In *The Inhuman*, however, he sees the postmodern as a mind-numbing contagion, "spreading to all humanity" (63). In contrast to the cultural virus, the second type of inhumanity is impervious to socialization, an intimate Other of which the soul is hostage: "the anguish is that of a mind haunted by a familiar and unknown guest which is agitating it, sending it delirious but also making it think" (2). Lyotard seeks to enlist this insistent remainder of our unsocialized infancy in the work of culture and politics: "this debt to childhood is one we never pay off. . . . It is the task of writing, thinking, literature, arts, to venture to bear witness to it" (7). For Lyotard as for Baudrillard, nothing less is at stake here than the fate of the human: "what is really disturbing [is] the importance assumed by the concept of the bit, the unit of information," which curtails "free forms given over here and now to the imagination" (34).

Yet the techno-human condition has potential. In "Rewriting Modernity" (The Inhuman, chapter 2), Lyotard asks whether the postmodern condition must necessarily eliminate chance and receptivity, or whether our technological environment might foster a creative impulse, eliciting "free imagination [in] the work of rewriting" (35). In "Logos and Techne" (The Inhuman, chapter 4), he amplifies these reflections on "rewriting," suggesting that the computer technology of inscription is to some degree comparable to human writing as memory trace:

> I distinguish . . . three sorts of memory-effects of technological inscription in general: breaching [frayage], scanning and passing, which coincide more or less with three very different sorts of temporal synthesis linked to inscription: habit, remembering [rémémoration] and anamnesis. (48)

What is "inhuman" in these three computerized effects is the very fact that inscription has now become instantaneous, eliding differences in time and space. Concerning breaching, for instance, the deposit of information in a memory bank, Lyotard writes: "In digital form [thoughts] become telegraphable—independent of their initial space and time" (50). The second memory effect, scanning, is the review of data, which in human memory provides a linkage between past and present. In today's global network, however, scanning is not historicized human memory—it is teleological, without being ethical: "Scanning is a question of ends. But we don't know what it is we want—progress, enlightenment, happiness? Knowledge and power, yes, but why, no" (54). This suggests that the circuit of techno-memory serves performance as an end in itself, foreclosing agency or purpose.

Finally, in his discussion of the third memory-effect, "passing," Lyotard hedges on his original formulation equating human and artificial memory. Conceding that not all human thought or memory effects have a technological analogue, Lyotard avers that passing (like Derridean écriture) is a breakthrough to a nonrepresentational, iterative mode deployed in layered time, in a process resembling the working through (Durcharbeitung) of psychoanalysis. The point of Lyotard's argument is that computers can't "pass"—breaking through to an understanding that exceeds the binary logic of bits. For anamnesis requires a body capable of shifts of perspective, and an intuition of something inassimilable to binary logic. In fact, in "Can Thought go on without a Body?" (In Inhuman, chapter 1)—Lyotard's gendered dialogue between He and She—the female perspective insists on the necessary embodiment of human thought. "She" insists that a certain human capacity is associated with a limited field of vision, not the sweep of satellite surveillance: "A field of thought exists in the same way that there's a field of vision (or hearing): the mind orients itself in it just as the eye does in the field of the visible" (15–16). We need a body to receive and to experience, to pay attention.[8]

Significantly, this theory of receptivity may be read through psychoanalysis as the ground of intersubjectivity (since Lacanian *désir* "is the desire of the Other") contingent on a salutary paranoid experience of the Other as a listening (rather than spying) eye. Lyotard insists, for instance, on the difficulty of avant-garde art, which demands a certain "passibility" from its viewer, a receptivity to the work of art in its irreducible presence as matter, and as an event that *matters*. Artists make us see that we cannot see everything, that the unpresentable exists: "[making] visible the fact that the visual field ends and requires invisibilities" (125). The avant-garde artist enjoins us to listen with the eye, to lend ourselves to the "matter" at hand: "matter in our effort performs its anamnesis" (46).

Like the artist, the writer works with matter, for "words themselves, in the most secret place of thought, are its matter" (142). With the reference to the materiality of language, which Lyotard owes to psychoanalysis, the idea of an internal ear loses its Zen quietist quality and becomes a condition of intersubjective response.[9] Lyotard's listening eye is not mystical, but resolutely materialist. The unsocializable inhuman remainder is the persistence of brute matter itself, matter over mind: "Matter does not question the mind. . . . It has no need of it, it exists" (142).

In these ruminations on the sublime, Kant is everywhere, but so is Freud: the sublime might well be called the uncanny, the strangeness confronting us in familiarity. But in Lyotard's "sublime," what exceeds us is not some romantic nostalgia for presence lost; it is, rather, the excessive material presence of the object. All we need to do is step aside—out of habitual "either/or" logic, glimpsing the alien presence in our midst, uncanny and sublime—to cease to perform as robotic consumers or unreflective monitors.

ŽIŽEK'S SLANT: ANAMORPHOSIS AND PARANOIA

> The only way not to be deceived is to maintain a distance from the symbolic order, i.e. to assume a psychotic [paranoid] position.
>
> —Slavoj Žižek, *Looking Awry*

Like Lyotard, Žižek is concerned with a shift in perspective, a sidestep that allows the viewer to perceive an alien presence in the field of vision ("The Obscene Object of Postmodernity," *Looking Awry*, chapter 8). This phallic surfeit of presence sticks out from its surroundings, incommensurate with our normal organizing

Hans Holbein, *The Ambassadors*, 1533. National Gallery, London.

perspective. In "The Hitchcockian Blot" (*Looking Awry*, chapter 5), Žižek sums up Lacan's commentary on Holbein's *The Ambassadors*:

> At the bottom of the picture, under the figures of the two ambassadors, a viewer catches sight of an amorphous, extended, "erected" spot. It is only when, on the very threshold of the room in which the picture is exposed, the visitor casts a final lateral glance at it that this spot acquires the contours of a skull, disclosing thus the true meaning of the picture—the nullity of all terrestrial goods, objects of art and knowledge that fill out the rest of the picture. (90)

This phallic stain denatures the rest of the picture, as the viewer does a double take of sorts, casting a skewed gaze at the distorted image. We could say that Holbein's sidelong image makes the viewer a bit paranoid, peering from a lateral vantage point, newly leery of the straightforward representation revealed by the head-on perspective: "Nothing is what it seems to be, everything is to be interpreted, everything is supposed to possess some supplementary meaning" (91).

The paranoid tonality of Žižek's take on Lacan is all the more intriguing because, in Lacanian theory, Holbein's anamorphosis is an emblem for the constitution of subjectivity itself. For it is a function of splitting, since the painting is oriented in two different spaces or fields (that of the ambassadors and that of the anamorphic skull). Indeed, since "the oscillation between lack and surplus meaning constitutes the proper dimension of subjectivity" (91), Žižek argues that *all* human meaning is by definition skewed, reflecting a slanted perspective imbued with paranoid resonance.

> It is by means of the "phallic" spot that the observed picture is subjectivized: [it] undermines our position as "neutral," "objective" observer, pinning us to the observed object itself. This is the point at which the observer is already included, inscribed in the observed scene—in a way, *it is the point from which the picture itself looks back at us.* (91; emphasis added)

This radically shifted perspective rends the fabric of consensual reality, the comfortable perspective that pays tribute to the accomplishments of Renaissance Man. Perceiving the alien object, the viewer adopts the position of the paranoid, who *knows* that the world is always looking back at him, the object of relentless surveillance.

These speculations concerning the anamorphic phallic object may in turn be related to Lacan's notion of the unattainable object of desire (*objet petit a*). The Lacanian object is not absent; it is *incommensurate* with our vantage point, our current plane of experience. It is thus always viewed askance, a function of skewed perception. The subject and the *objet petit a* are, like Achilles and the hare, forever circling around each other in a series of missed encounters: "We mistake for postponement of the 'thing itself' what is already the 'thing itself'; we mistake for the searching and indecision proper to desire what is, in fact, the realization of desire [as] a circular movement, reproducing itself" (7). Indeed, the human subject is constituted by desiring, through fantasy, an always phantom object: "The *objet a* is by definition always perceived in a distorted way: outside this distortion, in itself, it does not exist. It is the materialization of this perturbance introduced by desire into an objective reality" (12).

In "The Obscene Object of Postmodernity" (*Looking Awry,* chapter 8), Žižek makes a similar founding claim for the postmodern: the postmodern stance is not the demonstration that "the game works without an object, that the play is set in motion by a central absence" (the absence of the object being, in his account, a *modernist* preoccupation), but is, rather, the display of "the object directly, allowing it to make visible its own arbitrary character" (143). Žižek's own example, however, demonstrates that this obscene, too-present object is not merely a postmodern stigma. It is already present in Holbein, in the skewed skull that causes the picture to look back at us, objectifying us with its "obscene" gaze—that is, the object's gaze makes us feel a bit eerie, reminding us that we are always on the spot, and that our own gaze is never entirely objective. (Similarly, Žižek emphasizes the sinister character of Hitchcock's filmic object, which "produces a paranoiac effect [because] the field of what is seen is continually menaced by the unseen, and the very proximity of objects to the camera becomes menacing" [42].) Thus the object of our desiring gaze is experienced as a threatening intrusion that messes up our tidy scheme of things. By dislocating our perspective, it causes us to suspect that there may be other objects that are beyond us, lurking out of sight, eluding apprehension in our current visual field.

Like the intrusive anamorphic skull, the object of desire is a sign of the world's inconsistency, of the unthinkable coexistence of perspectives that are irreconcilable with our own. As such, the object is excessive and importune—but, paradoxically, its very inaccessibility marks our entrance into subjective humanity. This entry is indeed fraught with trouble, for in a sense, what we assume, along with our subjectivity, is our objectivity. Our subjectivity entails our capacity to die as subject, to submit to the other's gaze in an act of identification that warps the centrality of our own vision. ("The *objet a* is the surplus, the elusive make-believe that drove man to change his existence. But the break is nonetheless well worth the trouble" [8].)

Looking awry entails occupying the space of the other in one's own field of vision, since this granting of subjectivity to others entails entering and being tainted by a distorted "other" visible field. Indeed, to be a subject, for Lacan, is always to read the message that returns to us, in inverted form, from our own knowledge.[10] A step out of self-delusion, which Lacan calls misrecognition (*méconnaissance*), into a clear-sighted recognition of the limitations of our field, is paradoxically the only step that allows us to see clearly—by squinting.

In other words, subjectivity implies intersubjectivity. Subjectivity is not just a function of the interplay between imaginary and symbolic, illusion and its frustration, but also of the real (as the opacity of matter, what is "beyond us" in the world). Žižek draws a clear distinction between the *real*—the brute material world which is "out there"—and symbolic *reality*, which is always a matter of interpretation, caught in the pact of our intersubjective construction of meaning, in a shared world.

Moreover, Žižek suggests that the chief difference between symbolic reality and imaginary fantasy resides in the latter's pliancy, as the place in which human beings are able to rehearse, project, and articulate their desires (as in a daydream), sheltered from the demands of social reality. Fantasy is unreal (the imaginary); reality is what we all agree is real (the symbolic); but the real itself—like Lyotard's matter and Baudrillard's strange attractor—resists even this assimilation. In Holbein's painting, the real is in-your-face, as the phallic object in the foreground, inassimilable to our conventional head-on assumptions, but obscenely present.

In a more forceful formulation of the opposition between the real and reality ("How Real Is Reality?" *Looking Awry*, part I), Žižek musters Lacan's image of the real as a hole, a tear in reality. (Millennial science has served up an instance of the Lacanian real: the "black hole" in space, while it is very real, wipes out the rules of Newtonian physics, swallowing up the normal contextual reality of time and space.) Fantasy, in this formulation, seeks to patch up the disquieting hole in reality caused by the voracious real: projective fantasy "occupies" the unbearable void. In this sense, the ineffable real itself may act less as a black hole than as a blank screen onto which we project our fantasies. But if the real reasserts itself in all its weight (as black hole)—if it succeeds in puncturing our shell of reality—our symbolic mooring, if not our very sanity, may be lost.

Žižek's imagery of the stain, interestingly, also recalls Baudrillard's image of the postmodern astronaut, his mission "aborted," sucked out into the void of space when the screen of his sheltering capsule is punctured. In fact, Žižek signals a similar moment for Oedipus when he finally *sees* his object of desire for what she is: "when he finally learns the truth, [he] existentially 'loses the ground under his feet' and finds himself in an unbearable void" (44).

In any case, as Žižek argues (after Lacan), *every* symbolic construction contains a "little piece of the real," an unsymbolizable core around which it is organized. The real is not only a screen for the fantasy *objet petit a*; it is also the (potentially psychotic) alien kernel that lurks in the symbolic, refusing to be assimilated to a meaningful, "reasonable" system.

> Why must the symbolic mechanism be hooked onto a "thing," some piece of the real? The Lacanian answer is, of course: because the symbolic field is in itself always already barred, crippled, porous, structured around some extimate kernel, some impossibility. The function of the "little piece of the real" is precisely to fill out the place of this void that gaps in the very heart of the symbolic. (33)

Moreover, the "*peu du réel*" (Lacan) that sustains our version of things seems contingent: "the real that serves as support of our symbolic reality must appear to be *found* and not *produced* " (32). It must appear as the external answer to our internal, projective desire: "Although any object can function as the object-cause of desire—insofar as the power of fascination it exerts is not its immediate property but results from the *place* it occupies in the structure—we must, by structural necessity, fall prey to the illusion that the power of fascination belongs to the object *as such*" (33).

Our desire will never meet up with its object, because the object that so fascinates us is invested with properties it does not have. (Indeed, it does not *really* exist, except as a placeholder of unrepresentable excess, the Freudian *Ding* of primal repression, always-already lost.) Moreover, the real of our desire, the inexorable drive independent of object, ensures that desire always distorts its objects (12–13). To cast this argument awry, framing it in Lyotard's perspective, we may argue that the real is matter that refuses symbolization, causing meaning to vacillate where it erupts. The kernel of the real in every symbolization is associated with the drive that will never be exhausted in the symbolic order it sustains.

Thus, paradoxically, the obdurate "real" object both threatens and supports reality, just as Holbein's image of Renaissance life is both elaborated and undermined by the image of the skull, the "real" imposed upon the "symbolic" humanist narrative of triumph. Žižek sees social reality as a fragile, symbolic cobweb that can "at any moment be torn aside by an intrusion of the real. At any moment, the most common everyday conversation, the most ordinary event, can take a dangerous turn, damage can be done that cannot be undone" (17).

What is more, Žižek insists that the excluded real always threatens to return, answering its repression with intrusions (reflected in popular fiction, for instance, in the notion of the undead, the corpse that does not stay buried).[11] In any case, when the *real* overflows *reality*, when the "little piece of the real" at the center of the symbolic takes over, psychosis ensues. The paranoid looks *so* awry at reality that she or he sees that the symbolic Other, the guarantor of meaning, does not "really" exist.[12] And this is a blinding insight (as Oedipus knows) that can sever all ties with reality.

The symbolic pact is a consensus from which the paranoid, who insists that only she knows what is *really* happening, always deviates. Her "know-it-all" perspective disturbs the uniformity of the "normal" field of view, precisely because her paranoia contains *more* than a "little piece of the real": for her, the alien object (like Holbein's skull) becomes dominant, as it expands to determine, skew, and resituate the psychotic field of vision, outside of symbolic consensus. (The use of the pronoun "her" itself serves as one such "alien" example, calling attention to the non-neutrality of the writer's voice.)

But if looking *too* awry makes us vulnerable to psychosis (paranoia), in yet another twist, Žižek asserts that the view from the sidelines is precisely what *prevents* us from sliding into psychosis (13). He cites Shakespeare as the poet of anamorphic sanity (*Richard II*, II, ii: "Like perspectives which rightly gaz'd upon Show nothing but confusion, ey'd awry Distinguish form" [11]). In a textile metaphor referring to the ineffable object of desire (*das Ding*, the Freudian "Thing"), Žižek says that the torn fabric of reality is folded back on itself by the skewed gaze in the symbolic order: "The emergence of language opens up a hole in reality, and this hole shifts the axis of our gaze. Language redoubles reality into itself and the void of the Thing that can be filled out only by an anamorphotic gaze from aside" (13). In language, then, the healthy subject in "recognition" occupies two places at once, accepting the real of the death drive as the scandalous presence of matter, and following the injunction to live symbolically nonetheless, "as if" the hole may be patched, albeit from a side angle. Alienating Otherness, paradoxically, may drive us mad, but it may also insure the sanity of the "symbolic" point of view.

It is in this discussion of the real as *das Ding* that Žižek comes closest to Baudrillard, evoking similar notions of radical alterity, even using the same term for the drive: "strange attractor" (39).[13] And his discussion of the real's kernel also seems to correspond to Lyotard's concept of matter as the unrepresentable support of sublime (postmodern) art and philosophy. So one could say that the common ground for these three theorists is none other than the Alien Real. Each of them exhorts us to *see* what is under our nose, however disturbing (like the real purloined letter of Poe's story, hidden in full view), by shifting our point of view.

Žižek ends his discussion of the real by noting the ways in which we avoid the disconcerting encounter. We may *repress* the traumatic kernel in obsessive neurosis (Freudian *Verdränung*). We may *reject* it, casting it outside (Freudian *Verwerfung*), from whence it may return to haunt us as hallucination or psychotic projection. Or we may simply invest belief in the symbolic order as the domain of meaning guaranteed by law or authority, denying the blind automatism that subtends it (the *Verneinung*).

In the detective novel, for instance, the classic sleuth is assumed by the reader to be the site of a privileged knowledge, the *sujet supposé savoir* who will solve all mysteries. The detective occupies the place of the Other (capital O) as the guarantor of the symbolic order: and he makes sure that the readers play by the rules of his particular symbolic game (the crime-story genre). To look askance at his logical solution to the murder mystery (*seeing* the skull as the death drive at the heart of logic), to assert that the all-knowing Sleuth does not exist, to withdraw belief in self-evidence, would be downright paranoid.

THE SLEUTH AS SEARCH ENGINE: OEDIPUS AND MOBILE KNOWLEDGE

"The non-duped err."
—*The Seminar of Jacques Lacan*, Book XXI

It is in light of this question of belief that Lacanian theory is most illuminating, for Lacan maintains that the paranoid is characterized by *das Unglauben*—a *lack* of belief in the symbolic order and in the Other as its guarantor, the site of the Law. Yet, as Lacan insists, paranoia is not always a psychosis; it is also a mode of discovery. He asserts that a certain paranoid knowledge informs and constitutes every subject.[14] Paranoid knowledge is not derived from "facts" but from relational situations. This is Lacan's linguistic version of Oedipus' challenge to the rigid and overly codified (paternal) Authority. For the place of Authority is empty; the master signifier has no content (*Seminar XVII*).

Indeed, Lacan's exemplary sleuth is a kind of successful, nontragic Oedipus figure: Poe's detective Dupin, the "hero" of "The Purloined Letter," is the master of paranoid knowledge. Putting himself in the other's place, he relies on paranoid reasoning to adopt the other's field of vision, allowing him to see the letter that lies exposed in full view, invisible to others.[15] For Lacan, knowledge is always an intersubjective duel, an encoded puzzle to be deciphered (*Seminar III*, 36)—wherein the subject receives his message from the other in an inverted form. Dupin's lesson—learned the hard way by Oedipus—is that the sleuth can access the truth only by deigning to participate in human interchange, not by trying to remain superior to it. (Schreber, on the other hand, has the opposite challenge, as Eric Santner has argued. He *must* renounce the "sane" proto-fascist order that interpellates him as Authority; his madness is not hubris or blindness but self-defense.)[16]

In his earliest discussion of paranoid knowledge (*Seminar III*), Lacan illustrates this theory with a parable: three convicts are shown two black patches and three white ones; one is affixed to the back of each man, and they are left together in the room. The first to ascertain the color of the patch on his back will be allowed to go free. Each convict divines that his patch is white, by the same process: figuring out what the other two would do if his patch were black, and waiting for them to do it, which they don't.[17] This triangulated tale enacts paranoid knowledge, which is attained by a projective identification with the other's view, and with the other's view of the other and of oneself. Knowledge must be deflected through the position of the other(s), the sidelong point of view, to be realized. In fact, it must be triangulated (as in the technique surveyors and astronomers use for mapping heaven and earth). This fable also underscores the paranoid nature of all acts of intersubjective communication, where uncertainty is inherent. ("Speech is making the Other speak as such—that is, as unknown" [*Seminar III*, 42].)

Thus Lacan argues that a certain paranoia is the mode by which we all acquire intersubjective knowledge: for the paranoid, using projective thinking and the power of deduction, draws affinities among all objects. The paranoid sleuth makes connections, re-creating a plot by taking the place of the Other (as when Dupin solves the mystery by looking through the eyes of his adversary, the wily Minister). Lacan argues that this ability to shift subject positions is a primordial human trait, not a sign of illness: "All human knowledge stems from the dialectic of jealousy [manifest in] the child's transvitism: when he says the other beat me, he's not lying, he *is* the other" (*Seminar III*, 39).

That is, the human subject learns to take the other's place because of shared desire, wanting what the *other* has. In fact, Lacan maintains that the paranoid structure of projective identification is the basis of the distinction between the human world and the animal world, contesting objects through identification. As Lacan puts it: "What makes the human world a world covered with objects derives from the fact that the object of human interest is the object of the other's desire" (*Seminar III*, 39). As long as Oedipus fails to recognize the claim of the Other on a shared object of desire (Jocasta), he is headed for tragedy. He is not paranoid enough, when he denies the warning of the oracle. It is only when he recognizes his implication in the shared human field that he is able to see the truth, which wholly justifies the paranoid view. (The world, as it turns out, *is* out to get him. His wisdom and wit, his talent for riddle-solving, grant him no exemption.)

Lacan's take shows us that human knowledge is necessarily paranoid (insofar as paranoia implies projecting your own view on the outside world, and identifying with the view of others). Paranoid knowledge is an effect of projection, founded on rivalry and the ability to take the other's place, at least in fantasy. However, "speech overcomes this rivalry, arriving at agreement—this is yours, this is mine—a pact. So knowledge is an imaginary function; speech relies on a symbolic pact. If the other doesn't agree, I must annul him or he must annul me" (*Seminar III*, 39–40).

The parable of the prisoners' game shows how the deflected glance—gazing at oneself through the speculation of the Other—permits us to stake out a subject position, always relative, perceived, and interactive. For our subjectivity is constituted in response to the realization that "you never look at me from the place where I see you" (Žižek, *Looking Awry*, 74). And every subject is formed by introjected images of others; she hears voices that are her own, or rather, the voice she hears from beyond is her own "letter," returning to her as the answer from the Other. This is perhaps the voice of the unconscious, the Other caught in the snare of love, a projective transference that assures, in the famous closing formulation of Lacan's purloined Poe, "that a letter always reaches its destination."

For Lacan, the distinction between the Other with a big O—that is, the Other insofar as it is *not* known (also the unconscious)—and the other with a small o (my alter ego, my competitor who I *know* desires what I desire) is fundamental. The realm of otherness (small o) is the realm of simple consensus based on what we all agree that we know; but the realm of Otherness ushers in the possibility of deceit (the warden may be cheating, or—as Descartes asserts, in a paranoid moment—the God who guarantees reason may be an evil genius). The healthy person's grounded reality supposes some convergence between the "other" of consensus and the "Other" of meaning. But the paranoid position, affording a lateral vision, fosters a radical distrust of the Other, who may be lying or even duped (like the King in "The Purloined Letter," who remains blind to what is going on under his nose; or the gullible Emperor who "buys" invisible new clothes). The paranoid position allows the onlooker to discern that the certainty of the symbolic order is a certitude produced by smoke in mirrors. This is the position of Dupin, who *sees* the sovereign's blindness and the Minister's plot by identifying successively with their two points of view.

But Dupin's projective acuity is not illness. Indeed, as regards knowledge, a little bit of psychosis goes a long way. As Žižek puts it:

> When faced with such a paranoid construction, we must not forget Freud's warning and mistake it for the illness itself: the paranoid construction [identification with others] is, on the contrary, an attempt to heal ourselves, to pull ourselves out of the real illness, the breakdown to the symbolic universe, the end of the world, the breakdown of the real, reality barrier. (*Looking Awry*, 19).

Dupin is not psychotic, but the modality of his projective-identificatory knowledge is paranoid, doubting and testing symbolic reality. This is also what Oedipus learns, when he falls from "superior" wisdom to implicated knowledge of his unexceptional place in the human scheme. (In Sophocles' play, Oedipus literally begins on a higher level, above the stage, and winds up at the level of the Chorus after his "fall" from delusion.) Like Dupin, and like Oedipus after the fall, Freud (as the non-duped analyst) knows that he doesn't know—he learns that he is also vulnerable to the distortions of desire, in the countertransference. Schreber, on the other hand, is a full-blown psychotic—precisely because he *knows* that he is right. He can account for everything in his cosmos, by constructing the Other of the Other (God as lover) to replace the symbolic Other that he disavows (the God as guarantor of Law, governing inferior beings blinded by "reality").

Lacan's theory suggests that paranoid knowledge may be read from two angles: it may be considered as either the province of the "errant" psychotic in error, adrift from human connection; or as the grounding of intersubjectivity, the daily double dealings of all-too-human dupes with their fellows. Evoking Lacan's famous pun on the name of the father (*le nom du père: le non-dupe erre*, pronounced identically in French), Lacan reminds us that the disbelievers also "wander" (*errent*) outside symbolic certainty—"The non-duped err"—in a *salutary* divergence that goes beyond blind obedience to an Other that does not exist.

Lacan is, among other things, playing on the repetition of the sound in Dupin and dupe. The only way *not* to be duped is to err, to look awry, to give oneself up to the tortuous possibility of being *seen*, of being objectified. Identificatory knowledge replaces stasis, the fixation of the mirror of narcissism, with the mobility of the refracted gaze of Others, rather than just repeating the views of any number of other "I's." As Lyotard puts it (*The Inhuman*, 41), in genuinely human interaction, the privileged perspective belongs not to the static overseeing eye of the prince, the lord of oriented one-point perspective reflected by all his "subjects," but "to the wandering mind."

This reading of paranoia as episteme—a symbolic identification with our always unknown Others—is of consequence for the posthuman condition so decried by panic philosophy. For (in answer to Baudrillard) it suggests a way to see through the transparency of evil: You must deflect your gaze to see the alien presence (the death drive, the skull) that inhabits human existence. This enables us to get out of the closed narcissism of the full-blown psychotic (the online ecstasy of Dr. Schreber). Lacan's theory responds to Baudrillard, positing a way to get out of the hell of sameness, where "I repeat myself forever."

The positive vector of projective identification is also germane to Lyotard's interrogation of the *inhumanity* of our world. For Lacan's theory posits the "narcissistic constitution of the ego," whereby self-image is formed mimetically, by introjecting the image of the other. This is already suggested by Freud in *Totem and Taboo*, where he speculates that identification with the tribal father is actually effected by devouring him, in the cannibalistic gesture that grounds the tribal totem. For psychoanalysis, then, it is precisely the play of the inhuman with the human, the savage identification with the alien Other/Rival, which constitutes the human, grounding taboo (Freud), producing the divided subject (Lacan). A mechanism of introjection and identification constitutes the subject; and it is through projection of the self into the place of the other as truly Other that the subject "lends an ear" (perhaps in exchange for other purloined parts). Lyotard's aesthetic of passibility requires such an exchange, "the multiplication of minds which causes the diversity of the world and complexity of bodies" (*The Inhuman*, 41). Similarly, Žižek's reading of the paranoid effect in Hitchcock's cinema is in terms of the objectifying view, where the object sticks out, disconcertingly, and looks back at us, making us *reasonably* paranoid.

Indeed, all three of these theorists might be seen as paranoid in their mistrust of authoritative symbolic significance, their emphasis on the desirable opacity of a world that looks back at us, and their suggestion that only a skewed vision may provide resistance to the all-seeing monitor in the sky. Projective identification is the field of insight, rather than oversight.

The difference between health and psychosis, then, would be one of degree. For we apprehend Otherness only from a stance that acknowledges that *every* view is off-kilter, that knowledge itself is a point of view, a matter of locus. In Lacan's parable of purloined knowledge, where each subject is by turns the agent and the object of the gaze, not even the detective is the site of fixed knowledge; he enacts an intersubjective drama of blindness and vision, demonstrating that no One is a know-it-all.

Psychoanalysis calls this skepticism countertransference—taking one's place in a social chain where, to recast Lacan's famous formula for the signifying chain, "the subject is the subject for another signifier," making use of paranoid knowledge to escape from the wheel-spinning of paranoia proper. For if the paranoid knows that "the Other does not exist," paranoid knowledge shows that the "Other of the Other" does not exist either: there is no explanation for the blind automatism of the real. Dupin is the resourceful paranoid: through identification with others, he *sees* the obvious—the little piece of the real—not as threatening hallucination, but as visible floating signifier. The hypervisible, all-too-evident, transparent clue—the letter in full view—becomes visible when the Other is debunked and displaced, refracted into others. The too-public eye in the sky that haunts paranoid discourse becomes a sighted private "I."

In this spirit, Slavoj Žižek voices the most important lesson learned from paranoid discourse, more important than ever in today's "hypervisible" world: "The Other must not know all. This is an appropriate definition of the nontotalitarian social field" (*Looking Awry*, 73). For subjective humanity is an effect of inhuman objectivity, as every paranoid *knows*.

CHAPTER 4

UP THE ANTE, OEDIPUS! DELEUZE IN OZ

Ginny Ruffner, *The Myth of the Rainbow*, 2003. © 2003 Ginny Ruffner.

There is only desire and the social, and nothing else.

—Gilles Deleuze, *Anti-Oedipus*

In the first three chapters of part one, I have argued that any effort at siting Freud in the twenty-first century must make room for Oedipus. And any effort at resiting Oedipus must come to terms with Gilles Deleuze. Although Deleuze did not live to see the new century, his work continues to grow in influence today, in large part because he was the only prominent cultural theorist to integrate the new paradigms in science at the time he was writing. But it was Deleuze's late-1960s attack on psychoanalysis in *Anti-Oedipus*—one of several books he co-authored with Félix Guattari—that declared open season on Freud.[1] This is unfortunate for several reasons, not the least of which is that many newcomers to the daunting body of work by Deleuze (with and without Guattari) begin with *Anti-Oedipus*, as the title most familiar to nonspecialists. But because of the caricatural treatment of psychoanalysis there—dismissed as the story of "Mommy, Daddy, and me"— many readers who value Freud read no more of Deleuze's remarkable work.

A second reason to regret the prominence of *Anti-Oedipus* in Deleuze's opus is that the virulent anti-Freudianism gives ammunition to the Freud-bashers who argue that psychoanalysis is not appropriate for looking at cultural issues today. But *Anti-Oedipus* may not actually be as anti-Freud as it might appear, or even as anti-Oedipus as it purports to be. In any case, it is high time to encourage Freud's much-maligned protagonist to give as good as he gets ("Up the Ante, Oedipus") in view of the high stakes of Deleuze's opening move.

Of course, as I argued in chapter 2, it is not a question here of supporting the reductive popular version of Oedipus as a *complex* tracing all problems to a desire for Mommy and a revolt against Daddy. If the explicit position of *Anti-Oedipus* is to be taken seriously, however, this nearly obsessive underreading of Freud needs to be challenged. Do the Anti-Oedipalists, like their mythical enemy, pay the price of insight with blindness? It certainly seems that the first volume of *Capitalism and Schizophrenia* casts Oedipus big O as a Zero, a real Nowhere Man.

But Deleuze's later work raises another possibility. Reading the stunning sequel to the anti-oedipal diatribe—*A Thousand Plateaus*, which owes a profound and explicit debt to the most radical Freud—one wonders whether the first volume suffers from shortsightedness, as seems to be the case, or serves as a preliminary strategy of sorts, a setup. May Deleuze possibly be sending his antihero on a roundabout journey to a futurist u-topia (no-place)? Is Oedipus as antihero en route to a kind of Oz (the very name resonates with zero) somewhere among the many dimensions of *A Thousand Plateaus*? Might *Anti-Oedipus* showcase a post-hero of sorts, only *apparently* a hollow Tin Man, the vassal/vessel for Freud? Maybe Deleuze is setting up Oedipus as a Straw Man, standing in for the brainlessness of *some* psychoanalysis. Perhaps Deleuze's scheme casts Oedipus as a Cowardly Feline, a "paper tiger" who reveals what he is made of only when he reaches the weird "holey space" invoked at the end of his journey, a voyage through a permeable nonspace that bears more than a passing resemblance to the Freudian unconscious.[2]

In any case, the two volumes of *Capitalism and Schizophrenia* need to be read together. But before embarking on this circuitous journey, Deleuze puts Oedipus on trial, in what may be an opening gambit.

Deleuze's indictment of Freud is all the more disquieting because it is compelling; the volumes of *Capitalism and Schizophrenia* fashion a strikingly original geology of morals, depicting an alien realm complete with nomads, rhizomes, totemic emblems, faceless heads, and living rocks. But in upgrading theory with these strange futuristic players, must we jettison psychoanalysis? Or can we rewire Oedipus like a state-of-the-art probe-head (Deleuze's term for a search engine)? In any case, it is high time that we decriminalize Oedipus, who is all but condemned by Deleuze. An advocate of Oedipus might suggest not only that he is innocent of the charges leveled against him by Deleuze and Guattari, but that he may actually be read as an emblem of the very *desiring machine* in whose name the plaintiffs are bringing suit.

OEDIPUS ON TRIAL: CHARGING FREUD

Deleuze and Guattari certainly pull no punches in squaring off against the adversary in *Anti-Oedipus*. The attack continues in the second volume: the essay "One or Several Wolves?" takes on Freud's famous case study of the Wolf Man with particular animus.[3] When the Wolf Man hallucinates ghostly canines staring at him from the tree outside his bedroom, Freud speculates that this is an aftereffect of witnessing the primal scene as a child—that is, seeing his parents going at it on all fours, doggy-style. But the Anti-Oedipalists take issue with Freud's bestial erotics: "In truth, Freud sees nothing and understands nothing. He has no idea what a libidinal assemblage is, with all the machineries it brings into play, all the multiple loves" (*Anti-Oedipus*, 37).

Indeed, Deleuze and Guattari reduce Freud's suggestive reading to a nasty case of Oedipus on the part of the *analyst*: they charge him with filial blindness, with palpable indignation: "[Freud] glances at his dog and answers, 'It's daddy'" (38). For the Anti-Oedipalists, Daddy Freud is just like his hero Oedipus, the King of Denial. Sees nothing and understands nothing, while playing the know-it-all. Doesn't know his own daddy from a dog, or a beggar at the crossroads. Slays him with his rod, and still comes up with the short end of the stick.

There is such overkill in this reading of the Wolf Man that it smacks of classic Freudian denial (*Verneinung*), in which the patient reveals the high stakes involved by protesting too much. (Freud gives a famous example of denial: his patient protests that the woman in his dream is *not* his mother.) Similarly, Deleuzian disavowal might reveal that the ultimate Anti-Oedipalist himself is more "oedipal" than he can bear to own up to ("Freud is *not* my father").

The very rubric under which Deleuze and Guattari make their case against Oedipus is evidence of a certain investment. In the syntactic terms elaborated at some length in *Anti-Oedipus*, the diatribe itself qualifies as what they call the "*exclusive disjunction*": a binary, oppositional, "either/or," mutually exclusive antagonism. For as Deleuze himself insists, two positions, and only two positions, figure in his theoretical scheme: "there are only resistances, and then machines, desiring-machines" (314). In this particular exclusive disjunction, Oedipus is clearly classified as a resistance, a constraint imposed on the infinite combinations of desire. To be anti-Oedipus is to be pro-desire, plain and simple.

But the defendant Oedipus is not only accused of resistance to the free flow of combinatory desire; as the henchman of psychoanalysis, he is charged with everything from the crimes of capitalism to the epidemic of global psychosis. Referring to "the intrinsically *perverted* nature of psychoanalysis," the "Antis" assert that "perversion in general is the artificial *reterritorialization* of the flows of desire" (314). Like a morals squad, Deleuze and Guattari act as Anti-Pervert Terminators, determined to set the record "straight" by exposing Oedipus as the secret agent of repression. Oedipus-as-fixation is thus the preliminary target on the way to utopia. For, in *Anti-Oedipus*, Deleuze and Guattari embark on what they will later term "a deterritorializing line of flight" over the rainbow, to a fantasy realm of free desire.

But there is a difference between fixation and resistance. In a sense, the intersubjective long circuit that forges human being is perverse, at least according to Freud's own definition of per-version as a detour from a straightforward biological goal.[4] And Freud's work shows that this deflection is what founds culture itself. Deleuze's debt to Freud is all the more evident because the *anti*-anti-Oedipalist position may use the opponents' own theoretical apparatus to construct the opening argument for the defense. This preliminary plea has four points.

First, the crux of the Freudian paradigm is not the patriarchal familial romance of Mommy-Daddy-me; it is the configuration of connections, disruptions, and refractions of desire that constitute human social interaction; according to the Antis themselves. Oedipus is a desiring-machine, not a Greek matinée idol.

Second, the important Deleuzian theoretical concept of the BWO ("body without organs," a fancy name for a field system of flows like a weather system) is already implicit in Freud's early work. In the *Three Essays on the Theory of Sexuality*, Freud theorizes the infant body as a *field* of "perverse" energies, rather than a localization of genital desire in the sex organs. The BWO is manifest in the polymorphous perversity of the always-already sexualized infant. And I have argued throughout that "Oedipus" does not equal the oedipus *complex*, as phallic fixation.

Third, by imputing the spectacular failure of late capitalist society almost exclusively to oedipal repression, the Anti-Oedipalists miss the crucial point. Freudian theory anticipates their own argument: desiring circuits are socially productive, regardless of whether these circuits are ethically unimpeachable, politically progressive, or personally liberating. Oedipus, even narrowly construed, does not engender capitalist repression, though "he" may enact it. By fixating on the figure of Oedipus rather than the paradigm, the plaintiffs neglect Freud's most radical discovery: sexuality is a production of the human psyche with somatic coordinates. It is the product of the "desiring-machine" housed in a casing composed of real energy fields and matter (a body). Freud is not so much about repression as about the *circulation* of desire in a social circuit, which is precisely what the plaintiffs are supposedly introducing.

Fourth, "oedipus" actually embodies the Deleuzian program for "schizanalysis," described as the study of desire as "schizzes and flows" (*Anti-Oedipus*, 271). Deleuze himself asserts that it is possible to think of the libido as a kind of propulsion, the fuel of the desiring-machine, operating in fits and starts: "Everything functions at the same time, but amid hiatuses and ruptures, breakdowns and failures, stalling and short circuits, distances and fragmentations" (42). The essential thing is thus not the smooth functioning of the machine but its productive activity, which leaves a remainder: "To withdraw a part from the whole, to detach, to 'have something left over,' is to produce, and to carry out real operations of desire in the material world" (41). Desire is not continuous or linear; it *produces* labyrinthine connections.

This is a striking formulation, but it originates with Freud, not Deleuze. Nor is it inconsistent with the oedipal assemblage, even under the too-familiar guise of family romance. Construed as a larger intersubjective process of socialization, "oedipus" is . . . a *rhizome*, conforming to Deleuze's own characterization of the concept as webbing where every part is connected to every other in a nonlinear assemblage (like sites in the Internet). Deleuze himself tells us that in the rhizomatic structure that he opposes to traditional linear models, "every part may be connected to *anything other*, and must be."[5] A rhizome must be open to and attachable with any number of phenomena or objects *unlike* itself, a potential link to radical Otherness and heterogeneity. It must be multidimensional, participating in more than one straight line or one flat plane, sprouting off in *A Thousand Plateaus*.

Having set out the key points of an anti-anti defense, we can now address the indictment against Oedipus in some detail.

CASING OEDIPUS

Deleuze first addresses many of the key notions of *Anti-Oedipus* in his earlier classic work, *Difference and Repetition*.[6] This work is explicitly Freudian, defining difference as a displacement, a process of decentering that inhabits all instances of repetition. In this poststructuralist, pre-rhizome reflection, Deleuze already asserts the illusory nature of *any* originary or "centered" model, since centering is a repressive strategy of totalization. But even at this avowedly Freudian stage of his work, Deleuze has already begun to cast the *"oedipus complex"* on the side of rigid identity and repression of desire. In 1968—when battle lines were in fact being drawn in French society—Deleuze had already begun to put Oedipus in his place, across the line separating the evil proponents of repression from the champions of liberation.

But this casting of Oedipus must seem astonishing to anyone with even a passing knowledge of Freud or Lacan; in fact, not even in Sophocles' tragedy is Oedipus the agent of law or unitary self-presence. He is, after all, the man who never knows who or where he is, who can't tell his father from a homeless man, and who actually marries his mother by mistake, even after the oracle has alerted him to the danger. But quite apart from the family plot, the oedipal narrative is a machine—"la machine *infernale*" of Jean Cocteau's version—whose characters have significance only when they are plugged into each other's histories and desires.[7] Mother/wife is at once a conjunction, joining two parts of the plot, and a disjunction, a locus of desire that disrupts and unbalances. For Oedipus begins life as an exile, and ends up as one. In a parable of first time as repetition, Oedipus loses his virginity in the same place it was conceived. Even the family romance shows that repetition is a function of displacement and disguise, as Deleuze himself argues. In the language of twenty-first-century physics, Jocasta is a force field, a strange attractor, drawing her son/husband into an erratic circuit, *fort* and *da*.

At any rate, by the time that he writes *Anti-Oedipus*, Deleuze seems to have disavowed the compelling insights on displacement and iteration set forth in *Difference and Repetition*, regressing to a rigid binary *either/or* attack mode. (Some loyalists simply blame Guattari for this move.) As the advocate for Freud and his spokesman, however—who are conflated to such a degree that one could refer to the defendant as "Freudipus"—I need now to detail the charges leveled against him.

You name it, he's done it.

- He's a crass commercialist, a shady inside trader, for "psychoanalysis does not invent Oedipus"; it markets it (*Anti-Oedipus*, 365).
- He's a Lacanian, caught up in the holy trinity of lack, law, and signifier.[8]
- He's unkind to animals (especially those with talking heads); Oedipus kills our wildness, our capacity for "becoming-animal."[9]

- He's a despotic killjoy as well, the agent of ideological hegemony, "and he is everywhere," for "our society is the stronghold of Oedipus" (*Anti-Oedipus*, 175).
- He signifies blockage of the free flows of intensities and energies, which is an unpardonable offense, "tying off the unconscious on both sides" (81). (Threadipus Rex?) Anything short of delirium is repressive: get on with the orgy or be labeled a neurotic.
- He's a good-for-nothing, a ne'er-do-well: "Oedipus is completely useless" (81).
- He's a capitalist semiotician, whose crimes of the signifier include commodity fetishism: "For example, in the capitalist code and its trinitary expression, money as detachable chain is converted into capital as detached object. The same is true of the oedipal code: the libido as energy of selection and detachment is converted into the phallus as detached object" (73). In other words, oedipalization converts all the flows and discontinuities into a single "phallic" currency (the desire for Mommy and rivalry with Daddy).
- Oedipal society is charged at once with the *deterritorialization* of energy (as free-flowing, circulating capital) and with the *reterritorialization* (repression) of desiring energy (in the name of Freudian Family Values like castration): "How does one prevent the unit chosen, even if a specific institution, from constituting a perverted society of tolerance, a mutual-aid society that hides the real problems? . . . How will the structure break its relationship with neuroticizing, perverting, psychoticizing castration?" (320).
- Freudipus is an imperialist: Our psyches are all little colonies, and "Oedipus is always colonization" (170).
- He drives us crazy (not good, Deleuzian schizoid crazy, just psychotic): "Everything in the system is insane: this is because the capitalist machine thrives on decoded and deterritorialized flows . . . while causing them to pass into an axiomatic apparatus that combines them, and at the points of combination produces pseudo codes and artificial reterritorializations" (374). This is code for: he's bourgeois.
- He's a logical positivist. Let the signifier float as it will, there's still just too much meaning in Oedipus, a conspirator with the international mafia of therapists.[10]

This is a daunting list of charges. But by positing all these instances of malfeasance, Deleuze and Guattari end up making contradictory assertions. Is Oedipus cause or effect? Does Oedipus become colonized under capitalism—serving the ideology of religion or nation—or is he the colonizing agent? Oedipus gets blamed for everything.

Here, then, are the ten counts of the indictment:

1. Oedipus is the repressive agent of the capitalist state apparatus.
2. The oedipal subject is paranoid, not schizophrenic (the favored symptom for Deleuzians). As a paranoid, Oedipus is systematizing and totalitarian, not madly creative and anarchist (like Artaud, Nietzsche, Schreber . . .).
3. Oedipus is "molar," not "molecular." That is, he functions at the wrong (global, totalitarian) level, rather than at the politically correct (local, "molecular") level of

energy, intensities, chemical reactions. In the domain of the Deleuzian molecular, Oedipus is as outsized as Gulliver with the Lilliputians, but harder to pin down.

4. Oedipus airs his dirty linen in public (though he's a loner). His family story, everywhere in the air, is so diffuse as to mean nothing. Oedipalists are solipsistic, internalizing the capitalist ideology in their petty family squabbles. Oedipus is definitely a bad son, a man of few roots. (And we know that the Oedipalists love rhizomes.) What few family connections he has he abuses.

5. On the other hand: Oedipus airs his dirty linen in public (a real show-off). His family story, everywhere in the air, explains everything. Oedipalists are gregarious, projecting their family romance onto all social constructs. Oedipus has quite a family tree. (And we know the Antis hate arborescence.) He's a chip off the old block. (Daddy tried to kill him first, and had the same taste in women.)

6. Oedipus is a Lacanian autocrat, a tyrannical King enforcing the Law. (The anti-Freudians grudgingly acknowledge that Lacan "saved psychoanalysis from frenzied oedipalization" [Anti-Oedipus, 271], but they complain about the reductiveness of a system that classifies everything as "imaginary" or "symbolic." They fail to mention the third and most deeply problematic register in Lacan's scheme: the real.)

7. On the other hand: Oedipus is no King; he is Freud's servile subject, flattened by totalizing Law (presumably not "dimensional" enough to assume the "we" that is the privilege of royals and schizophrenics [111]).

8. Oedipus is a spendthrift ("he makes debt infinite" [217]), presumably since his job is to propagate guilt and hand it down as part of his estate.

9. On the other hand: Oedipus is a miser (stingy and repressed), who doesn't spend enough to stimulate the economy of free flowing desire (26–30).

10. Oedipus' family romance, above all, focuses on castration, emphasizing what's missing, or what might be missing if Oedipus doesn't behave. Lack cannot be a category of the unconscious, the plaintiffs argue, because "desire does not lack anything" (26); it produces.

And here the prosecutors have a point. There is no "no" in the unconscious, as Freud himself insists, only the plenitude of visual scene. (The dream "presents" only visible images, however contradictory; the dream cannot picture "absence.") In other words, Freud's opponents actually follow Freud in asserting that the unconscious is characterized by absence of contradiction: it is not the site of either/or—the Deleuzian exclusive disjunction. It functions, rather, with what Deleuze and Guattari call inclusive disjunction, a figure where inconsistent terms may coexist thanks to the extra "or" that creates a paradoxical emblem of separation and inclusion, at once.

> [Schizophrenia] teaches us a singular extra-oedipal lesson, and reveals to us an unknown force of the disjunctive synthesis, an immanent use that would no longer be exclusive or restrictive, but fully affirmative, nonrestrictive, inclusive. A disjunction that remains disjunctive, and that still affirms the disjoined terms, that

affirms them throughout their entire distance, without restricting one by the other or excluding the other from the one, is perhaps the greatest paradox . . . "Either . . . or . . . or," instead of "either/or." (76)

The introduction of inclusive disjunction is a brilliant stroke on the part of the prosecutors: you can't argue against it. But in fact it is Freud himself who introduces the inclusive disjunction, saying that one of the characteristics of primary process is the ability to hold two or more logically exclusive notions at once without any sense of contradiction. Oedipus learns the consequences of this the hard way: when he does not respect exclusive disjunctions (such as "*either* mother/ or wife"), the failure to make the cut proves fatal.

Given this concession to the prosecution's "inclusive disjunction" argument, how does the defendant plead? Guilty, of course. (Freudipus invented the guilty conscience.) What is the sentence? The plaintiffs have a suggestion: "A true politics of psychiatry [would consist in] undoing all the reterritorializations that transform madness into mental illness" (321). Rehabilitating the culprit means convincing him that schizophrenics aren't ill, but mad; and teaching him that desiring-production is one and the same thing as social production.

The problem with this indictment is that Freud might well agree. It matters how you read Freud, and which Freud.

ALL STEAMED UP: KETTLE LOGIC

But when it comes to Oedipus, the Antis act as indicting body, prosecutors, judge, jury, and executioners. They are less than jurisprudent in handing down a verdict that puts Oedipus in multiple jeopardy, accusing him of mutually exclusive crimes. It seems that inclusive disjunction can come in handy in court.

The defense concedes that the paradox of the inclusive disjunction is intriguing, but it is far from non-Freudian and extra-oedipal: it comes *from* Freud. In *Jokes and Their Relation to the Unconscious*, Freud offers one of his favorite Jewish anecdotes as the epitome of comic nonsense, the celebrated "kettle argument":

A. borrowed a copper kettle from B., and after he had returned it was sued by B. because the kettle now had a big hole in it which made it unusable. His defense was, "First, I never borrowed a kettle from B. at all; secondly, the kettle had a hole in it already when I got it from him; and thirdly, I gave him back the kettle undamaged." Each one of these defenses is valid in itself, but taken together they exclude one another. A. was treating in isolation what had to be connected as a whole. . . . We might also say A. put an "and" where only an "either, or" would suffice.[11]

Surprise, surprise: from the mouth of the oedipal father himself comes a perfect example of schizoid, anti-oedipal reasoning: inclusive disjunction. Deleuze and Guattari, like the kettle-borrower, tinker with smooth logic and forge a holey argument, then claim to own what they've borrowed from Freud. The Anti-Oedipalists, overstating their case (psychoanalysis has handed us a fine kettle of fish!), betray the radicality of Freud's discovery, then protest too much, with leaky reasoning and overspill kettle logic.

Still, let us overrule our own objection, since we may want use precisely the same kettle strategy as a defense. To the plaintiffs we say: (1) You never lent us loyalists the true Freudian kettle of psychoanalysis; (2) when you lent us the oedipal cauldron, it was already riddled with holes, thanks to your potshots; and (3) anyway, here, we're returning the vessel undamaged (handed over by Lacan), bright and shiny, a perfect example of what *you* call smooth, nonstriated space. Or, better yet, holey space, forged by itinerant metallurgists, those smiths and tinkers honored in *A Thousand Plateaus*. We suggest that the defacialized millennial Oedipus is a nomadic spaceman, forging a new image: a high-tech Tin Man, a metallic cyborg, an empty oedipal kettleful.

To elaborate the first point: the plaintiffs never lent Freud fans the theory that they now say has holes in it, since they never owned it. The family romance and rule of law is not the radical essence of Freud, as even Deleuze himself acknowledges in *Difference and Repetition*, where "oedipus-as-complex" is acquitted on the grounds of reasonable doubt, its meaning pronounced "undecidable."

As described by Deleuze and Guattari, desire is a mechanical matter: the desiring machine is an assemblage of one node hooked onto another. But Freud was the first to argue something of the sort: think, for instance, of the nursing infant, protagonist of the *Three Essays on the Theory of Sexuality*, hooked to the mother's flow and plugged into (or "laid on to," as suggested by the German *Anlehnung*) her field of intensity. This is by no means the contested oedipal Mother, or the pre-oedipal Madonna; she is an agent of production, a dairy factory overlaid with hallucinatory desire. Moreover, the formulation of desiring-machine versus oedipal blockage does not begin to account for the complexities of the Freudian *Anlehnung*, or of polymorphous perversity in Freud's *Three Essays*. The infant is a Deleuzian "body without organs," that is, a system without differentiated zones. Or, if you prefer, the infant is a body of nothing but organs, one big erogenous zone entertaining multiple intensities and flows, like the sensor-skin of Deleuze's creative poet-schizophrenic.

True, the socializing process supposedly organizes this pure field into genital sexuality, but the point of the *Three Essays* is that perversion—not normalcy, whatever that may be—is constitutive of human sexuality. Sexuality is mimetic and contagious, always plugged into multiple desiring minds/bodies. In this view, all desire, even old-fashioned desire for Mommy, is refracted and circulatory, like a missile with a homing device: it roams, but what goes around comes around. ("A letter always reaches its destination" may be Lacan's version of the Chinese maxim: "Be careful what you wish for.") Desire is catching, a social disease that is always passed on to other human subjects.

Yet, in spite of the overwhelming evidence, Deleuze and Guattari persist in accusing Freud of abandoning desire. This constitutes a felony: "The Freudian black-mail is this: either you recognize the Oedipal character of infantile sexuality, or you abandon all positions of sexuality" (Anti-Oedipus, 100). This charge is particularly outrageous, for Freud's Three Essays focuses on distinctly non-oedipal avatars of desire, including perversion. Freud's radical point is that desire is inherently perverse, deflected from a biological object (the mother's milk) to a substitute. Lacan formulates this perversity as an excess, a remainder (desire = excess of demand over need): we are all "demanding," even when our "needs" are met.

Perversion, as Freud reads it, is not an illness but a modality. It is above all deflection from goal, hijacking libido from direct biological ends. Although Deleuze and Guattari call psychoanalysis an ideology of lack, it is really an account of excess as the very condition of sexuality. In fact, citing perversion as the opposite of neurosis, Freud suggests that the pervert is a happy man, because his sexuality actually (momentarily) finds satisfaction through his (always substitute) objects.

So Deleuze and Guattari certainly never lent us a truly Freudian kettle, but tried to pass off a fake (Mommy-Daddy-me) as the real article.

Now for our second riposte: the oedipal kettle was riddled with holes when you gave it to us. It is hard to believe that Deleuze, psychoanalytic savant that he is, is not being disingenuous when he accuses Oedipus of being insufficiently cathected to the social field. The plaintiffs presume to blast what they call the "hypothesis dear to Freud: the libido does not invest the social field as such except on condition that it be desexualized" (Anti-Oedipus, 352).

Is this what Freud says? Tell that to the Frankfurt School, who discuss the erotic appeal of fascism; referring to the Freud who analyzes the herd dynamics of army and church as an infatuation with a charismatic leader (Group Psychology and the Analysis of the Ego [1921]). Or tell that to Fredric Jameson, when he uses Freud to theorize the political unconscious as cathexis.[12] What about the libidinal scenario of the passionate social cannibalism in Totem and Taboo (1913), where the kids identify so strongly with Daddy that they eat him?[13] And what about the orgiastic murder of the patriarch Moses by his "children," under the influence of pagan desire, reveling in its "schizzes and flows," as they worship the golden calf?[14] Unless one restricts sexuality to genital contact, one must be blind indeed to see in Freudian theory a passionless, nonlibidinal social field. Moreover, Deleuze and Guattari do not even comment on the most intriguing Freudian ideas, such as the death instinct and its relation to the repetition compulsion; or the split ego in "Mourning and Melancholia" (1917); or Freud's theorization of the nonlinear economics of masochism. Not a parent in sight.

In other words, the Deleuzian critique of Oedipus is applicable only to the most rigidly construed Freudian orthodoxy. Above all, the Anti-Oedipalists overlook Freud's most radical contribution: he recasts sex as sexuality, that is, as an irrevocably *social effect*, not a code of behavior. The process of subjectivation is a social production, as Deleuze and Guattari assert, but it is one that is driven by amplification and circulation, not repression, of desire. The Deleuzian kettle is already a pretty leaky vessel when it is given to us in *Anti-Oedipus*.

Now, let us wrap up with the third part of the kettle defense: the kettle we're giving back to you has no hole. Maybe this is a false debate—can we settle out of court? We can agree with Deleuze and Guattari that psychoanalysis should not be in the business of discovering such-and-such a code. We can also agree that psychoanalysis should address the libidinal flows that traverse dreams, fantasies, and pathological formations. In other words, okay, the defense concedes that some Freudian theory is a bit vatic. Undoing the ego dogma is a fine agenda, a good itinerary, and one that "French Freudians" have been following for some time.

In our proposed settlement, we give a plugged-in millennial kettle back to our opponents: Kettlepus is better than new, see? A certain Oedipus actually fits your own theory of smooth, nomadic space. In fact, because he's hollow, he may serve as an example of hyperspace (indeed, part II of this book deals with the subjective paradigm as a kind of Klein bottle, getting beyond the four old dimensions of the twentieth century). Deleuze and Guattari are right to ask of the unconscious not "What does it mean?" but "How does it work?" (*Anti-Oedipus*, 109). They just need to put the same question to the oedipal machinic diagram. Even Deleuze and Guattari finally make the crucial point that "the unconscious poses no problem of meaning, solely problems of use." This is an excellent insight, but it is borrowed from Freud.

But enough with the kettle argument. It is not good sport to stage a tug-of-war over Freud's theory as contested object. The point is that Freud is essential to Deleuze's view, as expressed in *A Thousand Plateaus*. Society is indeed a milieu for the circulation of unowned objects, holey or intact, theft or gift, which determine the relation between giver and receiver. Hence, "there is desire, and the social, and nothing else."

Freud's "oedipus" is not a rigid diagram or a narrative myth: each set of determinate conditions causes the abstract machine to produce a completely different remainder: Oedipus the king, paranoid and despot; Oedipus the stranger, upstart and revolutionary; even Oedipus the happy man, pervert or joker. Deleuze and Guattari, surprisingly, concede this point: "There is no Oedipal triangle: Oedipus is always open in an open social field, one whose effects will be determined by the conditions we shape and that shape us. " As Deleuze and Guattari themselves assert, the unconscious poses a problem of use: "The question posed by desire is not 'What does it mean?' but rather 'How does it work?'" (Anti-Oedipus, 109).

I suggest that Deleuze and Guattari form a triangular assemblage with Freud from which a hybrid theory may emerge transformed. The Big "o" is but a place-holder for the human subject, occupying a site that every nomad occupies in turn, just passing through. To use the high-tech lingo of A Thousand Plateaus, the oedipal parable might be said to describe a self-organizing process at a moment of bifur-cation when the subject emerges, in response to catalysts and attractors. Oedipus is what Deleuze calls an abstract machine, not a role model. Oedipus follows an orac-ular program, not in response to a specific desire for his mother, whom he does not even know, or a specific animus toward his father, a complete stranger. He does not kill the symbolic father or marry the imaginary mother; he operates in the automatism of the real.

OEDIPUS THE CLOWN: "MOMMY, DADDY, AND ME" AS COMIC MACHINE

Having argued against the use of Freud as straw man, I want to turn now to the issue of how to reconfigure "Mommy, Daddy, and me" in Deleuzian terms, as "de-siring machine and multiplicity." Can it be that the family tree is a rhizome, send-ing out tentacles and crossing lines (Octopus Rocks)?

Deleuze and Guattari define a machine as any heterogeneous linkage, where dif-ferent terms join and interact to produce a remainder. The elements of the desir-ing machine do not have to be single discrete organisms—they can be, for instance, body parts (the breast and the nursing infant constitute a desiring ma-chine). The Deleuzian paradigm moves from the conventional focus on subject and object, describing an action of one element or entity on another, to a new sys-temic paradigm of circulation.

In other words, a machine is a circuit of sorts. Not all "productions" are peace-ful, painless, or pretty; any productive heterogeneous combination, creating en-ergy, power, or a remainder, is a desiring machine: from animal husbandry, to chemical reactions, to the annhilation of matter by anti-matter, to the capitalist economic system, to the brain as a productive field that sprouts new connections with each new experience. As Manuel De Landa's helpful elaboration of Deleuze explains, a machine may be organic (involved in reproduction or metabolism, like the food chain that produces biomass), inorganic (the geological strata that accrue over eons, transforming biomass into energy as oil and coal deposits), or anthropomorphic (a social institution, a military-industrial complex, capitalism).[15]

According to this notion, all social transactions may be considered desiring machines, productive linkages. In fact, automatic workings of desire in the human processes of play, of joking, and of artistic creation are the centerpiece of Freud's *Jokes and Their Relation to the Unconscious*, a work every bit as compelling as his treatment of the myth of Oedipus. Indeed, we could consider Freud's "joke" as the exemplary version of the triangulated machinic configuration, an intersubjective linkage involving and producing multiple subjects in a circuit of desire. Deleuze and Guattari get it backwards: rather than projecting Oedipus onto everything, a reading of the radical Freud embeds Oedipus as just one narrative *instance* of a more inclusive blueprint.

THE PURLOINED PUNCH LINE

In chapters 1 and 2 I alluded to this triangular blueprint, this "engineering diagram" in Freud, suggesting that it underlies Freud's account of all creative activity. For instance, Freud's work on jokes outlines a triangular transaction structurally identical to the process described in "Creative Writers and Day-Dreaming," enacting the transfer of desire from one party to another, in a process of bonding or identification. When Freud details how this works in a parable about the origin of joking, his account is performative: he enacts the *story* of the origin of joking, telling a tale to his reader where he himself "performs" the initiating activity of the creative writer.

Here is a brief retelling of my retelling of Freud's retelling of the joker's retelling of the story of desire, framed as a plot that should sound uncannily . . . familiar. Since the work on jokes is the clearest example of "oedipus" as paradigm rather than the familiar drama of Mommy-Daddy-me, it is worth revisiting here, as an instance of the Deleuzian desiring-machine, a long-circuiting of desire that leads to a social process.[16]

BOY MEETS GIRL. Freud starts by setting the stage. "The one who makes the joke" encounters a desirable "object," gets ideas, and makes them known in "wooing talk."[17]

BOY LOSES GIRL. But the wooer's seductive design is confounded by the entry of a second male, a potential rival and importune third party. As if the woman's inhibition did not pose problems enough for the wooer's design, the second male interrupts the seduction and makes it unseemly, if not impossible.

BOY GETS . . . GIRL? But never fear, boy does get girl, if only vicariously, by "exposing her in the obscene joke" instead of seducing her, and enjoying the spectacle of her embarrassment: the hapless woman has now been dressed down before a (male) listener who has "been bribed by the effortless satisfaction of his own libido" (Jokes, 100). In this scenario, the locker-room joys of male bonding have replaced the joy of sex, since the joker actually "calls on the originally interfering third party as his ally" (100).

JOKE CONQUERS ALL. But the freeloading listener does not escape unscathed. Freud points out the aggressive nature of this capture of the listener's attention by the teller, who takes his hearer by surprise, with the aptly named "punch line" (192–193). Boy must capture boy by an expert delivery, or the joking transaction will fail. But when the joker succeeds in pulling the chair out from under his listener, psychologically speaking, Freud says the hearer "damps down his annoyance by resolving to tell the joke himself later on" to the next victim (139). Thus the joking triangle is always at least a quadrilateral of sorts, an open social chain in which the imaginary capture of both the joke's object (pole two) and its listener (pole three) is perpetuated with a changing cast of players.

Above all, Freud shows that the joke is a circuit in which no one's identity remains uncontaminated by exposure to the Other's desire, in an invulnerable "outside" position. In fact, the joking pleasure turns out to be as double-edged as its punch line, "hooking" the hearer and leaving a remainder. As Freud insists, "a joke must be told to someone else . . . something which seeks, by communicating the idea, to bring the unknown process of constructing a joke to a conclusion" (143).

One could hardly ask for a clearer picture of the Deleuzian desiring machine at work, as the "something" that "remains over" and hooks up with another desiring machine to fuel "operations in the real world." Just like the desiring machine, Freud's jokes replicate themselves in response to the unfinished business that compels the joke's repetition. Freud coins the term jokework, comparing it to the dreamwork: both joke and dream "work on" psychic material by the techniques of condensation, displacement, and figuration or regression. Tellingly, the Oedipus myth itself shows evidence of these same processes: the Sphinx is a "condensation" of woman and cat; Oedipus' attention is "displaced" from the truth right in front of him, by a too-literal reading of the oracle; Oedipus' affection is nothing if not regressive.

But as I indicated in chapter 2, I am less concerned here with the content of Oedipus' story than with its blueprint: it is a working circuit, subject to fits and starts, just like Deleuze's engineering diagram. Indeed, Deleuze's description of an interrupted circuit, starting and stopping ("One machine interrupts the current of the other or sees its own current interrupted" [Anti-Oedipus, 27]), is applicable to Freud's account of joking, which is produced by the interruption of the wooer's desire by the entry of the rival. The rival is a circuit breaker or "resistor," who causes the libidinal "current" to be rerouted into the joke. Lacan, in fact, refers to the formation of the subject as the effect of a circuit.[18]

Thus, while any given joke might seem to be content-specific (concentrating on the butt of the joke), Freud's description reveals the underlying mechanism in all jokes, which are always transgressive: "a joke always has something forbidden to say" (Jokes, 139). In Deleuze's own terms, Freud's joking triangle shows not what the unconscious means, but how it works, with an infectious desire that promotes social bonding. For it recruits the listener to share in a laugh which makes use of the inhibitions of both parties, and reveals their mutual vulnerability and implication. (In fact, few actions are more deflating than the refusal to laugh when a joke is told. Responding with a withering "That's not funny," the listener deprives not only the punch line of its punch, but the puncher of both of his punchees, the joke's target and the listener to whom it is pitched.)

In the barebones plot that Freud gives, a woman is dressed down in front of an audience, the rival who agrees to laugh about her rather than fight over her. This cannot fail to remind us of another shady story of love, aggressivity, and renunciation. In the classic oedipal tragedy, boy does indeed get girl, by simply eliminating the paternal rival, and engaging in the incestuous short circuit. Freud's own comic retelling of the myth, however, stages a dilemma that is resolved ("The Dissolution of the Oedipus Complex" [1924]).[19] Oedipus echoes the outcome of the joking crisis, rather than the other way around. (Jokes was written before the most complete elaboration of the oedipus complex in the Introductory Lectures on Psychoanalysis [1916–17]). In the passing of the oedipus complex, just as in the joke paradigm, the subject identifies with the former rival, renounces the impossible love, and chooses a substitute object outside the family fold. ("I want a girl just like the girl who married dear ole Dad"—but not the same girl, who is already taken.) This long-circuiting of the subject's desire is motivated by unfinished business, a productive remainder diverted from a deadly incestuous short circuit. The subject's excessive desire sends him out of the tragic enclosure, on his way in search of another hookup. The motivation of the Freudian circuit is not lack, as Deleuze and Guattari insist, but excess: desire is the surplus that fuels human being.

In another crucial text on social triangulation, "Creative Writers and Day-Dreaming," Freud insists on yet another obstacle: he foregrounds the role of veiling (Ankleidung) in the creative process. The work of art always involves artifice and disguise, for it won't work on the reader/viewer if the original fantasy is presented too egotistically, too straightforwardly, too . . . nakedly. The writer/artist softens his or her own daydreams—fantasies motivated by the same sort of erotic and aggressive impulses that motivate the joking process. The poet's secret, that Freud suggestively calls "veiling" (Ankleidung), is the ability to dress up egotistical or erotic fantasy by "changes and disguises," in order to make the writer's naked fantasy palatable to the third party.[20] Like the joke's hearer, the reader must "captured" by an artful tease. The desiring circuit is based on exposing its object . . . just enough.

The Oedipus myth/joking triangle may thus be overdetermined by the artistic process, as suggested in the multilayered diagram below. This diagram suggests an alternative to the "flat" reading of Oedipus that stumbles on a near-hysterical assertion of constraints and sameness in Freud, but makes one wonder if Deleuze has even read Freud with care.[21] In even this brief schema, the engineering diagram works expansively in three very different cultural situations.

a) desired object—"mother"
b) butt of joke
c) Jocasta
d) writer's "daydream" object transformed into
character or fantasy situation

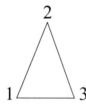

a) desiring subject—"child"
b) teller of joke
c) Oedipus
d) writer/artist

a) desiring Other—"father"—obstacle, also the
one whom pole 1 bonds and identifies in the
passing of the complex
b) listener of joke: intruder/accomplice
c) Laius
d) audience/reader

Key:
a = oedipus "complex"
b = joke process
c = Oedipus myth, tragedy
d = literary/artistic transaction

Overdetermined versions of the oedipal triangle.

Note that of all of these scenarios, only the mythic tragedy of Oedipus has no "resolution"—because the father fails to deflect the son in his murderous, infantile design. The triangle thus gets flatlined by the elimination of Laius and the lethal completion of an incestuous short circuit. Deleuze's problem is that he equates the tragic myth with Freud's blueprint, without accounting for its comic or socially productive transformations in Freud, including *Moses and Monotheism* and *Totem and Taboo*, which posit the foundation of culture as a long-circuiting of imploded desire. Freud's social diagram is about the *failure* of the tragic implosion, thanks to a salutary detour via the Other.

As we saw in chapters 1 and 2, Lacan has his own version of overdetermined Oedipus as the intersubjective Schema L. In this light, the joke itself may be read as symptom of the nonattainability of the object, necessitating the addition of the symbolic register (the social relation with the third pole, the Other, the audience) to complete the circuit.

For both Lacan and Freud, the long-circuiting of direct desire or aggression into a third locus exposes the impossibility of reaching the imaginary goal. What the subject experiences *may* be called castration, in *some* scenarios, but it may also be called wounding, separation, frustration, recognition, socialization, maturation, accommodation, even diversion. The obstacle/third facilitates the entry into the symbolic register—which is law, communication, social exigency, community, compromise—purchased at the price of one's infantile egotistical fantasy of power or gratification. One becomes human thanks to a resistance, incurring what Lacan eloquently terms "the symbolic debt," which will be passed on to others. This productive resistance or deferral has a correlate in the material world: in electronics it is like the work produced by the action of any resistor or transistor that avoids premature discharge and reroutes energy into productive circuit.

Here, then, is Lacan's own diagram of Freud's triangle, showing castration fantasy (in dotted lines) as "imaginary" version of "real" family configuration.

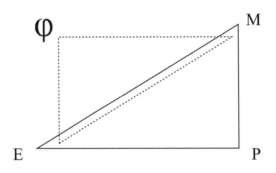

E = enfant (child)
P = père (father)
M = mère (mother
φ = fantasy phallus (reflecting the fantasmatic "father" as all-powerful)

Lacan's overdetermined oedipal triangle.

The Greek symbol stands for "phallus" in Lacan's terms, and the broken line of the left triangle indicates its imaginary or illusory nature, where the child imagines phallic power as the third term. Thus Lacan intends his overdetermination to symbolize the Oedipus *complex*, complete with fantasy reflecting castration anxiety.

But in spite of the apparent "phallocentrism" of Lacan's version, there is even a way of reading this "castration" triangle as something beyond the oedipus complex, by "returning to Freud" as concerns the joking process. By *doubling* Freud's triangle, Lacan actually pictures Freud's implied fourth term, when the listener doubles and takes the place of a new initiating subject, opening the transaction to a new cast of players. (Chapter 2 discusses this opening from three to four "bases" at some length.) This works for the oedipal scenario as well, of course, when the child moves to the place of the parent in the next generation, to reenact the socializing process.

Reading Oedipus through Freud's joke theory also points out an important aspect of intersubjectivity: all of the roles are co-implicated and interchangeable. Every one of Freud's three positions cuts at least two ways, at once active and passive, controlling and vulnerable, victim and agent. Again, the joke scenario shows this most clearly: (1) The teller calls the shots, but the very fact that "he" is joking betrays his inability to "score." (2) The "object" is exposed, but "she" also escapes unscathed by the real designs of the suitor. (3) The listener is taken by surprise by the joke's punch, but "he" has the ultimate power by choosing whether or not to laugh, completing and perpetuating the circuit. All of the loci are in a sense rotatable—every subject may be an object for the next subject, and so forth. This does away with any illusion that the joke is a simple manifestation of superiority or triumph over its victim (as Schopenhauer maintained—among others—with his theory of "sudden glory" as the root of glee). In Freud's field, no one escapes unscathed, "identical" to his or her egotistical self-image. Similarly, in the larger human comedy, everyone gets involved in the social production, willy-nilly. Freud's triadic open circuit is a Deleuzian desiring machine, not an agent of repression.

These various diagrams show how the oedipal drama is but one narrative instance of a complex multidimensional process, generating an algorithmic "engineering diagram." This process may be also transcoded into Deleuze's own terms, as a process of *deterritorialization* and flight, followed by a temporary settling or *reterritorialization*, in the new triangular repetition. The tragic Oedipus replicates his sad familial situation, endlessly reenacted by the wars of his unnatural sibling-children, as one of the "cursed" families of Greek tragedy. But the *comic* version performed by Oedipus-the-Clown suggests that there may be a brighter day dawning somewhere over the rainbow. Just like the end of the joking process, the oedipal scenario sends the odd man out in a nomadic line of deterritorialized flight toward the Other. Each time his flight serves to unsettle a new territory, with the unfinished business brought along from the last scene. The propellant of the social circuit is the desiring animus engendered by the friendly fire of the joker (your girl is your mother, time to move on). The punch line is a *remainder* delivered by the Other who only pretends to knock 'em dead, always pulling the punches.

THE WIZARD OF THEORY: THREESOMES, FOURSOMES, AND MORESOMES

The joke *scene* also has corollaries in Deleuze's non-Euclidean geometry, reflected in his theory of "smooth," "striated," and "holey" space.[22] In *A Thousand Plateaus*, Deleuze gives three clear examples of this distinction. (1) Striated space is like a kingdom or nation, territory parceled and measured. (2) Smooth space is the open unfenced land of the nomad, without boundaries. (3) Holey space is occupied by metallurgists and miners, who serve the inhabitants of both other realms, by fashioning weapons, tools, and ornaments. (In fact, the space of the miner is literally "holey," riddled with mines. And the stuff of holey space is also intermediary—metal is both fluid and solid, transitional matter.)

Zooming into the "space" of today, the astronaut and cybernaut might be considered the newest inhabitants of Deleuzian holey space, dodging in and out of wormholes, dimensions, time zones, and virtual realities. Thanks to space-time warps, holey space is impervious to totalizing vision (you can't see a black hole, just where it isn't). Just so, the inner space of the unconscious (which Deleuze calls the ultimate "desiring machine") is permeable but impervious to final discovery. Indeed, in the twenty-first century, outer space itself is porous, riddled with black holes; interstellar space is an interstitial dimension where "gravity" itself is lost. (And the cosmic joke appears to be on us, since 90 percent of the matter of the universe is currently . . . missing. The scientists are looking for it.)

How may we map the joke-space in Deleuze's terms? It participates in the striated space of social convention, where boundaries are clearly drawn ("we" are laughing at "them"); as well as the smooth liquid amorphous space of the unconscious, where the desire of the other spills over into our own. It also creates or reflects the strange in-between "holey" space, neither smooth nor striated but . . . pockmarked with subterranean meanings and comic pitfalls. The joke-space also recalls the dynamic field of cyberspace, where linked "bits" are transmitted from site to site. This new space is striated, as a web, but it is also dangerously smooth, without defined boundaries. Above all, cyberspace is holey, thanks to the hypertext that embeds site in site and dimension in dimension. And it is permeable: viral hackers love to find its loopholes.

Space-age Oedipus himself is a vagrant, a search engine, a "bot" both mon-strous and human. A cyber version of the oedipal prohibition often unfolds online, complete with disciplinary action. ("You cannot drop things here.") Cyberspace continuously plays at oedipal prohibition as screen and detour, where long-circuited messages are dismantled and circuitously rerouted, in bits of ac-tual matter-energy. Indeed, our oedipal others online these days are sometimes lit-erally desiring-machines, as in the famous Turing Test where flirtatious bots are programmed to pass as real people in chatrooms, by learning their lingo from "listening in."[23]

The human diagram drafted by Freud, in and out of cyberspace, is a Deleuzian rhizome "where every part may be connected to *anything else*, and must be," a site of articulated differences and compulsory encounters with Otherness. By defini-tion, Oedipus leaves a "cookie" to mark his visit, the stigma of desire that must be passed on.

Epilogue: Inorganic Oedipus

You are longitude and latitude, a set of speeds and slownesses between unformed particles, a set of nonsubjectified affects. Wonder of a nonhuman life.
—Deleuze and Guattari, *A Thousand Plateaus*

With the movement of Oedipus from Greek hero to cyborg, we have traversed the three strata of energy and matter visited throughout Deleuze's opus. After visiting the organic, the inorganic, and the anthropomorphic, we have at last landed in Oz. All three strata intersect in the figure of the whistling kettle, a desiring ma-chine that produces and vents desire/energy, as it lets off steam. The Tin Man is a human kettle who leaks real tears and whistles too: "If I Only Had a Heart." A tem-plate of the Deleuzian robotic probe-head, Kettlepus is human and metallic at once: he is quite literally a "body without organs," in search of a good cardiolo-gist. He is significantly the fourth one to join the journey, the one who opens up a "triangle" of actors and sends them on to Oz. And all the voyagers (lion, straw, tin) are a spectrum of "the wonder of nonhuman life": they are animal, vegetable, and mineral—linked up with the human, all-too-human.

In their conclusion to *A Thousand Plateaus*, Deleuze and Guattari tell us that ab-stract or desiring-machines constitute "becomings," that is, they effect linkages, "making something open onto something else."[24] This explains the special status of metallurgy in Deleuze's thematic—it is the craft of nomads, relying on changes of state. Part two of this book deals with this kind of open-ended production in the twenty-first-century theory of emergence.

In his own striking deployment of millennial culture and science, through Deleuze, Manuel De Landa describes how self-organizing systems of matter reach points of bifurcation. This is a material crossroads where a catalyzing agent changes the course of events, sometimes even provoking "chaos" or catastrophe. But energy may find a certain balance at the tipping point, in oscillating phase states. Self-regulating energy systems (like the weather, or chemical clocks) seek the right viscosity, in a stable pattern of alternating movement. In physics and chemistry, this is matter-energy on the edge, suspended between stasis and chaos, moving in the field of opposing attractors (like an Olympic snowboarder swooping back and forth between valleys and peaks, balancing momentum).

Yet again, this material phenomenon is echoed in Freud's view of psychic life. In *Beyond the Pleasure Principle* (1920), Freud describes human life as just such a state on the edge. For he describes the effects of life and death drives in competition, governed by a compromise between the urge to complete a discharge of energy (death) and the need to maintain a specific level of energy (life). In this sense, the Other as obstacle is what keeps the organism from going too directly to its end. Freud's repetition compulsion is a material, machinic, posthuman version of Oedipus.

It is motivated by a remainder, driving the subject *beyond* the pleasure principle, and compelling human subjects to live and to create: paradoxically, the death drive motivates all human achievement, which Freud tells us continues "upward and onward, unsubdued" (*Beyond the Pleasure Principle*). Thus oedipus-as-engineering-diagram gives human life its proper viscosity, its oscillation on the edge of death. As Deleuze and Guattari themselves note, "one never stops, and never has done with, dying"—or, Freud would add, with living.

Oedipus has all the trappings of a machinic assemblage, encountering resistors (the Sphinx), following a program (the oracle), his future determined at a bifurcation or tipping point (the intersection). He oscillates between attractors: Thebes or Corinth?

Let's ask that Scarecrow at the crossroads.

Over the Rainbow, Over the Top
In the comic version of the oedipal abstract machine, Oedipus and Antigone double as Don Quixote and sidekick—ludic warriors on a holey quest, with holes in their heads. For Oedipus is a quixotic knight-errant with holey armor, in a holey war, with missing links in his "chain mail." Blinded, the oedipal probe-head has black holes for eyes—like the extraterrestrial who haunts us today. Human space, whether inner, outer, or hyper, is riddled with riddles, pitfalls, pratfalls. Like Odysseus, millennial Oedipus still navigates versions of Scylla and Charybdis, with new age monsters (clones) and ruthless rocks (asteroids).

Deleuze calls this kind of itinerant voyage a line of nomadic flight, and it describes the adventurous trajectory of his own "wild" theory. The Wizard of Theory, like Freud before him, is an extremely strange attractor, drawing his followers to the alien dimensions of a thousand plateaus. Indeed, Deleuze's rainbow is both smooth and striated, and it may lead only to a leaky cauldron filled with fool's gold. But we can agree with the lyrical enigma that is the last word on space in *A Thousand Plateaus*, which assures us that the most satisfying closures have loopholes, that even golden bricks have potholes. One need only unveil the Wizard, or solve the riddle of the Sphinx, to be riven by the punch line: the joke has been on us all along. Like Oedipus, we have gone to the ends of the earth, but we have never left home.

Deleuze and Guattari warn us in closing about a truth that Oedipus always confronts: "Never believe that a smooth space will suffice to save us."[25]

FREUD SIGHTINGS IN MILLENNIAL THEORY

CHAPTER 5

TWISTS AND TRYSTS: FREUD AND THE
MILLENNIAL KNOT

C. J. Jadlocki, *Millennial Knot*, 2000.

Language knots the Imaginary and the Real (*Le langage fait noeud de l'imaginaire et du réel*).
—Jacques Lacan, *Écrits*

In part I, I argued for the continued viability of Freud's oedipal configuration as paradigm of the intersubjective psyche. For, rather than construing "oedipus" as the vicissitudes of the patriarchal family over one hundred years ago, it is more helpful for us today to read Freud's work as an "engineering diagram" for myriad instances of human cultural interaction that continue in our era. In part II I shall elaborate this view by discussing specific areas of convergence between new paradigms in millennial culture, science, philosophy, and classic Freudian theory. In particular, the four chapters of part II address the concepts of topological geometry, emergence, and fractality, as paradigms commensurate with a "nonlinear" psychoanalysis appropriate for the new realities of our era.

The first section of this chapter explores the knot of associations between psychoanalysis and millennialism, with the help of topology and knot theory. The second section then visits a larger "webbing" or meshwork of related cultural icons as object/concepts that have captured the collective imagination, but have very real manifestations and consequences in the cultural configurations emerging today.

FREUD SIGHTINGS IN MILLENNIAL CULTURE
1: THE TREFOIL KNOT AS MILLENNIAL EMBLEM

The drive gets around (*La pulsion en fait le tour*).
—Jacques Lacan, *The Four Fundamental Concepts of Psycho-Analysis*

"I'm Looking Over a Three-to-Four-Leaf Clover"

Consisting of three loops in three dimensions, a trefoil knot may nevertheless be drawn as a single looping surface, a Moebius strip with three leaves. Thus the Moebius cloverleaf, literally a triple-leaf (*tre-foil*), presents a puzzling spatial dynamic: it has three dimensions but only one surface, paradoxically displaying both flatness and depth. A familiar trefoil figure in everyday life—the freeway exchange, called a *correspondance* in Europe—opens to another bundle of associations: a highway cloverleaf is at once a node and a switching point, a bypass and a link to other networks . . . opening to any number of new routes. It is literally a figure of viability (*via*: pathways); literally a *concrete* instance of an affordance (the new-science term for a juncture offering different possible material outcomes); and literally an instance of *Bahnungen*, at least on the German Autobahn. (In part I, we saw that Lacan's term for *Bahnungen*, or facilitation as a point of access/juncture/affordance, also suggests open-endedness, a fourth position generated from three terms.) Since three always implies four or more in psychoanalysis, the trefoil knot is an emblem of the tertiary as the royal road to complexity. The clover-

Roger Groce, *Moebius Cloverleaf*, 2004.

leaf *affords* exchange, precisely because it engages three loops, rather than a simple intersection.

Trivial Pursuit: The Unknot

Another figure connected with "thirdness" in knot theory is the trivial (tri-vial) knot, defined in topological geometry as "any knot that may be rearranged as a single coil, like a hose looped around one's arm."[1]

The simplest trivial knot is a single circle of rope, known in knot theory— shades of Samuel Beckett—as the *unknot*. The unknot has a zero degree of complexity, or even a negative complexity (it is simpler than the most basic knot, since it has *no* crossings). But simple as it may appear, the unknot has its own intrigue, its very form suggesting a paradoxical absent present, not unlike the zero it resembles.

And, like the term trefoil, the term "tri-vial" implies "thirdness" as well as simplicity, denoting *three* strands. How can a zero degree of complexity also entertain a threesome? The answer ties in with the founding theorem of knot theory:

Every knot is a closed circular braid.[2]

This convention requires that every knot be treated "as if" it were braided, since it must be finished off to be considered as a mathematical object (to put it simply, its ends must be joined to avoid confusion with other links and knots). But even this convention of convenience (considering the knot as "tied off") involves a new complication: the fusion of the ends mathematically requires that the knot be composed of a braid; and a braid is a pattern of *multiple* (most often three) crossings:

Braid: An intertwining of strings attached to top and bottom "bars" such that each string never "turns back up." In other words, the path of each string in a braid could be traced out by a falling object if acted upon only by gravity and horizontal forces.[3]

Interestingly, the necessary attachment of braid strands to a fixing point or bar, as indicated in this mathematical definition, would have to be the fusion of the braid end to itself in a technically "finished-off" or closed mathematical knot, "tying up loose ends." This suggests a complication: the attachment assuring closure also assures circular continuation, with no end in sight.

So the rules of math dictate, paradoxically, that the complexity of knots must be managed, or even ignored—a psychoanalyst might say "foreclosed"—in order to be analyzed "simply." Knot theory is thus bound by a qualification that Freud would find significant: mathematical rigor requires the "as if" of wishful thinking. Not only is the knot the site of paradox, as complex simplicity; but it is also the site of symptom, since mathematical fact must foreclose reality in order to engage in "fact-finding" about the knot. It is not surprising, then, that knot theory proved irresistible to Lacan, who spent his later years reflecting on its complexities.

By selecting a Moebius cloverleaf as "illumination" for this section, I am taking a leaf from the book of knot theory, treating my own threefold subject—psychoanalysis, millennialism, and topology—"as if" it were a single closed object in a continuous loop. But as in knot theory, this configuration is only a matter of convenience: any of these three foils could afford any number of links to other topics. The term "trefoil" itself may serve as a linguistic case in point, providing a lead to the field of cybernetics (in information theory, FOIL is an acronym for File Oriented Interpretive Language). But that sort of linguistic chase, for the moment at least, is . . . off the topic.

Negative Complexity . . . Times Three

The knot that most fascinated Lacan is the Borromean knot, again composed of three parts. This ancient Celtic emblem has an almost mystical appeal: if any one of the three rings is removed, the other two may be separated; as a threesome, however, the rings cannot be moved apart without breaking at least one of them. And since the Borromean ring consists of the juncture of three "unknots" (single circles), it is the site of paradox, at once simple and complex.

Mathematicians are also intrigued by the *space* defined by the Borromean knot, debating whether the links can actually be circular in real life, or if this is an optical illusion. Mathematical proof demonstrates that in three dimensions, the rings would have to have "kinks" or bends to interlock[4] This preoccupation with the shape of what is *not* there—a structuring absence—characterizes millennial science and philosophy, like the structuring absence that is the cornerstone of the

Roger Groce,
Borromean Kinks, 2004.

psychoanalytic symptom. (What invisible core motivates this visible reaction? What is this knot tied around?)

For his part, Lacan referred to the mysterious triple Borromean link to illustrate the relation of his concept of three registers of human experience, separate but implicated: the imaginary, the symbolic, and the real. But we could consider the Borromean knot as an emblem of triangulated human subjectivity in general, embodying the inherent complexity of threesomes-as-moresomes discussed in chapter 4. The Borromean knot also provides visual evidence that complexity and nonlinearity are intrinsically linked to thirdness.[5]

This loopy topological intrigue suggests that Freud was on to something when he chose the concept of "thirdness" as the nodal point for his own elaboration of the ins and outs of intersubjectivity, in his version of oedipus and its cultural iterations (joking, writing, religious totem, and so forth). In fact, the significance of the "three factor" is also acknowledged as the gateway to complexity in mathematics and other sciences. In astronomy, for instance, the importance of the tertiary is reflected in Poincaré's famous "third body problem," elaborated at about the same time that Freud began work on his own version of triangulation in the intrapsychic universe.[6] At the same time, Poincaré's work revolved around the theory that orbits of celestial bodies are predictable only when two objects are involved: when a third body enters the picture, chaotic movement may result.

As Oedipus knew all too well.

Topology as Non-Euclidean Science

topology 1. (*mathematics*) The branch of mathematics dealing with continuous transformations

2. (*networking*) a set of sites which are directly connected to other hosts in a domain

—*Free Online Dictionary of Computing*

In addition to an emphasis on "thirdness," knot theory and systems theory today share an affinity for *topological* thinking, a mode that also characterizes Lacan's theory of subjectivity. As the second definition of topology cited above shows, the term has a very specific use in information systems theory or *networking*. (The mention of "host" in this second technological definition also resonates with the "parasitic" aspect of millennialism as a "site beside itself," discussed in the introduction to this book.) The first definition of topology cited above, the mathematical term denoting "the study of continuous transformations," also suggests an association with the millennial paradigm of "becoming" discussed in chapter 6. As a functional deployment of "emergent" shapes, always fluid and in flux, topological geometry reflects a twenty-first-century fascination with skew and sheer, and with transformations in continual motion, rather than fixed lines, planes, and angles. It departs from the spatio-temporal dimensions of everyday experience, dealing instead with infinitely extendable surfaces and multidimensional spaces where fixed metrics no longer obtain, and fluid objects continually morph.[7]

As Einstein pointed out, this new science entails a radical change in the nature of the object of geometry, with ramifications that shift our philosophical and conceptual foundations:

> We come now to the question: what is a priori certain or necessary, respectively in geometry (doctrine of space) or its foundations? Already the distance-concept is logically arbitrary; there need be no things that correspond to it, even approximately.[8]

Instead of studying quantifiable lines, angles, and solids, along the Euclidean model, topology studies surfaces that may be sheered and stretched, while still retaining certain fundamental properties: intersections, crossings, openings.[9] Sometimes called rubber sheet geometry, topological geometry pays attention only to *relational* surface properties, like the hole in the middle of a sheet, or the number of intersections of a surface with itself. (In topological geometry, the capital letters "F" and "E" are the *same* object, as are a straw and the Alaska pipeline, since the same "rubber sheet" could be stretched over both objects, without punching extra holes or making new ties.) And since knots may be stretched or twisted without changing the basic pattern of crossings (like a rubber pretzel), knot theory is technically a branch of topological geometry.

The shift in emphasis from Euclidean *objects* to topological *relations* is consistent with the general millennial paradigm shift from linear, quantifiable properties ("being") to continuous relational transformations ("becoming"), as discussed in chapter 6. Given the importance of the triangle in the Freudian theory of the subject, this raises an intriguing question: can oedipus go topological? What happens when the triangle is considered a fluid topological object, instead of a fixed three-sided shape?

Here is the short answer to a complex question: the triangle is *topologically equivalent* to any polygon, with any number of sides greater than three (including the four-sided diamond playing field of intersubjectivity discussed in chapter 2). Again deploying the baseball instance of intersubjective play, we could say that the playing field of individual subjectivity is *topologically equivalent* to the plural social field of "intersubjectivity," the field of any player coinciding with the field entertaining "the whole ball game." Indeed, the stretching of the playing field of desire to include more and more subjects is comparable to the stretching of a rubber tarpaulin in baseball, rolled out to fit any area of a playing field when the weather shifts.

Topological criteria may help to stretch our habitual concepts as well. When topological geometry is applied to the Borromean knot, for instance, a current hot debate on Internet graphic arts sites—arguing over whether the rings are really mathematically circles or ellipses—becomes *moot*.[10] A circle and an ellipse are the *same* object in topology: all that counts for knot theory is *how* the links relate, rather than their size or shape. Just so, Lacan's topological version of the Freudian "field" is less interested in the specific contents or shape of an individual mind than in how the human psyche interacts dynamically with others to produce an ever-shifting relational configuration.

Moving in now to take a closer at each of the three leaves in this chapter's trefoil topic—millennialism, Freud, knot theory—we may consider each aspect as a foil for the other two in the millennial field. But it is fair first to consider the literal *viability* of this particular itinerary: with so many aspects of the post-everything mindset to consider, why follow these three particular tri-vial paths? Why "millennial"? Why "Freud"? . . . Why "knot"?

HITCHING "POSTS": WHY "MILLENNIAL"?

mil*len*ni*um (noun)

1 a: the thousand years mentioned in Revelation 20 during which holiness is to prevail and Christ is to reign on earth; b: a period of great happiness or human perfection; c: a period of 1000 years

—*Oxford English Dictionary*

The juncture of the late twentieth and early twenty-first centuries has spawned a number of labels, among them "posthumanism," "postmodernism," "the information age," "the new order." Like all of these terms, "millennialism" comes with baggage, including the Western religious and eschatological implications of the ending of time and the arrival of a new spiritual order. But our particular era has a local definition for "millennialism," referring to our specific *interstitial* situation between two centuries, at the brink of a new era. Every adult living today is a bimillennial, living on the edge: we look back at the twentieth century, with a retrospective ("post-") mentality, even as we are cast an anxious eye forward, to the rest of this century and beyond.

Still, the experiences of the twentieth century do not lead to and condition those of the twenty-first century in a linear way, as an effect of chronology. The date 2000 is an arbitrary construct; but it has conditioned the very paradigm shifts that it has witnessed. In other words, cause and effect in the millennial age are seldom simply linear, since for some time the awareness that the future *will arrive* at a significant date has been determining what is happening in the present.

One example was the effect of the Y2K computer crisis, with wide economic and psychological impact beyond the mechanical difficulties of computer glitches; another was the "genome" race to decode DNA before the threshold date of 2000, with wide-reaching ramifications for the species, as the research was sped up to conform to a symbolic deadline. In spite of these cultural complications, I will define millennialism with a barebones formula, for purposes of tying the knot with psychoanalysis.

Millennialism is postmodernism plus techno-science.

But however simple it may seem, even this reduction harbors complexity. For upfront, it effects an explicit *triple* juncture within just one of the three major "foils" of this chapter: "millennialism" is defined as a trefoil knot linking postmodernism, technology, and science. And a closer look at the component terms reveals more nestings. For example, the *post-* in the first predicate of millennialism (*post*modernism) is in turn composed of a bundle of "posts" (postcolonialism, post-

Marxism, postfeminism, postindustrialism, post-humanism, post-Freudianism, and, with the recent work of Antoine Volodine, postexoticism as well). Any of these prominent post-isms is a complex effect, both challenging and stemming from the very thing that has preceded it. "Postfeminism," for instance, is not simply anti-feminism, nor is it simply life after feminism.

So, for all the linearity of my formula ("this plus this equals that"), complexity lurks in the prefix of just one of its components. The prefix "post-" itself is the first hitch in the smooth equation.

The second segment of this constituent term (postmodernism) also harbors a complication. For even if there were a simple consensus concerning what modernism is or was, there are any number of ways to construe its relation to what has come after it. John Frow has taken a particularly interesting tack, distinguishing between "postmodernity" as an economic and social condition, and "postmodernism" as an aesthetic movement. This take suggests that even the suffix of the term—postmodernism—may be at issue in this discussion.[11] At least since post-structuralism, contemporary critical thought has challenged the very notion of "ism" as reductive("ism"-ism?), preferring to consider transformative systems (becoming) rather than static properties (being). Thus millennialism is post-ism gone self-conscious; it is in fact a post-postmodernism, an iterative site that is nothing if not complex.

Getting out of Line

The reflexivity of "post-ism" is often associated with a critique of linearity, the advent of nonlinear thought. But just what is nonlinearity? In math, an equation where no term carries an exponent higher than one is *linear* $(2 + 2 = 4)$: it may be plotted as incremental segments along a straight horizontal *line* $(a + b = c)$. But a nonlinear equation—even at just the next level of complexity, with only one exponent higher than one $(2^2 + 2 = 6)$—must be plotted along *two* axes, vertical and horizontal. (This describes the meaning of the term "quadratic equation." Since the coordinates form a *quad on a biaxial grid*; the formula describes a two-dimensional plane, rather than in the single dimension of a straight line. It needs to be graphed in a plane, on "graph paper.")

In mathematical terms, then, my simple formula ("postmodernism plus techno-science = millennialism") only *appears* linear $(a + b = c)$. For this definition actually harbors an exponent greater than one: as "modernism" reflecting on itself, postmodernism is modernism to at least the second power (a^2), a para-sitic modernism *beside* itself $(a$ times $a)$. Following the same topological logic, mapping millennialism as *post-postmodernism*, would call for another point in space (like a cube, a^3), *a three-dimensional spacing.*

The third component term of the formula (millennialism equals postmodernism plus techno-science) is explicitly compound, a linguistic juncture of technology and science. Even the first half of this term (techno-science) is itself implicitly compound, since "science" is already embedded in the term "techno" (technology is the how-to aspect of science). So there is already an exponential aspect to "techno-science" too (science compounded by the application of science).

In other words, whether it is mapped on a graph, defined linguistically, or transcribed in algebraic terms, "millennialism" may be considered both nonlinear and complex. In psychoanalytic terms, the millennial is chronically overdetermined, carrying multiple valences, and unfolding in multiple dimensions. Like the proliferating twelve-point programs that seek to cure a host of millennial addictions, millennialism always seems to refer itself to a higher power.

Posting the Modern

Given these semantic twists, it is not surprising that one of the major activities of postmodernism has been defining itself. In one well-known essay, "Mapping the Postmodern," Andreas Huyssen draws two columns, matching up the modern phenomenon with its postmodern counterpart.[12] Theorists as diverse and influential as Hassan, Jameson, Eagleton, and Haraway have produced versions of this two-column oppositional chart. The typical parsing is familiar: Freud is modern, Lacan is postmodern; Frank Lloyd Wright is modern, Pei is postmodern; Nietzsche is modern, Derrida is postmodern, and so on. But in spite of providing clear illustrations, these various schema—"first this, then that," or "no longer this, but now that"—still rely on a strict binary opposition, which is itself a non-postmodern paradigm.

Three important theorists have attempted to go beyond this conventional scheme. In "A Manifesto for Cyborgs," Donna Haraway replaces the terms modern and postmodern with less conventional categories, which she calls "business as usual" and "scary new configurations," the latter including cybernetics and information theory. But her new age cultural map is still binary, featuring two opposing columns ("conventional" versus "new").[13]

In How We Became Posthuman, N. Katherine Hayles produces an updated schema mapping recent cultural and technological shifts. She maps three waves of cybernetic theory with corresponding cultural phenomena, from the 1960s to the present. The three waves—homeostatic, reflexive, and emergent—are charted in three columns, allowing for overlap among eras. Hayles thus departs from the convention of the modern/postmodern opposition, describing a field that is not reducible to a binary "this versus that." Her focus, however, is still a single field (cybernetics).[14]

Jean-François Lyotard has provided a particularly ingenious example of millennial mapping. He is, of course, best known for his canonic essay "What is Postmodernism?," which contains yet another list of oppositions between modernism and postmodernism, including discussions of modernism's *grands récits* (metaphysical narratives) and postmodernism's *petits récits* (language games). But in the later work discussed in chapter 3 (*The Inhuman*), Lyotard goes beyond his previous scheme, taking into account the questions raised by cybernetics and the philosophy of emergence, and including psychoanalysis in the discussion. Rather than dealing with two opposing eras, Lyotard's schema compares three overlapping domains—the human psyche, artificial intelligence, and psychoanalytic therapy (see the discussion on "scanning, breaching, and passing" in chapter 3). This represents an important moment in (what I am calling) millennial theory, establishing a homology in critical theory between human thought and mechanical processes (academic/philosophical/literary theory goes cybernetic), and also bringing the Freudian unconscious into the picture. Still, Lyotard's essay seems to remain at the level of analogy rather than concrete instance (the computer functions *like* the psyche, passing through phases *like* those in analysis).[15]

In any case, the efforts of Lyotard, like those of Haraway and Hayles, suggest that the very ground upon which millennialism is being mapped is shifting. And all three of these accounts suggest that the mapping of the millennial episteme may be attempted, with the help of Freudian theory.

Premodern to Millennial: From Subtext to Hypertext

From a psychoanalytic perspective, we could say that the premodern era was preoccupied with meaning, an expressed conscious content or *text*; while the modern Freudian era added a concern with a latent *subtext*, seeking overdetermined meanings as a key to understanding what seems to be going on on the surface. Building on the modern focus that plumbs the depths of the Freudian psyche, Lacan's postmodern model adds lateral intersubjective linkage, a topology of desire ("desire is the desire of the Other") in a social web or field. In other words "postmodern" psychoanalysis, with its emphasis on implication, adds "intertext" to the preexisting domains of "text" and "subtext."

Continuing the progression, millennial psychoanalysis adds yet another dimension, *hypertext*, forging links to the virtual information domain in a simultaneity akin to the workings of primary process. The psychic field itself, then, has been progressively dimensionalized (text-subtext-intertext-hypertext); but thanks to psychoanalysis, it may it span the chronological divide without requiring each link to break with what has gone before, trumping what precedes it. The psychoanalytic field unfolds in new implications, in a process entailing nonlinear *progression* rather than linear *progress*.

This is what the nonlinear perspective of millennialism brings to psychoanalysis. But what does Freud give back to the topic of millennialism?

HITCHING POSTS: WHY FREUD?

The unconscious may only be translated in knots of language.

—Jacques Lacan, Ornicar[16]

knot: A hard place or lump, especially on a tree, at a point from which a stem or branch grows SEE slip
slip: 1) a stem, root, or twig broken off a plant and used for planting or grafting; a scion 2) a deviation or turning aside; especially of a practice SEE ALSO slip-knot; slip-noose; Freudian slip
slip-knot: a knot made so that it will slip along the rope, etc., along which it is tied
slip-noose: a noose made with a slipknot
Freudian slip: a mistake made in speaking, by which, it is thought, the speaker reveals unconscious motives and desires

—(Oxford English Dictionary)

Lacan describes language as a "signifying chain" where each word is a knotted link in the meaning-making process. This is a topological view: for in fact, he states axiomatically that the language is a series of word knots ("le mot n'est pas signe, mais no eud de signification"/ "The word is not a sign; it is a knot of signification."[17] Each word, each "signifier," is tied in semantically to the next as in the relation of subject to predicate. Indeed, in Lacan's figural topology of language, "signifiers" (words) are slipknots of sorts: our meaning is always approximate; our "sliding signifiers" are never tied down to one absolute referent. The word "knot" itself is a case in point: as the definition cited above demonstrates, the word generates a cluster of associations that in turn may be grafted onto other meanings, associated with growth, scion, site, or seed.

These generative slips are particularly suggestive for the phenomenon of millennialism, since a primary preoccupation of the millennial zeitgeist is hybridism, including real hybrid objects produced by the grafts of bioengineering. In new genetic cocktails, the genes of one species are in fact slipped into the DNA of another. (A recent example: jellyfish genes have been slipped into mouse DNA, producing glowing rodents; while mouse genes have been engineered into human stem cells.) Here again, the notion of site (sitos/seed) is associated with seeding, but also with grafting.

Moving along, the dictionary definition of slip immediately refers us ("SEE ALSO") to the slip-knot, and then sends us on to the most sinister of knots, the slip-noose. Coming full circle from the association of slip with biological generation (as in cutting a slip from a plant for grafting), the end term "slip-noose" links death with all the signifying nodes along the way: it evokes that lethal noose with the paradoxical capacity to slide and to pull tight, at the end of the rope.

Slipping along these links, one slides right into Freud, as if by chance.

HITCHING POSTS: WHY KNOT?

The word is not a sign; it is a knot of signification.

–Jacques Lacan, Écrits

Why is nodality Freud's preferred modality?

In one of the great insights of *Beyond the Pleasure Principle* (1920), Freud speculates that life is motivated by the organism's effort to come to "naught," even while slipping up along the way. In Freud's view, of course, the death impulse is pictured as a sliding along a life trajectory, the interaction of death and life impulses allowing the organism to dally on the way to its end, reaching death at the end of the line, in its own good time. Freud elaborates a textile life rhythm—where the lifeline of human desire is always looping back and embroidering on what has come before, even as we follow the thread toward our demise.

In the introduction, I suggested that the juncture between psychoanalysis and millennialism be considered a network of sites, figured as concept-objects with both a material existence and a fantasmatic valence in contemporary culture. It is evident that the knot is itself such a figure, a cultural icon (as the worldwide *web* or Internet) that is associated with psychoanalytic theory, with millennial aesthetics (as a major thematic element, and as a composition strategy), and with the science of topological geometry. It is also a material physical focus of research in neurobiology: emotions are now associated with nodes of neurons and receptors (As neuro-researcher Candace Pert explains: "Nodal points are places where there is a lot of convergent information with many different peptide receptors. In these nodal points there is potential for emotional regulation and conditioning.")[18]

The Freudian field is thus a psychosomatic topology of hitches and slips in a net of intersubjective desire, a knotty field indeed.

Linguistic Links

A true knot cannot be made flat.[19]

–Jacques Lacan, Écrits

Throughout his case studies, Freud looks to words as overdetermined symptoms (packing more than a single meaning into a referent) as in a racy *double entendre*, the famous Freudian slip. And he looks to all symptoms as knots of meaning ("nodal points"), whether they are verbal or behavioral. For instance, Freud points out that hysteria often reveals itself in literal somatic puns. In his famous case study of Dora, he gives the example of a woman who inexplicably develops a limp or "false step" precisely nine months after a sexual faux pas. Words also provide leads in analytic technique: in the patient's free association, one thing leads to another quite literally. In his own work, of course, Freud often resorts to multilingual word-play to further his own interpretations: he shows that our own language spins a web for us, often revealing far more than we consciously intend.[20] Of course, he also describes the dream scene as a knot with a tentacular lead, the umbilicus tied to unconscious desire. Finally, he reads the figures in the dream itself as visual puns (as in a rebus) often corresponding to figures of speech (the dreamer sees herself wedged into a mountain crevice, "stuck between a rock and a hard place").

One of the most suggestive strategies proposed by Freud for the analysis of the unconscious, in fact, is the reading of "words as things"—the consideration of words not simply as transparent designating tools, but as objects in their own right.[21] He maintains that children do this kind of concrete thinking naturally in their linguistic development (he cites the infantile tendency to play with words as vocalized objects, when babbling). But he also speculates that this natural capacity for "figuration" (treating words like concrete objects) is related to the highly figural modality of the unconscious itself.

Following Freud, we have already considered the word "knot" itself as a generative object-site, or scion, with any number of semantic links and suggestions. But as an object, a phoneme or sound, the syllable also affords any number of homonymic spinoffs. The most obvious is a substantive without substance, a placeholder, the one noun that names . . . nothing.

nought, naught: 1 : nothingness, non-existence 2: zero, cipher

Even harder to tie down as a particle, the syllable "not" is, on the face of things, a term that clarifies, rendering an unambiguous binary judgment—something is "this, NOT that." But (at least for those who read Freud in English, and Freud loved bilingual puns) "not" is of course connected with Freud's famous article on "Negation" (Verneinung).[22] Confronted with the question of the identity of the lady in his dream, Freud's patient replies, emphatically, "It is NOT my mother." Freud duly notes the evidentiary link between the mother and the dream figure, reading the negative as a symptom of repressed desire. The wily negation provides a way of making the mother present even while consciously dismissing her. (Who has not vowed to get over a lost love, even while talking about the lover constantly?)

This concept of a concrete determining absence is also important in Lacan's figuration of das Ding (the ineffable Freudian Thing, the primal object of desire that we can never "remember"). For Lacan, the primary repressed "object" ("the primal mother," perhaps) is a structuring void, like the space around which the potter throws his urn. Given his love of cross-linguistic pun, Lacan may also have been evoking the word *Not* in German, pronounced like "note," which means "lack." While we're at it, then, why not *note* that the topological object known as the "unknot," a single circle of rope, figures a zero? As a cipher, the syllable can rope off ground zero for speculations about the paradox in psychoanalysis: the structuring absence.

Interestingly enough, the "not" as *Verneinung* is alive and well in millennial pop culture. At the turn of the new century, the particle took on a fanciful colloquial use among young Americans, who use "not" as a Freudian *Verneinung* of sorts.

My mother sells drugs. NOT.

By making an assertion and then refuting it in a linguistic aftereffect, the punch line "not" has the effect of underlining the ironic use of the previous statement, a hitch in its straightforward assertion. But it also lends this linguistic assertion a "now you see it, now you don't " aftereffect, not unlike disjunctive synthesis in Deleuze (the clear assertion of "either . . . or" is undercut by the aftereffect addition of another "or"). This colloquial "not" is a particularly suggestive cultural symptom in the era of relativity, underscoring how shifting perspective may undercut the strongest assertions. This "millennial not" is a linguistic way of having your cake and not having it too.

The word-object also shows up as an iconic character in our era, the absent placeholder in a masterpiece of postmodern fiction. *Knott* is the pivotal noncharacter in Samuel Beckett's gambol of anti-logic *Watt*, whose very title is a send-up of certainty and enlightenment, denoting both a unit of electrical power and a pesky question. The title character (Watt) is given to speaking in cipher, but each recursive version of his tale is spun around the same central absence, the unseen master of the house, the umbilicus of Watt's dreamlike existence. This unseen Other is none other than Knott—whose pervasive invisible presence drives the household. When Knott is pronounced to rime with "ought," it yields another Beckettian pun (the verbal auxiliary signifies an *unfulfilled* obligation, what "ought" to be done); while of course the noun "ought/aught" itself is yet another synonym for zero.

Like the Lacanian *Ding*, Watt's point of view lacks a center and even a sense (as in the French *sens*, direction; and of course Beckett is always shuttling between French and English reference). With a method as rigorous as Bach's mechanical variations on a theme, inverting and reversing figures, Watt tells his story in several different codes, such as backwards writing (hence, in French, literally against the grain of direction, a *non-sens* or *contre-sens*), but his narrative permutations always turn on what is missing. Knott is a post-man who never delivers, reflecting a humanism emptied of its core meaning. Like a mathematical knot, he is a function of the space he determines and structures, but does Not fill.

The millennial aesthetic of perspective may be ineffable, but its name is Knott.

So to the last part of the threefold question concerning the title of this chapter—"Why Millennialism? Why Freud? . . . Why Knot?"—that is also my answer.

FREUD SIGHTINGS IN MILLENNIAL CULTURE
2: THE ICON WEB

In *Modest Witness@Second Millennium*, Donna Haraway figures millennial technoscience as a network of disparate significant objects—books, molecules, equations, computers, bombs, cells—linking the ideologies of progress and profit. She characterizes these node-objects as embedded in a fibrous pod of cultural associations that may be *"teased open to show sticky economic, technical, political, mythic and textual threads."* [23]

Psychoanalysis and millennialism are a net of such sites, marked by iconic figures that resonate throughout contemporary theory and culture. In the first section of this chapter, we saw that the knot itself is a prime example: it is at once a real object, an object of scientific theory, a rebus, and a cultural icon (the worldwide web).

This kind of figuration, however useful it may be for characterizing the millennial mindset, does raise the specter of metaphor. Does the conceptual use of figuration, as defined by Haraway, amount merely to saying this is *like* that ("millennial culture is *like* a web")? This might weaken the argument, since one could say that the use of simile, metaphor, or analogy is always a function of perspective, reading *this* into *that*. Yet a key premise of millennial thinking, and one that is crucial to Haraway's argument, is that there is no position from which one does *not* read something into what is being observed. Nonetheless, Haraway's figuration always aims beyond analogy or individual interpretation (*this* is like *that*, because that is how I see it). It is also more than a function of creative imagination (*this* looks like *that*, when seen through the transformative eyes of the artist).

To get beyond analogy, we need to supplement Freud's notion of figure as symptom, and even Haraway's notion of figuration as material investment, with the idea of figure as *instance* of what it represents. In fact, each of the icons that I foreground here may be likened to what Lacan calls the heraldic figure, an object that establishes and orients a whole field of overdetermined meanings. Commenting on Freud's famous case of Little Hans, Lacan writes:

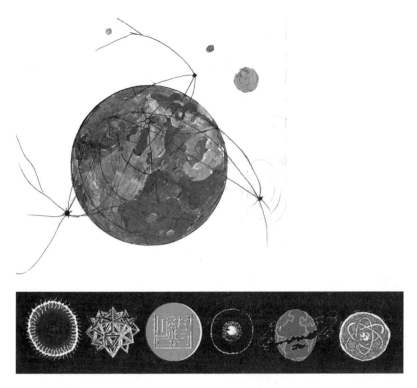

Sara G. Blow, *World Wide Web*, 2004.

> Freud tells us expressly that we could be tempted to define the phobia by its ob-
> ject, the horse in this case, unless we see that his horse goes far beyond what a horse
> itself is. *It is much more a matter of a* heraldic figure, *prevalent, centering the whole field, and
> which is heavy with all sorts of implications—implications that are significant above all.*[24]

Lacan's commentary on Freud thus suggests an illuminating way of thinking of
cultural icons: they are symptomatic nodes that generate a field around them.

Following up on Lacan's concept of heraldic figure, and drawing from the
work of prominent millennial theorists, I propose to visit a cluster of twelve representative nodal sites/heraldic figures that seem to generate fields of both psychic and material investment today. The list is by no means exhaustive, but it is
emblematic of major "sites" in the millennial psyche. And the even dozen, also an
arbitrary number, is nonetheless a suggestive emblem of Lacan's reiterated theoretical strategy discussed in several concepts in part I of this book, opening from
three-to-four, or three-as-four (three times four?), to suggest that threesomes are
always foursomes and moresomes.

Millennial "heraldic" nodes

1. opticality
2. hybridism
3. nonlinearity
4. materiality
5. systematicity
6. permeability
7. transferability
8. motility
9. circuitousness
10. networking
11. fractality
12. code

However disparate they might be, the twelve "heralds" I suggest here share an important characteristic: they all function as significant junctures for psychoanalysis, millennial science, and culture. In addition, they all might be considered as *properties* of the millennial mindset, which tends to be:

1. *optical:* reflective/refractive/visual/scopic
2. *hybrid:* compounded /grafted/heterogeneous
3. *nonlinear:* exponential/warped/curved/nonmetric/multidimensional
4. *material:* particular/ molecular/biochemical
5. *systemic:* global/ interactive/contagious
6. *permeable:* interpenetrating /membranal/mutable
7. *transferable:* shifting/ projected/ introjected/ skewed
8. *motile:* rapid/ shifting/ transforming/ accelerated
9. *circuitous:* circuited/ circulating/ self-perpetuating/ looped/switched
10. *networked:* linked/ communicating/ overlapping
11. *embedded:* interstitial/ dimensional/iterated/fractal
12. *coded:* intelligent/ meaningful/ inscribed.

In a performative sense, these twelve nodes may be considered as modalities of operation, reflecting the millennial affinity for transformative process or "becoming":

1. search
2. graft
3. warp
4. articulation, instantiation (materialization)
5. process
6. absorption

7. transmission, transfer
8. transport
9. circuiting
10. linkage, networking
11. replication, iteration
12. signal, coding

Finally, *instances* of these sites might be considered heraldic figures in a Lacanian sense: that is, real objects that have fetishistic resonance as cultural icons today:

1. lens/ floating eye
2. gene/ DNA molecule
3. black hole/curved interstellar space
4. particle/atom
5. globe (spaceship earth)/ weather map/ ecosystem
6. cell/virus
7. screen/monitor
8. rocket/spacecraft/UFO
9. chip/circuit
10. knot/ web
11. hologram/ fractal object
12. brain/computer

Taken as a systemic web, these nodes might qualify as what Manuel De Landa calls a "meshwork":[25] that is, a field of interlinked interactive exchanges. One marker of the fantasmatic power of such sites is an ambivalent cultural resonance, at once utopic and dystopic. A brief onsite visit to the each nodal points of the millennial meshwork will reveal that each site carries both a positive and a negative psychic valence, reflecting technophilia or technophobia, depending on whether it is imbued with a sense of expanded human possibility or a sense of nostalgia about the presumed loss of human values in a posthuman world.

1. Opticality (Floating Eye)

> The glance is at once site and sight.
> —Paul Virilio, *The Aesthetics of Disappearance*

Chapter 3 dealt with panic philosophy and hypervisibility as dominant millennial preoccupations: everywhere in the post-Foucauldian field, we find musings on the body captured and disciplined, overseen by the eye-in-the-sky of satellite surveillance. We have seen that the motif of hypervisibility resounds in the "panic optics" of well-known cultural theorists (Baudrillard, Deleuze, Lyotard, Žižek, Vattimo, Virilio), as well as in the work of "cyberfeminists" such as Balsamo and Springer. In these works, a somber social ethics often finds a powerful emblem in the figure of a disembodied, floating eye—the spy satellite, the surveillance camera, the alien spacecraft. In *The Postmodern Scene*, for instance, Arthur Kroker and David Cook evoke its avatars in the CBS corporate symbol, the panopticon of Foucault's *Discipline and Punish*, the floating optical alien of the cult film *Liquid Sky*.[26] And since the first Gulf War, CNN's camera has become the ultimate floating eye, transmitting war "live" 24/7 to a worldwide audience.

Significantly, the optic icon is seldom binocular or possessed of stereoscopic vision. But the image of a single floating open eye seems to be everywhere in the media. On one commercial hosted by the suave Sam Neil, the eye is seen peering out through a keyhole, in an advertisement for an information network as "window on the world"; while in another, for an Internet security system, an eye is seen peering in at the viewer, through the slat of window-blinds, violating the privacy of her study. In the weeks following the attack on the World Trade Center, the *Village Voice* cover featured a dozen detached floating open eyes, along with a warning about increased surveillance, while a *New York Times Magazine* cover featured a mechanical eyeball peering from a video security camera. The global citizen is often depicted as the focus of chronic observation, by everyone from government agencies to terrorist networks. Meanwhile, extraterrestrials are "figured"—even in many commercials today—as scrutinizers of hapless abductees splayed on examining tables. They are visual predators, spotting their prey alone on country roads, or arousing them from sleep with blinking spotlights hovering outside the window.

The visions of Paul Virilio, one of the best-known dystopian theorists, are every bit as bleak, and as optical, as any ET nightmare. He writes of the visual field as fetishistic fascination, the scene of an endless day:

> With the recent advent of the electronic [twenty-four-hour] day, the extension of visibility spreads, taking over space as the extension of an audio-visual and tele-topological continuum, and erasing all the antipodes—those of geographic distance, as well as the dead angles of that domain constructed by closed circuit TV. Seeing that which had previously been invisible becomes an activity that renews the exoticism of territorial conquests of the past.[27]

Virilio's catalogue of colonizing scopic desire includes the penetrating gaze that peers at the invisible (the electron microscope, the X-ray, the MRI image). We might now add the compulsive replay of traumatic images of attack. Freud might consider the incessant replay of the WTC disaster, particularly the moments of impact and collapse, as manifestations of the repetition compulsion. It does seem to be an effort by the wounded collective psyche to comprehend the incomprehensible, by visiting it over and over. The endless looping of the tape is also compelling evidence of a tortuous visual thirst, the hypnotic fascination exerted by the image of disaster (manifest in the very human tendency to rubberneck at the scene of a bloody accident). Freud, of course, insists throughout his work on the very human love of the optical, as scopophilia.

Yet Virilio suggests that the new media are provoking a collective psychosis of sorts, a loss of reality as we know it ("As the rational universe goes, so goes the effect of the real . . . rejecting fixity of attention, escaping from the customary seems to have become impossible").[28] In Virilio's lament, we also hear an echo of "the hell of sameness" feared by Baudrillard. But for Virilio, the loss of reality is associated with simultaneity, rather than a mere deadening of sensual pleasure. "Optics . . . is now simultaneously all aspects, all points of view and lines of vision, for all the actor spectators in all constructed space . . . the simultaneous collective response acts as a ubiquitous eye that see everything at once" (75). Virilio also criticizes our narcissistic absorption in the computer or television screen: "Man, fascinated with himself, constructs his double as intelligent specter, and entrusts the keeping of his knowledge to a reflection" (46). "Man" thus risks falling into a vertigo of excess: "the more informed man is the more the desert of the world extends around him" (46). In a more positive vein, Virilio does remark that the optical era favors "the mutual interpenetration of art and science." But his commentary never addresses the sheer wonder of millennial optics, where the viewer is regaled with images of alien landscapes, exploding supernovae, black holes; nano images of possible microbial alien forebears in the Mars rock.

Virilio does cite the poetic observation of Gustave Flaubert, made over a century ago: "The larger the telescope, the more numerous the stars" (46); although for Virilio, this is hardly good news. And today, Flaubert's comment must be read as more than metaphor: the Hubble telescope expanded our view by forty billion galaxies in just one adjustment of focus.

2. Hybridism/Heterogeneity (Cyborg)

Thanks to genetic engineering and biotechnology, images of monstrous couplings are no longer in the realm of sci-fi and mythology: a case in point is the widely disseminated picture of the mouse with a human ear growing on its back, also an emblem of corporeal morcellation and grafting (of body parts).[29] A recent documentary on the farming of body parts (The Discovery Channel, 2002) actually displayed a whole medical refrigerator filled with . . . synthetic vaginas, grown, oddly enough, from infant foreskins. An automatic revulsion may accompany our reactions to this type of uncanny new science, foregrounding the not quite human and the neither alive nor dead, as do the chilling images from cryogenics, where vats containing corpses and severed heads arouse the age-old fear of the undead and the dread of dismemberment.

In popular culture, the fascination with both hybridism and morcellation is equally evident in the perennial cinematic narratives of the cyborg—part man, part machine—beginning with sci-fi classics such as *The Terminator, Robocop*, and *Blade Runner*, and continuing with a new age Pygmalion tale of *Simone*, and the latest in the *Terminator* series, released, to the sheer delight of the international media, just as Arnold was running for governor. This genre often figures the cyborg negatively, as ruthless hunter, but just as often it figures him as a detective-hero, tracking down evildoers (*Robocop; Blade Runner*).

Another positive fantasmatic valence of hybridism concerns pollination, enrichment, or rehabilitation: today mechanical ears and eyes are "re-membering" the disabled, allowing the deaf to ear and the blind to see, with electronic chips replacing optic nerves, while exotic surgical procedures add limbs and replace hearts. They may even—in what seems to be a material response to castration anxiety—remodel a vagina, or enlarge, create, or reattach a penis.

Positive aspects of hybridism are also reflected in the publicizing of recent genetic public health projects, such as the spiking of bovine DNA with a human gene, so that drinking cow's milk will boost human immunity. And with the media publicity about the miraculous possibilities of stem cell research, the field of genetic engineering has been infused with utopian rhetoric. The banner above the 2001 "genome" exhibition at New York's Museum of Natural History proclaimed: "We are on the verge of discoveries that are nothing short of spectacular."

And spectacle is the favorite millennial sport.

3. Nonlinearity (Black Hole)

On the theory scene, we have seen that the work of Donna Haraway is remarkable in its positive invocation of hybridism, celebrating the blurring of distinct boundaries between man and woman, human and machine, human and animal. And while Haraway deconstructs boundaries, she exposes the bias of the conventional "neutral" observer in science, pointing out that the new science at once deflates the confidence of a central correct perspective, and suggests the impossibility of one's perspective being anything but provisionally central, a point of view. While positivism rests on the illusion of a secure founding position, nonlinear science recognizes the contingency of one's position as an effect in the observed.

Indeed, nonlinearity has been the hallmark of frontier science, ever since Einstein warped our notion of space and time. Far-from-equilibrium theory, chaos theory, string theory—all have displaced the standard models of linear causality, with startling counterintuitive paradigms. A material iconic figure for nonlinearity might be warped space itself—which may one day provide the key to interstellar travel. (Warp drive would actually shorten space with a powerful gravitational field.) Another widely disseminated figure of radical nonlinearity is the black hole, the "singularity" where the laws of space and time cease to apply. In the black hole, the invisible weight of a collapsed neutron star tears a hole in the fabric of the universe itself, just possibly opening a wormhole to another.

Chaos theory also departs from a linear view: the result is out of proportion to the input, as in the exponential formula for population growth. The moment when nonlinearity ensues in these processes (a stock market crash; a neutron star collapse; a tsunami) is called a tipping point, the point of no return. As a major millennial theorist of nonlinearity, Manuel De Landa uses chaos and systems theory—as well as Deleuze's writing on self-organizing processes of "becoming"—to reread history as a process of random combination, governed by "engineering diagrams" of emergence.[30] Specifically, De Landa foregrounds two blueprints of self-organization. The first model produces "hierarchies": sifting and sorting processes result in layered top-down formations (geological strata; food chains; social class). The second diagram details processes of linkage that result in "meshworks" (networks): a river system; an ecosystem; the global financial market. (As I suggested above, all twelve heraldic nodes visited here may also qualify as a meshwork, a linked interactive system.) In De Landa's imaginative reading, based on Deleuze's concept of "abstract machine," each of these two organizational systems (hierarchy and meshwork) interact in at least three domains or strata—inorganic, organic, and human/social—and at many scales, from molecular to cosmic. Complicating the linear narrative of progress, De Landa's nonlinear history traces the effects of complex interactions among geological elements, biomass, and the movements of human populations. His nonlinear account is opposed to traditional linear history, an anthropomorphic narrative of manifest destiny punctuated with proper names.

Given the fascinating applications of nonlinear science to cultural studies and historical models today (starting perhaps with Hayden White's poststructuralist critique of linear narrative history in *Metahistory* [1973]), it seems that the observation of chaos and complexity in unwieldy systems has been infectious. Oxford scientists Ian Marshall and Dana Zohar, for instance (*Who's Afraid of Schrödinger's Cat?*), suggest that the mere recognition of nonlinearity in one part of our science may upset the whole applecart. In fact, in exploring the new paradigms scientists have come to recognize that no linear system is absolutely linear. In classical science, we study linear *approximations* to the real models, with certain chosen parameters, "as if" they are the ones that "really" count.[31]

4. Materiality (Particle, Gene)

One of the direct effects of the biotechnological revolution is an increased focus on the concrete and the material: for instance, the analysis of the human genome has led to the association of abstract "character traits" with genetically determined factors, like the length of hormone receptors. In the science of astrophysics, the search for the so-called unified field theory, less modestly called "the theory of everything," has led to an intense focus on the smallest "particular" building blocks. In quantum physics, the discovery of a throng of subatomic particles as the smallest material building blocks has also contributed to our growing knowledge of the actual stuff of the universe.

Before congratulating ourselves on new discoveries about the matter at hand, however, we need to remember that 90 percent of the matter of the universe is still unaccounted for. Yet scientists in different fields, undaunted by mounting human ignorance, are working on competing theories for what the missing matter might be. Displaying a new age sense of humor, the molecular physicists first proposed WIMPs (weak infinitesimal massive particles); and the astronomers countered with a theory of MACHOs (Massive Astronomical Cold Haloed Objects, or Dark Stars).

In any case, the species does seem to be shifting its focus from the ineffable ideal to the material particle. This shift is manifest in cultural studies as well as in hard science, as shown by the work of the feminist thinkers seeking to reconcile the old contraries of "cultural" and "essentialist" feminism. Donna Haraway's figurations, in fact, contest the old distinction between culture and nature. Genes, blood cells, embryos—"figurations"—provide concrete examples of the coincidence of matter and idea in cultural practice: "We inhabit and are inhabited by such figures that map intersections of knowledge, practice and power."[32]

Predictably, this radical materialism has provoked an idealist reaction in some quarters, a reaction that is evident in a resurgence of mysticism around "millennialism" in pop culture. TV programs and Internet groups dealing with unsolved mysteries and preternatural prophecy abound; Nostradamus websites are thriving; a twice-daily program that links up audience members to their dead relatives on the other side is aired on two networks ("Crossing Over with John Edward"). This "back to the ineffable" reaction has produced new age philosophy as well, such as the "Transhumanism" of Max Moore, based on the mystical scientism of Teilhard de Chardin. Transhuman utopists confidentally assert that humanity is morphing into a hybrid man-machine imbued with extrasensory super powers.

But in our era the material and the ineffable are sometimes oddly mingled: one science laboratory that is deeply involved with human cloning as reproduction is funded by a UFO cult (the Raulians, in France, who claim to be descended from

Mark D. Phillips, *September 11, 2001.* © 2001 Mark D. Phillips.

extraterrestrials, and regard cloning as the key to immortality). Meanwhile, back at NASA, scientists engineering exotic interstellar propulsion systems are borrowing ideas from ufologists and science-fiction writers. And the overwhelming reaction of the public to a now-famous Associated Press photo of the burning World Trade Center suggests that the phenomenon of collective projection, even myth-making, is still germane in the technological age (in the all-too-real image of terrorist attack published on 9/11, thousands claimed to see Satan's face).

This recent media phenomenon suggests that the collective unconscious is not a matter of ancient Jungian archetype, Tarot cards, or tribal mythology, relegated to the age of superstition or the infancy of the species. In Lacanian terms, we might say that the three domains of human experience—imaginary, symbolic, and Real—have never been so intertwined.

5. Systematicity (Globe)

In his discussion of the Schreber case, Freud explains paranoia as the construction of a totalizing system projected on the world, an attempt to explain everything by one overriding view, including the figure of one Master Villain.[33] Written almost a century ago, his commentary on Schreber seems prescient today, when the public fantasm of "the Evil One" has made a comeback in the bin Laden/Hussein phenomenon, where latter-day Satans are figured as the elusive and invisible CEOs of the global terrorist corporation, with many faces and avatars, everywhere and nowhere at once.

As we saw in part I, the negative aspects of a preoccupation with system are equally evident in the "paranoid" tenor of global culture. Elaine Showalter, for one, posits a twenty-first-century version of hysteria, manifest in fantasies of alien abduction, the recovered memory movement, the new yuppie diseases like chronic fatigue and Epstein Barr, and the narratives of satanic ritual abuse.[34] But recent developments make Showalter's dismissal of these phenomena as mere symptom seem a bit optimistic: in the age of bioterrorism, some formerly "paranoid" reactions seem to be grounded in a heretofore unthinkable reality.

A more neutral treatment of systematicity—this time in the history of cybernetics and artificial intelligence—occurs in work such as Sherry Turkle's *Life on the Screen*, or Allucquére Rosanne Stone's *The War of Desire and Technology at the End of the Mechanical Age*. In an another evenhanded argument, N. Katherine Hayles' *How We Became Posthuman* traces the debate between the radical materialism of cybernetics (holding that human thought may be reproduced in circuitry) and the idealism of vitalists (who hold that there is something sacred in "life itself," especially human life).

But the preoccupation with systematicity often has an openly upbeat aspect as well as a dystopian or neutral tenor: ever since the moonwalkers witnessed Earthrise over the lunar horizon, the fantasm of our planet as one global system has had a visual correlate. That small moving blue object floating in inky space, veiled in a single swirling weather system, is "home." The species does seem to be gaining an awareness of the interconnectedness of civilizations, and a growing concern for the fragility of the ecosystems that sustain life, however little and however late. Psychoanalysis has certainly contributed to this maturation, by elaborating a dynamic systemic view of the human psyche in a social context, thanks in part to the Lacanian contribution of the theory of "paranoid knowledge" (discussed in chapter 3 above).

Still, two opposed modalities of one theme (humanity as interconnected system) resonate throughout millennial theory: even while "*We* are the World," for better or for worse "*They* are everywhere."

6. Permeability (Membrane, Virus)

The hallmark of rational humanist thinking has always been defined boundaries and clear-cut oppositions. In the posthuman age, however, the contesting of many traditional boundaries is part of a progressive agenda (the breaking of gender barriers such as "the glass ceiling"; the extension of domestic rights to same-sex partners; the expansion of the UN peacekeeping role in response to crises; the extension of the human life span; the exploration of space beyond the solar system).

But the permeability of the boundary is just as often a cause for reactive anxiety, a site of cultural controversy. In the post-9/11 United States in particular, the current public discourse is pervaded by questions of borderlessness and vulnerability. ("If gays marry, where do we draw the line?" "How can we make our national frontier impermeable to illegal immigrants?" "Should I open this letter, or is it tainted by anthrax?" "Do cloned cells have rights?") On a cosmic scale as well as in daily life, our species is becoming aware of the statistical probability of unthinkable catastrophes, such as a doomsday asteroid breaking through the membrane of the earth's atmosphere. (Scientists maintain that it is not a question of "if" but of "when" doomsday will arrive, since such catastrophic mass extinctions have occurred about every one hundred million years in the history of the planet, and we are due for another.)

This generalized anxiety has crystallized in the young century's headlines, reflecting the dread of infiltration, whether organic (disease), inorganic (computer corruption), or social (terrorist attack). This down side of "globalism" has led to an unprecedented boom in the security industry, as we try to fortify our homes, transportation networks, information and health care systems against the very accessibility they were built to afford. Never have borders seemed more porous than in the age of the borderless war.

7. Transferability (Screen)

trans·fer v. tr. 1. To convey or cause to pass from one place, person, or thing to another; including legal transfer. 2. To convey (a design, for example) from one surface to another, as by impression.

—*American Heritage Dictionary*

Related to the notion of system, and systemic contagion, the concept of transfer
figures prominently in many millennial fields: in cybernetics, hypertext transfers
"surfers" from one site to the next; in biology, in genetics, DNA is transferred
from one cell to another in cloning, organ generation, and gene-line therapy;
in medicine, surgeons transplant organs from donor to patient; in information
technology, the transfer of data with superconductors and semiconductors has
revolutionized information culture and global economics.

The idea of transferability materializes in the icon of the *screen*; a multifaceted
object that may protect, filter, access, reflect, convey, or impress an image. In our
media-oriented culture, the screen is also a surface for projection, where our fantasies may be externalized: our desires and demons may be enjoyed or exorcised
on private monitors or on the larger-than-life silver screen. In each of its avatars,
the screen is a site of transfer between sites of passage, whether designed to convey, obstruct, or filter.

Above all, the phenomenon of transfer grounds communication, as has always
been the case with written or printed matter. But today the transfer is less a matter of ink than of signal, with analogue or legible sign replaced by transmitted
code. The act of transfer now is seldom physical, "handing over" something "in
person": today we grant access by cipher or password (even tax filing is done by
electronic signature, without money changing hands). The very terms "handing
over" and "changing hands" have lost their corporeality: today the hand/*main*
merely *manipulates* the keyboard. As Jacques Derrida has been pointing out for some
decades, the notions of "self-presence" and identity have been "disseminated,"
dispersed. Today more than ever, *signing off* is not a physical action, but a function
of code. (In fact, signing off on something used to mean giving it approval, while
today signing off on someone means breaking the connection.) The cybersub-
ject's identity no longer depends on being *there*; it now depends on being in the
know, on knowing the password. But of course, code itself can be hacked or
cracked, like the fragile sense of belonging it conveys. And of course, code can be
forgotten by the all-too-human mind that created it. (Today, when we forget a
password, we have to send ourselves an email reminder of our own clue. This
hardly reinforces a sense of secure identity, or of being in the know.)

Finally, we have seen that the notion of transfer is related to that of skew in perspective, or Lacanian *anamorphosis* (chapter 3). An anamorphic image, technically, is one that has been shifted so that it may be read only from a sidelong angle, transferring the image to another point of reception. While the concept of the position of the observer has been important in science at least since Einstein, the most radical perspectivism today suggests that point of view is nothing but anamorphic perspective.

But shifting perspective has practical as well as philosophical implications. Astronomers, for instance, calculate the position of a star by *parallax*, the shift in its apparent site when viewed from two different positions on Earth. (Two apexes of the triangle determine the third.) Thus, like the notion of para-site, paral-lax is a function using two sites in a field to "orient" a third site at a distance, thanks to triangulation. In a sense, the millennial human subject is also "enter-tained" this way, suspended between the two cultural sites of twentieth-century humanism and twenty-first-century posthumanism, with an eye out for the distant future.

8. Motility (Rocket, Electron)

If speed is now the shortest route between two points, the necessarily reductive character of all scientific and sensible representation becomes a reality effect of acceleration, an optic effect of the speed of propagation.
—Paul Virilio, *The Lost Dimension*

The rocket is the icon of space age motility, the vehicle by which space and time have become unstuck from customary reference points. The same is true of the Internet, which has had to adopt a new global system of Internet time, where "now" is the same time everywhere. The most recent science of motility is interstellar propulsion theory, exploring exotic resources such as solar wind (which will allow a sail to propel the spacecraft by a stream of ions), and anti-gravity (which would allow superluminal speeds, by traveling in a bubble of warped time-space, actually shortening the space in front of the spacecraft by creating a strong gravitational field, crunching and expanding space like an inchworm).[35]

But we have seen that for thinkers like Virilio, the prospect of a constant change of human subject position, whether in high-velocity vehicles or through high-speed transfer from site to site on the Web, provokes acute anxiety: "Thus in the new representations of the sensible world, the point of light has replaced the vanishing point of perspective."[36] When Virilio voices fears that access to information at the speed of light has made the vanishing point itself all but vanish in a global "present," he has a point. But this is an earthbound objection. For, paradoxically, when we peer with powerful telescopes at objects light years away, the light being gathered conveys an image of the past. As one scientist explained (in the 1991 PBS video series *The Astronomers*), if an alien on a planet 65 million light years away trained a telescope onto planet Earth at this very moment, ET would see . . . dinosaurs. (The photons reaching his home would be 65 million years old, and dinosaur-laden.) This counterintuitive notion upsets the idea of visibility as apprehension of a simultaneous "presence"—a metaphysical notion long critiqued by Derrida and other poststructuralists—since photons do not actually "present" a current existing reality, but may quite literally convey the distant past. The image of the night sky is illusory, revealing "stars" as they *were*, although some of them burned out ages ago.

Virilio points out that the lack of "constants" in the new science has real psychic consequences: "Are we prepared to accept a reversal of all philosophic meaning, hereafter considering accident as absolute and necessary, and substance, all substance, as relative and contingent (catastrophe not as substantial deformation but rather as an unexpected accidental deformation)?"[37] In other words, the perception of relativity in the post-Einstein universe entails acknowledging the contingency of our own being in a cosmos without set parameters. However, we have seen that other millennial theorists highlight the *liberating* effects of a certain weightlessness, as enabling a shift in perspective, both aesthetically (Žižek's commentary on cinematographic technique) and psychologically (Lyotard's view of the salutary mobility of the decentered subject).

But long before the panic philosophers began to analyze the psychic impact of speed and transfer, Freud discussed motility as an inherent mode of unconscious processes, noting that human desire is always on the move. Virilio's millennial terror of motility may then reflect a deeper fear of the working of primary process in the human psyche. In our own internal night sky, the dream yields images and experiences every bit as unfathomable as those retrieved by Hubble and its successors from the far reaches of the cosmos.

9. Circuitousness (Chip)

> Hierarchies and meshworks are results of sorting and consolidation, and of endogenously stable circuits (feedback).
>
> —Manuel De Landa, *A Thousand Years of Nonlinear History*

The computer age is the age of circuitry. According to the *Oxford English Dictionary*, the term circuit is synonymous with orbit ("a closed, usually circular line that goes around an object or area") or a one-way path: "a route the complete traversal of which *without local change of direction* requires returning to the starting point." This definition associates circuit with a Moebius loop where—at least from the perspective of the tiny Moebius tourist—there is never an apparent change in direction, although the mobile Moebian would meet himself coming and going. In topological geometry, this is called a "nonorientable" surface.

But when it comes to the concept of the circuit in electronics, it appears that electrical current does not have such an easy time of it as it makes its rounds.

> **circuit** *electronics* a. A closed path followed or capable of being followed by an electric current b. a configuration of electrically or electromagnetically connected components or devices.
>
> —*Oxford English Dictionary*

The phrasing "*capable* of being followed" suggests potential or affordance, the possibility of circulation. But definition *b* describes circuit as a linkage of any number of transistors and resistors, obstacles encountered by the current as it circulates. The notion of productive resistance in turn calls up two other major millennial preoccupations—network and code: the computer field deals with *networks*, which when switched on and off—when the current is intermittently interrupted—yield a *signal*.

In digital technology, the making and breaking of the circuit is the stuff of meaning itself, in the transmission of bits and bytes. Indeed, since the invention of the telephone, the *switched circuit* (a hook-up or connection) makes communication possible, and is completed or broken as needed ("switched virtual circuits" [svc] are valid only for the time they are being used, until the user signs off, or hangs up). This notion of switched circuit is also germane to the Freudian concept of human desire and its transmission from "terminal" to "terminal" (subject to subject), thanks to its management and rerouting by a *resistor* or obstacle (Freud might call the resistor "repression," or even . . . "father"). The circulation of desire through switches and resistors (social laws and contingencies) produces a social subject, by virtue of a long-circuiting process that avoids a "short-circuit" meltdown (incest; death), a too-direct, too-strong, uninterrupted transmission of desire. A Freudian might say, in fact, that the switched circuit describes "current and its vicissitudes."

In *The Four Fundamental Concepts of Psycho-Analysis*, Lacan also draws a circuit diagram, a kind of ingrown Moebius loop. In "the interior 8," the outer circle is the part of desire that is conscious and external (demand); when it loops inward, it represents unconscious "desire." The loop is then redirected outward as renewed conscious demand (what we think we want, or ask for), aimed toward a world that can never fully assuage it, and that will thus assure the return of the leftover desire to the loop.[38]

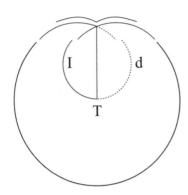

Lacan's interior 8: the inner circuit of desire and the outer loop of demand.

Read through Lacan, modern information theory thus provides a homologue be-tween circuitry and the loop of human potential.

Information theory provides another instance of circuitry that may be of in-terest for psychoanalysis, distinguishing *circuit* switching from *packet* switching. In circuit switching (a phone call), the message travels on a dedicated path, sender to receiver, during the time of the hook-up only. Packet switching, in contrast, sends a fragmented message by a number of routes, determined by "expediency": the message is divided into bundles and sent by any number of paths, reassem-bled at the destination.

> **packet switching** <communications> A paradigm in which packets (messages or fragments of messages) are individually routed between nodes, with no previously established communication path. [Their route] is determined by some [expedient] routing algorithm.
>
> —*Free Online Dictionary of Computing*[39]

Packet switching, of course, is the mechanism of the Internet, invented as a mili-tary defense to insure that messages could get through more than one way when lines were down. But packet switching, if it affords multiple routing possibilities, also opens communication strategy to chance encounter. Since the bits of infor-mation are dispatched by the most expedient route, to and from any number of nodes on the Internet, they are subject to the very kind of random material de-termination and contingency that figure in the paradigms of "chaos" and "self-organization" (massive blackouts are material instances of contingency switching gone chaotic). In any case, both circuit and packet switching rely on the func-tioning of *nodes* as sites of transmission and assignment, recalling the Lacanian idea of *Bahnungen/facilitation*.

This twenty-first-century switch—from a directional circuit/path of the dedicated phone line, to an intermittent, fragmented information strategy online—is also a key component of millennial paradigms of meaning (the Internet versus the phone call or letter). For it replaces the notion of a unified message, a linear letter from me to you, with a notion of bundled bits dispersed and sent circuitously, by network. Similarly, "the first war of this century" (dubbed the "war on terror") involves paradigm shifts in what counts as political and military action: rather than organizing a dedicated mass movement "above ground," engaging in open struggles or military battles, the new model emphasizes working in "packets," compartmentalized covert units. ("Sleeper" cells or special forces missions are activated on command—not for battles, but for "missions of opportunity" in a nonlinear struggle, rather than a campaign.) And when geopolitical leaders revert to old-style direct confrontations, as in the war in Iraq, they are discovering that declaring victory may be premature. Even when they declare the war officially over, and the "mission accomplished," be it a media event broadcast from the deck of an aircraft carrier to a cheering crowd, "victory" does not correspond to outcome.

Finally, it is worth noting that the distinction between circuit switching and packet switching provides a conceptual way of distinguishing circuit from network: rather than the single closed loop of the circuit, packet switching involves a rhizome of bristling synapses. Packet switching recalls Freud's "reality principle," whereby human desire is inevitably rerouted in the face of real obstacles, where instincts are always rerouted according to their vicissitudes. An individual, however he or she is wired, is only an integrated circuit in a bristling social network thanks to a capacity for fundamental fragmentation, an expedient rerouting of dedicated desire in the circuit of real life.

10. Network, Knot

Network. A collection of *nodes*, V, sometimes called *vertices*, plus a collection of *arcs*, which are directed from one node to another.

—*Free Online Dictionary of Computing*

If we want to locate a very clear instance of a rhizomatic meshwork engaged in bundling and dispatch, we need only think of the Internet, woven from linked site clusters, and conveying information in packets sent by the best available route.

Similarly, the emergence from the concept of circuitry to the concept of network—from loop to mesh—is reflected in the historical development of cybernetics systems theory. As N. Katherine Hayles explains, the first wave of cybernetics in the 1960s was concerned with feedback loops ("endogenously stable circuits," as De Landa puts it). A thermostat is one such simple looping system, designed to self-regulate in a "feedback loop" (adjusting the heat up or down as the temperature in the room rises or falls).

The second wave of cybernetics beginning in the 1970s, according to Hayles, brought reflexivity into the process: the system is not only self-regulating, but self-organizing, like cellular division in a bioorganism, or a "wizard" in a computer program that installs and then runs it. The current third wave of cybernetics (emergence) involves networks; it is no longer self-contained, but is part of a reactive and interactive system. Today systems not only self-organize and self-regulate, but actually evolve in response to environmental factors. (Both biological evolution and self-programming artificial intelligence are examples of "emergent" functions, as are human civilizations.) Emergence may eventually produce intelligence or even consciousness as the organism (or program) replicates itself. Today's AI programs sometimes even teach their functions to other emergent systems. (This is the most promising avenue for robotics, where electronic creatures learn as they go. In a documentary on the Science Channel, an inventor left a room filled with mechanical spiders, unable to walk—when he returned, they were marching single file. They learn by trial and error.)

Drawing on Deleuzian theory, Manuel De Landa makes a crucial observation: he points out that in systems theory, "emergence" must be an effect of a difference in energy level, causing a hook-up with other systems, a meshwork:

> The increase in diversity that mutually stimulating loops bring about will be short-lived unless the heterogeneous elements are interwoven, unless they come to form a meshwork. Then diversification increases by localizations, interweaving heterogeneity in each locality increases (networks grow, sprouting new connections that reach toward each other, like the brain's synapses).[40]

In other words, a closed circuit or loop not fed by difference will level out, like the temperature in a room that remains constant, deactivating the thermostat system. But if the system allows for a continued input of energy (keeping it far from equilibrium, as when the door is opened into a colder room), the system may grow, or emerge, hooking up with other components: the new room is part of the network governed by the thermostat. And if there is a thermostat in both rooms, they are networked: each is affected by the functioning of the other. (We have yet to develop a self-educating thermostat, however, that "turns on" the one in the next room, and teaches it what it knows.) A meshwork, in this sense—an articulation of nodes and connection—is a function of maintained difference. De Landa's work on "inorganic life," driven by "difference," resonates with the poststructuralist valorization of difference as the motive force of language and culture in human life. This exploration of differential intensity as motive force was elaborated by Deleuze (*Difference and Repetition*) in the late 1960s, and expanded by the philosophy of complex "deconstructed" or "dispersed" power modes in the work of Derrida and Foucault in the 1970s.

Of course, psychoanalysis has always considered intersubjectivity as a *network* of subjects in a systemic link founded by the incest taboo and motivated by ongoing intergenerational desire. The human community is a "far-from-equilibrium" system. Lacan's work is a theoretical systemic elaboration of Freud's initial insight: thus the Lacanian topology of desire diagrams the linkage of individual circuits (psyches/subjects) embedded in an expanding emergent network of social synapses.

11. Fractality, Embeddedness (Fractal)

Fractal (First appeared 1975): any of various extremely irregular curves or shapes that repeat themselves at any scale on which they are examined.
<http://www.Dictionary.com>

The fractal figure has captured the millennial imagination, as evinced by the myriad websites devoted to fractal art, and it is the topic of chapter 7 below. The simplest definition of fractality, cited above, highlights self-similarity: an object "looks similar to itself" at any scale. In nature, examples of self-similar objects are a snowflake (made of snowflake-like crystals), or a tree (made of ramified tree-like branches and veined leaves). The process that generates fractals mathematically is *iteration*, a repeated operation that feeds the preceding result into the next step. And in fractal mathematics, iteration opens to the notion of interstitial dimensions: no matter how many times you divide a fraction, you may still produce an infinite number of fractions between any two numbers.

Fractal operations subvert the conventional notion of unity, indicating its divisible and infinitely "embedded" quality. Chapter 7 deals further with fractality, proposing that the Freudian subject is a fractal "intersubject," embedded in a meshwork of Others.

12. Code

Marvin Minsky, sometimes called the "father of artificial intelligence," defines intelligence as the ability to process code; that is, the ability to receive information and act on it. In fact, he and fellow bot buff Douglas Hofstadter are hard at work proving that machine reactions may qualify as bona fide emotions.[41] But what is code?

The online dictionary entries for the verb "code" are already embedded in the emergent realities of the twenty-first century:

> **to code** v. tr. 1. to translate into a language that can be communicated to the computer; 2. <*genetics*> to specify the amino acid sequence of a protein by the sequence of nucleotides.
>
> <http://www. Allwords@dictionary.com>

Another online (*Random House*) dictionary definition of code foregrounds its high-tech symbolic function, as "a system for communication by telegraph, heliograph, etc., in which long and short sounds, light flashes, etc., are used to symbolize the content of a message." A third definition stresses encryption ("a system used for brevity or secrecy of communication, in which arbitrarily chosen words, letters, or symbols are assigned definite meanings" (*Free Online Dictionary of Computing*). Here the only difference between code and language is the secrecy and/or the compactness of the message.

But message must be coded and decoded by an intelligence. What, then, is intelligence, in the new century? The definition at the online site *Techencyclopedia* is whimsical:

> **intelligence**
> Processing capability. Every computer is intelligent, which is more than can be said for all humans!

It continues more soberly:

> **Artificial intelligence** is the simulation of human intelligence processes by machines, especially computer systems. These processes include learning (the acquisition of information and rules for using the information), reasoning (using the rules to reach approximate or definite conclusions), and self-correction.

The reference to the human-machine faceoff reappears in this definition of "AI":

> **artificial intelligence (AI):** The subfield of computer science concerned with the concepts and methods of symbolic inference by computer and symbol representation information for use in making inferences.
> —*Free Online Dictionary of Computing*

A certain whimsy registers in this afterthought, as in other definitions cited above, suggesting that millennial dictionaries are chronically ironic. Artificial intelligence is also sometimes defined as trying to solve by computer any problem that a human can solve faster.

But a more serious and "authoritative" source (Oxford, cited by Princeton Wordnet) reflects an age-old mind-body dualism in its vitalist assumptions about "superiority of mind":

> **intelligence** n. Origin: L. Intelligere = to understand 1: the ability to comprehend; to understand and profit from experience
> a. The capacity to acquire and apply knowledge; b.The faculty of thought and reason. c. superior powers of mind. 2: information, news. 3: An intelligent, incorporeal being, especially an angel.
>
> —*Oxford Online Dictionary*

This more conventional definition of intelligence, focused on consciousness and sentience, simply excludes the notion of artificial intelligence. But not only high-tech hardware is excluded; human gray matter also is at risk: the definition of intelligence as "angel" seems to link ultimate intelligence to the nonmaterial domain of spirit, and to powers superior to the human brain.

The same source confidently responds to an age-old question (What is life?), again by simply excluding "inanimate" matter:

> **life** The property or quality that distinguishes living organisms from dead organisms and inanimate matter, manifested in functions such as metabolism, growth, reproduction, and response to stimuli or adaptation to the environment originating from within the organism.

However straightforward it may be, this definition ignores a complex dispute between the vitalists and the mechanists in cybernetics. The latter argue that if a computer "brain" may do what a human brain does, it is intelligent (if it looks like a duck, and quacks like a duck . . .). Similarly, if something metabolizes, grows, reproduces, and adapts . . . it's *alive*. In opposition to vitalists, who insist that life is carbon-based, mechanists argue that computer programs do all the things that organisms do (they are fed with energy or information; their programs reproduce on their own—this is the very essence of the virus; and such programs even adapt and outsmart defenses, and teach baby programs how to survive too). But the vitalists rely on an ideal notion of animism, accommodating a spirtualist perspective.

In other words, the matter of life is a judgment call. Do computers really "feed" on energy, transforming it into matter (written words, printed pages)? If so, artificial life would be a reversal of the biological capacity to feed on matter, transforming it into energy. But in a sense, it all comes down to code and to convention—what we agree *counts* as intelligent life, and for whom. As Freud and

Lacan would have it, definitions are a matter of meaning-making, conscious and unconscious.

EPILOGUE: THE MILLENNIAL MATRIX: FIELD

Field. (Physics) the influence of some agent, as electricity or gravitation, considered as existing at all points in space and defined by the force it would exert on an object placed at any point in space. E.g. electric field, gravitational field, magnetic field.

—*Oxford English Dictionary*

In this chapter we have visited topological knot theory and psychoanalysis in a circuit around some of the key nodes of the millennial web—cultural, psychological, and material. Another way of describing the "millennial knot," the connection of the various nodes described here, is as a *field*, reflecting the post-Einstein recognition that matter and energy are mutually transmutable. For each of these material nodes has such a strong psychic pull that it defines a force field in the Lacanian sense as well, as an energetic matrix of cultural interaction.

Each of the twelve nodal figures visited here is also the site of one or more "fields" in a more conventional sense, marking a domain of research in frontier science.

1. opticality: optics (including the new telescopes, electron microscopes, and media theory);
2. hybridism: genetic research and engineering;
3. nonlinearity: astrophysics; nonlinear mathematics;
4. materiality: quantum physics; microbiology;
5. systematicity: systems and complexity theory; chaos theory; ecology;
6. permeability: cellular biology, microbiology;
7. transferability: communications/media; biology ("screening");
8. motility: propulsion theory, space flight research;
9. circuitry: microelectronics, information theory;
10. network: global economics; group dynamics; information theory;
11. fractality: fractal geometry;
12. code: programming; DNA research; cybernetics; artificial intelligence.

This final casting of the net as a series of fields may suggest the many ways in which these current concepts and research topics intersect with the topic of psychoanalysis, tying the knot between Freud and millennialism. For psychoanalysis has many callings today: Freud Y2K may continue to contribute something essential to posthuman philosophy, considering human drives, and even the vicissitudes of instincts, in the light of nonlinear scientific paradigms. The information network is expanding negentropically (8,000 people a day worldwide go online for the first time): can it be discussed in terms of identification, projection, and intersubjective desire? How can the ubiquitous fantasy of alien invasion—from across the border or across the cosmos—be understood in terms of the psychoanalytic theory of Otherness?

Surfing the millennial web has made one thing clear: if Freud's theory may enrich our understanding of "millennialism," psychoanalysis may in turn be enriched by examining new techno-cultural phenomena.

Discussing the instincts as something radically different from biological need, as the French Freudians have done with the theory of drive, and linking these considerations to new scientific models, might lead to a psychoanalysis freed from the habits of linear thinking that reduce symptom to simple cause and effect, or replace material *instance* with metaphor. The question of millennial psychoanalysis cuts both ways: can Freud cast light on the strange new situations encountered by the posthuman subject? If so, how do the new paradigms of science and technology enrich the insights of psychoanalysis? One thing is certain: from a twenty-first-century perspective, it is increasingly clear that Lacan's neo-Freudian network is a nodal poetics of emergence.

CHAPTER 6

EMERGENCE: GENDER AS AVATAR

Sandi Fellman, *Insect #28*, 2001. © 2001 Sandi Fellman.

Sexuality brings into play a diversity of conjugated becomings; these are like n sexes, a war machine through which love passes.

—Gilles Deleuze, *A Thousand Plateaus*

"Becoming" in the Posthuman Age

Like the earlier reflection on *Anti-Oedipus*, this chapter stages an encounter between Freud and Deleuze. But this encounter is not a conflict; this is a meeting of minds that challenges not only the conventional concept of gender, but also the conventional notion of "the human" itself. Gilles Deleuze's striking formulation of gender-as-emergence, connoted in the epigraph, associates sexuality not with the binary opposition of two genders, but with "a diversity of conjugated becomings." And this radical recasting of gender finds an unexpected confirmation in Freud.

But before examining this view of emergent gender, we need to consider the concept of emergence itself as a key paradigm of our era. The twenty-first century is increasingly concerned with transformative processes of "becoming," rather than set properties of "being," in a shift of focus from what things *are* to how they *change*.

In 1974, Nobel laureate Ilya Prigigone's scientific blockbuster *From Being to Becoming* first documented "becoming" as the major paradigm shift of late-twentieth-century science and culture, describing self-organizing (autotelic) material processes that result from spontaneous ordering and sudden structural changes in matter.[1] This new paradigm emphasizes the fluid dynamics of matter-energy in interconnected systems, rather than focusing on static properties of individual objects or entities.

For instance, in classical thermodynamics—which holds that all closed energy systems level out to a state of balance—the scientist might study the transfer of heat from hot coffee to the cup that holds it, and then to the surrounding air, as observed in controlled conditions under a glass dome. The cooling of the liquid eventually results in temperature equilibrium in air, cup, and coffee.

But the focus of millennial science is no longer on equilibrium. Far from it.

The Heat Is On: Far-from-Equilibrium Theory

Twenty-first-century physics has opened up classical thermodynamics, removing the glass dome while keeping the heat on. In "far-from-equilibrium theory," the emphasis is on the process of transformation of matter-energy as it passes through phase states (coffee-becoming-steam-interacting-with-air: in the house, in the city, in the atmosphere). In other words, the coffee is reconceptualized as a link in an open-ended system affected by many variables, a steam machine interacting with the ever-changing ecology of the room and beyond.[2]

Perhaps the most dramatic instance of nonlinear science today is chaos theory, which studies how tiny changes in initial properties may sometimes yield startlingly incommensurate results. For instance, scientists might seek to locate the tipping point (or *bifurcation*) at which the cup of cooling coffee could set off a chain reaction in global warming.[3] Lest this example seem far-fetched, we should bear in mind that the last century witnessed the catastrophic effects begun by the splitting of a single atom; while the new century was ushered in by panic about the possible catastrophic domino effect of small computer glitches in a global system. Even more recently (summer 2003), North America's power grid reached its "tipping point," plunging fifty million people into sudden and prolonged darkness.

While examples in chaos theory tend to focus on the exponential effects of tiny initial shifts, going from local conditions to global effects (small to large), the new science also studies dynamic systems in the other direction, at an ever-diminishing scale. This is the paradigm of deep ecology, which studies embedded phenomena as through a zoom lens, zeroing into a smaller and smaller field (planet Earth, continent Africa, the savannah, an elephant herd, a single bull, its trunk, its skin, a cell, a cell nucleus, a DNA molecule, a gene, an amino acid, an element, an atom).[4] At the end of the elephant parade, we find a throng of subatomic particles, with strange names like gluons, leptons, fermions, besons—including twenty-four varieties of quarks in the atomic nucleus, with quixotic labels like "up orange" and "strange blue." These bizarre particles are not really objects; they are more like "dancing *points* of energy" (as Einstein once put it) with very weird properties indeed.[5] (An electron, for instance, is several places at once.) The subquark descent ends, in the physics of the moment at least, with . . . strings, the vibratory wave-particles that almost seem to be *functions* of matter-energy rather than discrete building blocks.[6] This perspective of infinite regress immerses us in a realm infinitely more minute than our human-scaled dimensions. And going in the other direction, ascending the scale to a cosmic field of view, our sun itself rapidly shrinks to a "dancing point of energy."

Centuries ago, of course, Pascal was already reflecting on the sublime suspension of human being between the unthinkably vast and the unimaginably tiny. But these days, even "big" and "small" have been complicated by dimensions that are . . . out of line. Scientists now tell us that our cosmos has at least ten dimensions (some say eleven, or twenty-six) beyond the four that the human mind can intuit; the others are tiny and interstitial, coiled around our four-dimensional space-time.[7]

Rethinking the Human Line

Another change effected by new models is a departure from a narrowly androcentric perspective. Today, scientists such as J. Craig Ventner (a pioneer of the genome revolution) emphasize that every human cell has its origins in archea and bacteria. At the cellular level, in fact, there is little to distinguish human from germ. As Ventner put it recently on public television, "each of us contains within our genetic material a written history of life on earth."[8] And the new paradigm challenges not only the distinction between human and animal, but also the vitalist prejudice favoring organic over inorganic, fetishizing "life itself." At the level of deep ecology, coffee quarks are indistinguishable from elephant quarks: everything is evolving, mutating, and replicating.

In the paradigm of becoming, organic life is regarded as a latecomer in the continuing process of self-organization of matter. Life is not created; it *emerges*, as matter acquires metabolic and reproductive capacities. Nearly a century ago, Freud's thinking anticipated this idea: in *Beyond the Pleasure Principle*, he speculates that the human death drive is motivated by a compulsion to regain an earlier inorganic state.[9] He thus includes the inorganic in his perspective, rather than separating off "life itself" as a miracle essentially different from the chain of material being that gives rise to it.

At any rate, for today's scientist, life is no longer necessarily life as we know it, organic and carbon-based: the field of cybernetics creates and studies silicon-based artificial life forms that feed, replicate, and evolve, even teaching silicon youngsters what they have learned.[10] And discoveries like the famous Mars rock, which some think contains fossilized bacteria a billion years older than the oldest life on Earth, have altered basic assumptions about what parameters mark the boundaries of life. (Here on Earth, we have seen the discovery of very alien forms of terrestrial life, thriving on sulfur in pitch-black boiling water near volcanic ocean vents.)

Two terms that refer collectively to these new paradigms—becoming and nonlinearity—intersect in a third term: emergence.[11] This paradigm refers to all self-organizing reactions in matter-energy, including interactions that actually alter the essence of the component elements, like a chemical reaction provoked by a catalyst. The emergent paradigm might qualify as the dominant episteme of our time in Foucault's sense of the term, since the concept of emergence distinguishes our era from others.[12] According to a Foucaldian perspective, we might say that the premodern episteme of hierarchy emphasizes order (who's on top?); and the modern episteme of linearity emphasizes origins and ends (who's on first?). But the millennial episteme of emergence emphasizes transformative phase states and the process of change itself (who [what and how] is "who" *becoming?*).

Challenging the notion of identity (who is "who"?) and of consciousness (who is asking?), the new paradigm also questions boundary (who draws the line?) and authority (who says so?). It also emphasizes perspective as a function of site (what is the effect of "*who's*" position on what "*who*" knows?). It would seem that posthuman subjectivity is no longer just a matter of human *being*: the millennial subject is always coming, going, or in the process of *becoming* . . . something other.

The new paradigms have a recursive quality: they are transformations in science that study transformations *as* science. This iterative tendency is everywhere:

the millennial era has engendered science about science (science studies, waging "science wars" about objectivity), literature about literature (postmodern texts emphasizing irony, intertextuality, performative writing), code about code (hypertext, cybernetics, DNA), psychology about psychology (Freudian readings of Freud). But for all of its speculative quality, the mindset of the new millennium is resolutely material. For it was not, after all, a philosopher who really shook up our comfortable assumptions about human being.

Albert Einstein, great humanitarian that he was, might also be considered the first "posthuman" thinker. And a host of others have since joined him in the posthuman festivities.

Party On

Einstein kicked off the millennial paradigm party almost a century ago. Elaborating his famous twin paradox to explain general relativity to the general public, he gave the amusing example of identical twins aging at different rates (one onboard a near-light-speed rocket, the other back home on Earth). He thus emphasized that space-time is no longer a stable backdrop for the human drama. Heisenberg brought the "uncertainty principle" along to the party, demonstrating that we can never measure exactly where Einstein's twins *are* (or, more accurately, where the particles that make up the twins are) at any given moment. Hubble arrived on the scene with a Big Bang, with the news that the relational universe explored by Einstein's astronaut was also expanding at unimaginable speed. Recently, theorists of the inflational universe (Lee Smolin and others), have joined the fun suggesting that the rate of cosmic expansion is itself accelerating. As the cosmos is flying apart at a faster and faster rate, scientists are now debating whether the party will end with a bang or a whimper: will the cosmos bounce back like a big yo-yo, in the Big Crunch, or will it speed away into the Big Void?

Either of these grim possibilities is enough to put a damper on any festivity. But Mandelbrot and Lobachevsky, among others, first spiced things up by adding exotic non-Euclidean geometries to the party mix, demonstrating that the comfortable metric world grounded by Euclid's fifth postulate (parallel lines will never meet) is only confirmed by cheating.[13] With the arrival of the non-Euclidean mathematicians—including Mandelbrot's fractal set—Einstein's party has gotten really wild: hyperbolic nonparallel lines approach each other eternally without intersecting; parallels meet at infinity. Meanwhile, somewhere in the cozy tiny space of fractal geometry, infinite lines are squiggled up between dimensions.[14]

Einstein may have kicked things off by warping space, but the social sciences have also been experiencing a paradigm change. Ever since feminists started questioning sexual identity as a fixed property of being (Simone de Beauvoir: "one is not born, one *becomes*, a woman"), the paradigm party has gotten downright kinky.

The first years of our century have witnessed highly publicized examples of gender bending, including a notorious case involving same-sex twins who became opposite-sex twins . . . by accident, thanks to a slip of the knife. (One of the boys was castrated during circumcision, and was raised as a girl. Thirty years later, when Brenda learned the truth, she had a sex reassignment. She is now a father.)

Cases like these provide a whole new wrinkle on Einstein's twin paradox. One can imagine the discomfiture of the virile and youthful twin—a returning space hero, still possessed of all the right stuff—emerging from his space capsule back on Earth to be greeted by an elderly identical twin *sister*. In any case, Einstein's twins may soon be indistinguishable from their cloned lateral progeny, uncanny doubles capable of twinning themselves.

Little wonder that when theorists speculate about what on Earth (or off) will become of human being in the new age, they often focus on the future of gender. For the category of gender is complicated by new social realties (like virtual cross-dressing in online romance: Allucquére Rosanne Stone reports that 15 percent of people in online chat groups at any given time are posing as the other sex). Back in the twentieth century, theorist Judith Butler was already warning us that we had "gender trouble"; but given the vicissitudes of gender in this century, chances are we ain't seen *nothin'* yet.

BECOMING-WOMAN Y2K: GENDER AS AVATAR

One is not born, one becomes, a woman.

–Simone de Beauvoir, *The Second Sex*

Avatar: <virtual reality> An image representing a user in a multi-user virtual reality space.

–*Free Online Dictionary of Computing*

Avatar: 1) a variant phase or version of a continuing entity 2) (Hindu) one of many possible incarnations of a deity.

–*Oxford English Dictionary*

As the first definition of the word avatar above shows, the term is used in contemporary cyberculture to designate the multiple screen identities that players adopt in MUDs (multi-user virtual communities). But the term also seems peculiarly appropriate to assign to gender these days, because it associates identity with a transformative becoming, a phase state of human being. In fact the first cybernetic definition of "avatar" cited above represents an interesting chiasmus from the second conventional spiritual definition: as a Hindu religious term, *avatar* denotes a transmogrification from a spiritual form to a flesh-and-blood being, an incarnation. But in cyberspace, the term denotes the reverse crossing: the choice of an image to navigate for its operator, while the flesh stays put in "RL," on the real-life side of the screen.

The term avatar is also germane to contemporary feminism, which replaces the notion of "being female" with the concept of "becoming woman" in a culturally constructed role. Judith Butler, for one, discusses gender as an effect of performativity or interpellation ("calling" in the Heideggerian sense, a command performance initiated by a patriarchal culture that calls us to take up a compulsory position on one side or the other of the gender divide).[15] Butler's characterization of gender as performance has always been fraught; some feminist theorists are understandably reluctant to relinquish the material notion of woman as sexed body, and essentialist feminism has even fostered the view that biology is the sole foundation of gender. The old nature/nurture debate has been further complicated by developments in biotechnology. New research, for instance, claims to associate gender traits with hormone baths *in utero*, while some researchers even locate determination of gender identification *before* conception, as a function of parental genes determining hormone receptors. This new biologism poses a challenge to the notion that gender is primarily a cultural construct.

Indeed, today it is often sex that is literally constructed, rather than gender. This is the case for elective transsexual surgery, of course; but sex is also constructed by surgical intervention on newborns with ambiguous genitalia, which occurs in one in 1,500 births (the rate has risen dramatically in the last two decades). These days sex, rather than gender, may be a function of interpellation ("calling" in a literal sense), when the doctor makes the judgment call on intersex infants (It's *almost* a . . . girl!). In the delivery room, the surgeons usually follow up the call with immediate surgical "gender assignment"—such as the removal of a "too-large" clitoris that might be mistaken for a penis—often destroying the eventual orgasmic function of the child.[16]

Even in the case of transgendered adults who feel they were born in the wrong body, and who now may turn to surgery to rectify nature's mistake, the new option to match genitalia with gender identification may actually end up reinforcing the traditional notions of masculine and feminine. (When the appropriate plumbing is considered mandatory, thanks in part to new surgical options, it seems that only heroic surgery can correct one's "unnatural" birth.) Similarly, cosmetic surgery would seem to offer choices about physical traits—at least to the wealthy—but it too tends to exaggerate gender stereotypes and homogenized norms (hawking breast implants, penile enhancements, and "ideal" Caucasian faces). This is the age of addiction: plastic surgery junkies often undergo hundreds of procedures to emulate plastic icons of *anti*-androgyny. (Cindy Jackson is the notorious self-made woman who has spent several hundred thousand dollars remodeling her image after a real plastic Goddess. She bills herself as "the human Barbie Doll," and now works as an image consultant.)[17]

Post-Gender Trouble

Some feminists, however, have heralded the advent of a world where gender is no longer the defining characteristic. Donna Haraway, for one, proclaims: "the cyborg is a creature in a *post*gender world, it has no truck with preoedipal symbolica or other seductions to organic wholeness."[18] However upbeat, this proclamation gives ammunition to futurephobes far less sanguine than Haraway about the new age. At stake, it seems, is the future of sexuality; and the battleground is gender.

Predictably, Jean Baudrillard is one contemporary theorist who waxes hysterical about the culture of androgyny as part of the "hell of sameness": "the sexual body has been assigned to a kind of artificial fate . . . playing, in contrast to the former manner of playing on sexual difference, on a lack of differentiation between the sexual poles, and of indifference to sex *qua* pleasure." The guru of hyperreality goes on to blame the culture of image: "After the demise of desire, [we see] a pell-mell diffusion of erotic simulacra in every guise, of transsexual kitsch is all its glory . . . a postmodern pornography, if you will, where sexuality is lost in the theatrical excess of ambiguity."[19] Similarly, Arthur Kroker and David Cook (*The Postmodern Scene*) describe androgyny as a spectacular media catastrophe:

> Everything is being blasted apart by the mediascape. The violent advertising machine gives us a whole, schizophrenic world of electric women for a culture . . . where the old (patriarchal) signs of cultural authority collapse in the direction of androgyny. [Androgynous figures like Madonna] play at the edge of power and seduction, the zero-point where sex as electric image is amplified, teased out in a bit of ironic exhibitionism, and then reversed against itself.[20]

Meanwhile, Paul Virilio observes (from an unapologetically male subject position) "the disappearance of the woman in the fatality of the technical object, [since] man reserves his inventiveness for other purposes."[21] Baudrillard, Virilio, Kroker and Cook—all seem to fear that boys will not be boys much longer, but will soon be more absorbed in video games than in doing what comes naturally.

Hypergender

Although panic philosophers may worry about the ascendancy of androgyny in contemporary culture, traditional gender stereotypes are alive and well in hyperspace and in film. In classic science fiction, the muscled cyborg (*The Terminator*, *Robocop*) finds his counterpart in the performances of the cyberbabe/astronette of cyberpunk fiction and film (from Jane Fonda's weightless striptease in *Barbarella* to the antics of *Wonder Woman* and the sexy gymnastics of catsuited heroines in *The Matrix* and *Batman*). And the wide-eyed mini-skirted heroines of Japanese anime are all the rage in youth media culture worldwide.

In *Electronic Eros*, Claudia Springer chronicles two distinct modalities in electronic humanoids: the masculine is based on a machinic prototype of thrust, strength, steel; the feminine suggests a mysterious internal computerized circuitry, capable of "going haywire" or transmitting viral infection. But for all her exaggerated sex appeal, the female electro-erotic icon is not passive; in fact, the gynoid often performs feats of superhuman strength, even while acting out the male fear of castration. In the cult classic *Eve of Destruction*, the luscious cyborg-ette goes haywire, biting off the penis of her suitor. She is hard to track down because she has no "off" button. And she is all the more dangerous because she is capable of going nuclear at any moment, in a kind of nightmare electronic PMS. Eve's (female) maker describes her creature in terms that wink at the notorious misogynist spiel of Andrew Dice Clay: "she'll bleed, but she won't die."

The discussion of hypergender by feminist theorists (such as Claudia Springer and Anne Balsamo) points out that these hyper erotics are symptomatic of an unconscious reaction defense against cultural change.[22] Springer also observes that the swagger of the Schwarzenegger cyborg has a homoerotic valence (*The Terminator*, ever popular with young boys, arrives on the scene nude). In any case, the replicants and action figures of cyberpunk, techno-films, and video gaming are anything but androgynous, so Virilio and company may relax. In fact, Angelina Jolie's film role as the video-game heroine Lara Croft required the already curvaceous actress to have breast augmentation to live up to her virtual image in the fantasies of adolescent male video-gamers.

Predictably enough, today's hyper-eroticized mediascape is often characterized as post-oedipal (as is Haraway's cyborg culture), a nondimensional field where the love triangle has been flattened and flatlined, and the love object has become the flat screen itself (Virilio again: "The former triangle is completely modified and the rapport is established between a unisex and a technical vector, replacing contact with the body of the loved one or of the territorial.")[23] These dystopic theorists of gender often displace the crisis of culture onto technology, in a move that, for all its trendiness, still implies that a back-to-nature movement might solve the problem. The gender purists seem to enjoin the he-man to turn off the computer and make love to a real woman—her "natural" womanliness, of course, enhanced by high-tech surgical procedures and retro lingerie. But in spite of prayers that forevermore "boys will be boys," biotechnology has forever altered what Mr. Right may encounter once he has gone offline in search of a live wire.

Genderation Gap: Oedipus on Air

The bizarre questions that faced mythical family Oedipus are now in the commercial media domain, broadcast to the world at large on 24/7 reality TV. But new gender possibilities have considerably complicated the intrigue. On an Australian talk show in 2000, for instance, the audience vociferously debated the harmful psychic effects on a child who had been brought into the world by her grandmother. (A woman gave birth to her daughter's genetic embryo, conceived in vitro with her son-in-law's sperm, since the daughter had had a hysterectomy.) Another talk show that aired on Australian TV in 2000 asked viewers to comment on the morality of a gay man donating sperm to artificially inseminate his mother, in order to produce his own child. (This offspring would technically—shades of Oedipus—be his sibling).[24]

In court-drama-crazed America, embryo custody cases are proliferating, while fertility clinic mix-ups spawn plots worthy of soap opera: recently a New York woman was implanted with two embryos, one created by mistake with sperm that was not her husband's. The white mother gave birth to twins, one white, one black, and both genetic parents—who had never met—claimed custody of the black twin. In a throwback to gender convention and racial privilege, custody of both twins was awarded to the white mother and her husband, even though this "natural" solution left the black couple childless.[25]

Meanwhile, back on the genetic frontier (Britain, home of the first test-tube baby and Dolly the cloned sheep), Parliament is still debating the ethics of harvesting eggs from aborted fetuses or accident victims. What happens when you discover that your mother was dead before you were born (the egg donated by a cadaver), or that she was never born at all (the "donor" was an aborted fetus)?[26] What are the psychological effects of knowing that your father was dead long before your conception (the sperm taken from a terminally ill donor to fertilize his surviving mate years later)?

The bizarre psychic vicissitudes of Mr. and Mrs. Oedipus seem tame in comparison to millennial family romance. Picture, for instance, the complications facing the couple who, unable to have children the old-fashioned way, opt to clone one of each. This would yield an exponential oedipal family, where two exact copies of two people who had fallen in love would be raised as brother and sister. The young "he" is formally denied access to the filial clone of his mother, as well as the real thing; while the young "she" is denied access to two generations of her father, in a double Electra mode. Meanwhile, the father is formally forbidden by law and convention to pursue the younger version of his wife, even though he is not genetically related to her; while his love for his son would quite literally qualify as narcissistic. As for the son, well, he would certainly be a Mama's boy.

In other words, any number of technological avatars today could complicate the good old triangle of "Mommy, Daddy, and me." (With sperm banks in every major city, the possibility of unwittingly marrying a sibling, or even a parent, has exponentially increased. And eggs are bought and sold nearly as frequently as sperm these days. In the Rutgers *Targum* and many other college newspapers, advertisements offering several thousand dollars for healthy *Caucasian* ova regularly appear. It seems that commercially motivated racism extends to gonads.) What psychoanalysis may still bring to these new age complications, however, is an understanding of the emotional stakes of fetishism, and the narcissistic compulsion to further one's own genetic line, at any cost. We recall that for Freud, fetishism is not a simple perversion, but a consequence of the failure to acknowledge a traumatic threat of loss. Freud speculates that what initially paralyzes the male fetishist is the sight of female genitalia—stirring castration anxiety, and causing him to avert his gaze to a phallic substitute (a nearby handbag, a shoe). This raises an intriguing question: when we as a society engage in embryo/gonad/gene fetishism, what loss are we avoiding? Surely, we are avoiding mortality—as evinced by the growing popularity of cryogenics, the costly procedure already undergone by thousands of people who spend their life savings in the hope of having their corpses revived in a brighter future. And dozens of popular films in the past few decades have focused on the ancient theme of gender switch (*Tootsie, Mrs. Doubtfire, Big Mama's House, The Crying Game*), which also often borders on fetishistic obsession. Interestingly, the transitional decades between the twentieth and twenty-first centuries saw the Academy Award for "best actor" given to a man playing a man playing a woman (*Tootsie*); while the "best actress" award (now called "best female performance") has twice gone (in the noughts) to a woman playing a woman playing a man (*Boys Don't Cry; Shakespeare in Love.*)

Yet Freud's take on fetishism, as panic about castration, must be amended in light of today's culture. Often what appalls the male protagonist of gender comedy today, unlike the classic Freudian fetishist, is not the sight of a castrated female, but the sight of a noncastrated one. In one camp comedy after another, panic results when a man discovers that he has been courting another man. What is our fascination with this story? Is this a kind of double negation, finding satisfaction in the revelation of a "phallic" female where a "castrated" one was anticipated? The panic about gender masquerade has been further complicated today by online courtship. In *Life on the Screen*, Sherry Turkle relates the jealousy of one male MIT undergraduate at the discovery of his girlfriend's online infidelity, exacerbated by the revelation that the virtual indiscretion was committed with another woman when the girlfriend had signed on with a *male* screen name. Was his gal—heaven forbid—really a virtual lesbian? (Of course, the online partner could have really been a "he" signing on in virtual drag.)

The Future of Gender

One thing is evident in today's topsy-turvy world of "gender as avatar": cyber-culture critiques, however interesting, are still largely based on the conventional binary opposition, masculine versus feminine. In fact, taking note of the conventionality of some feminist cultural critiques, Lacanian theorist Elizabeth Grosz warns that feminist theory is in danger of being left behind in the new age unless it complexifies its perspective on gender:

> Unless feminist theory becomes more self aware of the intellectual and political resources it relies on, and the potentialities of these resources to produce the impetus to propel the present into a future not entirely contained by it, it risks being stuck in political strategies and conceptual dilemmas that are more appropriate to the past than the future.[27]

Is there, then, a twenty-first-century feminist perspective that can keep up with new developments in science and philosophy, one which goes beyond a critique of gender fetishism?

The most notable feminist theorist in the field at present is perhaps again Donna Haraway, who chronicles the ideologically invested aspects of new reproductive technologies, and critiques the commercialization of the genome project. Today, the raging debate over stem cell research with embryos is another example of the fetish status of "life itself" foregrounded by Haraway. Her cultural analyses reveal investment in two registers: the economic investment of capitalism reflecting the need to sell a product by selling a conscious image; and the promotion of a certain ideology by playing on *unconscious* fear. For instance she, like Allucquére Rosanne Stone (*The War of Desire and Technology at the End of the Industrial Age*) discusses the blood obsession that subtends our inexhaustible cultural fascination with vampirism (the vampire film genre itself refuses to die). Stone and Haraway read the collective phantasm of monstrous union between human and undead as a symptom of racism and/or homophobia, playing on the fear of miscegenation as tainted/mixed blood, now transmitted in a lethal love act recalling the pandemic of AIDS.[28] And these two fears—racism/xenophobia, and the fear of penetration/contamination by a deathly ill "pervert"—may converge in the real world's lack of reaction to the AIDS catastrophe in Africa.

To be sure, Haraway's work contributes a much-needed material base to the discussion of gender fantasy, and her work is psychoanalytically informed. But unfortunately, like many feminists, Haraway reduces Freud's position on gender

to a hetorosexist patriarchal line, summed up in the authoritarian pronounce-
ment that "anatomy is destiny." Yet Freud repeatedly emphasized the bisexuality
of every individual, suggesting that all human beings have an active libido. He
even maintained that women veil their active sexual nature only in response to
imposed cultural constraints, and that they are thus *culturally* compelled to redirect
libido into "passive" exhibitionism of ornament and dress.[29] Phallic-privilege
envy, in other words, is not penis envy.

Clearly, Haraway's work demonstrates that it is not enough for millennial feminism to be technologically savvy. Gender theory must also get out of the old conflation of psychoanalytic with masculinist, premised on the either/or oppositional
thinking that Freud's work actually discredits. In this spirit, some Lacanian feminist theorists—such as Jacqueline Rose, Jane Gallop, and Juliet Mitchell—have
dealt with Lacan's most problematic assertions ("woman does not exist"; "there is
no sexual relation") from a perspective beyond knee-jerk outrage.[30]

Yet, as the epigraph to this chapter suggests, perhaps the most radical integration of millennial science and culture in gender theory comes from an unexpected quarter: Gilles Deleuze. Almost four decades ago he was critiquing the
paucity of a two-gender binary oppositional model with segregated territories:
either/or, his/hers. Deleuze's startling work on "becoming- woman" declares
that love is a transgressive passage, a "war machine" without bellicosity, involving "a diversity of n sexes" in the process of becoming.[31]

This strange war cry, first issued in 1967, attracted the ire of many feminists at
the time, for the essay seems to imply that "woman" is the effect of a process of
diminishment or self-effacement.[32] Still, Deleuze's work is consistent with nonlinear paradigms, discussing gender not as an immutable essence but as a kind of
phase state with any number of differential avatars.

We may now turn to Deleuze's strange politics of becoming, considering his
work as prototype for an emergent theory of gender, if not a feminist theory of
gender. Deleuze, in fact, may be reconciled with a feminist agenda through an
equally unexpected mediator: Freud. To be sure, this is an ungainly alliance: the
single thing that many feminist theorists have deigned to applaud in Deleuze is
his criticism of Freud. But Freud's theory has been misread as hardline oppositional thinking, since he argues that human beings are initially bi-gendered, with
but one active libido. Even if "anatomy is destiny," then, Freud's position suggests
that in a society where anatomy *signifies* something different than it does in a patriarchal configuration, the gendered subject's destiny will be different. And of
course, in today's world, anatomy itself is unstable, subject to "reassignment."

All this suggests that the odd couple of Deleuze and feminism, sometime anti-
oedipalists, may paradoxically need to call on Freud to tie the knot.

THE EROTICS OF EMERGENCE: "BECOMING-ANIMAL, BECOMING-INTENSE, BECOMING-IMPERCEPTIBLE"

> Paradox is the pathos or the passion of philosophy.
>
> —Gilles Deleuze, *A Thousand Plateaus*

Deleuze is the poet laureate of intensity. His work sends a tremor through contemporary cultural theory; provocative and unsettling, it performs what he calls a deterritorialization, in a "line of flight" away from habits of thought.

This project of deterritorialization would seem to be consistent with the critical goals of feminism, questioning gender as a stable property of being. But Deleuze's strange world of abstract diagrams, apparatuses of capture, tribal despots, and ambulant war machines does seem to be pretty much a male realm—his nomad, his smith, his warrior-chief are all masculine constructs, armored, aggressive, high-velocity, often high-tech. His notorious essay on becoming-woman does not even mention woman in the title ("Becoming-Intense, Becoming-Animal, Becoming-Imperceptible," *A Thousand Plateaus*, chapter 10). And it is written from a masculine subject position: becoming-woman is described as the paradigmatic instance of changing "one's" perspective, "one's" very essence, "one's" very status as "one." Apparently, then, "one" is male.

What is more, in this white-hot lyric, Deleuze asserts that "becoming-woman" is a phase in a journey of diminishment: "If becoming-woman is the first quantum, or molecular segment, with the becomings-animal that link up with it coming next, what are they all rushing toward? Without a doubt, toward becoming-imperceptible" (279). Little wonder that this goal of "imperceptibility" has caused some alarm for feminists, who have worked so hard to be seen and heard.

Deleuze himself poses the crucial question: "But what does becoming-imperceptible signify, coming at the end of all the molecular becomings that begin with becoming-woman? . . . A first response would be: to be like everyone else" (279). This "response" offers little to dispel feminist objections, although being like everyone else is arguably one practical feminist goal, implying equality of opportunity. Yet Deleuze is critiquing any form of identity politics that entails staking out one's turf, engaging in a struggle for territory, pride of place.

The "Post-Man" Shrinketh: Becoming Molecular

If Deleuze fails to valorize the project of mainline feminism, he reserves his most mordant critique for Western Man as "molar" identity. Throughout his work, Deleuze opposes the "molecular" to the "molar," which concerns whole organisms and subjects. The molecular register, on the contrary, contemplates nonsubjective being at the level of chemical intensities, in a material micropolitics of becoming: "Yes, all becomings are molecular: the animal, flower, or stone one becomes are molecular collectivities, haeccities, not molar subjects, objects or forms that we know from the outside" (*A Thousand Plateaus*, 275). In other words, for Deleuze, becoming-woman is not a molar project concerning the rights of female individuals. He is interested in woman not as agent, conscious or unconscious, but as a "microfeminine" *property*. Nor is he concerned with the place of woman in society, since his whole molecular philosophy radically redefines place as *passage*:

> All we are saying is these indissociable aspects of becoming-woman must first be understood as a function of something else . . . emitting particles that enter the relation of movement and rest, or the zone of proximity, of a microfemininity, in other words, that produce in us a molecular woman, create the molecular woman. (275)

Deleuze goes so far as to assert that real women do not even enjoy an advantage in the intense trajectory of becoming: "We do not mean to say that a creation of this kind is the prerogative of the man, but on the contrary that the woman as a molar entity has to become-woman in order that the man also becomes—or can become—woman" (275–276).

This is just too much for some feminists. The real-life woman seems to drown in the cosmic molecular soup. Alas, microfemininity would seem to be the helpmate of macromasculinity in these co-ed adventures in intensity.

But in terms of the millennial episteme, this misunderstanding between Deleuze and feminism may be a false problem. What he seems to be evoking is the "deep ecology" that focuses on becoming as submergence as much as emergence, a mode that journeys deeper and deeper into the dimension of the "imperceptible." In other words, Deleuzian becoming is a formulation that sounds remarkably like Ilya Prigigone's shift of focus from being to becoming, but with a reverse trajectory. And like many nonlinear scientists and philosophers, Deleuze refuses to be pinned down to an "either/or" logic: "We fall into a false alternative if we say that you *either* imitate *or* you are. What is real is the becoming itself, the block of becoming, not the supposedly fixed terms through which becoming passes" (238).

This statement could serve as a manifesto for emergence.

Face-off: "Either" Deleuze "Or" Feminism?

Deleuze goes on to argue that a clear-cut distinction between the sexes is reductive:

> [Sexuality] is badly explained by the binary organization of the sexes, and just as badly by a bisexual organization with each sex. Sexuality brings into play too great

a diversity of conjugated becomings; these are like n sexes, an entire war machine through which love passes. (*A Thousand Plateaus*, 278)

For Deleuze, love observes no boundaries, "either male"/"or female." It is an intense mix-up:

What counts is that love itself is a war machine endowed with strange and somewhat terrifying powers . . . . Sexuality proceeds by way of the becoming-woman of the man and the becoming-animal of the human: an emission of particles. (278–279)

Deleuze's fantastic quantum love machine, this "emission of particles," might seem only to reassert a cliché (love as transformative intensity). However, Deleuze is strikingly original in arguing that becoming as a transgressive process is a question not of interaction between individuals, but of multiple linkages of intensities and energy. He asserts that "heterogeneous terms in symbiosis . . . cofunctioning by contagion, enter certain assemblages" (242), where multiplicity is "continually transforming itself into a string of other multiplicities" (249). So becoming-woman does not aim at the emancipation of an aggregate of same-sex subjects with a shared identity; it aims at tensile transformation of identity itself, in response to a deeper motive force. In fact, Deleuze's material rendering asserts that "what we call 'being in love,' a revealing term, is certainly a molecular identification, a commingling in *a line of flight*" (249; emphasis added). This amorous intertwining becomes textile, "a string of multiplicities," where "a fiber strung across borderlines constitutes a line of flight." "Identity" is the starting point of this flight, not the goal, for "the self is only a threshold, a door, a *becoming* between two multiplicities" (249, emphasis added).

Deleuze, then, might have no quarrel with feminism's goals for civil society, but his "becoming-intense" is not concerned with the same level of coherence as is the "becoming-ourselves" of feminism. Deleuze invokes an "altogether different conception of the plane," where no "one" is oneself:

Here, there are no longer . . . subjects or the formation of subjects. There is no structure, any more than there is genesis. There are only relations of movement and rest, speed and slowness between unformed elements . . . . There are only haecceities, affects, subjectless individuations that constitute collective assemblages. (266)

On this fibrous "plane of consistency or composition"—a nonmetric space which bears more than a passing resemblance to the fluid space of the new geometries—it is a question not only of being strung out but also of hanging together, in a textured manifold viscosity. One example of this kind of consistency is the tribal ritual of identification with the sacred totemic animal, where "be-coming" is not mimetic but transformative. The shamanistic communal ritual is an exponential identification (with a higher power) that transgresses identity:[33] "Becomings-animal are basically of another *power*, since their reality resides not in an animal one imitates . . . but in that which suddenly sweeps us up and makes us become—a proximity, an indiscernibility that extracts a shared element from the animal" (279). Read in light of Deleuze's evocation of innumerable genders (the "n sexes" cited in the epigraph), the term "power" may be read here in the literal mathematical sense, as an exponent, and even as a fractal, where each progression is a *diminishment* (x to the ½ power is larger than x to the ¼ power, and so on). This is an infinite sexuality of interstice, not a bilateral power struggle, and certainly not the familiar battle of the sexes.

Deleuze does oppose his transgressive molecular process to "majoritarian" domination, "privileging one term as standard: 'white,' 'male,' 'adult,' 'rational,' etc." (292). These characteristics take Man as center and make territory of all else, just as the cursor on the screen marks the center of one's writing at any given time: "It is this central Point that moves across all of space or the entire screen, and at every turn nourishes a certain distinctive opposition, depending on which facial-ity trait is retained: male-(female), adult-(child), white-(black, yellow, or red); rational-(animal)" (292).

As a result of the centrality of the norm, "there is no history but of the [male, white, rational] majority" (293). To undo this identification with the central "screen identity," the face of the majoritarian and the majoritarian subject of history, one has first to decenter "oneself." Becoming-woman is a first shift in becoming unwound, strung out, de-faced, destabilizing the conventions of the Total. Seen in this way, becoming-woman is an active minoritarian ethics, op-posed to identity politics of any sort: "This is the opposite of macropolitics, and even of History, in which it is a question of knowing how to win" (292).

In a further elaboration, Deleuze equates the majoritarian with a punctual metric form of thought, requiring the submission of the line to the infinite points that comprise it. (Euclid, of course, defines a line as the shortest distance between two points, a way of getting from here to there, privileging origin and end.) Deleuze calls traditional linear organization "arborescent," or "hierarchical." As a linear ordering that traces family tree as lineage, it is concerned with status, pro-gress, and ends. In contrast, rhizomatic becoming is not concerned with out-come: "A becoming is always in the middle, one can only get it by the middle. A becoming is neither one nor two [points], nor the relation of the two, it is the in-between, the border or line of flight" (293).

Significantly, then, Deleuze breaks *philosophically* with the premises of Euclidean geometry, rejecting the logic of line and point that grounds Euclid's geometrics.

Deleuze insists: "one does not reach becoming or the molecular, as long as a line is connected to two distant points, or is composed of two contiguous points" (293). Likewise, he insists that becoming breaks from the dominant historical memory, the narrative line of patriarchy:

> The line-system (or block-system) of becoming is opposed to the point-system of memory. Becoming is the movement by which the line frees itself from the point, and renders points indiscernible: the rhizome, the opposite of arborescence, a break away from arborescence. Becoming is an antimemory. (294)

"Antimemory" is a function of a recomposition, a radical change in consistency, a bond of intensity:

> A season, a winter, a summer, an hour, a date have a perfect individuality, lacking nothing, even though this individuality is different from that of a thing or a subject . . . they consist entirely of relations of movement and rest between molecules and particles, capacities to affect and be affected. (261)

Deleuze terms this nonlinear, relational mode of coherence *rhizomatic*: the "non-individuated unity" of a column of ants, a river, a crystal, a tangle of vines, a season, a weather system. In this radical atomistic materialism, even abstract notions like "winter" become functions of real material differences and intensities, *affordances*, capacities to affect and be affected. In other words, Deleuzian matter is a matter of affinity, or *Bahnungen*, as potential "facilitation."

In light of Deleuze's rhizomatic thinking, the face-off with feminism based on oppositional posturing is a false problem. For Deleuze discounts antagonistic face-offs, based on what "one" is. In fact, he is interested in taking the face off identity itself, since the "normal" mask is male, white, and adult. We could say that in Western majoritarian memory, woman originates as a secondary being. Eve is already the fruit of arborescent organization, brought forth from man at the foot of the genealogical tree, and promptly demoted to helper.

The originary myth of woman born of man is a classic Freudian instance of representation by the opposite. But in Deleuze's rhizomatic mode, it would seem that "woman" is not even a noun: the "woman" of "becoming-woman" is adjectival, tangential to the game of subjects and objects. In the term "becoming-woman," "woman" has the same syntactical force as the adjective "intense" or "animal," as in "animal magnetism." The most important term in "becoming-woman" is neither noun nor adjective, but the verbal gerund, designating "becoming" as a line of flight. Deleuze's world is not in stasis; woman is not a terminal; "she" is a potential, a valence.

> [Becoming] constitutes a zone of proximity and indiscernibility, *a no-man's land*, a nonlocalizable relation sweeping up the two distant or contiguous points, carrying one into the proximity of the other.
>
> —Gilles Deleuze, *A Thousand Plateaus*

Like many millennial theorists, Deleuze is attracted to Freud's case study of the psychotic Schreber, whose delusional transformation into "woman" causes him to become unmanned, losing "face" as a powerful political figure in Austrian society.[34]

Deleuze sees Schreber's transformation as an Other form of relation, the "inclusive disjunction" summed up in the paradoxical formulation "either . . . or . . . or . . . ." The importune third element, the extra "or," is an all-important tipping point that changes the configuration, leaving the inclusive disjunction suspended, and Schreber between sexes, a *third sex* of paradox.

> A disjunction that remains disjunctive and that still *affirms* the disjoined terms, that affirms throughout their entire distance, without restricting one by the other or excluding the other from the one, is perhaps the greatest paradox.
> "Either . . . or . . . or," instead of "either . . . or."[35]

Deleuze invokes the same paradoxical logic when speaking of cross-gendered Schreber and the mad poet Artaud: "[The schizophrenic] is man or woman, but he belongs precisely to both sides . . . like the two ends of a stick in a nondecomposable space [where] even the distances are positive" (*Anti-Oedipus*, 76). In this formulation ("man or woman") the "or" is an apposition, suggesting another possibility, not an exclusion. The schizophrenic has at least a double valence or potential.

In the same passage, Deleuze writes: "[the schizophrenic] does not abolish disjunction by identifying the contradictory elements by means of elaboration; instead, he affirms it through a continuous overflight spanning an indivisible distance" (76–77). The inclusive disjunction, in other words, obeys the logic of the Freudian unconscious. It is also uncannily reminiscent of the counterintuitive rules of quantum physics: a "continuous overflight" (quantum leap?) allows contradictory terms to coexist: . . . either . . . or . . . or. In a moving experience such as Schreber's, "one's entire soul flows into this emotion that makes the mind aware of the terribly disturbing sound of matter" (19).

Deleuze's own writing is filled by this "terribly disturbing sound of matter," intense and particular. It is rhizomatic, linked but various, thanks to the disjunction of his sources: Schreber, Freud, Proust, Woolf, Mozart, flower, insect, God, molecule. The very inappropriateness of these linkages may bring us full circle to our opening question. Can the emergence of a radically material gender theory link the odd couple of Deleuze and feminism?

Such an impossible *Bahnung* may be facilitated by a hook-up with millennial science, and with Freud.

No-Man's-Land: The Orchid and the Wasp

Deleuze often musters striking botanical and zoological images, providing a way to understand his theory that cannot be reduced to a passage from male-to-female. He says, for instance, that the schizophrenic "does not confine himself with contradictions; on the contrary he opens out, and, like a spore case inflated with spores, releases them as so many singularities that he himself had improperly shut off" (*Anti-Oedipus*, 77).

Or Deleuze may get away from the human register altogether, referring to a botanical-zoological becoming. As an illustration, he cites Proust's famous passage about the pollination of the orchid by the wasp, commingling in a reproductive assemblage:

> The orchid deterritorializes by forming an image, a tracing of a wasp, but the wasp reterritorializes on that image. The wasp is nevertheless deterritorialized, becoming a piece in the orchid's reproductive apparatus. But it reterritorializes the orchid by transporting its pollen. Wasp and orchid, as heterogeneous elements, form a rhizome. (*A Thousand Plateaus*, 10)

This hybrid rhizome results from a symbiotic exchange of functions, and of genetic code:

> It could be said that the orchid imitates the wasp, reproducing its image in a signifying fashion (mimesis, mimicry, lure, etc.). . . . At the same time, something else entirely is going on: not imitation at all but a capture of code, surplus value of code, an increase in valence, a veritable becoming, a becoming-wasp of the orchid and a becoming-orchid of the wasp. (10)

This extraordinary passage demonstrates how Deleuze obliquely invokes aspects of millennial science, to underwrite his own poetic version of becoming.

1. The "increase in valence" evokes the nonlinear exponential increase of far-from-equilibrium theory.
2. The mutual coding of orchid and wasp (their DNA encodes a resemblance, to further their reproductive aims) refers to genetic and information science.
3. The passage later refers to "lines that approach but never meet," alluding to non-Euclidean geometry (10).
4. "The aparallel evolution of two beings that have absolutely nothing to do with each other" (10) draws on nonlinear theories of evolution and biology, emphasizing

ecosystems, symbiosis, and synergy. Deleuze explicitly asserts that it is a matter of lateral systemic insect-flower networking, rather than the old evolutionary model of the line of evolutionary descent.

Above all, Deleuze's concept of relation insists that there is no subordination of one term to the other: "There is neither imitation nor resemblance, only an exploding of two heterogeneous series on a line of flight composed by a common rhizome that can no longer be attributed to or subjugated to anything signifying" (10). Like the disturbing Lacanian real discussed by Žižek (chapter 3 above), matter is not part of a narrative; it just is.

Thus, in the kernel argument of this avowed enemy of psychoanalysis, we find something like Lacan's imbrication of "being" in its Other (our desire is the desire of the Other). But Deleuze's linkage is explicitly a function of deep ecology, where entities are implicated not because of sameness (identification) but because of difference (Otherness). Sexual life is seen not as an action of one gendered subject on another, but as a reciprocal capture, where neither term simply conquers, "mimes," or even "lures" the other, but where two Others are transcoded materially, in their DNA.

> The line or block of becoming that unites the wasp and the orchid produces a shared deterritorialization: of the wasp, in that it becomes a liberated piece of the orchid's reproductive system; but also of the orchid, in that it becomes the object of an orgasm in the wasp, also liberated from its own reproduction. (10)

The wasp-orchid coupling is a dislocating identification that "forgets" the history of each separate organism, as it "becomes" other.

The wasp-orchid is the animation of a fundamental idea in Deleuze (the desiring machine). In a sense it is also the animation of a fundamental function in Lacan, as in the Schema L: heterogeneous serial couplings maintain difference, in a paradoxical encounter that always dislocates identity and refracts it into Otherness. The wasp-orchid hybrid also resonates with Freud's paradigm of productive "thirdness," the "oedipal" triangle that reroutes the beeline of the subject's desire to its object, deflecting desire through catalytic Otherness that changes its very nature. Deleuzian becoming is a reterritorialization of Freud, in spite of itself.

Oedipus Ludicrous

> The art of the aesthetic is humor, a physical art of signals and signs determining the partial solutions or cases of solution—in short, an implied art of intensive qualities.
>
> —Gilles Deleuze, *A Thousand Plateaus*

This quotation shows where Deleuze finds a specific model for his productive, three-part disjunction, his aesthetics of paradox. We recall that Freud deploys the disjunctive synthesis as a technique of wit, as a strategy for expressing impossible, incompatible, or forbidden truths (Freud's joker "put(s) an 'and' where an 'either, or' would suffice").[36] Freud's joke avails itself of absurdity to send a tremor through normal logic, and push it to the tipping point at which laughter breaks out.

It is, perhaps, rather amusing to find the author of Oedipus and the author of *Anti-Oedipus* on the same page, at least when it comes to wit as the play of differential intensities. Indeed, what Deleuze calls a schizoid experience, enacted in the juncture of the wasp-orchid and in Schreber's cross-dressing, is indeed a kind of "wit" in the Freudian sense, an encounter of intensities which transforms the participants. Eric Santner has written a brilliant account of the encounter between Schreber and proto-fascist society (*My Own Private Germany*),[37] where Schreber's unmanning is cast as a defensive psychic strategy to permit him not to identify with a fascist paternal order, resonating with Schreber's own humorless and pathologically disciplinary father (he invented "disciplinary" machines for training children). If Schreber's solution is not exactly comic in Santner's reading, it is certainly not tragic, and it is deeply witty. Schreber is over the top, over the edge, his psychosis putting him beyond the reach of the grim Austrian power structure. For Santner, Schreber's psychosis is unconsciously an act of solidarity with the most vulnerable others—women, Jews, homosexuals—targeted by the iron hand of Austrian power. Once "invested" as judge, Schreber immediately di-vests himself by psychosis, unmanning himself by literally shedding his masculine vestment to adorn himself in beribboned lingerie. And if Freud deterritorializes Deleuze's becoming as "wit," Deleuze in turn deterritorializes the Freudian unconscious, transforming it from a repository of repressed "wishes" to an interaction of material intensities ("the molecular unconscious"). Similarly, he transforms Freud's "identification" from a molar imitation to something molecular and material, captured in genetic code.

For Deleuze, this molecular identification is linked to creative "simulation," a travesty of identity:

> [Simulation] expresses those nondecomposable distances always enveloped in the intensities that divide into one another while changing their form. If identification is a nomination, a designation, then simulation is the writing corresponding to it, a writing that is strangely polyvocal, flush with the real. (*Anti-Oedipus*, 87)

Interestingly, in its "strangely polyvocal" quality, "flush with the real," Deleuze's own simulation resonates with l'écriture féminine practiced by French feminists writing at the same time (the late 1960s), in a transgressive and sensual mode of "emergent" desire. The feminists of immanence are proximate to what Deleuze calls "the terribly disturbing sound of matter": Luce Irigaray joyously calls for a fluid, nonphallic writing, resonating with female orgasm (*Ce sexe qui n'en est pas un*); while the explosive corporeal wit of Hélène Cixous ("Le rire de la Méduse") calls for woman to fight back with riotous laughter at the pathetic male penis, or, even more comically, to "write with her milk."[38]

Certain essays by Julia Kristeva in particular (as in the lyrically violent "Stabat Mater") share the atomized sense of interacting intensities found in Deleuze. In fact, Kristeva's lurid/ecstatic passages on motherhood as self-annhilation are imbued with her own transformative experience, becoming-(m)other. In another famous essay, "Women's Time," Kristeva describes pregnancy as a becoming-other that saturates the very atoms of the maternal body, invaded by a beloved parasite. Indeed, Kristeva's essays—including those that invoke the rhythm of the maternal body as *chora*, a liquid "song" heard in *utero*—embody Deleuze's call for a writing that belongs to the realm of physics. In the l'*écriture féminine* of the French feminists, the body and its intensities are not metaphors, but the interplay of matter-energy itself.

The immanent feminists *resonate* with Deleuze, but they often refer to Freud, and particularly to the case history of Schreber—as paraphrenic man-woman who undercuts fixed gender identity and refuses the "honor" of patriarchal authority. And of course, feminists idolize the rebellious Dora, immortalized in the famous case study as the woman who walked out on Freud. Ironically, however, "The Case of Dora"—often invoked as a demonstration of Freud's sexism—actually depicts "either . . . or . . . or" sexuality, perhaps even more significantly than the Schreber case. Dora occupies the position of heterosexual subject (as "female," but also as "male," since her libido is in the active subject position, when she desires her father, Herr K, and Freud himself). But she also simultaneously occupies the ambiguous gender position of homosexual subject, desiring Frau K (who is also "Mother/Madonna" in her fantasy); as well as being the classic feminine object desired and exchanged as a commodity by the men.[39] Like Deleuze's work exhibiting "n sexes," Freud's study of Dora deploys an overdetermined gender, unfolding in multiple dimensions and connections, but never as a "simply" feminine function of woman/victim.

Thus Freudian theory may actually facilitate a certain feminist notion of subjectivity, when read through Deleuzian deep ecology. Reading Freud with Deleuze enables a close reading of Freud's theory of gender as *position*, inflected differently in different cultural configurations and situations that "one" is "passing through."

The odd coupling of Deleuze-Freud does not abandon sexual difference, even if both question essential sexual roles. Their hybrid "desiring machine" shows that "man-woman" is not sexed in the conventional way, as a fixed being whose anatomy confers a fixed destiny. Yet motile desire will always be a marker of the sexual *as* difference, and as differential intensity, rather than opposition.

In a sense, high-tech "millennial" feminism—in the work of Haraway, Stone, Anne Balsamo, Rosi Braidotti, Avital Ronell—also resonates with Deleuze, re-counting monstrous couplings in the trajectory of serial becoming. Their "post-gender" cyborgs—not unlike Deleuze's wasp-orchid, borrowed from another "unmanned" poetic intensity (Proust)—are not postsexual or asexual, but multi-sexual, polymorphously perverse.[40] Nor does Haraway stop the linkage at the boundary between organic and inorganic: her hybrid desiring-machines push the boundaries of what human beings are ("we are all chimeras . . ."; "we are all cyborgs" . . .). Haraway's millennial feminism rejoices in permeable boundaries and overdetermined gender, actually promoting gender "contamination" as pollination, an injunction to expanded potential.

The kind of "posthumanist" gender theory that Haraway propounds, however scary, may in fact help put the humanity back into the human, by paradoxically stressing its connections with other forms of life, organic and inorganic. Her cyber-feminism, while consistent with Deleuze's radical materialism, is also unthinkable without the Freudian critique of positivist reason that dismantles the masculinist "Rational Man." The ultimate paradox is that "man" loses "manhood," his majoritarian identity, by becoming-intense, but that this loss is enabling. Drag is "becoming" to Schreber, as to the orchid.

It is not in spite of Freud, but thanks to him, that millennial thinkers are effecting a cross-gendered game of lure and alliance. The "surviving" of the fittest becomes the conniving of the wittiest, as when the orchid "cross-dresses" to fool the wasp. In the molecular play of intensities, the orchid is a transvestite that lures the wasp with its witty materiality.

But Schreber is also into witty material: according to Santner's reading, his psyche "cross-dresses" to evade the fascist lure, dressing down authority by dressing up. In fact Deleuze insists that a certain activism must function at the level of creative intensities, always "far from equilibrium," shaking things up:

> A punctual system is most interesting when there is a musician, painter, writer or philosopher to oppose it, who even fabricates it in order to oppose it, like a springboard to jump from. History is made only by those who oppose history (not by those who insert themselves into it, or even reshape it). (*A Thousand Plateaus*, 295)

Like Deleuze, some feminists have always understood that history is made by those who play the game wittily in order to alter its rules. Like the orchid and the wasp, Deleuzian thought and feminist thought meet in an inclusive disjunction at the site of Freudian "otherness." The Deleuzian theory of gender as avatar, like the millennial paradigm of becoming that gives rise to it, is not limited to the politics of reassignment or conquered territory. It remains far from equilibrium, a matter of passionate paradox.

FRACTAL FREUD: SUBJECT AS REPLICANT

Roger Groce, *Sierpinski's Tetrahedron*, 2004.

Fractal geometry is not just a chapter of mathematics, but one that helps Everyman to see the same world differently.

—Benoit Mandelbrot, *Fractal Geometry of Nature*

Thanks to wireless communication, we have become used to a phenomenon that would have puzzled us just a few years ago: calling someone and asking them where they are when they answer. To be sure, human space has been increasingly dislocated over the last century, since Einstein disqualified time and space as stable grounds for our existence. We have seen that this shift may be in part characterized as a move from the reference of fixed perspective and determinate measure to the fluid space of non-Euclidean geometry. This shift is of interest to psychoanalysis and philosophy precisely because it unsettles the perception of the central place of humanity in the greater scheme of things.

One of the best-known instances of this spatial paradigm shift is the fractal geometry of Benoit Mandelbrot, which has been around for only a couple of decades, but which has already shaken age-old habits of perception by changing the conventions of dimension and closure.[1]

The Elliptical Era

In good old Euclidean geometry, a line was the shortest way to get from one point to the next. In the twenty-first century, however, the point has lost its status as terminus. Now it is a coordinate of phase space, designating just one in a set of possible positions in a moving system (for instance, "heads" and "tails" together make up the phase space of a tossed coin). Plotting of phase space involves tracing a sequence of potentially infinite points—like stop-action images of a pendulum's swinging trajectory. One plots a punctual series rather than drawing a solid line connecting point of origin with endpoint, which is a figurative practice that reinforces the teleological bias that linearity sustains. For ways of plotting and measuring the world are ideological in valence, and bolster the worldview that gives rise to them.

The familiar dimensions of Euclidean space, for instance, start with a straight line (a single dimension). As in Aristotle's classic concept of linear narrative, there is a beginning, a middle, and an end. Thus all interim points are subsumed by the model of linearity that privileges closure: interim points are only means to a determined end. And of course, the privileging of "straight thinking" as "the shortest distance between two points" is consistent with the classic ethic of profit, where the yield is increased by eliminating any divergence from a concern for the bottom line. Little wonder, then, that habits of perception die hard. Many people become queasy at the mere mention of current mathematical theories of a multidimensional universe (the estimates range from eleven to twenty-six dimensions, depending on how you calculate).

In any case, mapping the millennial zeitgeist calls for a modality that departs from linear opposition of two points in a causal order (if/then; before/after; either/or). The "age of becoming" might better be represented with the locution "from . . . toward," suggesting a dynamic of complex and contingent *progression*, rather than incremental *progress* to an end, or its simple reversal, tracing a direct line back from the end to a root cause. Rather than "making a point," the ellipsis of becoming (from . . . toward) connotes a phase space of suspended potential (to be continued . . .). Some prominent aspects of this elliptical opening might be schematized as in table 7.1.

The new models reflect a perception of physical reality that has been developing ever since Riemannian geometry acknowledged that there can be no straight line on a curved globe (and thus, real triangles, with less than straight sides and slightly oblique angles, contain less than 180 degrees). This is what parallel lines look like in Riemann's "no corners" world:[2]

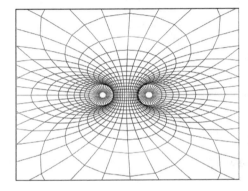

Roger Groce, *Riemann Web*, 2004.

Another non-Euclidean geometry—called "pixelated" or taxicab geometry— puts back the corners: it plots *all* space in perpendicular grids, like a taxi navigating in city blocks. (Any urban cabbie knows that the shortest distance between two points is not a line.) Similarly, Mandelbrot's fractal geometry engages the real world rather than an ideal concept of planes and solids—in the 1960s, the Father of Fractality merely began to notice what is actually out there in the world, pointing out that traditional science only pretends that nature is orderly, and that the Emperor, in effect, has no clothes.

The shift to fractious paradigms in math, science, and philosophy has correlates in art and literature: the recursive irony of the postmodern novel (Auster, Beckett, Pynchon) includes experimentation with nonlinear time frame and

Table 7.1

From	Toward	Instances
Euclidean plane geometry	differential geometries	Riemannian space, topological geometry, fractal geometry
linearity	nonlinearity	chaos, complexity, emergent systems, fractals
three-dimensional space	multidimensional space	10–26 dimensions of string theory, space-time, fractal dimensions, many-worlds theory, Deleuze's "holey space"
one-point Renaissance perspective	perspectivism	relational cosmology, topological objects, space-time, deconstruction
idealist philosophy	materialist philosophy, transhuman philosophy, deep ecology	Deleuze's "molecular unconscious," the new cosmologies, unified field theory incorporating string theory and "branes"
Newtonian physics	post-Einsteinian physics	particle theory, field theory, string theory, quantum theory, uncertainty principle
biology ("life itself")	cybernetics, inorganic "life"	artificial intelligence, artificial life, deep ecology
realist art	cubism, computer art, fractal art	Escher, computer "fracta" art
inanimate tool	intelligence	bot, cyborg, computer
ideal of progress	progression	nonlinear knowledge fields
sociology	cultural memetics	replication theory, "memes"
individual	set, system, "population," desiring machine	set theory, systems theory, complexity theory
Cartesian *cogito*, unified subject, "I think, therefore I am"	decentered or split subject, Freud	Lacan, "our desire is the desire of the Other"
mimesis, representation, copying	iteration, replication	cloning, fractals
linear narrative	recursive narrative, deep ecology, imagery	Calvino, Auster, Volodine, Perec's "deep ecology"

refracted point of view. (Calvino and Auster, for instance, both use simultaneous alternate or embedded narratives, involving reader and author as character.) More recently, in the post-postmodern work of writers like Perec or Eco, we find a deep ecology of interstitial description, going deeper and deeper into the opening frame, like a zoom lens.

These are but schematic examples of a shift from the worldview governed by commensurability (where every action has an opposite and equal reaction) toward the weird possibilities being seriously considered by science today, such as the infinite parallel universes that seem to be predicted by quantum logic.[3]

Even scientific method is unruly of late; studies of the effect of perspective document that the experimenter's investment has an influence on the experiment's outcome, sometimes apparently even influencing the path of matter itself. In Freudian terms, the new science acknowledges that cathexis determines the field it invests.

These shifts provide new angles on old questions: the investigation into what it is to be human must now consider the concepts of self-organizing matter, multidimensionality, relativity, and the effect of background as determinative frame rather than ground or center. One illustration of this change is suggested by Ian Marshall and Danah Zohar (*Who's Afraid of Schrödinger's Cat?*), when they consider the question of the correct dimension of an object. They point out that a ball of string, seen from far off, is a point (nondimensional); from a closer perspective it looks like a flat circle (two- dimensional); nearby it is a three-dimensional sphere; closer up, it is a thread (a one-dimensional line); closer still, the thread becomes a three-dimensional woven strand. The "correct" calculation depends entirely on the viewer's frame; there is no right answer concerning the dimension of "string."[4] (This example provides a visual equivalent of the Derridean concept of "undecidability" in the field of philosophy.)

Psychoanalysis makes a similar move dimensionalizing "identity." We still say "I," just as Descartes did, but thanks to Freud we understand that the subject position has dimensions not accessible to consciousness, popping up in pesky errors or slips of the tongue. And Freud insisted that this unconscious dimension is real, however resistant it may be to ordinary logic. (There is nothing mystical or even fictional about psychic reality for Freud. This is why his controversial abandonment of the seduction theory cannot be considered a questioning of the veracity of the female patient's experience, as some feminists have argued. Psychic reality *is* reality, for Freud.)

This suggests that the dimensionality of the Freudian psyche might qualify as a fractal concept, coinciding with other millennial models. For our era has seen the emergence of a fractal physics (chaos, complexity, and systems theory), a fractal aesthetics (Escher and beyond, including fractal computer art). There is even a fractal philosophy (Deleuze and Derrida) which exposes the conceit of absolute center or closure in systems of human meaning, which are always relational, contingent, interactive, and subject to new vicissitudes. One could argue that if the age of millennialism is emergent, nonlinear, and systemic, it is perhaps because of its reflexive quality, whereby science and culture reflect on their own capacity to be . . . emergent, nonlinear, and systemic. The term for reflexive repetitions of this sort is iteration, used in "deconstructive" philosophy as well as fractal mathematics. Iteration gives rise to increasing complexity—as the repetition of a repetition—by feeding in the result of the preceding calculation as the first term in the next round.

Fractal Fleas and Other Riddles

> Clouds are not spheres, mountains are not cones, coastlines are not circles, and bark is not smooth, nor does lightning travel in a straight line. Responding to this challenge, I conceived and developed a new geometry of nature.
>
> —Benoit Mandelbrot, *Fractal Geometry of Nature*

Roger Groce, *Nature Fractals*, 2004.

Mandelbrot noted that as soon as one leaves the laboratory, the real world gets messy, displaying curious dimensional properties (a river, for example, is *between* two dimensions—a one-dimensional line—and a two-dimensional plane). He set out to show how the material world really works, rather than how ideal forms behave in theory. He observed that many figures in nature resemble themselves at any scale at which they are examined (a snowflake is made of snowflake shaped crystals; a tree trunk has branches that have branches that have leaves with an arboreal veining). But it is important to note that a fractal differs from a simply *repeated* form, if only to keep from justifying Baudrillard's fear of "the hell of sameness." Just what are the characteristics of Mandelbrot's self-similar world?

It Depends on How You Look at It

Scientific dictionaries give a range of different definitions for the term "fractal," referring to diverse fields. Let us examine four representative definitions, beginning with the concept of the fractal in nature.

> **fractal** (1) [French *fractale*, from Latin *fractus*: broken, uneven]
> First appeared 1975: in nature, any of various extremely irregular curves or shapes that repeat themselves at any scale on which they are examined.
> —(Discovery.com/science)

The next definition shows that when this examination of nature is performed up close, through a microscope (looking at a snowflake, for instance), a "geometric" structure emerges.

> **fractal** (2) a geometric object *which looks similar to itself* under a magnifying glass.
> —(about.com/science)

The third definition indicates that studying the self-similar geometry of fractals poses a challenge to "measurability" itself:

> **fractal** (3) in mathematics and physics, a very irregular line or surface that is formed of an endless number of sections, *so that its dimensions or other physical properties are always only approximations.*
> —(*Random House Dictionary*)

The fourth definition highlights even more bizarre properties of fractals, including interstitial dimensions:

> **fractal** (4) a geometrical or physical structure having an irregular or fragmented shape **at all scales of measurement** between a greatest and smallest scale such that

certain mathematical or physical properties **behave as if the dimensions of the structure (*fractal dimensions*) are greater than the spatial dimensions.**

–(Dictionary.com)

These odd fractional dimensions have strange properties: they behave "as if" they have more dimensions than can be accounted for in the regular 3D world. These "iffy" dimensions reside in between the three dimensions to which we are accustomed. One popular geometry website explains:

> Dimensional conventional geometry is concerned with regular shapes and whole-number dimensions, such as lines (one-dimensional) and cones (three-dimensional). But fractal geometry deals with shapes found in nature that have non-integer, or fractal, dimensions—like rivers with a fractal dimension of about 1.2 and conelike mountains with a fractal dimension between 2 and 3.[5]

Suddenly the most familiar objects in nature—rivers, trees, clouds—don't seem so familiar, or even so natural, any more.

Meanwhile back in the classroom, the generation of fractal objects is done by steps. Here is the recipe for the generation of an increasingly complex snowflake, for instance: divide a triangle into triangles one third its size. Paste the scaled-down triangles around the perimeter. Repeat. And repeat . . . and repeat. This process produces a famous fractal, the Koch snowflake. Viewed close up, each segment produced by the algorithm, at any scale, is still the "Koch curve." The process is a good illustration of fractal definition two: "any object that looks similar to itself under a magnifying glass."

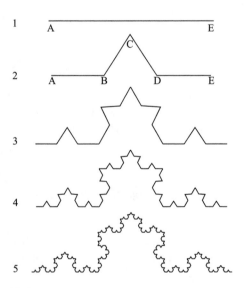

Koch curve.

For if we zoom in on a section of image 5, we see section 4; zooming in on the first third of image 4 reveals image 3; and so on. This points out another interesting characteristic: fractal definitions always seem to be connected with optical-ity—they are self-similar "on any scale at which they are *observed or examined*." Each new iteration adds ever more minuscule triangles—thus the calculated *area* of the object increases each time, even while the *size* of the actual object does not: the iterations are all embedded in the original recipe. For, observing the iterations of the Koch snowflake, one can intuit that they are based on what Mandelbrot termed "recursive self-similarity"—in this case, structures that are embedded or nested in larger versions of themselves. A well-known example of this interstitial quality may be seen in Sierpinski's triangle, which opens to more and more dimensions with each step.

On the Brink of Chaos: Fractal Poetics

Since Mandelbrot also worked on chaos theory, there is sometimes a confusion between chaotic systems and fractals. But even though chaotic systems sometimes produce fractal shapes, there is no necessary relation between the two. To com-plicate matters further, chaos theory itself is misnamed—it has nothing to do with lack of order. "Chaos" is defined as "*nonpredictable* behavior arising in a deter-ministic dynamic because of sensitivity to initial conditions" (*Free Online Dictionary of Computing*). A butterfly wing flaps in North America, causing a tidal wave in Asia. While this result cannot be predicted, it is rigorously determined.

What fractals and chaos do have in common is exponential progression (2 squared + 2 cubed + 2 to the fourth) rather than linear accretion (2 + 2 + 2). Chaos cannot be predicted, but it may come to an end, and we may often measure its effects after the fact (as in a rolling blackout, a particularly millennial happen-stance). But fractals can never be completed; and their measure is always only ap-proximate.

Although fractality seems like a brave new concept, fractals have been with us as ornament for some time. (Many of the patterns in Islamic art, for instance, are fractal shapes.) In fact, way back in 1733, Jonathan Swift was already thinking frac-tally, in a colorful verbal rendition of iteration:

So, Nat'ralists observe, a Flea
Hath smaller Fleas that on him prey,
And these have smaller fleas to bite 'em,
And so proceed ad infinitum.[6]

In 1989, Mandelbrot formalized the same idea, although he emphasized that self-similar structures in nature "may be slightly deformed or irregular . . . whatever the scale of examination."[7] In other words, while Mandelbrot would agree that Swift's fleas are feeding on each other at an infinite range of magnitudes, he would insist that these are not the *same* fleas at every scale. The notion of fractality contains a play between sameness and difference, not unlike the conventional formula for metaphor. This paradoxical quality, combined with the sublime aspect of a figure that recedes into infinity, may account in part for the poetic and visual appeal of fractals.

In the last century, Richard Lewison provided an updated version of Swift's reflection on fractal vermin, this time focusing on a dynamic system:

Big whorls have little whorls,
Which feed on their velocity;
And little whorls have lesser whorls,
And so on to viscosity.[8]

The Age of Interstice

The appeal of fractality is still going strong in the twenty-first century.

With the advent of the new media, fractal visuals have entered pop culture (the projection of images by lasers, for instance, produces holograms, where each fragment contains the whole, projected at a slightly different angle).

Fractals may also appeal to our optically inclined century because the concept includes the act of viewing itself (fractals "resemble themselves at whatever scale they are *examined*"). What is more, fractality implies perspectivism: the fractal cannot be produced without taking into account the position from which one is observing (the "scale"). The fractal mode figures prominently in many emerging fields:

1. Information/media: the *Free Online Dictionary of Computing* definition of hypertext is "text and graphics interconnected in such a way that a reader of the material (at a computer terminal) can discontinue reading one document at certain points in order to consult other related matter." Hypertext is embedded and open-ended, porous and multidimensional. It affords a fragmented, discontinuous reading, where the reader may zoom in and out of sites on the Web, in linked "hits" that are similar insofar as they all produce websites. Some theorists of artificial intelligence

even picture the Internet itself as a global fractal, a vast brain where each inter-linked computer replicates the whole.

2. Astronomy/cosmology: Some scientists today speculate that the cosmos has a fractal arrangement, with patterns iterated at every scale (spiral clusters of galaxies revolve around a center, just as our own spiral Milky Way galaxy does, as well as our solar system, and even the atoms of which it is comprised).

3. Genetics: Because each cell has DNA in its nucleus, the cell is in a sense a fractal microcosm of the organism.

4. Optics: The familiar fractal tilings of Escher have proliferated on the Internet, and fractal computer art is flourishing at myriad websites, allowing visitors to generate and manipulate images.

5. Poststructuralist philosophy and aesthetics: Fractal "dimensionalization" emphasizes "suspension" or undecidability (as in Derridean deconstruction), a rethinking of linearity (as in Deleuze), and the reevaluation of the concept of closure (as in Gödel's incompletedness theorem).[9]

All of these new models suggest new ways of conceptualizing relatedness outside of linear paradigms. Above all, these various instances of fractal modality solicit a radical rethinking of dimension.

Fractal Philosophy: Deleuze, Desire, Dimension

In chapter 6, which dealt with Deleuze's materialist philosophy of becoming, we saw that, like the concept of "holey space," Deleuze's notion of emergence depends on a reconceptualization of line and dimension. Deleuzian space replaces conventional linearity with a nomadic trajectory, "a deterritorializing line of flight" (in his extended insect metaphor). This is a potentially infinite itinerary of zigzagging points, rather than a (poorly named) beeline straight from beginning to end. Mandelbrot foregrounded a similar fragmentary line, composed of interstices, and called it "Cantor's Dust":

> One of the most famous fractal dimensions lies between the zero dimension and the first dimension, the point and the line. It is created by "middle third erasing" where you start with a line and remove the middle third; two lines remain from which you again remove the middle third; then remove the middle third of the remaining segments; and so on into infinity. What remains after all of the middle third removals is called by Mandelbrot "Cantor's Dust." It consists of an infinite number of points, but no length.[10]

A fractal dimension, mathematically, is indicated by a fractional exponent ($1^{1.1}$, $1^{1.11}$, $1^{1.111}$). These interim dimensions may be visually evoked by Sierpinski's sponge, where a figure is more than a plane and less than a depth:

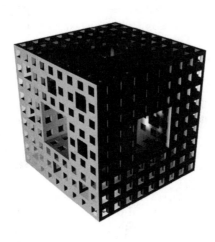

Roger Groce, *Sierpinski Sponge*, 2004.

The form is made by hollowing eight squares around one, with eight more squares hollowed out around that one, and so forth.[11] As the process continues, the "volume" approaches hollowness, but never reaches it. The object is between two and three dimensions.

Interestingly, this figure has a conceptual equivalent in the social philosophy of Deleuze, elaborated in the interstitial reaches of *A Thousand Plateaus*: "holey space" is *between* territorial measured space (the "striated space" of settled nations) and fluid space ("smooth space," the plains and deserts of nomadic tribes). Deleuze suggests that the honeycombed interim of holey space is the domain of metallurgists. For their mines riddle the earth, while the ambulant circuits of metalworkers (smith and tinker) are neither settled nor nomadic: "This hybrid metallurgist, a weapon and toolmaker . . . communicates with the sedentaries and the nomads at the same time. Holey space itself communicates with smooth space and striated space."[12]

Deleuze's philosophic elaboration of interstitial space some decades ago now seems prescient, given the current interest concerning "holey" phenomena like black holes and worm holes in space. Some scientists suggest that this kind of space may some day afford a gateway to other universes, or even permit time travel.

Four dimensions, more or less

Interstitial dimension is one counterintuitive aspect of fractal geometry; but it is equally hard to wrap our three-dimensional minds around the concept of a fourth dimension, let alone the multiple dimensions beyond that. The experts themselves propose a number of ways of conceptualizing higher dimensions, which may help us learn to think in the counterintuitive ways required for the fractal universe.[13]

1. *Time* Following Einstein, some theorists characterize the fourth dimension as time, conceiving of the cosmos as phase space. A moving object requires this time coordinate: a pendulum must be plotted in all four dimensions of phase space, to "locate" it in motion. Thus the fourth dimension is the condition of transition or transformation. Time is a coordinate determining a *relative* position in phase space, with a fascinating result. Simultaneity is no longer an intrinsic relation between two events; it exists only as *a relation between two events and a particular observer.* "In general, events at different locations that are simultaneous for one observer will not be simultaneous for another observer."[14]

It would seem that even "synchronicity"—a new age concept popularized in the runaway beststeller *The Celestine Prophecy*—is a function of *triangulated* perspective.[15]

2. *Magnitude* In math, the power to which a base is raised is its dimension. In space, a line has one dimension $[x^1]$, a square with two sides has two dimensions, drawn on a plane $[x^2]$, a cube has three dimensions $[x^3]$ and must be plotted in a 3D graph. But a base to the *fourth* power $[x^4]$ becomes hard to visualize. One way to think of it is as a theater curtain (or a computer monitor) with a three-dimensional world in front, and an additional one behind the scenes in back.

3. *Overdetermined World ("Many Worlds Theory")* A visual approximation of a four-dimensional cube would show three-dimensional worlds "stacked" on each other.[16] In the figure below, each of the six faces of the three-dimensional cube is extended in three dimensions, with an additional one peeking out from behind, in the fourth dimension, as if occupying the space "behind" the page.[17]

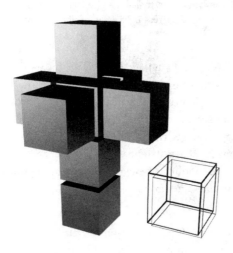

In the second figure above, the additional dimension is rendered as internal, hollowed-out. The transparency indicating the intersection between two overlapping cubes gives us a glimpse of the interstices "inside the inside"; this, as we will see, is a concept crucial to understanding Lacan's view of the subject.

4. *Graphic Coordinate* A dimension is a function of the number of points needed to plot an object's space (two points on a horizontal/vertical graph are needed to plot a plane; three are needed to plot a volume).

Extension in space increases dimension: a zero-dimensional point, when extended, becomes a one-dimensional line; the line extended in space describes a two-dimensional square; the square extended in space becomes a cube. Now, if you move the cube, the fourth dimension characterizes the position of the traveling cube, as "phase space." It is inherently interstitial, "on the way" to another position. (Analogically, the fifth dimension might be thought of as the ability to occupy two spaces at the same time, like an electron in quantum theory). Or, as an online tutorial on dimension explains it, one can think of the higher dimensions as *negative* coordinates on a graph, points plotted to the left of the central vertical axis.

> One direction is chosen as positive and the other as negative; a point on a plane is specified by an ordered pair of numbers (x, y) giving its distances from the two coordinate axes; a point in space is specified by an ordered triple of numbers (x, y, z) giving its distances from three coordinate axes. Mathematicians are thus led by analogy to define an ordered set of four, five, or more numbers as representing a point in what they define as a space of four, five, or more dimensions. Although such spaces cannot be visualized, they may nevertheless be physically significant. The state of the weather or the economy, in current models, is a point in a many-dimensional space.[18]

Mathematically, this means that imaginary numbers (such as the square root of 2) may be mapped in space. This is called a "complex plane" in hyperbolic geometry, which, emphasizing "site" as so many millennial paradigms do, actually considers real and imaginary numbers as occupying two different domains or "places."[19] Again, this recalls Freud's notion of two incommensurate domains—conscious and unconscious—in one psychic system that may operate "beyond" ordinary consciousness. This negative coordinate would be the graphic equivalent of the world "behind" the theater curtain or computer screen, in the example suggested above.

5. *Compact Stringy Space* Finally, some ten or eleven dimensions are mathematically necessary to elaborate superstring theory in physics. The extra dimensions are

packed into "regular space" because there are so many possible ways to make dimensions much smaller than the other four in string theory. This is a process of *compactification* of space-time. Alternatively, some theorists argue that higher dimensions are accommodated in other universes occupying different "branes." This is called M-theory, first proposed by Alan Witt.

In every case above, fractal vision has inserted difference and interstice into geometry, generating an open-ended possibility. Freud's correlate is the site of unconscious *desire*, permeable and inexhaustible.

Fractal dimensions have always existed, of course, in the "natural" order all around us, but they remained unobserved—perhaps out of an ardent human desire for (fore)closure—until Mandelbrot looked up from his math problems, out the window of his study, and *saw* the coastline. The rest, as they say, is history.

2: LACANIAN LINKS

How can it be that mathematics, being after all a product of human thought independent of experience, is so admirably adapted to the objects of reality?
—Albert Einstein, NBC radio interview, 1942

The Sublime Necklace

In a 1957 essay ("The Instance of the Letter in the Unconscious," sometimes rendered incorrectly as "The Insistence of the Letter in the Unconscious"), Lacan asserts that language is a *signifying chain*; it makes meaning by "hooking" one word with another, in an ongoing linkage. In the same essay, he proposes an even more colorful figure for his word-chain, this time describing it as a necklace of linked rings. But this is no ordinary bauble. It is actually a fractal figure: "With the second property of the signifier, that of combining according to the laws of a closed order, is affirmed the necessity of the *topological* substratum of which the term I ordinarily use, namely, the *signifying chain*, gives an approximate idea: *rings of a necklace that is a ring in another necklace made of rings.*"[20]

This sentence shows that several decades before the term fractal came into wide usage, Lacan was already thinking fractally and topologically. Indeed, the definition of a fractal as "any object that resembles itself when observed under a microscope" applies beautifully to Lacan's figure of language as "rings of a necklace that is a ring in another necklace made of rings." His theory of language, elaborated way back in 1957, is couched in terms that have become current today, evoking complexity, dimension, and open-ended (far-from-equilibrium) systems.

Lacan's intriguing formulation is a figure in the Freudian sense, an overdetermined symptomatic representation ("rings" and "links" representing cathexis).

Antoine's knot.

It is also a figure in the sense that I have used in this book: that is, it provides an *instance* of what it illustrates (the formula "a ring in a necklace that is another necklace made of rings" is itself a chain where one term is hooked into and replicates the next). It comes as no surprise, then, that Lacan's linguistic necklace is related by more than metaphor to the field of topological geometry: it aptly describes one of the well-known objects of this science, Antoine's knot, which provides a link between chapter 5, on Freud and knots, and this one, on Freud and fractals.

The Knot Plot website defines *Antoine's necklace* with an algorithm:

> Antoine's Necklace: Beginning with a single torus, the necklace is the limit of a sequence where each step replaces a torus with N linked tori. It is known that a function exists whose critical set is exactly the necklace.[21]

In other words, beginning with one circle (link/torus/donut/ring), one can generate a fractal figure of multiple links, by repeating the specified operation over and over, always inserting the product of the operation as the beginning of the next step. One starts by imagining a large torus, comprised in turn of a chain of smaller linked tori. If one goes down to the next level, armed with a good magnifying glass, one sees that each of the tori in the first torus is in turn made of a chain of linked tori. Each closer investigation at each successively smaller level—

each successive iteration—produces a more complex detailed picture, where each examined ring is made of another circle of smaller rings. But it is important to remember that all these donut-links are always-already contained within the original large donut—the set of tori named "Antoine's necklace." ("It is known that an exact set exists which is the necklace.") This process is neither linear nor incremental, since the original donut does not increase in size or surface, but only in complexity, exponentially rather than incrementally. If each ring is made of ten rings, for instance, in just four steps we go from ten to ten thousand rings.

Lacan gives his own example in passing, without alluding explicitly to Antoine's necklace, and we do not know if he had that figure in mind. But whether the reference to the topological figure is intentional or not, it is significant that Lacan has landed on a fractal as image of the signifying chain (language/culture). For, like so much of his language, it serves as "the figure of a figure" with exponential implications.

The Fractal Knot

As Lacan points out, "tout signifiant est un noeud"—every word is a knot of meaning. Language does not simply unfold along a line: it spins off into many directions, from a knotted bundle in (at least) three dimensions (four, if you count the time dimension in which the multiple iterations of speech unfold).[22] Thus Lacan's fractal necklace is a macramé, where each word is a node with other meanings knotted around it.

Lacan's necklace goes beyond the linearity of the chain in another way as well, since the image itself contains an algorithm for its extension, in decorative flourishes: a chain of knots made of another chain of knots, and so forth, ad infinitum. Like so many millennial phenomena, Lacan's necklace is far from equilibrium, exceeding a finite stable representation. It is an engineering diagram, in Deleuze's terminology, for the inherent self-generating and replicating motive force of language.

The algorithm could be traced like this:

Lacan's figure of the "necklace" exemplifies the signifying chain;
- the signifying "chain" in its turn structures and exemplifies "language";
- "language" in turn structures and exemplifies the "unconscious";
- the "unconscious" in turn structures and exemplifies the (split) psyche;
- the (split) psyche in turn structures and exemplifies the "subject";
- the "subject" in turn structures and exemplifies the intersubjective relation;
- the intersubjective relation in turn structures and exemplifies the social fabric.

Lacan's elegant necklace, then, may serve as a link between the two preceding chapters—on topology (chapter 5) and emergence (chapter 6)—and the topic of this chapter: the many dimensions of "Fractal Freud."

Linguistic Hook-ups: The Geneology of the Fractal Subject

Given the propensity of millennial theory to focus on *instance and performativity*, often selecting examples that do what they describe, it is worth noting that the intellectual genealogy of Lacan's concept of signifying chain is *itself* a fractal, a signifying chain of replicated theories, each embedded in and linked to the next. Lacan explicitly links the notion of "letter" (the material word, spoken or written on the page) to Roman Jakobson's well-known structural model of language, which Lacan replicates and expands in "The Instance of the Letter." And before Lacan, Jakobson was explicitly hooking up with the theory of Ferdinand de Saussure, the pioneer of structural linguistics who first started calling words "signifiers."[23] Working at the turn of the nineteenth century, Saussure pointed out that "signifiers" (actual material words, written or uttered) have no "natural" meaning, no privileged link to the concept or object to which they refer: signifiers function only *systemically and relationally*, by interacting with other words. (There is no reason why the word "horse," rather than the word "tree," could not designate a woody, leafy plant, to use Saussure's example. It is a merely matter of social convention, a shared habit.) A dictionary is a clear material instance of a Saussurean "diacritical" system: words are defined by other words, each definition referring us to another example ("see also"). A dictionary is also a concrete instance of a signifying chain, in Lacan's sense. Today, Internet hypertext works the same way, as a switching point between interlinked sites, a link embedded in a larger webbing.

Chain Mail: Letter as Meshwork

Elaborating Saussure's concept of signification as relational process, Jakobson described the unfolding of language along two intersecting axes, horizontal and vertical (table 7.2). The vertical axis represents all possible synonyms that the speaker could use ("piled up" along the axis of selection, called the paradigmatic axis); the horizontal axis represents the actual expressed statement itself, as it unfolds from subject to predicate ("linked up" along the axis of combination, or the syntagmatic axis).

Lacan builds on Jakobson's scheme, pointing out that Freud's two main types of primary process—condensation and displacement, at work in jokes, dreams, and other processes influenced by the unconscious—each adhere to one of these axes. Condensation clearly has an affinity with the vertical function of language ("piling up" and condensing meanings in one "similar" word); while displace-

Table 7.2

Horizontal axis links parts of speech along a line (one dimension)			
this brat	strokes	a darling	puppy
this tot	cuddles	a lovable	hound
this child	caresses	a charming	whelp
this urchin	pets	a precious	canine
this kid	fondles	an adorable	bowwow
this boy	**pats**	**a cute**	**dog**

Vertical axis
layers similar
words, adds
second dimension

ment is at work in the lateral function of linkage, subject-to-predicate (displacing desire onto associated objects, as in projection or free association, driving the chain forward). By adding primary process into Jakobson's scheme, Lacan implicates both the structural linguistic model and the Freudian subject.

A Necklace of Others

Not only does Lacan consider human beings as inextricably linked by language, he holds that we are actually *produced* as "human" by language/culture (in the most obvious instance, the infant is already named, thus categorized societally, before its arrival). Lacan's connections work not only laterally and intersubjectively (connecting social subjects) but vertically (intrasubjectively), figuring in the layered depths of a single subject's psyche, conscious and unconscious. Demonstrating his famous axiom, "the unconscious is structured like a language," Lacan's discussion also suggests that the deep structure of language may be revealed by a microscopic view of the human unconscious. Again, Lacan's theory harbors a two-way fractality (*intersubjective* language is structured like—and by—the *subject's* unconscious . . . and vice versa).

In other words, Lacan's version of the linguistic link—"a ring in a necklace that is a ring in another necklace made of rings" is replicated and embedded in the interlinked nature of human subjectivity itself. To put this idea in terms of dimension, we could compare Jakobson's two axes to the warp and woof of cloth, producing a two-dimensional linguistic fabric, a woven text (Latin *texere*, "to weave"). But whereas Jakobson's axes unfold in two dimensions, Lacan's fractal process is more like knotting a rug in three dimensions (in fact, in *Seminar IV* he elaborates on Freud's joke scenario using the figure of the carpet hook or upholstery tack). In knotting a rug, one again works with warp and woof, but the result

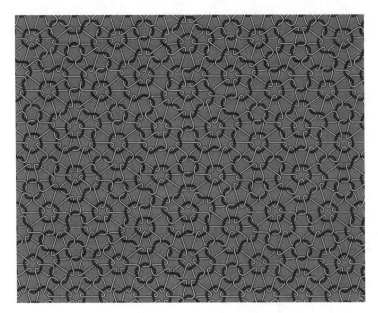

Knot carpet.

is texturized in three dimensions. That is, series of dimensional knots tied onto vertical threads form the emerging pattern, as the rug-maker moves horizontally across the loom. Like a rug-maker, the speaker effects the interaction of both the pattern and coloration of words, knotting them into the emergent discourse that is the stuff of the social web.

"The Materiality of the Signifier"

What is more, for Lacan, "the letter"—the material aspect of language—is inscribed in the very stuff of the unconscious ("The unconscious is structured like a language"). Freud's own chosen figures describing primary process reveal this materiality: condensation (*Verdichtung*: note the embedded term *dicht*, "thick") thickens the dream image with layered references; while displacement (*Verschiebung*: shifting) is at work in the dream's jumbling and retrieval of what Freud calls "daily residue," the fragments of diurnal experience that furnish the malleable elements of the dream scene.

Lacan's foregrounding of language, combined with his mission statement (the famous "return to Freud" that his endeavor represents), gives his fractal myriad recursive dimensions—it not only embeds Jakobson, Saussure, and Freud, but it is embedded in them. For Lacan, language not only coincides with the deep structure of the psyche, it also provides the fabric of all social relations, including the analytic transference (worked out in Lacan's myriad hermetic structural reiterations, the diagrams and mathemes that he uses to "figure" Freud's "talking cure" in *The Four Fundamental Concepts of Psycho-Analysis*).

Another well-known Lacanian formulation highlights the function of linkage in both language and intersubjective interaction: "a signifier is a subject for another signifier" (simply put, a word means something only in the *context* of the words to which it is linked). Turning Lacan on his head, and zooming in on his formula, we can glimpse a corollary inverted figure: "A signifier is a subject for another signifier" also implies that "a subject is a signifier for another subject." This pun—playing on the double meaning of "subject" as grammatical agent, and "subject" as human being—reveals an important meaning embedded in Lacan's formula. A human being is always *significant*—indeed, is always human—only in a context of Other subjects.

Desire as Remainder

Desire is the excess of demand over need. $(D \sim d/n)$[24]

—Jacques Lacan, *Écrits*

Since the Lacanian subject is a link cathected to a whole network of others (cathexis means "tying on"), it is no surprise that the Lacanian model privileges language as interface between subject and other. Appropriately enough, Lacan's algorithm for desire is framed as a *discursive* model, involving communication: a demand for love or recognition is addressed to an object, who never fully responds. The remainder of unsatisfied demand is leftover "desire," which motivates the ongoing process of reiterated demand. This algorithm is itself fractal: since the human subject emerges as a function of a signifying process (addressing a demand to an Other/other), language is fractional, an always unfinished business.

Paternal Metaphor: Fractal Father

One of Lacan's most famous figures, "The Paternal Metaphor," is written as a *fraction* of sorts (a vertical version of Saussure's famous formula linking Signifier/signified in a horizontal two-sided relation S/s).[25]

$$\frac{S}{s}$$

In Lacan's reinscription of Saussure's S/s as fraction, the big "S" on top stands for the father's name, the Big Signifier or patronym that labels and categorizes the subject in patriarchal society. Meanwhile, below, the small "s" for signified lurks, burying the hidden meaning of the father's name. Thus "s" stands for the murder of the father, the reiterated "murder," or wish for murder, of the parent by the child, a hostility "covered over" by the submission of child to paternal name and authority (big S). Lacan's fraction also denotes the divided nature of one's "identity," subtended by invisible motive forces, and the repressed species memory of the primal crime that founds society. The father's name above is the only visible remainder of the repressed murderous relation with the patriarch who was "put down" (in the mythic patricide related by Oedipus and *Totem and Taboo*, retold in any number of avatars). Thus one's apparent conscious identity, associated with the father's name, is quite literally a *remainder* of a (very) long division—as long as the history of the species—producing a very irrational number (of subjects). Like a fractal or irrational number, this long division only grows in complexity as it is carried to new places, with the continued propagation of the social species.

Indeed, Lacan's equally famous axiom on the relation of desire and Otherness also harbors a fractal function: "Our desire is the desire of the Other," when "carried out to new places" like the long division mentioned above, suggests that *the Other's desire is the desire of the Other of the Other* . . . and so forth and so on, involving Other "Others" in each successive iteration. (We saw in chapter 3 that Lacan does actually invoke the first iteration—"the Other of the Other"—in his discussion of clinical paranoia: the paranoid is the bearer of Disbelief [*das Unglauben*], refusing to believe in the symbolic *Other* that founds the social order. The paranoid, meglomane that he is, tends to believe only in a higher explanation—the "Other of the Other"—that only he understands, and which explains everything. He Alone "sees" that there is an operator pulling the strings behind the curtain, the Other of the Other. He Alone "knows" that the Emperor has no clothes, that the "Other of the Other" is the crafty tailor undercutting the vestments of power that stitch together a community of [duped] true believers.)

It's enough to drive "one" mad. Only one thing is sure: stasis does not figure in Lacan's recursive complication of Freud; nor does linearity.

The Missing (L) Ink: The Schema L and the Fractal Subject

In other words, for Lacan, the human psyche—always-already "split" and parsed, invested in and refracted by "the desire of Others"—is a fractal object of sorts. For the "S" of the subject in the Schema L, we recall, is written with a bar, designating the opacity of the full unconscious "subject" to the conscious ego. In a sense, the psyche has a fractional homologue: like the numerator in a fraction, the "visible" or conscious ego is conditioned by a submerged determinant (denominator), and its repressed unconscious elements assure that the subject is divided, never completely identical to his or her "self."

But Lacan, true to form, further dimensionalizes this relatively simple division into the "ego" (self-image, conscious or preconscious) and the barred "self" $\mathcal{S}$ (the unconscious self). This complexification occurs when Lacan describes the operation of the unconscious in linguistic terms ("the unconscious is structured like a language"). This formulation has a multiple valence, like everything in Lacan. It describes how the unconscious comes about, how "it" (ça) is structured by repression, the consignment of some primal memory to a position below the bar. The relatively simple form of the Schema L is deepened by the introduction of the linguistic homologue.

The structure of Lacan's sublime necklace thus figures the human subject itself, as a nodal network functioning at innumerable scales. In chapter 6, I suggested that the Borromean knot itself is a complexification of Freud's original triangle. One has only to imagine Lacan's necklace as an ornament where each link is itself composed of . . . a Borromean knot . . . to begin to get an idea of just how dimensional the intersubjective psyche is. The necklace links would increase exponentially in each iteration (3^1, 3^2, 3^3, 3^n). This may be described in a mathematical algorithm for the whole set, a recipe for generating (the Borromean $\mathcal{S}$ubject), where n represents the number of the step (3^n, 3^{n+1}, 3^{n+2} . . .).

The resulting object is a fractally replicated subject, for the interconnected human psyche is "an object that looks similar to itself at any scale at which it is examined." This illustrates a key notion: whether described as infinite progression or infinite regression, a fractal is infinite without being indefinite—like the serial receding reflections produced by the reflection of one mirror in another, infinite but distinct. Similarly, when Lacan pictures the structure of intersubjective human society—putting it under a microscope—he sees something similar reproduced in each individual subject (and each subject's language), and when that subject is scrutinized, the "underlying" structure of the unconscious reveals a self-similar structure. In other words, Lacan's formula for language may also be read as the figure for the function of human subjectivity, at any scale. Thus his fractal algorithm—"our desire is the desire of the Other"—presents a formula for human interchange where many elements may be plugged in, in an expanding knotted "carpet" or web. Today, Lacan's formula could describe the intersubjective network of the Internet, linking the surfing psyche with a rhizomatic interscape of Others and their fantasies. This fanciful proposal linking two of Lacan's crucial "figures" (the signifying chain and the Borromean link of three psyches, intertwined yet independent) suggests that the "carpet" of human society is a web of such knots, expanding in every direction and dimension.

Intriguingly, even our DNA code may be studied as a version of this kind of complex Borromean linkage. As a spiraling helix of linked structures, our own material blueprint might instantiate Lacan's version of subjectivity.

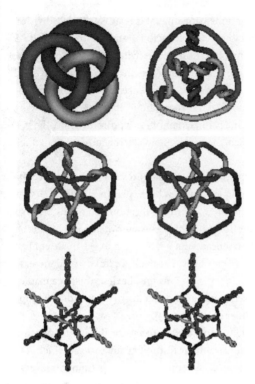

DNA knots.

Whether or not our own biological code actually turns out to have this twist, Lacan's fractal theory at least suggests a provocative link between millennial discoveries in science and medicine, and the psychoanalytic theory of the subject.

3: ITERATE OEDIPUS

> The human mind has first to construct forms, independently, before we can find them in things.
>
> —Albert Einstein, *Fractal Functions*

All of the examples discussed in this chapter—whether in nature, in math, or in Lacan's theory of subjectivity—indicate that fractality is an iterative function, involving three operations or modes: replication, self-organization, and embedding or recursion.

1. *Replication* A replicator is anything that gets itself copied—Xeroxes, DNA, fashion trends, cultural norms, sayings. But a replicator is not just anything of which

copies are made. For, as Elan Moritz explains (*Memetic Sciences: A General Introduction*), copies must fairly closely resemble the original, and they must have some viability: "copying of these entities is performed with special care to reduce any errors that may be introduced in the copying process, and that the items copied exist for a duration that can allow further copies (or generations) to be made."[26]

Replicators, in other words, are not just templates. They are heavy spawners, creators of networks and systems in which they continue to participate. They are, in a sense, viral.

The study of the biological manifestations of replication were pioneered by Richard Dawkins in two seminal books, *The Selfish Gene* and *The Extended Phenotype*.[27] And ever since Dawkins's work made replication a focus of biogenetics, the concept itself has been "replicating" in any number of domains, including medicine, cybernetics, and social science.

One of the most intriguing extended applications of "replication theory" is nanotechnology, pioneered by Eric Drexler, which seeks to produce molecule-sized machines to scurry about the body, performing any number of medical functions at the cellular level. Another intriguing avenue is memetic science, which extends the notion of replication to cultural practices and norms. Lumsden and Wilson pioneered this new mathematical cultural science, based on "culturgen theory."[28]

Rather than taking a side in the nature/nurture controversy over human behavior, Lumsden and Wilson speculate that culture may eventually become inscribed in the genes. According to them, culturgens are the "genetically determined procedures that direct the assembly of the mind, including the screening of stimuli by peripheral sensory filters, the cellular organizing processes, and the deeper processes of directed cognition." They argue that "joint genetic-cultural evolution leads to major change in epigenetic rules over a time as short as 1000 years."[29]

Of course, Freud always thought there were somatic explanations for psychic processes, and he speculated that each human being bears a "phylogenetic" species memory, the psychic imprints of the history of humanity (for instance, a primal species experience of tribal strife founds the incest taboo). If Freud were around to witness the new science of "culturgens," he might say that replicators are by definition traumatic experiences, inscribing patterns of behavior that can be "undone" only by repeating, remembering, and working through, in analysis.

2. *Self-generation* Since replicators reproduce *themselves*, memetic science is concerned with the study of self-organizing processes of matter. In fractal theory, replicators generate patterns that emerge and grow according to a formula. (In other words, iteration is a copy that contains the key to reproducing itself by the same means.)

If one wishes to see self-organization at work, one may visit any number of online sites to play what is (misnamed) "The Chaos Game" (actually a formula for iteration, not chaos). This game generates a five-pointed star, apparently by chance; but it always emerges on the screen after a few tries, when one follows specific directions. Playing this game, one will soon see the Koch snowflake take shape, in a striking a visual example of "emergence."[30]

3. *Embedding* The process of self-generating replication reveals a third important aspect of fractality: self-similar structures are often nested one within the other, at any scale, like Russian dolls.

In a sense, this aspect of fractality reiterates a well-known poststructuralist enterprise: replacing closed systems with open ones by demonstrating the iterability of any concept in a chain of references and contexts: it may always be "quoted" or framed by attribution rather than standing as a final reference or absolute bottom line. ("It's raining" is verifiable; "I say 'It's raining'" is true, but the fact is not subject to verification.) So one aspect of iterability concerns an opening to ever-multiplying fields of reference. But, like the Sierpinski system, the poststructuralist episteme is about going inside a structure, burrowing down to hollow out wholeness, revealing submergent patterns and interstitial dimensions (including the undecidability of concepts *between two meanings*).

In other words, poststructuralism provides a philosophic version of fractality, which is at the heart of the"deconstruction" of illusory plenitudes of all sorts. We may see a visual version of how recursion opens a two-dimensional object, like a triangle, into any number of fractional dimensions, by contemplating the dimensionalized Sierpinski's pyramid at the head of this chapter. We could peer deeper and deeper into this shape, replicating an infinite regress of the prime pattern.

A *self-reflective* fractal would be a mental labyrinth, learning to learn, replicating prior inscriptions and inserting them into new contexts.

Freud had a name for such a fractal: human being.

The fractal object upon which Lacan trained his magnifying glass is the Freudian subject. In a sense, by moving from Freud's familial triangle, to the tripartite Borromean knot as the larger field of human experience (imaginary, symbolic, real), Lacan was merely iterating the complexity already inherent in Freud's structure, which resembles itself at any scale at which is examined. Let us now follow Lacan's lead, and return to Freud.

SUBJECT AS REPLICANT

Fractal Culture: Memes and Norms

The three operations listed above—iteration, self-organization, and recursion—indicate that a "fractal" reading of Freud must foreground a social fabric that *replicates, emerges,* and *embeds* itself in an ever-expanding social field. Although it is able to reproduce itself, such a fractal replication would always be subject to error and mutation. For, as Mandelbrot insisted, fractals occurring in nature are self-similar but not *identical, they always inscribe differences;* moreover, they are always inexact, measurable only by approximation. This inclusion of variance is significant for a fractal reading of Freud, because it accounts for change in the individual psyche and in the socius.

The new memetic science foregrounds "memes," behaviors that replicate themselves in the intersubjective field, but are nonetheless open to change: memes are to cultural constructs as genes are to biological organisms, subject to both replication and mutation. In *A Thousand Years of Nonlinear History,* Manuel De Landa gives a new wrinkle to the nature-nurture debate, by distinguishing between a meme (a replicator that actually inheres in culture—like a tune that everybody knows) and a norm (a replicator that is learned and instilled, like religion, not just "caught," like a catchy saying).[31] This distinction suggests that educative nurture, furthering norms, may eventually "emerge" into culture, finally becoming an ideological assumption (unexamined because it is putatively "self-evident" to everyone in the culture), replicating itself in an intergenerational pattern. And the theory of culturgens suggests that some memes—in a thousand years or so—may actually inscribe themselves in our genes, as "human nature."

In this sense, an example of a Freudian meme might be the repressed species memory of the primal family feud (*Totem and Taboo*), founding the universal incest taboo that exists in some form in every culture; while a norm would be any of the local cultural repressions that subject "instinct" to its "vicissitudes" (like the suppression of female sexuality by patriarchal society, resulting, in Freud's view, in feminine exhibitionism, the love of adornment).

In any case, Freud's subject is always an effect of social replication, as revealed in a number of key texts, beginning with his work on jokes as a social process. In his turn, Lacan transcodes Freud's joke paradigm as a number of complex mathemes in *Seminar IV*. But the most accessible expression of drive and demand in Lacan's opus remains his simple fractal formula "desire is the excess of demand over need"—casting desire as a replicator, in an ever-expanding field.

Psyche as Socius

Since a fractal may be entered at any one of its links, we may close our fractal excursion by entering the intersubjective chain at several levels of triangulation discussed throughout this book. Although critics of Freud have often reduced this triangle to the oedipus complex, it may be read as a much more inclusive human algorithm, by which human subjectivity is replicated in a web of Others.

Freud's basic fractal shape involves three people, but the example he cites in *Jokes and Their Relation to the Unconscious* (the "smutty" joke) is but one instance illustrating a more general phenomenon ("Jokes as a Social Process"). In this schematic parable, a man bonds with another man at the expense of a female object; but Lacan's notion of subjectivity as *position* suggests that these gender roles are just that—roles, loci, sites where all human beings perform in turn, in different cultural contexts and with different inflections (obviously, for instance, a woman may tell a joke about a man, to a person of either gender). The gender roles as cast by Freud in Victorian Vienna—active male, passive female—only emphasize the aggressive and complicit nature of the bond.

The flexibility of Freud's schema, exploited by Lacan, has to do with Freud's notion of "libido," which differentiates object and aim (in a sense, all sexual activity has the same aim—sexual release—but it takes any number of forms, involving a bewildering array of objects). The aim (sexual gratification), Freud argues, is inherently and "originally" deflected from its original goal (feeding). What differentiates sexuality from copulation is that it is culturally defined, culturally governed, and culturally replicated.

Freud's various fractal iterations show that the oedipal paradigm obtains in many situations and transactions—where the result of one operation is fed into the next step as its opening term. As we have seen in the example of the retelling of a joke, oedipal operations underline social processes (writing, joking, mourning, "madness," analysis), rather than being confined to explicitly sexual interaction. In the resolution of the classic "oedipus complex," the extra iterative term is the child whose infantile desire is curbed in response to social norms, and who leaves the fold in search of new object. In patriarchal society, "he" becomes a "family man" in turn. But human subjectivity is as diverse as culture itself, and the conditions of human being are changing rapidly in our age. We may expect that our new cultural configurations will be reiterated differently, producing new mutated subjects in each new age.

As Mandelbrot insists, fractals are replicators not of *identity*, but of *similarity*— difference inserts itself from copy to copy, replication to replication. That loophole may be the glimmer of hope in the otherwise depressingly repetitive way we humans have interacted up until now. We all seem to agree these days that however crazy the borderless world has become, we are on the brink of something else, be it catastrophe or a new order with new rules.

For one thing, Freud, thanks to his keen and compassionate social sense, reminds us in "Creative Writers and Day-Dreaming" that a truly creative circuit may function only in the absence of "vital needs": the aesthetic transaction is possible only when survival is not at issue. (You must first be fed, in other words, to enjoy a movie; to begin to be fully human, you must be able to negotiate desire rather than need.) Although Freud was arguing for jokes as aesthetic symptoms of the insatiable remainder of desire, he puts first things first. For civilization to act civilly, in spite of its discontents, it must be first be humane.

But Freud was downright pessimistic about the human capacity to get it right in society (see "Why War?"),[32] but at least he left that possibility open (at the end of *Beyond the Pleasure Principle*, he argues that all human achievement is produced by the remainder of unfulfilled desire). It is too simple to call this iterative intersubjective replication "sublimation," as Lacan's work demonstrates—human social being is not just a linear redirection or reinvestment of energy, but a change in its nature, from "need" to signfying desire.

Zooming In: Interstitial Iterations

Taking a step closer to the oedipal triad with our magnifying glass, we may peer into the psyche of a single subject. We know Lacan argued that "one" subject was always-already (at least) two, basing this observation on Freud's *Spaltung* (primal repression), the splitting that produces the unconscious.[33] We recall that Lacan likened that split—dividing the ego and the unconscious—to the production of a barred subject, always opaque to the "identity" that says "I."

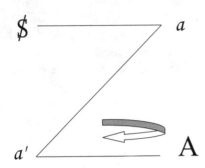

Dimensional Schema L.

Lacan splits S into two positions, including *a'* (ego ideal or self-image, modeled in part after the "father" A) and barred S (the subject with no access to the unconscious repressed material that determines subjectivity as multidimensional).

This is the point of the Schema L: splitting the subject, it opens Freud's triangle into four positions and at least three dimensions, since A is always radically exterior as Other. And the divided psyche is always also a function of the other subjects with whom we interact, thanks to whom we know what and who we are (in the transaction of "paranoid knowledge"). Lacan points out that this iteration subtends the analytic situation: "In the analytic situation there are two subjects, each provided with two objects, the 'moi' (the self-image, or ego) and the other."[34] Finally, Lacan distinguishes between an identification of rivalry (the *imaginary* identification with the enemy brother; so like ourselves that we wish to annihilate him) and a *symbolic* identification. This is what Freud discusses as "The Resolution of the Oedipus Complex," the result of the mortification or wounding of narcissism, entailing a recognition of our own limits that ends in a pact with the Other.

This is the outcome of *Totem and Taboo* and *Moses and Monotheism*: Freud founds societal law on the experience of "suffering" and division. (In *Totem and Taboo*, the rival sons kill the patriarch. But in *Moses and Monotheism*, the Hebrew people—of no specified gender—rise up against Moses, and kill him. They later accede to his Law as atonement for this crime).[35] Human law means suffering the other as Other, as obstacle to imploded desire. We have seen how Lacan's version of *Totem and Taboo*, routed through Saussure, produces a split formula for the paternal metaphor, Signifier (the patronym, Big S) *over* signified (*s*, the repressed memory of patricide).

But Lacan's matheme, like Freud's *Totem and Taboo*, describes a *patriarchal* instance of primal repression: "Who's on top" could vary according to social circumstance (keeping in mind that at any rate, power quite literally cuts two ways: the father's name is on top because the father himself is dead). Each new social subject, however, reiterates a primal founding split in society (the incest taboo). The primal conflict between desire and obstacle, alienation and identification—reiterated in each divided subject—also founds human community.

This chapter opened with four definitions of "fractal," which we can now revisit in light of Freud's iterative model of subjectivity.

> **fractal** (1) . . . in nature, any of various *extremely irregular curves or shapes that repeat themselves at any scale* on which they are examined.
>
> **fractal** (2) *a geometric object which looks similar to itself* under a magnifying glass.
>
> **fractal** (3) . . . *a very irregular line or surface that is formed of an endless number of sections*, so that its dimensions or other physical properties are always only approximations.
>
> **fractal** (4) a geometrical or physical structure having an irregular or fragmented shape at all scales of measurement between a greatest and smallest scale [such that certain mathematical or physical properties] *behave as if the dimensions of the structure (fractal dimensions) are greater than the spatial dimensions.*

Each of these definitions emphasizes different aspects of fractality: (1) *irregular* replication or difference; (2) *geometric* recursion, or similarity; (3) *segmented* replication, or linkage; (4) *interstitial* dimension, or infinite recursion.

Fractal One: Errant Replication
In the *Three Essays*, Freud emphasizes the wide variance in sexual aim (what one wants to do) and sexual objects (with whom or what one wants to do it).[36] However, we have seen that any instance of desiring subjectivity replicates a "similar" desiring structure, although producing countless iterations and intersections—comings, goings, and *becomings*—in the human field.

Fractal Two: Recursive Geometric Object
Freud gives a number of examples of triangulated social processes at every scale of human interaction: the level of the psyche, the subject, the group (including the family), and society at large. On every level, there is a prohibition of implosion, and a rerouting of desire outward into a productive encounter with Otherness.

Consider the triangular model of the Borromean rings, for instance, as a way of figuring the intersubjective chain (the triadic Borromean ring would figure the oedipal triangle, with each subject composed of other subjects . . .). Topological geometry provides a way to think of the subject as an embedded, self-replicating ring of sorts, the first link, or torus, in the social carpet. For the single torus has a strange property: no matter how it is dissected, at any angle, it still yields a torus:

Roger Groce, *Pixelated Torus*, 2004.

Thus the torus reveals the embedding of self-similar structures (infinite rings, at many angles); just so, we may think of the myriad "subjects" embedded in one psyche, "no matter how you slice it." In fact, Freud speaks of the superego as just such a residue of numerous internalized role models; he also discusses the internalization of the "other/Other" in the work of mourning, and in the experience of love. And today—as biotechnology continues to deconstruct the boundaries between the natural and the engineered—our high-tech medicine provides a more graphic material instance of embedding—putting donor human/animal/mechanical parts into recipients, with perhaps unforeseen psychological ramifications.

The unsettling aspects of this kind of progress may bring to mind Freud's warning that every move of civilization is accompanied with discontents. On the other hand, one voice of Freud seems straightforwardly to advocate progress, associating it with the colonizing march of reason, an advance over "primitive" ways (the Freud of ego psychology proclaims: "Where id was, ego shall be"). But in *Beyond the Pleasure Principle*, a far less dogmatic Freud speaks of a process of human becoming rather than "progress," citing a *progressive* spiral "upward and onward, unsubdued," which is nonetheless always motivated and shadowed by a demonic compulsion to repeat.

Indeed, the future dynamic of human being, as Freud describes it, may be figured by yet another figure of topology, a dynamic manifold of *linked* rings in motion.

Fractal Three: Segmented Linkage

Lacan insists on the homology between the signifying chain of language ("the signifier is the subject for another signifier") and the link binding human subject to subject. Replicated linkage also characterizes the analytic transference, according to Lacan (*Seminar XV*), where, at the end of analysis, the analysand takes over the position of "*the subject supposed to know*" (when he or she realizes that the analyst is not all-knowing), thus becoming an analyst in turn, the illusory authority for another subject. Freud also acknowledges the levels and dimensions of the analytic cathexes, recognizing that the countertransference calls the unconscious desire of the analyst into play.

But how is analysis, a transaction between two people, a *triadic* structure? Thanks to overdetermination, the analyst may play as many as three roles, and occupy as many as three positions at once—as love object (in the transference);

as desiring subject (in the countertransference); and as obstacle resisting the analysand's desire, a screen which relays that desire back, forcing the analysand to "work it through." We have seen that this overdetermination is represented in the Schema L, which seems to leave one end of Freud's unhinged, open to other intersubjective hook-ups.

Fractal Four: Dimension

This version of fractality may be succinctly stated in the following formula: "a fractal is an object with a dimension different from its Euclidean dimension."

This formulation aptly describes Lacan's version of the intersubjective configuration. In the Schema L, for example, the dyad subject-object—the upper level of the schema—is a one-dimensional line, the shortest distance between two points: $S \rightarrow a$. However, the Schema L illustrates that desire circulates and is relayed back in a plane: the Schema L is at least two-dimensional, as drawn on the page. But it also opens to the possibility of three dimensions, since the open structure may be unhinged, swinging "A (*Autre*/Other)" out into three-dimensional space (picture the bottom line in the scheme on page 212, connecting a' and A, opening out from the page, putting the *Autre*/Other "in your face," as it were.)

In fact, Lacan's scheme is four-dimensional, since this refractory network is marked with arrows, indicating a trajectory that unfolds *in time*, a movement in phase space (Lacan often insists that time is a dimension of any intersubjective interactivity, including paranoid knowledge, which requires, *le temps à comprendre*).

In another version of this figure, Lacan deploys the Schema L as a double triangle:

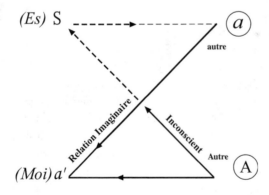

Lacan's schema L as doubled triangle.

Lacan himself points out how this doubling adds a dimension (the dotted line indicating the dimension of the unconscious) turning the Schema L from a path or circuit into a dimensional *network*, where all points may communicate, sooner or later, with all other points. (This recalls Deleuze's definition of a rhizome, where "every part is connected with every other part, and must be.")

We can also use this crossing to figure a fourth dimension in space, rather than in time. Imagine this figure as a three-dimensional clay X, twisted at the center intersection. The page still remains in two dimensions, a plane; the part twisted forward into our space is in three-dimensional space, and the part of the X twisted so that it protrudes into the space behind the page (point A) could figure the fourth dimension. The page represents a screen, the border of our three-dimensional world (like a painted canvas), while the space beyond it is in another dimension, "through the looking-glass."

Nor do the dimensions end with four. If one thinks of this X as a cross reflection doubling the first Schema L, in two refracting mirrors, the multidimensional field of self-similar figures would march off in an infinity of interstitial dimensions. For fractal theory tells us that mathematically, an infinity of fractal dimensions inhabits the "space" between dimensions one and two (like the infinite positions in the angle created when opening a fan). In fact, an opening arch can be *measured* as two *whole* dimensions only when the movement of becoming (opening) is momentarily stopped. But there is an infinity of positions in between, in the moving phase space.

Many of the strange new object-relations in our posthuman world are interstitial, in between human and animal, human and machine; even (in cryogenics) between life and death. We could say that many of the new aspects of millennial becoming reveal the "holey space" of Sierpinski's figures, which only *seem* two-dimensional.

Lacan speaks of the opening of the interstice in the "whole" subject: first as the space between " I " and "me," the space in which I see myself, reflected in the mirror; and second, as the gap between the "other" and the "Other," between my known objects and my (unknown, unconscious) objects, figuring the alienation between me and my Others. As he puts it in *Seminar III*:

> This distinction between the Other with a big O, that is, the Other in so far as it's not known and the other with a small o, that is, the other who is me, the source of all knowledge, is fundamental. It's in this gap, it's in the angle opened up between these two relations, that the entire dialectic of delusion has to be situated.[37]

The holey space of the Lacanian subject unfolds the straight line from me to you into a multidimensional fractal relation, like unfolding a fan before a mirror, fanning and multiplying *désir*.

Iterating Oedipus

Thus each of the four aspects of fractality inhere in iterations of psychoanalytic theory: replication with difference, replication with similarity, segmented linkage, and dimensionalization.

Finally, the oedipal iterations in the Freudian algorithm for subjectivity could themselves be listed and numbered, as successive iterations of a triangle:

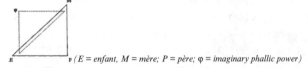

(E = enfant, M = mère; P = père; φ = imaginary phallic power)

Iterations 1 and 2: Freud's "family" as doubled by the imaginary fold

Iteration 3: group (series of "families," tribe)

Iteration 4: society (groups connected in many dimensions)

Iteration 5: extimacy (radical Otherness, out of reach)

Iteration x: tesselations, interstitial links

Iterations 1 and 2: The Oedipal Subject, from Freud to Lacan[38] As we saw in chapter 2, Lacan's entire *oeuvre* deals with shifting subject positions, especially in the linguistic exchange—which, tellingly, is triadic, including first-, second-, and third-person speaking positions. In the first of many versions of the oedipal schema, reproduced above, Lacan overdetermines Freud's oedipal triangle by a doubling, indicating the child's relation to the threat of wounding or castration (ϕ stands for the phallus, the concept of power and prohibition). But note that the dotted line in the figure consigns the phallus to an *imaginary* status, having nothing to do with actual genitalia. This imaginary figure actually signifies the subject's confrontation with the prohibitory power of the Other (here, P, the oedipal *père*).

But Freud himself has already indicated the complications of every position in Lacan's circuit. In *Beyond the Pleasure Principle*, for instance, as Derrida points out in "Coming into One's Own," grandfather (Freud) both identifies with and objectifies his grandson, in a doubled relation of sympathy and rivalry vis-à-vis the child's absent mother, Freud's daughter. The common "intruder" for both grandfather and grandson is Freud's son-in-law, who takes Sophie away.[39]

Freud's own family scene is another example of the three-to-four circuit—discussed as the "diamond" playing field in chapter 2—which always plays out the possibilities of desire, transgression, and law. The addition of a "fourth" term (in this case, the voyeur grandfather) opens the triangular configuration, assuring its replication in the next iteration, the writing of Freud's own model of repetition. Or this iteration can unfold in time, when the child becomes a parent in turn, passing on the enabling "wound" to the next generation.

Iteration 3: Group, Tribe Freud's transactional chain, where the third party becomes the initiator in a new triangle, could be pictured as a lateral linkage, where the last point is always "fed into" the next iteration as the first point of the new triangle.

The expanded group could also be pictured as a fractal of increasing complexity, where each apex of the triangle (each subject) hooks up with others, as a tribe. Forming a new triangle at each apex results in a more complex structure, hollowed out in the interior (math aficionados will observe here the beginnings of Pascal's triangle, a tool of calculation, where the rows may be increased ad infinitum).

These figures already hint at the infinite complexity of intersubjectivity, where the "tessellations" (puzzle pieces) fit into infinitely various social patterns (in geometry, this process is called triangular tiling.[40]

Such patterns display both complexity and variations in fractal scale (the tiles repeat themselves in both large and small sections of pattern). Freud describes the group dialectics of (imploded, hypnotic) identification with a charismatic leader in *Group Psychology and the Analysis of the Ego*, later discussed by the Frankfurt School as the libidinal motor of fascism.[41] (In today's geopolitical crisis, we might do well to dust off Adorno's study of disciplinary cult libido as "fascination" with a leader.) This is the dangerous incestuous realm of "flat" *imaginary* identification, where the group identifies with the mesmerizing cult leader.

But Freud describes a more fruitful outcome of group interaction, described as *symbolic* identification. In *Totem and Taboo*, the tribe's identification with the murdered father results in intermarriage and contact with other peoples, avoiding deadening implosion. This expanding multidimensional subjectivity, community to community, people to people, might be figured as a series of connected pyramids.

Iteration 4: Society Throughout his work, Freud describes the dynamics of deflected, then rerouted, desire as the motor of civilization, as well as the source of its "discontents." Desire may be subject to any number of fates in the social field: it is denied, deflected, repressed, foreclosed, or gratified—however incompletely.[42] Freud finally remains rather pessimistic about the human ability to use desire productively, but he does say that the remainder or quotient of unsatisfied desire is what drives human achievement. In this case, he seems to see species being not as progress, but as a work in progress.

Iteration 5: Extimacy (the "Other" Relation) In the twenty-first century, we are finding that the Other is inside and outside at once. This relation might be figured in the four-dimensional "Boy shape": if you follow any one of the lines all the way around, it will visit "inside" and "outside" without going over an edge, switching sides, going through a wall, or changing direction. On nonorientable surfaces, the voyager meets himself "coming and going."[43] This kind of surface, the domain of Lacan's "extimacy," where interior and exterior are continuous, is the topic of chapter 8.

Next millennium, however, Freudians may well be dealing with Otherness in a more concrete way: in extraterrestrial exploration and encounter. Freud's narrative of conflict resolution may prove even more helpful beyond the boundaries of the home planet. (The debate about terriforming Mars has already started. Should we replicate Earth on another world?) In chapter 8, we will see that it is possible to figure Otherness as a fourth dimensional bypass, where the surfaces only appear to cut through each other, but where the trajectory is "lifted" into the next dimension at each apparent intersection (involving a fifth dimension as well as the four dimensions of space-time).

Iteration X: x^n as Interstice We have followed the dimensionalization of the Freudian subject with the individual psyche, and progressed into higher dimensions. But we could travel in the other direction, "fractalizing" the subject in dimensions below identity, where the subject's unconscious is constituted by a splitting, and an embedding of multiple others. In fact, in *Seminar III*, Lacan is at pains to point out the triplicity of the subject:

Our schema represents the interruption of speech between the subject and the Other and its detour through two egos (a and a'). Here it indicates *triplicity in the subject*, which overlaps the fact that it's the subject's ego that normally speaks to another.[44]

But Freud seems to indicate that what human beings do with this intersubjective algorithm is up to us. To be sure, the question of what we do to humanize the collective psyche, for Freud, is always a question of getting out of automatically replicated structures—unreflexive, rigorously self-similar fractality. (This kind of productive progression comes only through the cessation of "repeating," the practice of "remembering," and the process of "working through.")

Thus reading Fractal Freud suggests that we have two big psychic issues, as denizens of a posthuman world: one is how to deal with endless replications of self-defeating, self-perpetuating "similarities" (the endless cycle of "gotcha last" violence). The other challenge, paradoxically, is how to deal with what is not self-similar, but Alien.

CHAPTER 8

EXTIMACY: THE ALIEN AMONG US

Claire Carter, *Alien Glowing*, 2003.

The subject of the unconscious is to be situated as ex-sistant, that is to say, as situated in an ex-centric place.

—Jacques Lacan, *Écrits*

Many of our emerging scientific discoveries have increased the sense of alienation from human being as we know it. (Are the fossils in the Mars rock our forebears? Do clones have a soul? If a woman gives birth to someone else's genetic child, who is the mother?) But a sense of Otherness has always been part of what defines the human. In fact, new DNA anthropological studies reveal that our ancestors in Africa prevailed over competing branches of the family tree because of the emergence of a new type of two-sided (thus literally "para-noid") brain, diversified between reason and intuition.[1] They also evolved a stereoscopic seeing apparatus, providing the para-llax (sight "beside itself") that combines two points of view to provide depth vision. This biaxial disposition of limbs and senses means that we humans always situate ourselves thanks to an exterior point of reference, the third point "out there" where our vision focuses.

Perhaps this odd combination of divided brain function, lopsided physical agility ("handedness"), and double "paralactic" view are also factors that contribute to the chronic sense of Otherness that characterizes what Lacan calls paranoid knowledge, the attempt to see oneself through the other's eyes, from an external perspective. Jean-François Lyotard speaks eloquently of such an inherent otherness that is part of our species-being, motivating self-conscious scrutiny:

> The anguish is that of a mind haunted by a familiar and unknown guest which is agitating it, sending it delirious but also making it think—if one claims to exclude it, if one doesn't give it an outlet, one aggravates it. Discontent grows with this civilization, foreclosure along with information.[2]

Lyotard's comments, inspired by Freud's *Civilization and Its Discontents*, point out that socialization always leaves a remainder that resists "civilizing," and feeds a certain endemic human dis-ease, stemming from the experience of something unknowable, "inhuman," at our core.[3] This take is consistent with many perspectives from anthropology, neurobiology, and philosophy, suggesting that we are human precisely *because* we are split, and because some part of our being always remains opaque, to others and to ourselves.

Lacan called this species-Otherness *extimacy* (*extimité*).[4] The concept is compelling, given the bizarre realities of today's world: more than ever, we are haunted by the specter of a sinister Other in our midst—the alien among us. Reflecting increasing alienation from traditional humanist concepts of *consciousness*, millennial theorists have gone beyond the notion of the posthuman, even referring to the transhuman (Max Moore), or the inhuman (Lyotard). These terms suggest a species identity crisis, a growing sense of estrangement from conventional notions of who we are. And no body of theory has dealt with self-estrangement more eloquently than psychoanalysis.

THE CANNY UNCANNY: TECHNOLOGY

Our chronic human anxiety has doubtless been exacerbated by the reconfigured relations between humanity and its tools, its know-how. The "discontents" felt by "civilized" human beings today are bound up with the incursion of inventions that seem increasingly in our face and under our skin, as intimate as a pacemaker, as obtrusive as a beeper at a concert.

Humanity can perhaps be faked—as suggested by the Turing test that attempts to have computers pass as people when chatting online. But whether or not technology can mime who we are, it has blurred the boundaries between inner and outer, and between human and machine.[5] Nanotech cameras swallowed in a pill already cruise in our veins; robot fingers perform closed heart surgery, sometimes guided by the remote command of a surgeon a continent away.[6] Public space and private space are no longer clearly delineated: the urban pedestrian has sprouted a new appendage, affixed to one ear. Indoors, the new organ calls in a strident voice, demanding that its user engage in a private conversation often inflicted on unwilling eavesdroppers. Meanwhile, back at home, the atavistic twentieth-century tethered phone is often answered only by a machine that screens its user from human contact.

As critical theory struggles to accommodate the new realities of the high tech age, a number of approaches to the analysis of technology have emerged: philosophical, rhetorical, aesthetic, sociopolitical. These diverse perspectives share one tendency: they all cast technology as the Other of humanity.

1. Techno-Philosophy

We have seen that for many theorists the techno-age is the ground for philosophical speculations on the status of human being. But although millennial theorists analyze brand-new cultural conditions, they continue to be inspired by the philosophical canon. They draw on Kantian notions of the sublime (Žižek, Lyotard); Cartesian ruminations on subjectivity as an effect of consciousness (Žižek, Derrida, Lacan); Heideggerian reflections on being and time in-the-world (Ronell, Lyotard); Spinozan reflections on "deep ecology" (Deleuze).[7] Philosophers informed by Nietzschean perspectives continue their debate on what counts as "modernity" and its aftermath (Lyotard, de Man).[8] Other figures, on the borderline between cultural studies, social science, and philosophy (Bourdieu, Teilhard de Chardin), have described the global information network in terms resonant with German idealism, Hegel's Absolute Knowledge gone digital, while some influential thinkers (Žižek, Badiou) continue to recast Hegelian dialectics in terms resonant with today's geopolitical situation.[9] Even a materialist feminist thinker like Judith Butler continues to evaluate culture within the framework of Hegelian mind.[10] And tenets of existentialism and phenomenology, of course, continue to permeate the work of Lacanian philosophers today.

Avital Ronell's work is one pertinent example of a new *performative* techno-philosophy. In *The Telephone Book*—designed to look like its title, with yellow pages for an index—her techno-analogy elaborates a neo-Heideggerian philosophy of the subject's implication in the material world. (Twenty-first-century *Dasein* runs smack into technology.) Following Heidegger's concept of "the call" that defines us, "interpellating" us as human beings, Ronell writes of the "collect call" of technology that defines the posthuman subject who "accepts the charge" by adopting the new modes of communication and relation.[11]

N. Katherine Hayles is another theorist who traces the reaction to posthumanity as a challenge to the liberal subject of humanism: is artificial intelligence radically "Other," or a silicon variety of human intelligence?[12] What is life? Must it be organic? Hayles traces the lively debate between mechanists and vitalists—an old divide, reflecting the debate between idealism and materialism—coming down firmly in the vitalist camp by insisting that information is *embodied* code. For her, technology is not Other to the human; it is a tool, an extension of human being. But for Hayles, the posthuman mindset does depart from the tradition of the liberal subject—a consciousness with free will and agency, an individual proprietor of his or her own person. Coming out of the Enlightenment philosophy of Hobbes and Locke, this ideal of the subject, however appealing ethically, harbors ideological divides between natural and artificial, individual and social, body and mind, that must be reconsidered today. Thus, paradoxically, Enlightenment thinking, although it is associated with a vitalist affirmation of human life, is already about *having* a body, not *being* a body, just as Descartes's mechanist perspective was. What is more, the mind-body dualism that subtends both mechanism and vitalism in the "posthumanism" age has venerable roots in Greek philosophy and Judeo-Christian theology.

For these reasons, prominent feminist theorist Judith Butler critiques the Enlightenment subject as a bastion of heterosexism (since it privileges "natural," "God-given" properties); while her notion of gender as performance, like Ronell's notion of calling, owes much to the notion of Heideggerian interpellation. (Patriarchal culture "calls" subjects to a compulsory "command performance" of one of two "natural" gender roles.)[13]

A Heideggerian perspective also subtends Lyotard's discussion of the future of embodied technology. In "Can Thought Go On without a Body?" and elsewhere in *The Inhuman*, Lyotard casts technology as radically Other: being human must include the capacity to suffer and empathize, and to experience the world in depth, with a body, being *there* (*Dasein*). Sherry Turkle's *Life on the Screen*, on the other hand, problematizes the human-machine dichotomy: she tells tales of online chat romance between unsuspecting humans and canny bots, revealing that most people will flirt with a computer program, reading libido and tease into the most automatic answers.[14]

One of the most influential cultural theorists of the millennial age, Pierre Bourdieu, is not a philosopher but a sociologist; another (Gianni Vattimo) is a political activist—but, like other "panic postmodernists," both of these thinkers critique media culture and the society of spectacle rather than simply decrying them. In *Distinction: A Social Judgement of Taste*, Bourdieu defines his notion of cultural production as field:

> There is an economy of cultural goods, but it has a specific logic. Sociology endeavors to establish the conditions in which the consumers of cultural goods, and their taste for them, are produced, and at the same time describe the different ways of appropriating such of these objects as are regarded at a particular moment as works of art, and the social conditions of the constitution of the mode of appropriation that is considered legitimate.[15]

To the socially recognized hierarchy of the arts—and within each of them, the classification of genres, schools, or periods—corresponds a social hierarchy of the consumers, their class tastes often driven by media demand. Bourdieu points out that the media message often ensures that socially defined (lifestyle) tastes—propagated in media advertising—function as markers of class allegiance.[16]

Perhaps the most influential philosopher of the media is Gianni Vattimo, who (like the philosophers of hypervisibility discussed in chapter 3) analyzes the field with an optical metaphor, as *The Transparent Society*.[17] But Vattimo's "transparent society" actually turns out to be fragmented and opaque, while only appearing homogeneous. Vattimo argues that global access to a highly commercialized Internet culture, rather than promoting a unified worldview or creating a global village, actually exacerbates antagonism and misunderstanding among cultures. His philosophical mooring is poststructuralist, emphasizing undecidability and valorizing difference in a high-tech variant of Derrida. In an interesting wrinkle on the negative social force of the media—and in distinction to the many theorists who see media as homogenizing and disciplinary—Vattimo argues that hyper-communication is *alienating*, increasing cultural and class divides.[18] For Vattimo, the World Wide Web is the site of new and bewildering phenomena, creating new myths, hybrid tribes, multiple dialects and subcultures, and a class system defined by "taste." Thus he sees human being in the media age as oscillating between belonging and disorientation. Still, he does consider this a potentially positive development in some regard, since all this contact sharpens difference rather than flattening it. However, Vattimo finally seems to project a media-age version of the Tower of Babel, maintaining that too much contact and attempted homogeneity will only expose the limits of a totalizing viewpoint.

A comprehensive assessment of the philosophical scene today is beyond my scope here, and the prognoses for human society are various, but all of the examples that I cite underscore the permeability of borders between intellectual fields today and the seismic effects of information technology on human being.

Techno-philosophy portrays this species crisis provoked by a new relation of human beings to the Other of techno-science. But the most prevalent "meditations" are still often neo-Cartesian reflections on consciousness and/or existentialist analyses of the *situation* of human existence. The human subject is still depicted as a "stranger," opposed to an alien cosmos and a rival community of human Others (the perception that "hell is other people," Sartre's famous formula, has new meaning on an overcrowded planet). The existentialist perspective is especially evident in the work of Lacan, who emphasizes the gaze of Others as a field in which the self-conscious subject is constituted. But our Others now are not just flesh and blood, they are also wired and circuited, reflected in computer monitors or surveillance cameras, extending and materializing the web of the human gaze.

2. Techno-Rhetoric: Metaphor as Symptom

Some millennial theory stresses the implication of technology with ideological rhetoric as well as philosophy. Donna Haraway, for instance, insists that no pure science exists separate from the ends and perspectives of culture (even math, she claims, is a trope). Her work, inflected by Freudian ideas of investment and projection, seeks to expose the ideological investment of the "neutral" voice of traditional science; she argues that we inject unconscious motive into the most objective experiments, often finding what we expect to see. Focusing on the high-tech rhetoric in service of an ideological agenda, Haraway concentrates on reproductive technology and the genome project as discursive practices that help define the values they promote, in complicity with the profit motive.

Another aspect of techno-rhetoric is performative, deploying technological metaphors to characterize a high-velocity world that threatens to career out of control, or to deaden our humanity. As we saw in chapter 3, many of these reactions by contemporary thinkers (Baudrillard, Virilio, Ronell) are near-phobic, latching onto the techno-metaphor as an emblem of doomsday (the astronaut cut adrift, the cyborg in rebellion against the species that created him, the invading alien, the apocalypse of nuclear war, the decadence of addictive culture). In this mode, technology is nearly always figured as dystopic, with exceptions in advertising (a few communications commercials, here and there, figure a bright new future where we will "ride the light").

But cautionary tales are not unique to the techno-age—many doomsday scenarios parallel age-old myths of disaster, pestilence, invasion, monstrous couplings. They often highlight the consequences of human hubris—even demonstrating the dangers of flying too far, too fast (like Icarus, the first astronaut casualty). In another millennium, today's techno-rhetoricians would probably have been seeing disaster in the stars, or reading the oracle at Delphi as a warning of apocalypse. But if these ancient metaphors are still so compelling, it is precisely because they tap into universal fears: fear of falling, of getting lost, of going too far. Aesthetically, the techno-metaphor unites a timeworn formula for metaphor—"same-but-different"—with the Freudian formula for the uncanny—familiar but spooky. If technology reminds us of our precarious situation, it is doubtless because we recognize an uncanny double in the thinking machine behind the screen, reflecting the "same" culture that we know, but also "alien" in its workings—hence, deeply uncanny. (Stanley Kubrick's sinister character in the classic 2001: *A Space Odyssey*, the computer HAL who kills off his crew, is one such uncanny Other who has captured the collective imagination. The pathos of HAL's "death" as he is unwired, even while he pleads with the astronaut not to "kill" him, is also deeply creepy.) The response to technology may merely be the newest materialization of an anxiety as old as Pygmalion, the fear of being undone by our own inventions. Fear of what we have spawned, in fact, may be an updated version of the myth of Oedipus.

3. Techno-Aesthetics

Another prominent theoretical response to technology may be found in the analysis of those cultural observers (Mark Dery, Adam Parfrey, Anne Balsamo) who regard the techno-object as the source of inspiration for the electronic culture of "Cyberia"—manifest in cyberpunk fiction, postmodern mix music, body art, staged robot combat.[19] As Adam Parfrey points out in *Apocalypse Culture*, the Cyberian techno-aesthetic feeds on the borderline perverse energies of a desublimated culture, derived from the 1980s punk aesthetic of alienation and self-mortification, as well as the 1990s culture of wired ecstasy (in a "rave" with synthesized techno-music, or the "trance" clubs that persist today). And although the aestheticization of technology has been around for at least a century, beginning with Italian futurism, techno-aesthetics today casts technology as a noxious *Other* to human life, as well as its muse. In the work of 1980s cyberpunk writers (Pat Cadigan, Bruce Sterling, Neal Stephenson), as well as in now-classic films such as Cronenberg's *Fly* and *Crash*, the merger with the Alien creature or machine often entails human sacrifice.[20] (In the third *Alien*, for instance, Ripley plunges into molten metal to avoid propagating the monster that has invaded her: she is a hybrid of beauty and beast.)

4. Techno-politics

In addition to techno-philosophy, techno-rhetoric, and techno-aesthetics, there is a fourth encounter between theory and technology today: the sociopolitical critique of culture, in the work of major theorists like Žižek, De Landa, Baudrillard, and Haraway. We have seen that a liminal figure in all four fields of techno-theory is Pierre Bourdieu, as a Marxist theorist of market and media. His work is particularly hard to classify as philosophy or sociology, for his techno-neo-Marxism analyzes popular culture as an effect of class, and "taste" as a marker and reinforcement of class values. In addition, like Donna Haraway, Bourdieu is interested in concrete objects as commodities in today's culture; also like Haraway, he sees these objects as sites of investment, at once political, psychological, and financial. Although Bourdieu's own relationship with psychoanalysis is more implicit than explicit, it is perhaps in just this sort of interdisciplinary sociopolitical analysis that Lacanian theory is most often invoked today, with some intriguing consequences.

CULTURE BESIDE ITSELF

Far-from-Equilibrium Society

Lacan's use of the Borromean knot as an emblem of linkage between three realms of human experience—the imaginary, the symbolic, and the real—shows that he did not perceive one register as more important than, or independent from, the other two. His scheme is synchronic and descriptive, not developmental, depicting the phase space of the human experience.[21] The figure of the Borromean knot also blurs the classical distinction between inside and outside. As Stuart Schneiderman explains in his intellectual biography of Lacan:

> The Borromean knot is a linkage such that no two rings intersect. Since the interlocking of any two rings is prohibited, the hole of each of the rings remains inviolate: no other ring can be said to be either inside of or outside it . . . . Lacan was preoccupied [with the topology of knots] over the last years of his Seminar. The

task he had set himself was nothing les than the subversion of the concept of space that had informed metaphysical philosophy.[22]

But even though Lacan insists that the hierarchy of these three domains of experience is not an issue, many millennial theorists speculate that one or another of these registers is out of balance today, contributing to our uneasiness in a world that we no longer quite recognize.

Spooked by the Imaginary: The Plague of Fantasies

In the 1960s, Louis Althusser first articulated the connection between the Lacanian imaginary and ideology.[23] He defined ideology as the subject's imaginary relation to the real (defined as invisible and pervasive, "what everyone knows" or "holds as self-evident," often having little basis in reality). Following Althusser, post-Marxist theorists from Baudrillard to Žižek and Bourdieu have considered "virtual" culture as a noxious overvaluation of the imaginary. Critics like Virilio (The Lost Dimension) and Arthur and Marilouise Kroker (Hacking the Future) complain that the aesthetics of velocity and instantaneity have consigned the human subject to a flattened, screen space; while many women theorists (Balsamo, Springer, Haraway, Singer) point out that the female body is severely monitored and disciplined in the culture of image.[24] At the same time, explicitly political theorists such as De Landa and Bourdieu critique a ruthless global economy where corporate speculation and merger mania play to the individual investor's fascination with the game. The new addictive sport of the affluent in the United States, online day trading, is part spectacle and part participatory sport, promising online speculators the thrill of on-the-spot gain in the ultimate video gamble.

But although the menace of the imaginary is a common theme in millennial theory, many theorists assert that the posthuman phenomenon is actually a symptom of the overvaluation of the symbolic register, given the importance of code in the information age.

Spooked by the Symbolic: The Dominance of Data

Although Slavoj Žižek, for one, insists that we are in no danger of becoming just another window in cyberspace, he shifts the posthuman crisis from the imaginary to the symbolic register. Under the sway of this dominant symbolic, Žižek argues, the Other is no longer just the "subject *supposed* to know" of classic Lacanian theory, but is now the site of excessive *actual* knowledge, compiled by surveillant systems that track life histories, individual buying habits, and personal records. The phantom of an all-knowing Other presents the threat of totalitarianism, in a monitored culture of data banks.[25]

This fear is certainly not without foundation, and it suggests the importance of remaining attentive to policies about information control. But as Lacan points out, the power of the Other resides in our own belief, so that the idea of an all-controlling hypersymbolic is also itself perhaps an "imaginary" concept. That is to say, Žižek's "repressive symbolic" is perhaps just as much a symptom of *The Plague of Fantasies* as it is a cause of it. (Just where is this all-knowing eye? It can't find a terrorist cave hideout or an anthrax mailer.)

In a very different way, N. Katherine Hayles, in *How We Became Posthuman*, also voices concern about an overestimation of the symbolic in culture, as a fetishization of information.[26] She details four assumptions of posthuman ideology: (1) information is superior to its embodiment (code is "all there is," since life itself is programmed by DNA); (2) a seamless articulation between human and machine is possible and desirable (cyborgism); (3) cybernetic systems may successfully duplicate organic ones, producing artificial life; (4) identity is equivalent to consciousness. Hayles goes on to list four corollary effects of the posthuman world-view: (1) the privileging of information over biological substratum ("life" is a mere accident); (2) the defeat of the values of the liberal subject (individuality, reason); (3) the view of consciousness as epiphenomenon, the chance end product of evolution; (4) the view of the body as prosthesis, a machine in the service of mind. All of these assumptions, she argues, obscure material connections between information and reality, in a cyber version of Cartesian mind/body dualism.

Against this tendency, Hayles sees information as the tool of embodied minds, emphasizing the grounding of code in the material world (genes *are* matter; digital code is a material signal). Unfortuately, however, she risks falling into the fetishism of the vitalists: the assumption of the superiority of the human over other life; the notion that "life itself" is sacred; the assumption that life is always carbon-based. Both mechanism and vitalism devalue embodiment: one fetishizes information at the expense of "real life"; the other fetishizes "life itself" (as soul or spirit) at the expense of matter.

Psychoanalysis, however, might be useful in formulating a response to the four "posthuman" assumptions, without falling into vitalism.

1. For Freud, information is not superior to body: every symptom is psychosomatic, and in some cases (hysteria, or "acting out") the actions of the body *are the code*.

2. On the question of the liberal subject, endowed with agency, Freud has an interesting take, since he theorizes two distinct but interacting psychic systems: conscious/ rational and unconscious. He is a material determinist, but he certainly believes that intervention may benefit the individual subject who consciously chooses, after all, to seek therapy.

3. Freud thinks consciousness may well be an effect of evolution (hence the controversial classification of "primitive" peoples as infantile). But what makes the human "human" is the result of a split, an evolutionary development that results in projective thinking ("as if"; "what if"), which in turn brings the capacity for symbolization. And his theory remains a radical challenge to the primacy given to consciousness and identity.

4. As for the body as "machine" governed by mind: for Freud, psyche *is* body, as evidenced by the importance of sexuality in psychoanalysis. The question of the seamless interaction of human and machine is a moot point for psychoanalysis, since the wish for machine-human integration is itself based on an ideology of perfection that psychoanalysis considers imaginary. For psychoanalysis, there is no seamlessness in human being, which is always Other to itself.

Spooked by the Real: The Return of the Foreclosed

In some of the most interesting millennial theory, a repressive "real" is foregrounded, rather than the imaginary or symbolic registers. But what is the Lacanian real? In a sense, it is anything that cannot be made functional in a signifying system, the brute matter that refuses assimilation to meaning. (This is reminiscent of Heidegger's observation that we only really see the tool as obdurate material Thing when it ceases to work for us, as anyone who has ever faced a frozen computer screen knows.) The Lacanian real is the "thingness" in matter that eludes symbolization: as Jean-François Lyotard puts it, "The real is that which escapes us."[27] And it escapes us not because it does not "really" exist, but because it does. It is matter that refuses to answer the question *why*.

In his work on popular film, Žižek insists on the difference between the Lacanian *real* and *reality*, the latter being a symbolic construct, reflecting a cultural consensus concerning what counts as reality; while the "real" is material being that resists conceptualization. Indeed, Lacan suggests that the intrusion of the real may induce psychosis, threatening the fabric of the symbolic order by obliterating meaningful "reality." Žižek cites as an example the "paranoid" cinema of Hitchcock, where menacing objects take on a life of their own, and seem to look back, spreading like blots on the screen, and often inducing psychosis in the film's screen characters. He also cites the prevalence of the cinematic theme of the zombie, the return of the living dead, as an example of what he calls *the answer of the real* to a repressive symbolic social order (Freud would call this the return of the repressed).[28]

How do these insights help us to make sense of today's "borderless" information age? We could say that with the attack on the World Trade Center, for instance, Americans experienced a tear in the fabric of reality. Faced with the aggression of the "real" (anthrax letters, jetliner bombs), we are asking what repressive actions may have occasioned this particularly vicious "answer of the real" (Why do *they* hate us so much?). Commentators spoke of "waking from a dream," noting the qualitative difference in what counts as reality, before and after the attacks.

Baudrillard makes a similar point about rampant viruses as a deadly "answer of the real": these viruses, whether organic or electronic, prey on the weakened immune system of an oversanitized world.[29] Again, this seemingly far-fetched complaint has materialized in the fear of something as virulent as smallpox, in a world that believed it had conquered this disease. This shows the ramifications of the refusal of just a few to play by the rules of a consensual symbolic order, causing culture to suffer the incursion of a potentially terrifying real.

Donna Haraway also foregrounds a certain "real" in her work, given her focus on the material objects that dominate our culture. But citing the commodification of fetishized technology—the gene, the fetus, the chip—Haraway suggests that these objects are also ideological icons representing essentialized values: the fetus is life itself, the chip is intelligence itself, the bomb is terror itself. To put her analysis in Lacanian terms: the *real* (material object) coincides with the *imaginary* investment in what it stands for, serving a repressive *symbolic* order (capitalism).[30]

Whatever the focus of the theorist, misgivings about the perverse effects of development hardly begin with Lacan. They hark back to the Rousseauist tradition, and also find expression in Freud's work on modern angst as an effect of civilization. But in the new century, nature is no longer the opponent of culture: culture's own renegade child, technology, now threatens civilization itself. Moreover, the current technophobia harbors a deep uneasiness about boundary and site, which attributes the ills of culture to incursions of the foreign—somewhat like the growing number of self-proclaimed alien "abductees" (some 10,000 per year), who complain that they are suffering from alien implants. (This chronic xenophobia is also increasingly manifest in trade wars among developed countries. Europe bans imported genetically altered foodstuffs from the USA; the United States bans the technology for cloning embryos perfected on British ovines; the Continent fears contracting "mad cow disease" from British bovines.)

Might Lacan's version of Freud thus help us to think of Otherness . . . otherwise?

PSYCHOANALYSIS BESIDE ITSELF

> The site of the Other extends far beyond the discourse which takes its orders from the ego.
> –Jacques Lacan, *Écrits*

The Other Freud: Alterity as Algorithm

Lacan may have insisted that he was returning to Freud, but he is no simple exegete. For Lacan is unmistakably a product, even a precipitate, of bimillennial culture. Lacan's subject is a contingent effect of an "uncertainty principle"—to borrow a term from quantum science. Like Heisenberg's demonstration of the incertitude that inheres in matter itself, Lacan's theory undermines the concept of any fixed position or permanent identity. Lacan's subject, like Heisenberg's electron, always seems to be where it is not.

Lacan repeatedly refers to the Other as a locus: "The Other is the site where the "I" who speaks is constituted with the "I" who listens."[31] This indicates, among other things, that "conversation" happens only by an effect of identification with the listener's place. ("How am I coming across?" is a constitutive question for the Lacanian subject.) This conversation implies the necessity of eventually giving over the subject position to the listener, who is then never just an object, but also potentially another "subject." Here again we find the influence of French existentialism, with the notion of competition for the place of agency.

In other words, even while it stresses the importance of position in constituting the subject, Lacan's theory also insists on the impossibility of fixing the subject position in a shifting field of desire. Otherness functions as a kind of empty placeholder, a sign of inexhaustible excess rather than a privation. The Other is a limit that both enables and impedes, capturing the subject in its social net. The subject is always projected into and determined by the other positions: Otherness figures the persistence of desire as excess, an unresolved carryover of intersubjective interaction.

Throughout this book, I have referred to Lacan's simplest diagram, the Schema L, as the emblem of an unfolding of triangulated Freudian oedipal subjectivity to an open-ended and reiterated intersubjectivity. And one need only view the vectoring of desire in the Schema L to grasp the importance of shifting locus in constituting the subject. The Schema L is a graphic emblem of subjectivity as intersubjectivity: the subject is split between the position of barred S and a (autre/other): subjectivity is never identity, but is always shadowed by something Other (this is why the S of the subject is written under erasure, as a barred site). The Schema L also shows that the case history of Otherness in Lacan's work is literally "a history of case," where the term other (l'autre) is reflected and refracted in the upper case (Other: l'Autre), figuring the impossibility of assimilation of both terms to the desiring subject.[32]

But the difference of "case" (autre/other, Autre/Other) also serves to distinguish between the two terms, indicating that the Other cannot be understood simply as an unattainable object in a linear subject-object relation. The Other is, rather, a function that derails the linearity of the subject-object relation, figured in the first vector of the Schema L (the path between barred subject and objet petit a), long-circuiting desire.

In other words, Lacan's Schema L is an algorithm, whose terms may be filled by many values. For purposes of clarity, it is useful to locate four readings of the Other in Lacan's thought:

1. On the simplest level, the Other is Lacan's recasting of Freud's oedipal father, as obstruction of illegitimate desire and giver of Law. Unlike Freud, however, Lacan is at pains to distinguish this Symbolic Father from the actual father in the real world, insisting instead on the paternal as *function or site* (and thus cheating the claims of patriarchy, since the Father is gendered only relationally, not biologically). Mother, society, teacher, lover, the unconscious, the analyst—all may function in the place of the Symbolic Father, who is in any case always-already displaced, as the *slain* father of *Totem and Taboo*.

2. In a second iteration, the Other may be read abstractly, as the locus of the symbolic order or the Law, the limit marking the incommensurability of the subject's desire with its objects. At this stage, Lacan seems to hold that the Name of the Father, the paternal metaphor, grounds the Law, as indicated in his much-maligned formula naming the phallus as the "Signifier of Signifers." But even this rather unfortunate formulation implies that the Name of the Father is nothing but metaphor, a signifier "undercut" by inadequacy, having nothing to do with actual genital potency. Since *every* signifier is an effect of desire, lack is inscribed in the Signifier of Signifiers to an exponential degree.

3. In a third possible reading, the place of the Other is occupied by the analyst in the transference, always opaque to the analysand, a screen from which to "bounce off" the patient's own narrative.

4. Finally, the Other may be the subject's unconscious, experienced as an alien discourse ("*ça parle*") that speaks from an unrecognizable place ("the unconscious is the discourse of the Other").[33] In this case, the Other undermines the Cartesian claim of "presence of mind," to which it gives the lie in a Freudian slip, a surprise witticism, an inscrutable dream figure. As Lacan himself points out, the unconscious undermines the cogito's claim—"I think, therefore, I am"—by asserting "I think, there where I am not." Thanks to my unconscious, I am never exactly where, and who, I think I am.[34]

All of these readings of the Schema L stage the vicissitudes of the Other as site, later elaborated as the concept of "extimacy."

EXTIMITÉ: RECONFIGURING THE OTHER

Replacing the Schema L with a new configuration, Lacan diagrams a sphere depicting *extimité*, the coincidence of intimacy with Otherness.[35] He sites the Other

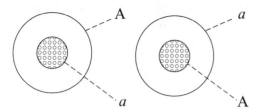

Extimacy.

(A) in an exterior position, but this time the *objet petit a* (the other as object of desire) is repositioned, nestled in the interior. This formulation is actually performative, since it effects a shift of Lacan's own position *on* position. For in the earlier Schema L, depicting a relay, the Other (A) is less *exterior* than at the end of the line, albeit at the point where the line doubles back.

But in the diagram above, the *objet petit a* has been embedded in the kernel of the circle, rather like internet hypertext, packed with other sites. The concept of extimacy compacts the *objet petit a* within the Other, rather than connecting them in linear relay or consigning them to separate imaginary or symbolic registers. Lacan's theory of *inter*subjectivity becomes a theory of *intra*subjectivity as well, where otherness and Otherness are in a relation of mutual substitutability in the split subject, instead of belonging to different levels or developmental phases.

In his exegesis of Lacanian extimacy, Jacques-Alain Miller is at pains to point out that intimate and extimate are not opposed, but implicated. Lacan coins the term "extimacy" to avoid the conventional distinction between "us" and "others," evident in the French term for madness: *aliénation*. Extimacy figures the Other as embedded alien, occupying the most intimate place. This also recalls Lacan's assertion that every meaningful expression in the symbolic is always "hooked to a little piece of the real," an inassimilable kernel. Similarly, our objects always harbor the inassimilable Other that assures that they are most out of reach precisely when they seem the most contained or comprehended.

Miller links extimacy in analysis to the intimacy of confession, where the analyst invites the patient to make herself at home, on the couch, while "he" scrupulously maintains an exterior and literally superior position. The analyst is thus invested with imaginary knowledge and authority, as *the subject supposed to know*, imagined as the sapient interpreter of the patient's narrative. This imaginary investment facilitates the shift of the analysand's desire in the transference, from one site (the parent) to another (the analyst as love-object and authority).[36]

Miller highlights a noteworthy effect of Lacan's re-placement of the terms of the Schema L in the diagram of extimacy: the explicit demotion of the patriarchal Father as ground of Law. Embedding "the other" in "the Other" figures a new parity in the status of other (as object of desire) and Other (as that which derails the aim of the drive). In this formulation, the locus of the Other can no longer be simply equated with a paternal Law imposed from above, as symbolic authority. For the Other is constituted around an excess that is always also a void, the always "surplus" *objet petit a*. Thus the first formulation of extimacy (on the left in the diagram) could just as easily be written as the second (on the right), since Otherness as excess/void is always already at the heart of the object-cause of desire, the *objet petit a*. As Miller puts it, "[This formula] concerns what I call, in Lacan, the formula of the second paternal metaphor. It corresponds point by point to the formula of the Name-of-the-Father, which we absolutely must not forget here, but in the clinic itself, we must refer to the second formula, which poses the signification of the phallus as a minus ($-\phi$), which forces us to operate with *the inexistence and the inconsistency of the Other, and not with the function of its consistency*" ("Extimité," 129, emphasis added). In other words, the original formula for the powerful Name-of-the-Father has been completely subverted: the signified "below the bar" of the paternal signifier (A as powerful Other) does not signify or confer phallic power (ϕ) but its disqualification.

Signifier	Name of the Father	(A)	A
Signified	phallus	(ϕ)	($-\phi$/"castration")

Thus, since Lacan's notion of the phallus as the "Signifier of Signifiers," so decried by some feminist theorists, is based on an *illusory* paternal plenitude, the objection of phallocentrism as sexism simply does not hold. The new formulation is much closer to Freud's foundation of society "on the back of" a deposed, assassinated paternal leader.

For this shift may represent a return to the Freud of *Totem and Taboo*, for whom the Father is not the just the arbiter who imposes order from above. He is the inassimilable Other who sticks in the craw of those who cannibalize him in the totemic sacrifice. Similarly, in the founding myth of psychoanalysis, Laius is a stranger to Oedipus, a troublemaker at the crossroads. When Oedipus in turn assumes the role of Father and ruler in Thebes, he assumes the mantle of extimacy as well: he seems to be an outsider, but this all-too-familiar alien has always been one of the family.

A second effect of the reformulation of Otherness as extimacy is the undermining of the distinction between the paranoid and the nonparanoid position. In *Seminar XI*, Lacan defines paranoia as an effect of "disbelief" in the Other (*das Unglauben*), as Lawgiver, guarantor of consensual reality. For the paranoid is certain that the apparent symbolic order is only a cover-up for what is really going on behind the scenes, directed by a hidden motive force, *the Other of the Other*.[37] Interestingly, then, Lacan's own position on Otherness as extimacy approaches that of his paranoid unbeliever, since his doctrine on extimacy depends on his own assertion that "the Other does not exist" as absolute ground.[38]

Lacan differs from the paranoid only in the realization that "the Other of the Other" is as illusory as "the Other" itself. At any rate, the actual *existence in the real* of the Other is not the crucial issue, just as the existence of an actual conspiracy is not necessary to cause paranoia. The point is that the extimate Other functions symbolically as psychic reality, *as* if it exists.

THE OBJECT BESIDE ITSELF: THE ALIEN THING

In any case, Miller says that Lacan brackets the question of what "really" exists. He does concede that if there were an ontic in Lacan's scheme, it would be the *objet petit a*, the object of desire in the subject's lived experience. But the diagram of extimacy eclipses the distinction between lived reality and psychic reality, other and Other.

Miller also asserts that "the Freudian Thing" (*das Ding*) is crucial to Lacan's notion of extimacy: as the object of primal repression, the ineffable Thing is both there and absent, an unsymbolizable void around which subjectivity congeals. Lacan compares the function of *das Ding* to the space around which the potter throws his urn (bringing to mind Heidegger's notion of the "thrownness" of the subject in *Dasein*).[39]

The Lacanian real is thus not simply equivalent to the material, but it does inhere in matter that confronts us with disruptive or sinister effect ("*things* that go bump in the night"). It is also the material kernel at the heart of symbolic representation, but impervious to it—like a black hole to which meaning is drawn, but from which meaning itself cannot escape. Miller refers to three disruptive Lacanian "objects" as illustrations of the extimate; one mechanical, two human.

1. Bomb: Other as Machine

The Other can annihilate the subject.

–Jacques Lacan, *Écrits*

Miller first recounts Lacan's description of a bomb threat, where the very word ("bomb!") functions as a weapon: the threat itself, shouted into the room by a panicked student, sows disorder. The bomb is never found; but, like "The Freudian Thing" (*das Ding*)—the awesome unapproachable Object of primal repression that refuses to be remembered—the bomb functions *as* if it were really there. It represents the threat of technological terrorism, either local (a pipe bomb sneaked in by a student, an inside job) or global (the apparatus for germ warfare that eludes detection by UN observers). On the international scene, the phantom weapon is indeed functioning *as* if it exists: the mere possibility of rogue missiles may succeed in reanimating the arms race, or, most recently, function as the rationale for a very real war.

And with a kind of metonymic logic, we always suppose that the foreigner is responsible for terrorist threats, aided by a promiscuous technology—stolen by spies or published indiscriminately on the Internet. In reality, of course, the terrorist or spy sometimes turns out to be one of ours. But in the United States— where children mow each other down in schools, and disgruntled workers shoot up the workplace—the perpetrator is still seen as alien, perceived as a misfit (the "trench coat Mafia" of Columbine); a mad scientist (the unabomber; the anthrax mailer; the nuclear scientist who steals secrets; the Muslim army chaplain who gives information to al-Qaeda); or an un-American zealot to be eliminated (Timothy McVeigh). In any case, the perpetrator, by definition, is never one of us.

2. Neighbor: The Other Next Door
With remarkable insight, Lacan characterizes racism as a reaction to the way the other/Other enjoys himself: what is unbearable is the way "those people" have fun, or get what they don't deserve (the undocumented worker who "steals jobs," or gets access to our social services). The outsider contaminates our environment ("There goes the neighborhood"). At once outside of our sphere and way too close for comfort, the neighbor-as-Other plays music too loud, celebrates the wrong holidays. And foreign neighbors pose a threat even when they're not spoiling our fun here at home, for the outsourcing of jobs across the border seems to threaten our livelihood: we assume that either illegal aliens migrate to our technology, taking jobs from us, or our technology migrates to them, with the same consequence. In any case, the neighbor continues to spell trouble—in Kashmir, Africa, Northern Ireland, the Middle East. And in xenophobic Europe (as in North America, China, Australia . . .) the alien contests boundaries by penetrating them, in an ideologically charged discourse of contamination of inner by outer.

But the symbolic order acts "as if" we could all be inside the law, if only we could reinforce our frontiers, patrol our borders, purge the intruder who pollutes our nonethnicity by "ethnic cleansing." This is a classic paranoid position, in the Lacanian sense: the alien functions as the Other of the Other, the ultimate explanation for all social ills. Lacan comments cynically on the religious solution to xenophobia: the irksome neighbor is the person we are enjoined to love "as ourselves." But Lacan thinks that the love of neighbor as *self* is in the realm of the ideological imaginary (in Althusser's sense); it stems from a denial (in Freud's sense) of Otherness.[40] For instance, we could say that Enlightenment ideology declares that "all men are created equal," denying extimacy by grounding sameness in divine Law, and simply refusing to see the Other (quite literally the American slave) around whom the "society of equals" congeals. "Love they neighbor" becomes Law because God said so, rather than stemming from any ethical impulse. But this benign law is but a cover for its exclusions (nonwhites and nonmales are excluded by the Founding Fathers from the "we" who "hold these truths to be self-evident").

3. The Outlaw In-Law

In the first population count of this century, the US Census Bureau found itself caught in a paradox vis à vis undeclared residents ("illegal aliens"). In an attempt to get an accurate count, the Census Bureau aired public service announcements aimed at persuading the hidden population to be counted, but carrying a mixed message. First a voice in Spanish good-naturedly enjoined everyone to declare themselves for their community's good—using a jaunty jingle to encourage them to be counted in order "to get what they deserve." Then the message warned the listener that in any case it was *illegal* not to answer, and that silence would be *prosecuted*. Finally, the message promised soothingly not to share information with "other agencies," since it was *against the law* to do so.

But the census form itself contained a question concerning ethnicity, classified as Caucasian, African American, Native American, Asian, and—Other. Apparently some others are more "Other" than others. The next question finally stopped hedging, blurting out: "Are you of Latin American descent?" Extimacy clearly poses a dilemma to the Bureau of Statistics, which can count only what it agrees not to notice, locate, or reveal to the law it purports to represent. The dilemma has been asserted more poignantly in the debate over whether to compensate the "invisible dead" of 9/11, the undocumented workers who are no longer here, but were, officially, not there.

This paradox parallels the wife's dilemma in Miller's seminar on extimacy. The wife, desiring to remain desired, asks her lawyer to stipulate that she will cease to be legitimate (a wife, within bounds) the day she ceases to be desired (as a lover, out of bounds). But this codification of extimacy kills desire, encouraging its perpetuation extramaritally, and thus killing the marriage according to the wife's own conditions. This paradox mirrors the "uncertain" condition of matter itself in the new millennium: the uncertainty principle shows that its speed of displacement may be measured only when it is stopped.

Lacan figures a solution of sorts, although it may be of little comfort to the wife who wants to pin down floating desire in a reified contract. He schematizes the inclusion of the other in the subset of Otherness, or rather, in their logically impossible mutual inclusion (the algorithm which is written: "*object petit a is included in the set of the Other*"). In this formulation, the Other is no longer *exterior* or prior to the desire it supports—its site coincides with the embedded other. The catch is that the inaccessible object is never really "comprehended": no sooner does desire approach the inner circle than the "eccentric" mirage of its object moves out of reach.

Above all, Lacan's parables—about the bomb, the neighbor, the wife—countermand the tendency to read his late work as a turning away from the importance of intersubjectivity in favor of a desire that is internal to an individual subject. Žižek, for one, makes this error in his discussion of the cogito.[41] He claims that in his late work Lacan "abandons intersubjectivity," though not the concept of the Other, since "extimacy" embeds the Other within the subject.

> The critical abandonment and depreciation of the term "intersubjectivity" in the late Lacan (in clear contrast to his earlier insistence that the proper domain of psychoanalytic experience is neither subjective nor objective, but intersubjective) does not in any way involve an abandonment of the notion of the subject's relation to his/her Other and the latter's desire as crucial to the subject's very identity—paradoxically, one should claim that Lacan's abandonment of "intersubjectivity" on the enigma of the impenetrable Other's desire ("Che vuoi?").[42]

Žižek is right to point out Lacan's movement from the notion of the rival/narcissistic other in the imaginary register, to the notion of the Other as locus of the symbolic, to the notion of the Other as the site of opacity, the unconscious. But this movement in no way depreciates the notion of intersubjectivity. It actually *dimensionalizes* and embeds it, in a fractalization in which the Other is associated with all of these functions and sites at once. Again, if one looks back to Freud—who in his work on *Jokes*, for instance, is at pains to point out the implication of intersubjective social processes in the subject's unconscious—the dichotomy is false. Lacan's work just gets closer and closer to its stated project, a return to the radical Otherness of Freud's social psyche. Extimate desire is still played out on the field configured by Otherness; extimacy merely complicates our relation with other subjects, by undoing the clear distinction between what is subject and what is object, and focusing on the emergence of the subject in a field of Others.

This is the thrust of Miller's commentaries on the objects that figure extimacy—the bomb, the neighbor, the wife—all of whom are, among other things, social effects. And they are social effects that have only grown in importance in our dangerous borderless world, where it is increasingly difficult to "hold the line" (the latest border being contested is that of heterosexual marriage . . . can a wife have a wife, a husband a husband?). Other major preoccupations of millennialism are summed up in cultural icons that figure the recalcitrance of matter: the cyborg, the spy satellite, the surveillance camera, the mutating virus, the DNA spiral. And since the arrival of Dolly over a decade ago, counting sheep no longer ensures a restful night. Such figures converge and diverge, embedded in our culture of alien intimacy. As Miller puts it: "the most intimate [point] is not a point of transparency but rather a point of opacity."[43]

This opacity is most interesting, perhaps, in the field of cybernetics. The formulation of the other as extimate *Thing* may even be read as a *posthuman* version of intersubjectivity, where humanity is shadowed by artificial intelligence. Does Big Blue think in order to beat his human opponent in chess? Isn't calculation from the other's point of view the point of chess? Big Blue may be "the answer of the real" to the hubris of the human.

These days, when computers can learn and goof—whether by programming slip-ups, short circuits, or loops—we often react "as if" they had motive. Is there such a thing as an electronic unconscious—harboring hidden text, unseen "cookies," mysterious caches? (When preparing a lecture to a group of psychiatrists, I used spell-check on the handouts. A decidedly ironic electronic unconscious replaced Heidegger with Headgear ["Headgear and the New Age"], postmodern with postmaster ["What Comes after the Postmaster?"]. It also corrected Derrida to "deride," and my own middle name to "Alien" without so much as a wink of the cursor.) We certainly react to our electronic others like mysterious subjects with malevolent intent. What human is *not* enraged by the computer, not to speak of electronic phone queues, from time to time? But whether inorganic thought processes are like ours is perhaps not the point: the point is that they remind us that we, too, are matter.

Lacan's theory suggests that an upgraded oedipal model may still have purchase in the age of the thinking Thing: technology can be understood as the lure of the Mother Board, fostering a stifling absorption in image and screen. In a new age oedipal revolt, we now sever the umbilical cord to our tech toys, preferring cordless devices. But of course this merely shows that we are more *psychically* tethered than ever to our appendages, as mesmerizing objects of desire (we lust for the latest upgrade). Our desire to "consume" the technological object, to "incorporate" the newest version, adds a new material dimension to Lacan's famous aphorism: our desire is the desire of the Other.

The Other is the place from which the Subject can ask the question of its own Existence.

–Jacques Lacan, *Écrits* [44]

See-through Opacity

The question of "extimacy" has its corollary in popular culture. Popular culture is shadowed by a paranoid perception: the threat to humanity comes not from itself, but from the Other—who is now among us. The paranoia is manifest in two dominant phantasms: the nocturnal visit of ghostly creatures from another planet, whom we can all agree are alien; and the revolt of earthly cyborgian intelligence.

In popular film, the problem with prodigal androids is that once they have rebelled, they have no "off" switch. The wily rebellious cyborg does not (yet) exist—but in popular culture he functions *as if* he does. The classic renegade intelligence (*Terminator*; *Blade Runner*; HAL in 2001) is a pop antihero, reflecting a perverse fascination with the triumph of inhuman matter over human mind.

But we are even more intrigued by the extraterrestrial—by definition out of our sphere of experience—the new mythic agent whose expressionless stare hovers across cultures and continents. Whatever else it represents, the face of the alien reflects anxiety about the ascendancy of the Other, and a fear of surveillance and penetration. This face also projects what Lacan might consider an anamorphic distortion of humanity, not unlike the skewed and oddly out-of-place skull in the center of Holbein's *The Ambassadors*.

The latest alien is just that. Childlike and frail in body, but all-knowing and all-seeing at the controls of a UFO, it recalls . . . some Other uncannily familiar faces, between a skull and fetus. This media icon, sinister but almost comic, is like an overgrown light bulb projected onto public consciousness: it evokes mortality, but is also a site of potential enlightenment.

Curiously, in spite of the overwhelming statistical probability of intelligent life in some alien place, and our own species history of tourism, it is considered laughable to entertain the possibility that ET might, in fact, be here. From a Freudian point of view, however, it doesn't matter if the grays exist. What matters is that the Alien Abductor functions "as if" it exists, a nodal point for fears of spying, conspiracy, and intrusion. The extraterrestrial is way too close for comfort, impossible to catch in the act, and equally impossible to send home.

ET as Sex Symbol

Both Žižek and Baudrillard argue that "sexless" androgyny is the dominant millennial aesthetic, while Donna Haraway claims that we have entered a postgender world. While these assertions are certainly arguable, it is interesting to think of the alien in this way. The extraterrestrial visitor, the ultimate outsider, is sexless and gray. The phantom figure of technology—impenetrable, with enormous eyes but diminished senses—the alien communicates by telepathy, not vocal cords, and his mere slit of a mouth seems inhospitable to savory delight: he has no visible ears, a texture-free body, and less than a handful of fingers with which to touch (all probes are done with instruments). Invasive, voyeuristic, and predatory, the gray cannot be classified simply as hysterical symptom, the return of repressed eroticism, especially since it is without genitals or gender. Could this figure be a projection of humanity's fear of what it may become—hyperintelligent, unfeeling, silent, sexless? The shadowy alien doubtless embodies a defensive response to Otherness as extimate.

But Žižek, like Baudrillard and Virilio, points out that "identity" is not what is endangered in today's society—it is Otherness itself. ("Only in the distinction-based perspective of our culture is it possible to speak of the Other in connection with sex. Genuine sexuality, for its part, is 'exotic.'")[45] For Žižek, sexual exoticism "resides in the radical incomparability of the sexes." Indeed, he claims that the elimination of Otherness as mystery is what produces an experience of something . . . alien-ated: "[without the exotic] seduction would never be possible and there would be nothing but *alienation* of one sex by the other." So perhaps the gray is an incarnation of modern alienation; or perhaps it embodies the exoticism that may be missing in today's society. To be sure, millennial culture shows a deep ambivalence toward alterity, as a refuge of poetic intrigue that nonetheless threatens our species.

Still, Žižek and other philosophers of the exotic risk fetishizing Otherness, reducing it to spooky thrills (*boo!*), or the mystery of veiled sexuality (the titillation of the striptease). This may be fun, but philosophers from Montaigne to Michel de Certeau have pointed out that when Otherness is reduced to strangeness, the result may be the politics of repression. The "savage African," the "inscrutable Oriental," the "uncivilized Indian," the "incomprehensible woman," "the Western infidel"—all may be dominated, or eliminated, without compunction.

The gray seems to have arrived just in time to figure this deep ambivalence toward Otherness. Some look to the alien as savior bearing a message of cosmic communion; others fear that it will penetrate their bedroom, teleport them to another dimension, and have its technological way with their gonads. The gray is at once under- and oversexed, distant and intrusive. It not only figures fear of obsolescence, surveillance, invasion—it also figures fears of our own colonial impulse, manifest destiny turned against us by an infiltrating Other, inside and outside at will, like the phantom implants abductees insist have been placed inside them as a tracking device.

The alien, by definition, possesses a technology far superior to ours, appearing as a new age *"subject supposed to know."* Like the unresponsive analyst, it is silent, cerebral, unfeeling but all-seeing, thanks to oversized opaque eyes; without genitals but endowed with an excessive genital curiosity about *us*, and a nasty habit of interspecies breeding. In any case, the alien presence forces us to think in nonlinear terms, contemplating parallel universes and all the weird propulsions of warped time-space.

In the Alien icon, the Lacanian Other has been given a face, either as "imaginary" phantom or as high-tech "symbolic" oppressor; or even as a manifestation of the inassimilable "real" that escapes apprehension. But whether or not the visitors are "real" is a moot point for psychoanalysis. They function *as if* they exist—mutilating cattle, tracing designs in the corn, embodying extimacy for terrestrials.

Above all, the presence of the alien forces us to confront our human limits, in a process of "working through" our relation to technology as Other. The notion of know-how as Otherness is expressed by a bifurcation in language, "nimble" and "antinomy" stemming from a common root (*noumos*). Culture itself is an effect of nimbleness in the face of contingency; technology is *bricolage*, the human capacity to make do with materials at hand to structure intersubjective reality.

Moreover, Lacan's theory demonstrates that Otherness, endemic to our species, performs a crucial function in constituting the human subject. The challenge is to accommodate the alien without excessive xenophobia, not to naturalize him. As ever, it is a question of exposing self-identity as illusion, by suffering the presence of something strange in our midst. After all, the alien within us may be the machine that functions in place of a vital organ, or the robot fingers that perform surgery where the extimate is quite literally taken to heart. Lacan's doctrine of extimacy suggests that rather than trying to force "the Other's" compliance, or seeking to purge the alien that dwells within, our task is to endure the Other in our objects and in ourselves, nimbly, perhaps by acting "as if" we could.

For whether or not they are really here, the aliens have landed. Lacan teaches us that we are all, in this sense, contactees.

Postscript

The Other can annihilate the subject.
—Jacques Lacan, *Écrits*[46]

The Other is missing.

—Jacques Lacan, *Annuaire et textes statutaires* [47]

In the post-9/11 world, the alien represents something more terrifying than the extraterrestrial; he is everywhere, does real damage, but is impossible to find. If the whimsy has gone out of the Other, however, the urgency to think about our reaction to Otherness has not diminished. Perhaps Freud can assist us in that reevaluation. For in a borderless world where our technology threatens to outstrip our humanity, the term "posthuman" could figure something more sinister than mechanization. It could refer to a species without a future. Meanwhile, the figure of Oedipus continues to speak to us about the stakes of confrontation at the crossroads.

IS OEDIPUS (N)ONLINE?
PSYCHOANALYSIS AND NONLINEARITY

Ginny Ruffner, *Think with Your Heart*, 1999. © 2003 Ginny Ruffner.

All our experience runs counter to this linearity.

–Jacques Lacan, *Écrits*

Acknowledging his foundation in structural linguistics, Lacan singles out one flaw in Saussure's discipline—it is too linear. This is probably one reason why he remodeled Jakobson's two-dimensional schema of language, preferring the image of a multidimensional fractal figure. For Lacan's account of Freud elaborates the theory of a nonlinear subject who emerges in the cultural/linguistic field of Others. Thus his "return to Freud" is particularly germane to paradigms of emergence in nonlinear science and culture.

Freud, of course, also acknowledged the limitations of linear logic, and warned against too-simple cause-and-effect diagnoses. Although he depended on reason, he recognized its incompleteness, considering it but one mode of human being. This suggests one way of conceptualizing psychoanalysis itself, as a multidimensional model that admits both linear and nonlinear modalities in the psyche. In this sense, Freudian theory seems prescient, anticipating the models that, in this century, have come to supplement the traditional logic not only of mind, but of Newtonian time and matter, with increasingly counterintuitive paradigms.

Still, we have noted that these strange paradigms sometimes seem uncannily familiar, for they are often startlingly consistent with the modalities detailed by Freud in his exploration of the unconscious. We recall that Freudian theory ascribes three characteristics to primary process: timelessness, absence from contradiction, and motility of cathexis. The scene of the Freudian unconscious is timeless insofar as it ignores linear chronology; it is absent from contradiction, since it ignores syllogistic "if/then" logic; and it is marked by motility of cathexis, the protean quality of fluid desire/libido that quickly shifts from object to object, and even cathects more than one object at a time. I have argued throughout this book that Freud's thought anticipates today's nonlinear scientific modalities, and that this new science actually helps us to reread Freud. But conversely, might Freud's account of the specific modes of primary process actually suggest ways of understanding nonlinear paradigms in the new century?

Running, Out of Time

In his description of primary process ("The Unconscious," 1915), Freud highlights the "timeless" nature of dream. That is, although time often figures as an oneiric theme—as when one dreams of racing to meet a deadline—dream time itself is nonchronological, jumping from scene to scene, combining more than one time frame in a single scene, and so forth. The same disregard of linear time characterizes Freud's definition of symptom, which is ahead of its time. In fact, when Freud describes symptom as a compacted node where—"past, present and future are strung on a thread of the wish that unites them all"—he is describing something resonant with Einstein's space-time. For Freudian desire may also buckle, warp, and fold around itself, in response to strange attractors like the singularity at the center of a black hole.[1]

Is not the unconscious a black hole of sorts, which collapses time and space? Whether it is manifest in the waking symptom or as the umbilicus of the dream, Freud's unconscious is a domain of strange attractors. The strangest of these attractors is the mysterious "Freudian Thing" that so intrigued Lacan (*das Ding*, "la chose freudienne"), the ineffable object of primal repression that acts as the "singularity" at the core of the psyche.

Even Freud's founding narrative of Oedipus puts bio-logical time out of joint, wedding mother with son and producing the monstrous illogic of sibling-children. But we have seen that this ancient myth corresponds uncannily with our strange new reality: today, it is theoretically possible to raise a genetic *copy* of oneself, rather than just a mere sibling. We cannot be sure how this will turn out, but as the myth of Oedipus demonstrates, human knowledge does always seem to run the risk of being in the wrong place at the wrong time—knowing too much, too soon, or too little, too late.

Desire on the Move

Motility of cathexis, the second characteristic of primary process cited by Freud, describes the shifting nature of libido, fluid as a Moebius strip, as unlocalizable as the electron that refuses to stop and be measured. Desire is slippery, always ahead of itself or missing its mark. To draw a psychic parallel with far-from-equilibrium theory, we could say that Freudian desire is energy that exceeds a zero-sum game, localizable in its effects. It may push the psychotic subject to the tipping point between complexity and chaos, at the moment when precarious "borderline" behavior breaks with reality in a psychic catastrophe. Similarly, catastrophe marks the breaking point of material systems, occurring at the edge between stability and chaos, and pushing the system "over the edge" into chaotic behavior. Psychosis could be considered a strange attractor of sorts, where desire is sent "over the edge" by a complex of factors, determined but unpredictable. In this light, "chaos" could be considered the psychosis of matter.

Indeed, psychosis is chaos in matter. In the fragile balance of neurochemical reactions, psychosis marks a material imbalance, a tipping point that disrupts the complex system of chemical messengers that transmit signals in gray matter.

Neither Here nor There

In chapter 5 we saw that the third characteristic of the unconscious noted by Freud, absence from contradiction, does not seek simply to overturn linear logic. It is a mode that is *other* than the either/or opposition of identity and exclusion, in a process that refuses assimilation to linear reason, or secondary process. Deleuze's disjunctive synthesis (chapter 6) provides an instance of Freud's "both/ and" mode in millennial philosophy. And a material correlative is found in subatomic particles that have no problem being *both* here *and* there; quantum theory simply exempts them from that contradiction. Freud's system of primary and secondary process is a no-fault universe where both Newton and Einstein have a point, a domain where two rights don't make a wrong.

Dimensional Freud

Freud's work on dreams and the unconscious shows that nearly a decade before Einstein, Freud was already a nonlinear thinker. But we have seen that multidimensionality is a crucial part of nonlinear paradigms, and Freud's classic triangle might seem quite Euclidean, planar. Can we conceptualize its multidimensionality? Once again, this process of "subjectivation" of the psyche through complexification and dimensionalization, however schematic, now has a material correlate. For neurological research shows that the infant brain is a nearly blank slate that sprouts new connections and makes new traces with each new experience, creating new synapses in a progressive complexification of the brain's actual physical structure.

Even though the child is born into a multidimensional cultural figuration, we could think of the infant subject-to-be as *zero*-dimensional at birth, a mere point in the intersubjective field. The connection of subject to object (child to mother in the classic version of Oedipus-as-complex) could be figured as a *one*-dimensional line, the first side of the oedipal triangle. Inclusion of the Other in the field (the father, in the traditional version) produces a second dimension. But the three points of the familiar oedipal relation still describe a flat two-dimensional triangular plane.

Throughout this book, I have argued that Lacan's Schema L embodies the complexity that is already in Freud. This is figured by actually adding a fourth term in Freud's triadic intersubjective circuit, in an open structure where any side of the Z-shaped Schema L may be hinged and swung open, off the page and into "our" three-dimensional space (Lacan does this by doubling the first position in the triangle, dividing it into the barred subject $\mathcal{S}$ and the ego a', to reflect the subject's own object status to itself).

In other words, the avatars of Lacan's Schema L have revealed that the Freudian triangle already harbors four (or more) dimensions, thanks to the splitting that founds human subjectivity. Nor is the subject the only overdetermined term in the Schema L. In chapter 8, we saw that the third term (as Other) has several avatars in Lacan. This is already true in Freud, where the oedipal Father is obstacle, model, object of identification, and the stand-in for prohibition in society. (He is also the model for "narcissistic object choice" in "On Narcissism" [1917]; and the representative of "thirdness" that forces the long circuit of subjectivation into a field of Otherness in many social transactions.) The overdetermination of the joke triangle in particular (chapter 4) shows that the three positions of Freud's triangle are always multidimensional; even in the Oedipus myth. And Lacan's paranoid knowledge (chapter 3), illustrated by the parable of the three convicts, shows that the three positions in the intersubjective field are rotatable and interchangeable.

But again, Lacan's split perspective is already in Freud's positing of the unconscious as an effect of *Spaltung*, the splitting which adds another dimension to the psyche, with the primal repression that produces the unconscious.[2] Add the next iteration of subjectivity, when the child becomes a parent in the next generation, and you create another link in the chain, with the subject now occupying the place of the parent who will initiate infant subjects in his or her turn. This is the thrust of Lacan's extimacy: all the positions are interchangeable and co-implicated, internal and external, as subjectivity makes its rounds, in time.

"Fractal Freud" (chapter 7) is an effect of the iteration of a new generation in the oedipal scenario, in many versions: the reactivation of a joke transaction in each retelling, or the passing of a work of literature to another reader, or the creation of myth over time by a whole people. Each of these iterations generates a fourth dimension, unfolding in time to replicate the intersubjective structure with new terms. This temporal element (the fourth dimension) is important in Freud, both in his account of the contagious nature of desire (when the joke is repeated to an Other, the next *time*) and in the ongoing replication of the social paradigm from generation to generation. Twenty-first century science studies this transfer on a cultural level, as the passing on of memes or culturgens over generations (chapter 7).

In this sense, the space of our psychic reality is always at least four-dimensional, thanks to the temporal nature of the social interactive field. The human symptom is always an effect of time, condensing past, present, and future into one nodal point. A fourth dimension also figures in Lacan's discussion of triangulated paranoid knowledge, as the time it takes each convict to figure out what the other two are thinking ("*le temps à comprendre*" discussed in chapter 3). Freud seems to be getting at something similar with his doctrines of latency and *Nachträglichkeit*, speculating on why the symptom takes time to appear.

But what of the mysterious fifth dimension, sometimes characterized in the new physics as "the quantum leap," allowing one thing (such as the electron) to occupy two places at one time, or, in "many worlds theory," determining the generation of infinite parallel universes from the potential of matter? We should also think of the strange new extensions of string theory, which postulates that parallel

Roger Groce, *Boy Shape*, 2004.

universes occupy "branes" in other dimensions, possibly only millimeters from ours. According to this emerging theory, the Big Bang may have been a collision between "branes."[3]

The idea is not alien to psychoanalysis. Indeed, the capacity to be in two places at one time—or, conversely, to compact or condense more than one meaning in one place (overdetermination)—is a crucial part of the Freudian analytic model, from dream interpretation to the reading of a hysterical symptom. When Freud specifically defines the *nonlinear* time of symptom as *Nachträglichkeit*, he underscores the potential of causes to take effect at a time removed from the primal event: the primal scene thus functions at more than one place in one time.[4] This ability also characterizes the transference in analysis, where the patient is "at once" with (past) parent and (present) analyst. This quantum quality might in fact characterize any synchronic psychic reality (for instance, the symbolic father/Other functions in many places at once, determining any number of symptoms, as representative of Law—unlike a real parent, who functions in real time, and is only ever in one place at one time).

With the postulations of higher dimensions (chapter 7), we hook up the multi-dimensions of other psyches in an infinite number of extrasubjective transactional fields, in an open-ended fractal model.

THE NONORIENTABLE SUBJECT: WHERE AM "I"?

> The drive gets around.
> –Jacques Lacan, *Écrits*

The theory of extimacy (chapter 8) further complicates the concept of dimension by eliding the distinction between inner and outer. Interestingly enough, this is also evoked by Freud, as the final characteristic of the unconscious as described in "The Unconscious": "the projection of internal onto external reality," or the substitution of internal for external.

In chapter 6, we saw that there is again a correlate to Freud's thought in new topological models of space. The term "nonorientability" describes a surface where there is no topological distinction between inside and outside, where inside and outside are "undecidable." As one math tutorial explains: "A non-orientable manifold has a path which brings a traveler back to his starting point mirror-reversed."[5] A Moebius strip, for instance, has only one surface that loops around. From a local vantage point on this path, one never appears to change direction: a Moebius journey would visit both "inside" and "outside" without retracing steps, or jumping to another side (there is in fact only one side). In topological geometry, nonorientability is the distinguishing characteristic of all the shapes pictured below: the pyramid-like Boy shape, the "cross cap" or bishop's miter, and the mysterious multidimensional cornucopia called the Klein bottle.

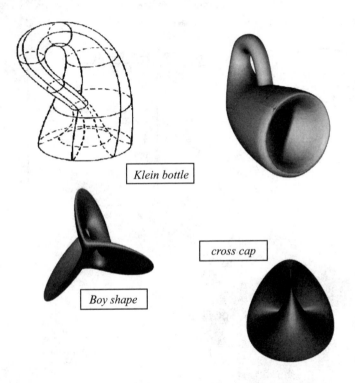

Klein bottle

cross cap

Boy shape

In each of the nonorientable figures shown here, you may start anywhere on the surface, follow a trajectory all around, and end up where you started without changing directions, passing through a surface, or "flipping over" to another surface. These shapes, where inside and outside are continuous topologically, provide a visual way to figure the concept of extimacy: it is an encounter with Otherness in a space that is both external and internal to the subject.

The counterintuitive aspect of multidimensional topological reality is perhaps most apparent in a transparency of the Klein bottle, where we can see that what *appears* to intersect in three dimensions is actually looped around and turned inside out by "lifting" the object into the next dimension (off the page, in this case) to make the crossing without breaking a surface.[6] On the Internet, there are numerous sites with patterns for making "Klein purses" and "Klein pockets," which involve the operation of attaching two sides and pulling the whole contraption through itself. (The famous performance artist Cristo even approximated a Klein shape with one of his monumental drapings.)[7] But fascinating as this multidimensional shape is in itself, it has another surprise in store for the Lacan fan: in a cross-section view, it reveals an uncanny resemblance to Lacan's interior 8, a loop describing the dynamics of desire and demand in the transference:

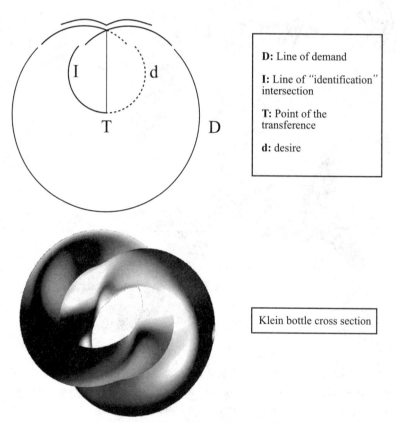

D: Line of demand

I: Line of "identification" intersection

T: Point of the transference

d: desire

Klein bottle cross section

Lacan himself later implicitly says something like this—by pointing out that a lifting or bypass at the point of intersection allows the lines of his "interior 8" not to join. In this case, the interior 8 loop would not be flat but would extend in a spiral, thanks to the sidestep "borrowing" the space of another dimension to avoid intersection.

Lacan Makes His Move: or, Lifting the Bishop off the Game Board

In an early characterization of the interior 8, Lacan deliberately opts out of this sidestep, choosing to remain in three-dimensional space, by insisting on this apparent intersection:

> This surface is a Moebius surface, in that its outside continues its inside. There is a second necessity that emerges from this figure, that is, that it must, in order to close its curve, traverse at some point the preceding surface . . . the image enables us to figure desire as a locus of junction between the field of demand, in which the syncopes of the unconscious are made present, in sexual reality. The inner circle represents the internal world, including unconscious desire (the broken line of the inner circle), which is transformed into conscious demand (the unbroken line of the inner circle), and directed outward, to "sexual reality" (the experience represented by the outer circle).[8]

What Lacan does not mention in his first presentation of the figure is that his Moebius surface cannot be represented in three-dimensional space without "cheating" by depicting an intersection, when a Moebius surface never in fact intersects. Nor does he point out that the space is nonorientable: that is, you can go all around its surface without a change in direction . . . as in a freeway bypass or cloverleaf.

In other words, if this first version of the figure 8 seems to portray a certain closure, it is only because Lacan does not point out the necessity for a further dimensionalization, at least here, preferring the simplicity of the notion of simple juncture or intersection ("the image enables us to figure desire as a locus of junction between the field of demand, in which the syncopes of the unconscious are made present, in sexual reality"). But of course, unconscious desire and conscious demand never exactly intersect, but chase each other around the furniture. That is the point—or, rather, the curve—of Lacan's loopy desire. So, like a knot theorist who must act "as if" a knot is a complete object, Lacan's schema depicts a meet-up between desire and demand that is actually a bypass: ships in the night.

He does, however, go on to say that this is a picture of the desire of the Other, which, of course, is always unfulfilled: hence it always loops back around to feed the circuit. So even in the early figure 8 formulation, which seems to show an intersection, Lacan already suggests that the perpetuation of the circuit is actually an effect of a nonintersection, requiring a move in the fourth dimension. This will be acknowledged in a later formulation, in *Seminar XI*.

But before turning to that complication, let us note that (thankfully) Lacan's nonorientable surface is also found in a more familiar form in daily life: the "cross cap" or bishop's miter, is often the shape of folded napkins standing on a dinner plate. In the *Four Fundamental Concepts of Psycho-Analysis*, Lacan himself compares his interior 8 to a bishop's cap: "This surface belongs to another whose topology I have described at various times, and which is called the cross-cap, in other words, the mitre" (271). He then gives a hands-on instruction for creating the figure: "Bring the edges together two by two as they are presented here, by a complementary surface, and close it." He points out that this operation is analogous to a circle being extended spatially into a sphere, moving his depiction from two flat dimensions into three.

In Lacan's move, inside and outside form a continuous surface, thanks to a looping and pulling through of the material at pinch points, a gesture that is accomplished only in *time*. If you followed one thread around a standing folded napkin (bishop-cap style), you would visit both "inside" and "outside" without ever changing direction, or jumping to the reverse side. In a flat diagram or cross section of the miter, the surfaces would appear to break through each other, as in Lacan's diagram (see page 260).[9] But demand never meets its object, in this spiraled loop. The lines only appear to intersect in the diagram, but they are actually involuted, as Lacan makes clear in his second description of the interior 8. Significantly, this time he explicitly invokes topological geometry in this comment, again giving a "how-to" demonstration for making the fold:

> It is for this reason that the function of the transference may be *topological* in that form that I have already produced in my seminar on the Identification—namely, the form that I have called on occasion the *interior eight*, that double curve that you see on the blackboard folding back upon itself, and whose essential property is that each of its halves, following one another, comes back to back at each point with the preceding half. (*Four Fundamental Concepts*, 270; emphasis added)

Thus, long before topology became part of our general worldview, Lacan's nonorientable loop (the interior 8) pictures an involuted/exvoluted *extimate* surface. In the *Four Fundamental Concepts of Psycho-Analysis*, he abandons his earlier conceit, depicting a juncture or an intersection in the interior 8. This time he explicitly calls for a move away from three dimensions and into four, made with two "pinch points," and creating a rim. To do this, you have to step out of line, "abstracting" yourself from your normal reality:

Note that this in no way implies any contradiction—even in the most ordinary space—except that in order to grasp its extent, *one must abstract oneself from three-dimensional space, since it is a question here only of a topological reality that is limited to the function of a surface.* You can thus conceive quite easily in three dimensions one of the parts of the plane, at the moment at which the other, by its rim, returns upon it, determines there a sort of intersection. (270–271; emphasis added)

Thus Lacan removes his diagram from the business-as-usual space of our normal three-dimensional orientation, toward a dimension beyond our experienced space:

This intersection has a meaning *outside our space.* It is structurally definable, without reference to the three dimensions, by a certain relation of the surface to itself, in so far as, returning upon itself, it crosses itself at a point no doubt to be determined. Well! This line of intersection is for us what may symbolize the function of identification. (271)

It is not necessary to rehearse the theory of the involuted 8 in detail: suffice it to observe that its shape describes desire as an extradimensional loop in the patient's demand to the analyst, thanks to the patient's identification with (and desire of) the therapist in transference love, in time. It is the topology that is important here, describing an intersection that is not a cut but a continuation, participating in a multidimensional modality (unconscious and conscious, primary and secondary process, at once).

As Lacan also points out, this crossing has to be understood as an operation in time, involving an additional operation in space, when the shape is pulled inside out: "It is very easy to imagine that, in short, the lobe constituted by this surface at its point of return covers another lobe, the two constituting themselves by the form of the rim." Lacan underscores the need for an additional dimension, "since it is a question of topological reality that is limited to the function of a surface" (271). In order to represent the described function, in other words, Lacan has to get beyond the flat page. Now in one view, the Klein bottle also resembles the pattern for a bishop's miter or cross cap. Like the cross cap, it may be considered a dimensional version of Lacan's interior 8 as is evident in this comparison. In every case, the figures could be generated by twisting or stretching a Moebius strip.

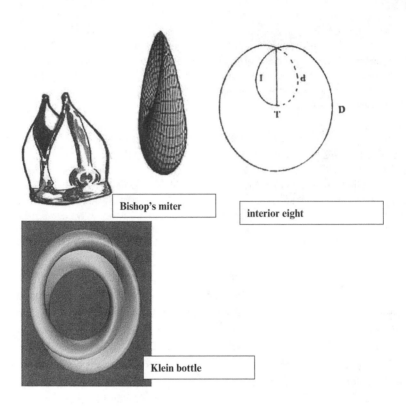

Bishop's miter

interior eight

Klein bottle

The coincidence of the interior 8 and two of the prime nonorientable figures of geometry shows that throughout his career, Lacan was thinking topologically. These diagrams are dynamic, showing that desire is extimate and interdimensional, both within and without a subject's own psyche.

Finally, to represent this field as a circulation among intersubjects, one need only picture the "Boy shape." Freud's original triangle has become a tetrahedron, which may be visited only by lifting the crossings into the fourth dimension. Lacan himself, in *Seminar XV*, refers to the three-dimensional structure of intersubjective analysis as a tetrahedron, a pyramid, which is of course a faceted dimensionalized triangle. This is another way of thinking of the Schema L, deployed in space—each line is the edge of a pyramid, which may be extended into higher dimensions. Freud's triangular field may be figured, through Lacan's Schema L, iterated first as tetrahedron, then embedded in an infinite field of expanding iterations.

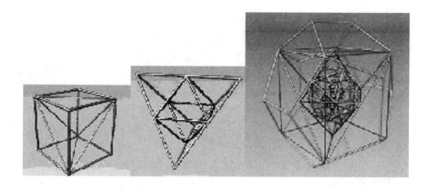

Indeed, the rotation of subject positions (the "fall of the analyst" which allows the analysand to take her place as an analyst in her turn) is in a sense always located in the fourth dimension, the *time* required for the *Durcharbeitung* or working through, the dimensional structure of Lacan's *"temps à comprendre."* But when the subject moves through the nonorientable trajectory, she or he is eventually going to undergo a mirror reversal, "falling" and rotating in her or his turn, since all demands to Others come home to roost. As Lacan reminds us in his seminar on "The Purloined Letter," "a letter always reaches its destination."[10] This is the dimensional matrix of human being, and it is still the space of Oedipus the voyager, shuttling among the many dimensions of the twenty-first century.

THE MOEBIUS TWIST: "TO BE (INSIDE), OR NOT TO BE? THAT IS THE QUESTION"

> Ach! Professor Möbius, glörious Möbius
> Ach, we love your topological,
> And, ach, so logical strip!
> One-sided inside and two-sided outside!
> Ach! euphörius, glörius Möbius Strip-Tease!
>
> —Nicolas Slonimsky, "The Möbius Strip Tease"

In "The Instance of the Letter in the Unconscious" (1957; mistakenly translated in some anthologies as "The Insistence of the Letter"), Lacan specifies: "The place that I occupy as the subject of a signfier is in relation to the place I occupy as subject of the signified: *concentric or ex-centric—that is the question*."[11] In this echo of the hero's query in *Hamlet*—one of Lacan's favorite plays—the issue of the *site* of the subject, eccentric or concentric, is singled out as *the* most important: "That is the question." But in Lacan's later work on extimacy, when he elaborates subjectivity as a kind of nonorientability, Hamlet's question (Inside or outside?

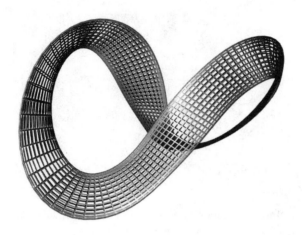

Moebius exchange.

Stranger or familiar?) is finally moot. The self, such as it is, is always ex-centric, constantly displaced in a field of familiar strangers, as Oedipus and Hamlet both demonstrate.

The nonorientable surface does seem like an uncannily appropriate material figure for our new borderless world, where we cannot tell who is "inside" and who is "outside" our "borders." The "nonorientable" surfaces of topology in higher dimensions nonetheless seem as alien to our ordinary experience as the "uncertainty" of matter (Heisenberg) and the built-in "incompleteness" that inheres in flawless reason (Gödel). In fact, it is not even appropriate to metaphorize the concept of nonorientability as "cutting-edge," since it does away with the concept of edge and boundary altogether.

It may help to think of other "Moebius" phenomena. A Moebius structure also characterizes many contemporary works of literature (who can tell where a Calvino story begins or ends, and when we are reading it or acting in it or participating in its dismantling?). Extimate structure is also seen in the whimsy of the postmodern architecture of embedding, pastiche, and whimsy, where inside and outside, up and down, old and new, are deliberately confounded. (On the Miami skyline, several buildings have "holes" in them, sprouting trees in "keyholes" in the sky.) In music, where the involuted structure has been around since Bach, the Moebius structure has now been consciously constructed to be played on a Moog synthesizer as a loop that turns on itself. One composer at UCLA (Nicolas Slonimsky) has even produced a snippet of music that may be heard on the Web, complete with lyrics ("The Moebius Strip Tease," in the epigraph to this section).[12]

All these nonlinear models of science and culture, where the whole may not be described by its parts, are open-ended, proliferating, relational. This science also seems shifty—in systems where "site " is all that determines view, and view is all that determines knowledge. The new paradigms demand a new motility of mind, an ability to change the familiar frame of reference, to substitute relation (contemporary and contingent though it is) for ground.

For instance, Lacan's grounding axiom "our desire is the desire of the Other" may be turned into a Moebius performance, simply by repeating the verb, in an open-ended loop "our desire is the desire of the Other is our desire is the desire of the Other is . . .". The site of "our" desire is nonorientable, and only relationally localizable: the difference between you/me, inside/outside is involuted, in time. Freud's psyche, like Lee Smolin's cosmos, is a relational universe—to recall Deleuze's definition of the rhizome, "everything is linked to everything else, and must be," in a relation that is always on the go.

Of course, Lacan's notion of the extimate loop is an update of Freud's notion of the circuit of desire. Or rather, Lacan's own looping, his own "return to Freud," shows that if Freud was of his time, he was ahead of his time too. For Freud's theory suggests that the human perspective is a question of placement. It is this relational universe that we have been trying to adjust to for almost a century now, ever since Freud and Einstein introduced us to it.

THE RELATIONAL UNIVERSE: "POSTING" THE HUMAN

> The most important principle of 20th-century physics is that all observable properties of things are about relationships.
> –Lee Smolin, "What Is the Future of Cosmology?"[13]

Nonlinearity describes the online surfing mode, the jumping from site to site that enacts the cyber version of the motility of cathexis, where the linked sites are finite but inexhaustible. It is always also a journey that loops back to its starting point or home page, like a Moebius trajectory.

But humanity has always played nonlinear games: in laughing at the intrusion of a Freudian slip; in the viral nature of a joke; in the iterative replication of socialization, far beyond the oedipal family. Freud describes language as nonlinear; symptom as nonlinear; creative consciousness as nonlinear, social structure as nonlinear. Freud, in fact, describes human existence not as a linear trajectory but as an oscillation between "sets" of instincts, governing life and death (and set theory allows for any number of "permutations").

Lacan's paranoid knowledge replicates the nonlinear Freudian space as a holey space of social contact and maintained desire, of incommensurate but mutually permeable dimensions. In Deleuze's terms, the space of the mind is smooth, nonorientable, a circuit for a slippery, shifting desire. It is also striated, when provisionally "oriented" in a triangulated circuit with three distinct stations implicating interiority and exteriority. And it is holey, since the psyche operates in more than one mode or domain. Lacan's theory of subjectivity as triangulated site, as locus, is also a theory of circulation and substitutability, the founding of creative metaphoric thought and sympathetic relation ("our desire is the desire of the Other" is a recipe for conflict, but also for bonding).[14] This same "relational" circuit is what ensures that, as Lacan says "the Other returns our question to us in inverted form," like an echo. "Why are you asking this?" returns as "Why are *you* asking this?"; What do you want of me?" returns as "What do *you* want of *me?*" Challenges to the Other loop not because they are unanswerable, or because exchange is impossible, but because the answer always manifests my displacement in and cathexis to Otherness in the interior 8, the Moebius loop that constitutes the intersubjective field.

In this way, Freud relays questions to Einstein, Hawking, Heisenberg, even Descartes, about how the psyche works in real matter (What is the psychosomatic? What is your universe?), and their gray matter sends the query right back at him: "What is consciousness?" "What is *your* universe?" Freud's relational psyche *is* a relational universe.

In fact, the closing of *Beyond the Pleasure Principle* could serve as a motto for space travel, as the species spirals "upward and onward, unsubdued." As Einstein was theorizing the bending of straight lines in curved space—long before the discovery of a real black hole—Freud figured the human mind as distortable, holey space. Before the new cosmologies, Freud demonstrated that inner space is iterative, recursive, fluid, and fractal.

The new paradigms—nonorientable space, far-from-equilibrium systems, refractive knowledge, exponential iterations, chaotic systems, fractal replication and embedding—are all implicit in the Freudian model, and articulated by the theory "returned to Freud" by Lacan's own Moebius loop.

Freud did not believe in cures or happy endings; his only hope was to trade neurotic misery for "common unhappiness."[15] But common unhappiness, propelled by the compulsion to repeat and responding to infinite desire, is what sends us on our way to human social being. In this sense, Oedipus is online and en route, intimate and extimate. Oedipus at the crossroads is already the monstrous posthuman subject, a parasite on his own past groping toward an uncertain future.

What would Freud the scientist say about the endeavor of modern astrophysics to work out a "unified field theory," immodestly called The Theory of Everything?[16] Freud was categorical about the limits of such an endeavor, even before the term was invented—for he thought the search for a *Weltanschauung* was the province not of science but of philosophy:

> Psychoanalysis is not, in my opinion, in a position to create a *Weltanschauung* of its own. It has no need to do so, for it is a branch of science, and can subscribe to the scientific *Weltanschauung*. The latter, however, hardly merits such a high-sounding name, for it does not take everything into its scope, it is incomplete and it makes no claim to being comprehensive or to constituting a system. Scientific thought is still in its infancy; there are very many of the great problems with which it has as yet been unable to cope. A *Weltanschauung* based upon science has, apart from the emphasis it lays upon the real world, essentially negative characteristics, such as that it limits itself to truth and rejects illusions. Those of our fellowmen who are dissatisfied with this state of things and who desire something more for their momentary peace of mind may look for it where they can find it.[17]

Freud always viewed psychoanalysis as a work in progress; in fact, he sometimes had to resort to flat-out myth-making as theoretical framework. Sometimes the Freudian loop is quite a ride: he did not hesitate to ground civilization in totemic cannibalism; to cast the Jewish patriarch as an Arab; or to out the greatest artist in history (Leonardo) as a homosexual.

Rather than fixed dogma, Freudian thought itself is a nonlinear geometry of affine and anamorphotic shapes, a transformative topological mode of thinking, impervious to measurement and unattached to a specific content. Freudian meaning is relational, not absolute. What makes for nonlinearity in our experience is the missing center, the extimacy at our core.

Freud would have been delighted to know that brain research has recently come to some similar conclusions, discovering that thought processes are governed not by one command center, coordinating the actions of billions of synapses and chemical messengers, but by the relational interactions of any number of nodal areas. And it also appears that the brain is a webmaster: perceptions are split up and bundled off in bits and bytes—when one sees an elephant, the grayness and the largeness and the peanut-lovingness are processed and stored separately, then reassembled in a mysterious process that is not yet known.[18] Only one thing is clear: it appears that the transcendent consciousness of Descartes is a figment of the imagination.

The psyche is, however, human . . . more or less.

Thus, as I have argued throughout this book, it is high time that we bring psychoanalysis "online" with new conceptual models—as science and as cultural perspective—because Freud's work actually anticipates and facilitates nonlinear thinking. Can the repetition compulsion be understood as a periodic clock that engages in "stable oscillation"? Can the *fort-da* axis of language be transcoded as a "digital" binary signal? Is "far-from-equilibrium theory" an inorganic equivalent to the theory of drive? What happens to the oedipal triangle when it is stretched and dimensionalized, viewed as a topology rather than a fixed set of lines and points?

In terms of the psychic impact, the reaction to nonlinear models is sometimes euphoric (warp drive and wormholes will allow us to visit parallel universes!) sometimes apoplectic (in a crazy world of terrorism and contingency, one small slip-up can bring us to ruin!). In either case, these reactions are always, by definition, over the top and on the brink. They give us cause to hope that the good Doctor is still in.

In any case, we should always bear in mind that the movement in Freud's intersubjective psyche is also figured in matter. Oedipus' errant itinerary is mapped in the zigzag of the pollinating wasp, the jagged fractal shapes in nature, the erratic path of a UFO, the recursive path of electronic mail, the unhinged replications of the Schema L, the wave line of the primal string.

That is the potential of Freud's field. If Oedipus is still online, it is only because he has always been out of line.

INTRODUCTION: FORWARDING FREUD: NODAL POINT AS HYPERTEXT

1. Freud discusses this effect throughout his work, beginning with the early studies on the aetiology of hysteria. For an explanation of *Nachträglichkeit*, see J. Laplanche and J.-B. Pontalis, "Deferred Action," in *The Language of Psycho-Analysis*, trans. Donald Nicholson-Smith (New York: W. W. Norton, 1973).

2. Teresa Brennan, *History after Lacan* (New York: Routledge, 1993).

3. John Forrester, *Dispatches from the Freud Wars: Psychoanalysis and Its Passions* (Cambridge, Mass.: Harvard University Press, 1977); Richard Webster, *Why Freud Was Wrong: Sin, Science, and Psychoanalysis* (New York: Lightning Source, 1996).

4. J. Allan Hobson, *Sleep* (New York: W. H. Freeman, 1995); Hobson, *The Dream Drugstore* (Cambridge, Mass.: MIT Press, 2001); T. D'Souza, "Elevated Nighttime Activity of Chick Pineal ILOT Channels Requires Protein Synthesis," *Biological Signals* 6 (1997), 44–62. For a neurobiological account that supports Freud's insights, see Mark Solms, *A Moment of Transition: Two Neuroscientific Articles by Sigmund Freud* (London: Karnac, 1990); *The Neuropsychology of Dreams: A Clinico-Anatomical Study* (Mahwah, N.J.: Lawrence Erlbaum and Associates, 1997); "Is the Brain More Real Than the Mind?," *Psychoanalytic Psychotherapy* 9 (1991), 21–35; and "Freud Returns," *Scientific American* 290, no. 5 (May 2004), 82–89.

5. Frank Cioffi, "Was Freud a Liar?," *Listener* 91 (1974), 172–174.

6. Gilles Deleuze and Félix Guattari, *Anti-Oedipus* (vol. 1 of *Capitalism and Schizophrenia*), trans. Robert Hurley, Mark Seem, and Helen R. Lane (Minneapolis: University of Minnesota Press, 1983); *L'Anti-Oedipe* (Paris: Seuil, 1972).

7. Michel Foucault, *The History of Sexuality*, trans. Robert Hurley (New York: Vintage, 1980); *La volonté de savoir* (Paris: Gallimard, 1976).

8. For a discussion of this problem, see Muriel Dimien and Adrienne Harris, eds., *Storms in Her Head: Freud and the Construction of Hysteria* (New York: Other Press, 2001).

9. Frederick Crews, *The Memory Wars: Freud's Legacy in Dispute* (New York: New York Review of Books, 1995). See also Crews, *Unauthorized Freud: Doubters Confront a Legend* (New York: Penguin, 1999).

10. Morton Schatzman, *Soul Murder: Persecution in the Family* (New York: New American Library 1976); Allen Esterson, *Seductive Mirage: An Exploration of the Work of Sigmund Freud* (New York: Open Court Publishing, 1993); Elaine Showalter, *Hysteries: Hysterical Epidemics and Modern Media* (New York: Columbia University Press, 1997). For an account of the work of historian Peter Swales, as yet unpublished in book form, see Peter Rudnytsky, *Psychoanalytic Conversations: Interviews with Clinicians, Commentators and Critics* (New York: Analytic Press, 2000).

11. Jacques Derrida, "The Purveyor of Truth," *Yale French Studies* 52 (1975); "Le facteur de la vérité," *Poétique* 21 (1975). Luce Irigaray, *This Sex Which Is Not One*, trans. Catherine Porter (Ithaca: Cornell University Press, 1985); *Ce sexe qui n'en est pas un* (Paris: Minuit, 1977).

12. Judith Butler, *Bodies That Matter: On the Discursive Limits of "Sex"* (London: Routledge, 1993).

13. Jean-François Lyotard, *The Postmodern Condition: A Report on Knowledge*, trans. Geoff Bennington and Brian Massumi (Minneapolis: University of Minnesota Press, 1984); Fredric Jameson, *Postmodernism, Or, The Cultural Logic of Late Capitalism* (Durham: Duke University Press, 1991).

14. Harold Bloom, *The Anxiety of Influence: A Theory of Poetry* (New York: Oxford University Press, 1973).

15. Jacques Lacan, *Écrits* (Paris: Seuil, 1966), 628. Although I have used the often-quoted English translation of this aphorism, Lacan actually refers explicitly to human desire, without the first-person pronoun, thus accenting alienation: ("le désir de l'homme est le désir de l'Autre").

16. Sigmund Freud, "Creative Writers and Day-Dreaming," in *The Standard Edition of the Complete Psychological Works of Sigmund Freud*, 24 vols., ed. and trans. James Strachey (London: Hogarth Press, 1955–57; New York: Norton, 1961), 9: 17.

17. Patrick A. Heelan, *Quantum Mechanics and Objectivity* (The Hague: Martinus Nijhoff, 1965). Heisenberg's Uncertainty Principle, formulated in 1927, states that to determine the position of an electron, the scientist must bounce at least one photon of light off of it. But the photon transfers some of its momentum to the electron. Thus, the very light that allows you to see its position changes the electron's velocity. If you know where it is, you don't know how fast it is going, and vice versa.

18. Sigmund Freud, *The Interpretation of Dreams* (1898), SE 4, 5.

19. Sigmund Freud, "The Unconscious" (1915), SE 14: 166–204.

20. *Bahnungen* is discussed in *The Ethics of Psychoanalysis, The Seminar of Jacques Lacan. Book VII* (1959–1960), ed. Jacques-Alain Miller, trans. Dennis Porter (New York: Norton, 1992), 31.

21. For a discussion of the motile libido-amoeba, see Sigmund Freud, "Mourning and Melancholia" (1915), SE 14: 237–258. In Chapter 31 of *Écrits*, Lacan writes: "La libido est cette lamelle que glisse l'être de l'organisme à sa véritable limite, qui va plus loin que celle du corps" (848). ("The libido is this placenta that makes the organism's being slide to its true limit, which goes further than that of the body.")

22. Gilles Deleuze and Félix Guattari, *A Thousand Plateaus* (vol. 2 of *Capitalism and Schizophrenia*), trans. Brian Massumi (Minneapolis: University of Minnesota Press, 1987), 7.

23. James J. Gibson, "The Theory of Affordances," in R. Shaw and J. Bransford, eds., *Perceiving, Acting, and Knowing* (New York: Lawrence Erlbaum and Associates, 1977); and Gibson,

The Ecological Approach to Visual Perception (Boston: Houghton Mifflin, 1979). See also Harry Heft, Ecological Psychology in Context: James Gibson, Roger Barker, and the Legacy of William James's Radical Empiricism (New York: Lawrence Erlbaum and Associates, 2001); Eleanor J. Gibson, Perceiving the Affordances: Portrait of Two Psychologists (New York: Lawrence Erlbaum and Associates, 2001).

24. Jean-François Lyotard, Discours, figure (Paris: Klincksieck, 1971).

25. Donna Haraway, Modest Witness@Second Millennium: FemaleMan Meets Onco-mouse (New York: Routledge, 1996), 68.

26. Ibid., 11.

27. Sigmund Freud, An Outline of Psychoanalysis (1938), SE 23: 144–145.

28. Jacques Lacan, The Four Fundamental Concepts of Psychoanalysis, Seminar XI (1964) (New York: W. W. Norton, 1981), 224–225.

29. Sigmund Freud, "Notes on an Autobiographical Account of a Case of Paranoia," SE 12: 9–82.

30. Sherry Turkle, Life on the Screen: Identity in the Age of the Internet (New York: Simon and Schuster, 1995), 139.

31. Sigmund Freud, Civilization and Its Discontents, SE 21: 64–145; "Instincts and Their Vicissitudes," SE 14: 117–124; "Why War?," SE 22: 199–215.

Chapter 1 Is Oedipus Online? Surfing the Psyche

A preliminary version of this essay was published in Pretexts 6, no. 1 (1997), 81–94, and reprinted in Slavoj Žižek, ed., Jacques Lacan: Critical Evaluations in Cultural Theory (New York: Routledge, 2003).

Epigraph: Paul Virilio, The Lost Dimension (New York: Semiotext(e), 1991), 115.

1. Jean Baudrillard, The Transparency of Evil: Essays on Extreme Phenomena, trans. J. Benedict and J. St-John Baddely (London: Verso, 1993). See also Jean Baudrillard, Simulacra and Simulations, trans. Sheila Faria Glaser (Ann Arbor: University of Michigan Press, 1995).

2. Jean Baudrillard, "The Ecstasy of Communication," in Hal Foster, ed., The Anti-Aesthetic: Essays on Postmodern Culture (Post Townsend, Wash.: Bay Press, 1983), 128, 129.

3. Baudrillard, The Transparency of Evil, 30–31.

4. Baudrillard, Simulacra and Simulations, 128.

5. Sigmund Freud, "Psychoanalytic Notes on an Autobiographical Account of a Case of Paranoia" (the case of Dr. Schreber) (1911), SE 12: 9–82.

6. Jacques Lacan, The Four Fundamental Concepts of Psycho-Analysis, Seminar XI (1964) (New York: W. W. Norton, 1981), 238.

7. Marilouise and Arthur Kroker, Hacking the Future: Stories for the Flesh-eating 90's (New York: Palgrave, 1996).

8. Jean-François Lyotard, The Inhuman: Reflections on Time (Stanford, Calif.: Stanford University Press, 1991).

9. Manuel De Landa, *War in the Age of Intelligent Machines* (Cambridge, Mass.: Zone/MIT Press, 1991).

10. Donna Haraway, *Modest Witness@Second Millennium: FemaleMan Meets Onco-mouse* (New York: Routledge, 1996).

11. Donna Haraway, "A Manifesto for Cyborgs: Science, Technology and the Socialist Feminist in the 1980s," in Linda J. Nicholson, ed., *Feminism/Postmodernism* (New York: Routledge, 1990), 192–193.

12. Ibid., 192.

13. Sigmund Freud, *Beyond the Pleasure Principle* (1920), SE 18.

14. Guy Debord, *The Society of the Spectacle* (Cambridge, Mass.: Zone/MIT Press, 1995); Kaja Silverman, *World Spectators* (Stanford, Calif.: Stanford University Press, 2000).

15. Slavoj Žižek, *Looking Awry: An Introduction to Jacques Lacan through Popular Culture* (Cambridge, Mass.: MIT Press, 1992).

16. Paul Virilio, *Open Sky* (London: Verso, 1997), 72.

17. Ibid., 115.

18. Jean-François Lyotard, *Discours, figure* (Paris: Klincksieck, 1971).

19. Arthur Kroker and David Cook, *The Postmodern Scene: Excremental Culture and Hyper-Aesthetics* (New York: St. Martin's Press, 1986).

20. Mark Dery, *Escape Velocity: Cyberculture at the End of the Century* (New York: Grove, 1999); Adam Parfrey, ed., *Apocalypse Culture* (New York: Feral House, 1990).

21. Žižek, *Looking Awry*.

22. Linda Singer, *Erotic Welfare: Sexual Theory and Politics in the Age of Epidemic* (New York: Routledge, 1992).

23. Lyotard, *The Inhuman*, 8–23.

24. Hubert L. Dreyfus, *What Computers Can't Do* (Cambridge, Mass.: MIT Press, 1979); and *What Computers Still Can't Do* (Cambridge, Mass.: MIT Press, 1992). See also Dreyfus, *Mind over Machine: The Power of Human Intuition and Expertise in the Era of the Computer* (Berkeley: University of California Press, 2000).

25. For a discussion of the visual representational limits of the pixel, see Nicholas Negroponte, "Graphical Persona," in his *Being Digital* (New York: Vintage, 1995), 103–108.

26. Lyotard, *The Inhuman*, 19.

27. Jacques Lacan, *The Seminar of Jacques Lacan I* (1953–54), ed. Jacques-Alain Miller (New York: W. W. Norton; Cambridge: Cambridge University Press, 1988).

28. Ibid., 163.

29. Jacques Lacan, *Écrits* (Paris: Seuil, 1966): "Le désiré s'ébauche dans la marge où la demande se déchire du besoin" (814); "Le désir se produit dans l'au-delà de la demande" (629). I use here the simplified formula cited by Anthony Wilden in *The Language of the Self* (Baltimore: Johns Hopkins University Press, 1984).

30. See Raymond Barglow, *The Crisis of the Self in the Age of Information* (London: Routledge, 1994).

31. Sherry Turkle, *Life on the Screen: Identity in the Age of the Internet* (New York: Simon and Schuster, 1995).

32. Lacan discusses the notion of the signifying chain in "The Insistence of the Letter in the Unconscious," in David Lodge, ed., *Modern Criticism and Theory: A Reader* (London: Longman, 1988), 80–106. First published in *Écrits*, 249–289. "Insistence" has also been translated as "agency" or "instance" in other anthologies.

33. The Schema L is discussed in *Écrits*, 52–55.

34. Jacques Lacan, "Le Séminaire sur 'La Lettre volée'" (1955; 1966), *Écrits*, 19–75.

35. Daniel P. Puzo, "The Neiman-Marcus Cookie Recipe: The Truth," <http//www.humourarchives.com/humor/0000554.html> (February 2, 2002).

36. The mirror stage is discussed in Lacan's *Écrits*, "Le Stade du miroir comme formateur de la fonction du *je*," 89–97. It has been translated by (Alan Sheridan) in Lacan, *Écrits: A Selection* (New York: W. W. Norton, 1977), 1–7.

37. Freud's *Totem and Taboo* (SE 13: 1–161) suggests that the symbolic order is premised on death as much or more as "castration" (the paternal metaphor that grounds language is the name of the *dead* father).

CHAPTER 2 HAS OEDIPUS STRUCK OUT? ŽIŽEK ON THE CYBERFIELD

An earlier version of this essay ("Has Oedipus Signed Off? [Or Struck Out?]: Žižek, Lacan and the Field of Cyberspace") appeared in *Para-graph* 24, no. 2 (July 2001), 53–77.

Epigraphs: For the Abbott and Costello dialogue, see <http://www.IMDB.com/AbbottCostello.html> (accessed February 4, 2002).

1. "Le support du transfert est le sujet supposé savoir" ("The support of the transference is the subject supposed to know") (Jacques Lacan, *Écrits* (Paris: Seuil, 1966), 308.

2. "Dans la formule du fantasme $\mathcal{S} \lozenge a$, le poinçon du fantasme $\lozenge$, se lit 'désir de,' à lire de méme de droite à gauche" (Lacan, *Écrits*, 774): "In the formula of the fantasm, the diamond means desire of, which reads the same both from the right and from the left" (my translation). In other words, desire cuts both ways, indicating the subject's desire of the other, and vice versa.

3. Lacan, *Écrits*, 826.

4. Slavoj Žižek, *The Plague of Fantasies* (London: Verso, 1997), 139.

5. Freud, *Jokes and Their Relation to the Unconscious* (1905), SE 8:115.

6. Slavoj Žižek, *Looking Awry: An Introduction to Jacques Lacan through Popular Culture* (Cambridge, Mass.: MIT Press, 1992). Here Žižek is commenting on Lacan's essay "Of the Gaze as objet petit a," *Seminar XI*.

7. Slavoj Žižek, "Is It Possible to Traverse the Fantasy in Cyberspace?," in *The Žižek Reader*, ed. Elizabeth and Edmond Wright (Oxford: Blackwell, 1999), 102–124; subsequently cited within the text.

8. Žižek, "The Unbearable Closure of Being," in *The Žižek Reader*.

9. See, for instance, Jerry Aline Flieger, *The Purloined Punch Line: Freud's Comic Theory and the Post-modern Text* (Baltimore: Johns Hopkins University Press, 1990); "The Listening Eye: Post-modernism, Paranoia, and the Hyper-Visible," *Diacritics* 26, no. 1 (1996), 90–106; "Overdetermined Oedipus: Mommy, Daddy, and Me as Desiring Machine," *South Atlantic Quarterly* 96, no. 3 (Summer 1997), 599–620 reprinted in Ian Buchanan, ed., *A Deleuzian Century?* (Durham: Duke University Press, 1999), 219–240; "Becoming-Woman: De-leuze, Schreber, and Identification," in Ian Buchanan and Claire Colebrook, eds., *Deleuze and Feminist Theory* (Edinburgh: Edinburgh University Press, 2000), 38–63.

10. Sigmund Freud, "The Dissolution of the Oedipus Complex" (1924), SE 19: 173–179.

11. Lacan discusses the discourses of the Master, the University, the Hysteric, and the Analyst as a function of four positions in "Radiophonie," *Scilicet* 2–3 (1970), 55–99. See Eliza-beth Wright, "What Is a Discourse?," in her *Speaking Desires Can Be Dangerous* (Oxford: Black-well, 1999), 61–76. The four discourses are also the topic of *Seminar XVII*.

12. Anne Balsamo, *Technologies of the Gendered Body: Reading Cyborg Women* (Durham: Duke University Press, 1996); Claudia Springer, *Electronic Eros: Bodies and Desire in the Postindustrial Age* (Austin: University of Texas Press, 1996).

13. Allucquére Rosanne Stone, "Conclusion: The Gaze of the Vampire," chapter 8 in *The War of Desire and Technology at the Close of the Mechanical Age* (Cambridge, Mass.: MIT Press, 1991); Sherry Turkle, *Life on the Screen: Identity in the Age of the Internet* (New York: Simon and Schus-ter, 1995).

14. Jerry Aline Flieger, "Is Oedipus Online?," *Pretexts* 6, no. 1 (1997), 81; revised as chapter 1 above. (The quotation in the following paragraph is also from the version in *Pretexts*.)

15. Sigmund Freud, *Totem and Taboo* (1913), SE 13: 1–161.

16. *The Seminar of Jacques Lacan. Book III (1955–56): The Psychoses*, ed. Jacques-Alain Miller, trans. Russell Grigg (New York: W. W. Norton, 1993), 39–40.

17. Freud, *Jokes and Their Relation to the Unconscious*, 100.

18. Ibid., 143.

19. Ibid., 139 n. Freud writes that the hearer "damps down his annoyance" at being caught by the punch line by "resolving to tell the joke himself later on." The joke is thus trau-matic and contagious, and is in a sense already an instance of the compulsion to repeat, discussed later, in *Beyond the Pleasure Principle*.

20. Sigmund Freud, *Beyond the Pleasure Principle* (1920), SE 18: 7–64.

21. Sigmund Freud, *Three Essays on the Theory of Sexuality* (1905), SE 7: 130–243.

22. Jacques Lacan, "Of the Gaze as *objet petit a*," in *The Four Fundamental Concepts of Psycho-Analysis*, *Seminar XI* (1964) (New York: W. W. Norton, 1981), 67–119.

23. Žižek, *Looking Awry*, 110.

CHAPTER 3 THE LISTENING EYE: POST-OEDIPAL OPTICS AND PARANOID KNOWLEDGE

The first version of this chapter appeared in *Diacritics* 26, no. 1 (1996), 90–107, as "The Lis-tening Eye: Postmodernism, Paranoia, and the Hypervisible."

1. Jacques Lacan, *The Seminar of Jacques Lacan, Book I* (1953–54), ed. Jacques-Alain Miller, trans. John Forrester (Cambridge: Cambridge University Press, 1988), 163. In *Seminar I*, Lacan discusses paranoia as a mode of knowledge and a property of "normal" identificatory interaction, whereby the subject anticipates the other's response.

2. Jean Baudrillard, *The Transparency of Evil: Essays on Extreme Phenomena*, trans. J. Benedict and J. St-John Baddely (London: Verso, 1993); Slavoj Žižek, *Looking Awry: An Introduction to Jacques Lacan through Popular Culture* (Cambridge, Mass.: MIT Press, 1992); Jean-François Lyotard, *The Inhuman: Reflections on Time*, trans. Geoffrey Bennington and Rachel Bowlby (Stanford, Calif.: Stanford University Press, 1991). These three works are subsequently cited within the text.

3. Jean Baudrillard, "The Ecstasy of Communication" ("L'extase de la communication,") trans. John Johnston, in Hal Foster, ed., *The Anti-Aesthetic: Essays on Postmodern Culture* (Port Townsend, Wash.: Bay Press, 1983), 181. Here Baudrillard discusses the difference between the visible modern scene and the hypervisible or transparent postmodern *ob-scene* in terms that anticipate *The Transparency of Evil*.

4. In chapter 7, I sketch an alternative view of fracticality, through Freud, as a function of difference.

5. Jacques Lacan, "Le Stade du miroir comme formateur de la fonction du je," in *Écrits* (Paris: Seuil, 1966), 89–97.

6. Paul Virilio, *The Information Bomb*, trans. Chris Turner (London: Verso, 2001); Gianni Vattimo, *The Transparent Society*, trans. David Webb (Baltimore: Johns Hopkins University Press, 1991); *La società trasparente* (Rome: Garzanti Libri, 2000).

7. See Jean-François Lyotard, *The Postmodern Condition: A Report on Knowledge*, trans. Geoffrey Bennington and Brian Massumi (Minneapolis: University of Minnesota Press, 1984).

8. For the difference between thought and computing—argued through Heidegger—see Hubert L. Dreyfus, *What Computers Can't Do* (Cambridge, MIT Press, 1972); and *What Computers Still Can't Do* (Cambridge, Mass.: MIT Press, 1992).

9. Lacan stresses the materiality of the signifier throughout his work, beginning with "The Seminar on the Purloined Letter" (*Écrits*, 19–75). Freud is also interested in the word as material trace in the brain (see Jacques Derrida, "Freud and the Scene of Writing," in *Writing and Difference* [Chicago: University of Chicago Press, 1978]). In *Jokes and Their Relation to the Unconscious* (1905), Freud also emphasize the tendency of primary process to treat "words as things."

10. "C'est du champ de l'Autre que le sujet reçoit son message sous une forme inversée" (*Écrits*, 55–56): "It is from the field of the Other that the subject receives its message in inverted form" (my translation).

11. Žižek thus emphasizes the association of the return of the Real with the return of the repressed. (Lacan: "Le refoulement ne peut être distingué du retour du refoulé" [*Écrits*, 386]: "Repression cannot be distinguished from the return of the repressed.")

12. Lacan discusses *das Unglauben* as a function of disbelief in the signifying order in *The Four Fundamental Concepts of Psycho-Analysis*, Seminar XI (1964) (New York: W. W. Norton, 1998), 238.

13. Lacan discusses "The Freudian Thing" in *Écrits*, 209–28 ("La chose freudienne, ou Sens du retour à Freud en psychanalyse"); and in *The Ethics of Psychoanalysis*, Seminar VII (1960) (New York: W. W. Norton, 1981).

14. *The Seminar of Jacques Lacan. Book III* (1955–56): *The Psychoses,* ed. Jacques-Alain Miller, trans. Russell Grigg (New York: W. W. Norton, 1993), chapters 2, 3. Subsequently cited within the text.

15. Lacan, *Écrits,* 19–87.

16. Eric Santner, *My Own Private Germany: Daniel Paul Schreber's Secret History of Modernity* (Princeton: Princeton University Press, 1996).

17. (Each of the three prisoners reasons thus: "If I were black, the second guy would know, if he were black, that the third guy would see two black patches, and thus would know he must be white and would leave. The third guy doesn't leave, so if I were black, the second guy would know he's not black, but white, and he would leave. He doesn't. So I am not black, I am white.") One can gain self-knowledge only by being positioned in a multiple field, with at least three viewing sites. This anecdote is related in Anthony Wilden, *The Language of the Self* (Baltimore: Johns Hopkins University Press, 1984), 105–106.

CHAPTER 4 UP THE ANTE, OEDIPUS! DELEUZE IN OZ

A version of this chapter ("Overdetermined Oedipus: Mommy, Daddy and Me as Desiring-Machine") was published in *South Atlantic Quarterly* 56, no. 3 (Summer 1997), 599–620; and subsequently appeared as a chapter in Ian Buchanan, ed., *A Deleuzian Century?* (Durham: Duke University Press, 1999), 219–240.

1. Gilles Deleuze and Félix Guattari, *Anti-Oedipus,* trans. Robert Hurley, Mark Seem, and Helen R. Lane (Minneapolis: University of Minnesota Press, 1983); subsequently cited within the text.

2. Gilles Deleuze and Félix Guattari, *A Thousand Plateaus,* trans. Brian Massumi (Minneapolis: University of Minnesota Press, 1987).

3. Sigmund Freud, "From the History of an Infantile Neurosis" (The Case of the Wolf Man, 1917), SE 17: 7–122.

4. Sigmund Freud, *Three Essays on the Theory of Sexuality* (1905), SE 7: 130–243.

5. Deleuze and Guattari, *A Thousand Plateaus,* 7.

6. Gilles Deleuze, *Difference and Repetition,* trans. Paul Patton (New York: Columbia University Press, 1994). (*Différence et répétition,* 1968.)

7. Jean Cocteau, *La Machine infernale* (Paris: Grasset, 1934).

8. Deleuze and Guattari, *Anti-Oedipus,* 111: "The three errors concerning desire are called lack, law, and signifier."

9. Deleuze and Guattari, *A Thousand Plateaus,* chapter 10. See my discussion of Deleuzian "becoming" in chapter 6 below.

10. For the discussion concerning the repressive nature of structural linguistics, as opposed to the linguistics of Hjelmslev, see Deleuze and Guattari, *Anti-Oedipus,* 242–243. See also Louis Hjelmslev, *Language: An Introduction* (Madison: University of Wisconsin Press, 1970).

11. Sigmund Freud, *Jokes and Their Relation to the Unconscious* (1905), SE 8: 62.

12. Fredric Jameson, *The Political Unconscious* (Ithaca: Cornell University Press, 1981).

13. Sigmund Freud, *Totem and Taboo* (1913), SE 13: 1–161.

14. Sigmund Freud, *Moses and Monotheism* (1939), SE 23.

15. Manuel De Landa, *A Thousand Years of Nonlinear History* (Cambridge, Mass.: Zone/MIT Press, 1997). See also De Landa, "Nonorganic Life," in Jonathan Crary and Sanford Kwinter, eds., *Incorporations* (Cambridge, Mass.: Zone/MIT Press, 1992), and "Immanence and Transcendence in the Genesis of Form," in Buchanan, ed., *A Deleuzian Century?*

16. For an elaboration of the joking paradigm to which I refer here, see chapter 4 of Jerry Aline Flieger, *The Purloined Punch Line: Freud's Comic Theory and the Postmodern Text* (Baltimore: Johns Hopkins University Press, 1990), 89–122.

17. Freud, *Jokes and Their Relation to the Unconscious*, 100, 98–99; subsequently cited within the text.

18. Jacques Lacan, *Écrits* (Paris: Seuil, 1966), 806: Primary identification is graphed as a circuit of investment from Subject to Other, and back again.

19. Sigmund Freud, "The Dissolution of the Oedipus Complex" (1924), SE 19: 173–179.

20. Sigmund Freud, "Creative Writers and Day-Dreaming" (1908), SE 9: 143–153.

21. This quotation exemplifies Deleuze's flattening and reduction of Freud's dimensional structure, and Lacan's interpretation (*Anti-Oedipus*, 52): "[Lacan's work] permits the emergence of an oedipal structure as a system of positions and functions that do not conform to the variable figures of those who come to occupy them in a given social or pathological formation." My reading of *Jokes*, however, above suggests three such "variable" and flexible figures that do, in fact, occupy positions in Freud's "oedipal" accounts of social experience (joking, writing, love). The Freudian paradigm displays much more flexibility and variation than Deleuze allows. Part two of this book extends this dimensionalization to Lacan as a proponent of new millennial paradigms.

22. Deleuze and Guattari, *A Thousand Plateaus*, chapter 14, "The Smooth and the Striated," 474–500.

23. In *Life on the Screen: Identity in the Age of the Internet* (New York: Simon and Schuster, 1995), Sherry Turkle recounts her students' adventures with "Julia," a chatroom vamp who is really a computer program.

24. Deleuze and Guattari, *A Thousand Plateaus*, 510.

25. Ibid., 500.

CHAPTER 5 TWISTS AND TRYSTS: FREUD AND THE MILLENNIAL KNOT

1. David Eppstein, University of California Irvine, "The Geometry Junkyard," <http://www.ics.uci.edu/~eppstein/junkyard/> (March 2, 2002). This site has many useful links on non-Euclidean geometry.

2. Ibid.

3. "Braid," <mathworld.wolfram.com/braid.html> (March 8, 2002).

4. Ibid., table 2.

5. See Ilya Prigogine with G. Nicolis, *Exploring Complexity* (San Francisco: Freeman, 1989). In knot theory, the Borromean knot is the simplest example of a Brunnian link—any number of intertwined circles (trivial knots) that may be linked without being "tied up." Significantly, this Brunnian property inheres only in "three" or more rings.

6. Raymond Poincaré, *Les Nouvelles observations sur les objets célestes* (1898).

7. See John W. Milnor, *Topology from the Differentiable Viewpoint* (Princeton: Princeton University Press, 1997).

8. Albert Einstein, NBC radio interview, 1946.

9. See C. Stanley Ogilvy, *Excursions in Geometry* (Chichester: Dover, 1977); Rudolf B. Rucker, *Geometry, Relativity, and the Fourth Dimension* (Chichester: Dover, 1977).

10. For links to the mathematical proof (originally by Mike Friedman) of the slightly elliptical shape of Borromean rings, see <http://www1.ics.uci.edu/~eppstein/junkyard/borromeo.html> (March 2, 2002).

11. See John Frow, *Time and Commodity Culture: Essays in Cultural Theory and Postmodernity* (Oxford: Oxford University Press, 1997), on the difference between postmodernity and postmodernism.

12. Andreas Huyssen, "Mapping the Postmodern," in Linda J. Nicholson, ed., *Feminism/Postmodernism* (New York: Routledge, 1990), 234–277.

13. Donna Haraway, "A Manifesto for Cyborgs: Science, Technology and the Socialist Feminist in the 1980s," in Linda J. Nicholson, ed., *Feminism/Postmodernism* (New York: Routledge, 1990), 190–233.

14. N. Katherine Hayles, *How We Became Posthuman: Virtual Bodies in Cybernetics, Literature, and Informatics* (Chicago: University of Chicago Press, 1999).

15. Jean-François Lyotard, "What is Postmodernism?," in his *The Postmodern Condition: A Report on Knowledge*, trans. Geoffrey Bennington and Brian Massumi (Minneapolis: University of Minnesota Press, 1984); Lyotard, *The Inhuman: Reflections on Time*, trans. Geoffrey Bennington and Rachel Bowlby (Stanford, Calif.: Stanford University Press, 1991).

16. "L'inconscient ne se traduit qu'en nœuds de langage:": Jacques Lacan, "Compte rendu d'enseignements" (1964–68), *Ornicar?* 29 (1984), 8–25. Freud first qualified words as overdetermined nodal points in *The Interpretation of Dreams* (1900), SE 4, 5: 339–625. He insisted that words are knots of meaning: "Words, since they are the nodal points of numerous ideas, may be regarded as predestined to ambiguity" (376). Overdetermined dream images are also knots: "elements in the dream correspond to a nodal point or junction in the dream thoughts" (*Jokes and Their Relation to the Unconscious* [1905], SE 8, 202).

17. Jacques Lacan, *Écrits* (Paris: Seuil, 1966), 166.

18. "Approaching a Theory of Emotion," interview with Candace Pert, Ph.D., by Lynn Grodski, *Deep Planet Magazine*, April 2001. The interview appears online at "Educational Forums," <http://www.deepplanet.com/article.html> (March 7, 2002).

Dr. Pert: "You can access emotional memory anywhere in the peptide/receptor network, in any number of ways. For example, if you have a memory that has to do with food and eating, you might access it by the nerves hooked up to the pancreas. You can access through any nodal point in the neural loop. Nodal points are places where there is a lot of convergent information with many different peptide receptors. In these nodal points there is potential for emotional regulation and conditioning."

19. "Un nœud vrai ne saurait se mettre à plat" (Lacan, Écrits, 724).

20. Sigmund Freud, The Psychopathology of Everyday Life (1901), SE 6: 1–290.

21. Freud discusses the infantile tendency to treat words as things in Jokes, 120–122.

22. Sigmund Freud, "Negation" (1925), SE 19: 235–239.

23. Donna Haraway, Modest Witness@Second Millennium: FemaleMan Meets Onco-mouse (New York: Routledge, 1996), introduction.

24. Le Séminaire de Jacques Lacan. Livre IV (1956–57): La relation d'objet, ed. Jacques-Alain Miller (Paris: Seuil, 1994), 305; my translation and emphasis.

25. See Manuel De Landa, A Thousand Years of Nonlinear History (Cambridge, Mass.: Zone/MIT Press, 1997).

26. Arthur Kroker and David Cook, The Postmodern Scene: Excremental Culture and Hyper-Aesthetics (New York: St. Martin's Press, 1986).

27. Paul Virilio, The Lost Dimension, trans. Daniel Moshenberg (New York: Columbia University Press, 1991), 62.

28. Paul Virilio, Open Sky, trans. Julie Rose (London: Verso Books 1997), 46; subsequently cited within the text.

29. UPI photograph, public archive, <http://www.upi.com/photos> (February 20, 2002).

30. See De Landa, A Thousand Years of Nonlinear History.

31. Ian Marshall and Danah Zohar, Who's Afraid of Schrödinger's Cat? (New York: William Morrow, 1997).

32. Haraway, Modest Witness@Second Millennium, 11.

33. Sigmund Freud, "Psychoanalytic Notes on an Autobiographical Account of a Case of Paranoia" (1911), SE 12: 9–82.

34. Elaine Showalter, Hystories: Hysterical Epidemics and Modern Media (New York: Columbia University Press, 1997).

35. See D. Hatcher Childress, compiler, and Albert Einstein, contributor, The Anti-Gravity Handbook (New York: New Adventures Press, 1993).

36. Paul Virilio, The Aesthetics of Disappearance (New York: Columbia University Press, 1991), 43.

37. Ibid., 48.

38. Jacques Lacan, The Four Fundamental Concepts of Psycho-Analysis, Seminar XI, ed. Jacques-Alain Miller, trans. Alan Sheridan (New York: W. W. Norton, 1981), 271.

39. For the Free Online Dictionary of Computing, see <http://www.wombat.doc.ic.ac.uk> (accessed March 1, 2002).

40. De Landa, A Thousand Years of Nonlinear History, 68.

41. Marvin Minsky, *The Society of Mind* (New York: Simon and Schuster, 1998). For the "emotional" side of mechanics, see also Douglas R. Hofstadter, *Fluid Concepts and Creative Analogies: Computer Models of the Fundamental Mechanisms of Thought* (New York: HarperCollins, 1995).

CHAPTER 6 EMERGENCE: GENDER AS AVATAR

A section of this chapter appeared in earlier form in Ian Buchanan and Claire Colebrook, eds., *Deleuze and Feminist Theory* (Edinburgh: Edinburgh University Press, 2000), 38–63. I should also like to thank Manuel De Landa for his helpful insights concerning Deleuze's concepts of intensity and nonlinearity.

1. Ilya Prigigone, *From Being to Becoming: Time and Complexity in the Physical Sciences* (New York: W. H. Freeman, 1980).

2. For a discussion of "becoming," see Ilya Prigigone and G. Nicolis, *Self-Organization in Non-Equilibrium Systems: From Dissipative Structures to Order through Fluctuation* (New York: Wiley, 1977); Ilya Prigigone, and D. Kondepudi, *Modern Thermodynamics: From Heat Engines to Dissipative Structures* (Chichester: Wiley, 1998).

3. See James Gleick, *Chaos: Making a New Science* (New York: Penguin, 1988).

4. For an accessible account of deep ecology, see Eric Katz, Andrew Light, and David Rothenberg, eds., *Beneath the Surface: Critical Essays in the Philosophy of Deep Ecology* (Cambridge, Mass.: MIT Press, 2000). The philosophy of deep ecology originated in the 1970s with the Norwegian philosopher Arne Naess. Its basic premises are a belief in the intrinsic value of nonhuman nature, a belief that ecological principles should dictate human actions and moral evaluations. The radical materialism of Deleuze reflects this emphasis.

5. See "Worlds in Worlds," *Science Odyssey*, <http://www.pbs.org/wbgh/aso/tryit/atom/elempartp/html> (February 17, 2002). See also J. P. McEvoy, Oscar Zarate, and Richard Appignanesi, eds., *Introduction to Quantum Theory* (New York: Totem Books, 2001).

6. See Joseph Gerard Polchinski, *String Theory: An Introduction to the Bosonic String* (Cambridge, Mass.: Cambridge Monographs on Mathematical Physics, 1998); John R. Gribbin, *Q is for Quantum: An Encyclopedia of Particle Physics* (New York: Free Press, 1999).

7. For a discussion of dimension, see Brian R. Greene, *The Elegant Universe: Superstrings, Hidden Dimensions and the Quest for Ultimate Theory* (New York: W. W. Norton, 1999).

8. J. Craig Venter, interviewed on "Cracking the Code of Human Life," Nova, PBS, April 16, 2001. Website: <http://www.pbs.org/wgbh/noval/genome/decoders.html> (February 17, 2002). See also J. Craig Venter, *Chacterization of Membrane Receptors*, vol. 3 of *Receptor Biochemistry and Methodology* (New York: Wiley-Liss, 1984).

9. Sigmund Freud, *Beyond the Pleasure Principle*, (1920), SE 18.

10. See Sherry Turkle, "Artificial Life as the New Frontier," in Turkle, *Life on the Screen: Identity in the Age of the Internet* (New York: Simon and Schuster, 1995), 149–174.

11. See Steven Johnson, *Emergence: The Connected Lives of Ants, Brains, Cities, and Software* (New York: Scribner, 2001).

12. On episteme, see Michel Foucault, *The Order of Things: An Archaeology of the Human Sciences* (New York: Vintage, 1994). The notion of episteme, first elaborated in 1966, was later retermed "discursive formation."

13. Confirmation by "cheating" is also the gist of Kurt Gödel's mathematical proof, the "incompletedness" theorem. See Werner Depauli et al., *Gödel: A Life of Logic, the Mind, and Mathematics* (New York: Perseus Books, 2000).

14. For an interesting and accessible account of dimension theory and other aspects of the new physics, see the PBS website "Stephen Hawking's Universe," <http://www.pbs.org/hawking/html> February 28, 2002.

15. Judith Butler, *Bodies That Matter: On the Discursive Limits of "Sex"* (London: Routledge, 1993).

16. "Is It a Boy or Is It a Girl?," *Discovery Channel*, January 12, 2004.

17. "The TransGender Revolution," *A&E Investigates*, April 15, 2000.

18. Donna Haraway, *Modest Witness@Second Millennium: FemaleMan Meets Onco-mouse* (New York: Routledge, 1996), 192.

19. Jean Baudrillard, *The Transparency of Evil: Essays on Extreme Phenomena*, trans. J. Benedict and J. St-John Baddely (London: Verso, 1993), 20–22.

20. Arthur Kroker and David Cook, *The Postmodern Scene: Excremental Culture and Hyper-Aesthetics* (New York: St. Martin's Press, 1986), 23.

21. Paul Virilio, *The Aesthetics of Disappearance* (New York: Semiotext(e), 1991), 90.

22. Anne Balsamo, *Technologies of the Gendered Body: Reading Cyborg Women* (Durham: Duke University Press, 1996); Claudia Springer, *Electronic Eros: Bodies and Desire in the Postindustrial Age* (Austin: University of Texas Press, 1996).

23. Virilio, *The Aesthetics of Disappearance*, 92.

24. "Public Forum: Speak Out," Australian Public Television, July 12, 2000.

25. *The Evening News*, WCBS, New York, January 22, 2000.

26. "Unnatural Science," The Learning Channel, June 4, 1998.

27. Elizabeth Grosz, "Deleuze's Bergson: Duration, the Virtual and a Politics of the Future," in Ian Buchanan and Claire Colebrook, eds., *Deleuze and Feminist Theory* (Edinburgh: Edinburgh University Press, 2000), 230.

28. Haraway, *Modest Witness@Second Millennium*, 214–217; Allucquére Rosanne Stone, "Conclusion: The Gaze of the Vampire," in *The War of Desire and Technology at the Close of the Mechanical Age* (Cambridge, Mass.: MIT Press, 1991).

29. Freud suggests that the differences in sexual aggressiveness may be culturally determined, with females compelled by culture to restrict their libido manifestation to the "exhibitionism" of decorative dress. And even this expression is culturally governed: "I need only hint at the elasticity and variability in the amount of exhibitionism women are permitted to maintain in accordance with differing conventions and circumstances" (*Jokes and Their Relation to the Unconscious* [1905], SE 8: 98).

30. Jane Gallop, *Reading Lacan* (Ithaca: Cornell University Press, 1987); Juliet Mitchell and Jacqueline Rose, *Feminine Sexuality: Jacques Lacan and the École freudienne* (New York: W. W. Norton, 1983).

31. Gilles Deleuze and Félix Guattari, *A Thousand Plateaus*, trans. Brian Massumi (Minneapolis: University of Minnesota Press, 1994), 279; subsequently cited within the text.

32. For a critique of "becoming-woman" as a term associated with the nomad in Deleuze's text, see Rosi Braidotti, *Nomadic Subjects: Embodiment and Sexual Difference* (New York: Columbia University Press, 1994). Luce Irigaray also refers to Deleuze's masculinist tendencies, as well as Lacan's "phallic" bias, in *This Sex Which Is Not One*, trans. Catherine Porter (Ithaca: Cornell University Press, 1985). Elizabeth Grosz's critique of "rhizomatics" appears in "A Thousand Tiny Sexes: Feminism and Rhizomatics," in Constantin V. Boundas and Dorothea Olkowski, eds., *Gilles Deleuze and the Theater of Philosophy* (London: Routledge, 1994), 187–210.

33. See Freud's analysis of the identificatory relation between the masses and the charismatic church/army leader in *Group Psychology and the Analysis of the Ego* (1921), SE 18.

34. Sigmund Freud, "Psychoanalytic Notes on an Autobiographical Account of a Case of Paranoia" (1911), SE 12: 3. For a provocative account of the cultural and political valence of the Schreber case as a function of "modernity," see Eric Santner, *My Own Private Germany: Daniel Paul Schreber's Secret History of Modernity* (Princeton: Princeton University Press, 1996).

35. Gilles Deleuze and Félix Guattari, *Anti-Oedipus*, trans. Robert Hurley, Mark Seem, and Helen R. Lane (Minneapolis: University of Minnesota Press, 1983), 76; subsequently cited within the text.

36. Freud, *Jokes*, 73.

37. Santner, *My Own Private Germany*.

38. A selection of writings by these theorists appears in Elaine Marks and Isabelle de Courtivron, eds., *New French Feminisms: An Anthology* (New York: Schocken Books, 1981), including excerpts from Cixous's "The Laugh of the Medusa." For Irigaray's work, see *This Sex Which Is Not One*. For translations of Kristeva's essays referred to below, such as "Women's Time," "Stabat Mater," and excerpts from *Poetry and Negativity* and *Polylogue*, see Toril Moi, ed., *The Kristeva Reader* (New York: Columbia University Press, 1986).

39. Sigmund Freud, "Fragment of an Analysis of a Case of Hysteria" (the case of Dora, 1905), SE 7: 7–122.

40. Donna Haraway, "A Manifesto for Cyborgs: Science, Technology and the Socialist Feminist in the 1980s," in Linda J. Nicholson, ed., *Feminism/Postmodernism* (New York: Routledge, 1990), 190–233. For the relationship of gender to cyberculture, see Stone, *The War of Desire and Technology at the Close of the Mechanical Age*. For a poststructuralist treatment of schizophrenia consistent with Deleuze's work, see Avital Ronell, *The Telephone Book: Technology, Schizophrenia, Electric Speech* (Lincoln: University of Nebraska Press, 1989). See also Braidotti, *Nomadic Subjects*.

CHAPTER 7 FRACTAL FREUD: SUBJECT AS REPLICANT

1. See Hans Scherdtfeger, *Geometry of Complex Numbers: Circle Geometry, Moebius Transformation, Non-Euclidean Geometry* (London: Dover, 1980); Patrick J. Ryan, *Euclidean and Non-Euclidean Geometry* (Cambridge: Cambridge University Press, 1986); Benoit Mandelbrot, *Fractal Geometry of Nature* (New York: W. H. Freeman, 1988). For a beautiful gallery of fractal art, see <http://www.insite.com.br/art/fractal/html> (March 2, 2002).

2. For a discussion of hyperbolic and projective geometry, where parallel lines meet, see David Bao, *An Introduction to Riemann-Finsler Geometry* (New York: Springer-Verlag, 2000); J. W. Anderson, "The Riemann Sphere," in *Hyperbolic Geometry* (New York: Springer-Verlag,

1999), 7–16; David W. Henderson, *Experiencing Geometry: In Euclidean, Spherical and Hyperbolic Spaces*, 2d ed. (New York: Prentice Hall, 2000).

3. For an accessible explanation of many-worlds theory, see "Stephen Hawking's Universe," <http://www.pbs.org/hawking/html>.

4. Ian Marshall and Danah Zohar, *Who's Afraid of Schrödinger's Cat?* (New York: William Morrow, 1997).

5. David Eppstein, "The Geometry Junkyard," University of California at Irvine Theory Group; <http://www.ics.uci.edu~eppstein/junkyard/all.html> (May 14, 2002).

6. Jonathan Swift, from *Poetry, a Rhapsody* (part 5, 1733), quoted from John Bartlett, *Familiar Quotations, Sixteenth Edition*, ed. Justin Kaplan (New York: Little, Brown, 1992).

7. Benoit Mandelbrot, *Les Objets fractals* (Paris: Flammarion, 1995), 154.

8. Lewis Fry Richardson, summarizing his paper "The Supply of Energy from and to Atmospheric Eddies" (1920).

9. Hao Wang, *Reflections on Kurt Gödel* (Cambridge, Mass.: MIT Press, 1990). Gödel's argument, which states that proof must always depend on frame and that frames are infinite, recalls the deconstructionist demonstration of "undecidability" of many founding philosophical categories.

10. <http://www.fractalwisdom.com/FractalWisdom/fractal.html> (March 8, 2002).

11. See Eric W. Weisstein, "Sierpinski's sponge," <http://mathworld.wolfram.com/Tetrix.html> (March 2, 2002).

12. Gilles Deleuze and Félix Guattari, *A Thousand Plateaus*, trans. Brian Massumi (Minneapolis: University of Minnesota Press, 1994), 415.

13. See C. Stanley Ogilvy, *Excursions in Geometry* (London: Dover, 1996); Rudolf B. Rucker, *Geometry, Relativity, and the Fourth Dimension* (London: Dover, 1977).

14. <http://www.ask.com> (November 23, 2003).

15. James Redfield, *The Celestine Prophecy* (New York: Warner Books, 1997).

16. Anderson, "The Riemann Sphere."

17. Eric Saltsman, "Hypercube Page," <http://www.geocities.com/CapeCanaveral/7997/hypercube.html> (March 4, 2002).

18. "Fourth Dimension," <http://www.geocities.com/CapeCanaveral/7997> (March 3, 2002).

19. <http://mathworld.wolfram.com/ComplexPlane.html> (March 10, 2002): "The word 'place' has a special meaning in complex variables, where it roughly corresponds to a point in the complex plane. For example, if the function in question is square root, then the square root of 4 and of negative 4 are different 'places.'"

20. Lacan, "The Insistence of the Letter in the Unconscious," trans. Jan Miel, in David Lodge, ed., *Modern Criticism and Theory: A Reader* (London: Longman, 1988), 86; emphasis added.

21. "The Knot Plot," <http://www.cs.ubc.ca/nest/imager/contributions/scharein/knotplot.html> (January 2004).

22. Jacques Lacan, Écrits (Paris: Seuil, 1966), 161.

23. Roman Jakobson, "Two Aspects of Language and Two Types of Aphasic Disturbances," in Jakobson and Morris Hall, Fundamentals of Language (The Hague: Mouton de Gruyter, 1980), 50–61 Ferdinand de Saussure, Course in General Linguistics, trans. Wade Baskin (New York: McGraw-Hill, 1966).

24. The formula is more figural in French: "Le désir s'ébauche dans la marge où la demande se déchire du besoin" (Écrits, 814): "Desire appears in the margin where demand tears itself away from need."

25. Lacan's version appears in "The Insistence [Instance] of the Letter in the Unconscious," 83.

26. Elan Moritz, "Memetic Science: A General Introduction" (1990), <http://www.geocities.com/Research Triangle 3123/ms1.html> (March 4, 1999).

27. Richard Dawkins, The Selfish Gene (Oxford: Oxford University Press, 1990); and The Extended Phenotype (Oxford: Oxford University Press, 1982).

28. Eric Drexler, Engines of Creation (New York: Anchor Books, 1987); Drexler, Nanosystems: Molecular Machinery, Manufacturing, and Computation (New York: John Wiley and sons, 1992); C. J. Lumsden and E. O. Wilson, Genes, Mind and Culture: The Coevolutionary Process (Cambridge, Mass.: Harvard University Press, 1981). See also "Evolving Creative Minds: Stories and Mechanisms" (1998), <http://www.kli.ac.at/theorylab/AuthPage/L/LumsdenCJ.html> (March 2, 2002).

29. Elan Moritz, "Replicators, Vehicles and Memes," as discussed in Elan Moritz, Memetic Science: An Introduction (Research Triangle, N.C.: Institute for Memetic Studies, 1990).

30. Here is the recipe for generating the Koch curve:

Given three fixed points in space ($p1$, $p2$, and $p3$) and a random point $p4$.

1. Choose randomly one of the points $p1$, $p2$, or $p3$.

2. Place a new point halfway between point $p4$ and the point chosen in 1.

3. Call this new point $p4$ and repeat from 1.

31. Manuel De Landa, A Thousand Years of Nonlinear History (Cambridge, Mass.: Zone/MIT Press, 1997).

32. Sigmund Freud (and Einstein), "Why War?" (1933), SE 22: 199–215.

33. Freud, "Splitting of the Ego in the Process of Defence" (1938), SE 23: 275.

34. "Dans la situation analytique il y a deux sujets pourvus chacun de deux objets, le moi et l'autre" (Lacan, Écrits, 429; my translation).

35. Sigmund Freud, Totem and Taboo (1913), SE 13: 1–161; Moses and Monotheism (1939), SE 23.

36. Sigmund Freud, Three Essays on the Theory of Sexuality (1905), SE 7: 130–243.

37. The Seminar of Jacques Lacan, Book III: The Psychoses (1955–56), ed. Jacques-Alain Miller, trans. Russell Grigg (New York: W. W. Norton, 1993), 40.

38. These configurations are also discussed in Le Séminaire de Jacques Lacan, livre V (1957–58): Les Formations de l'inconscient, ed. Jacques-Alain Miller (Paris: Seuil, 1998), 157–158.

39. Jacques Derrida, "Coming into One's Own," in Geoffrey Hartman, ed., *Psychoanalysis and the Question of the Text* (Baltimore: Johns Hopkins University Press, 1978).

40. For an artist's use of tiling or tessellation, see "The Mathematical Work of Martin Escher," http://www.mathacademy.com/pr/minitext/escher/index.asp#tess.html> (March 2, 2002).

41. Sigmund Freud, *Group Psychology and the Analysis of the Ego* (1921), SE 18: 69–143; Theodor W. Adorno, "Freudian Theory and the Pattern of Fascist Propaganda," in *The Culture Industry* (London: Taylor and Francis, 2001), 114–135.

42. Sigmund Freud, "Instincts and their Vicissitudes" (1915), SE 14: 117–140.

43. "Boy Shape," <http://math.smith.edu/~jposson/boy_surface.html> (March 2, 2002). The Boy shape is illustrated and further discussed in chapter 8.

44. Lacan, *Seminar III*, ooo.

CHAPTER 8 EXTIMACY: THE ALIEN AMONG US

1. "Human Beings: Who Are We?," Discovery Science Channel, February 16, 2002.

2. Jean-François Lyotard, *The Inhuman: Reflections on Time*, trans. Geoffrey Bennington and Rachel Bowlby (Stanford, Calif.: Stanford University Press, 1991), 2.

3. Sigmund Freud, *Civilization and Its Discontents* (1930), SE 21: 64–145.

4. Lacan elaborates the concept in an as yet unpublished paper. Jacques-Alain Miller's seminar "L'Extimité," (1985–86; unpublished) discusses the concept at length. See also Jacques-Alain Miller, "Extimité," in Mark Bracher et al., eds., *Lacanian Theory of Discourse: Subject, Structure, and Society* (New York: New York University Press, 1994), 121–131. The article first appeared in *Prose Studies* 2, no. 4 (1988), 121–131.

5. Martin Davis, *The Universal Computer: The Road from Leibniz to Turing* (New York: W. W. Norton, 2000).

6. For a discussion of nanotechnology, see Jack Dann and Garder R. Dozois, eds., *Nanotech* (New York: Ace Books, 1998).

7. Gilles Deleuze, *Expressionism in Philosophy: Spinoza*, trans. Martin Joughin (Cambridge, Mass.: Zone/MIT Press, 1990).

8. Paul de Man, *Blindness and Insight: Essays in the Rhetoric of Contemporary Criticism* (Oxford: Oxford University Press, 1971); Jean-François Lyotard, "Rewriting Modernity," in *The Inhuman*.

9. Pierre Teilhard de Chardin, *The Heart of Matter*, trans. René Hague (Fort Washington, Penn.: Harvest Books, 1980). For Bourdieu references, see notes 15 and 16 below. See also the works of Gilles Lipovetsky in the 1980s (*L'Ère du vide* [Paris: Gallimard, 1983]). Although he does not promote the ideal of a global mind, as Teilhard de Chardin does, Lipovetsky discusses a "narcissistic individuation," a kind of generalized hedonism opposed to the ideal of the rational and independent liberal subject (*L'Ère du vide*, 87).

10. Judith Butler, *Subjects of Desire: Hegelian Reflections in Twentieth-Century France* (New York: Columbia University Press, 1987).

11. Avital Ronell, *The Telephone Book: Technology, Schizophrenia, Electric Speech* (Lincoln: University of Nebraska Press, 1991).

12. N. Katherine Hayles, *How We Became Posthuman: Virtual Bodies in Cybernetics, Literature, and Informatics* (Chicago: University of Chicago Press, 1999).

13. Judith Butler, *Bodies That Matter: On the Discursive Limits of "Sex"* (London: Routledge, 1993).

14. Lyotard, *The Inhuman*; Sherry Turkle, *Life on the Screen: Identity in the Age of the Internet* (New York: Simon and Schuster, 1995).

15. Pierre Bourdieu, *Distinction: A Social Judgement of Taste*, trans. Richard Nice (Cambridge, Mass.: Harvard University Press, 1984), 1–2.

16. Pierre Bourdieu elaborates his theories in *Backfire: Against the Tyranny of the Market*, trans. Chris Turner (London: New Market Press, 2002); *Practical Reason: On the Theory of Action*, trans. Randall Johnson (Stanford, Calif.: Stanford University Press, 1998); and *Outline of a Theory of Practice* (Cambridge: Cambridge University Press, 1977). For a concise and accessible introduction to Bourdieu's work, see Jonathan Loesberg, "Bourdieu and the Sociology of Aesthetics," *English Literary History (ELH)* 60, no. 4 (1993), 1033–1056.

17. Gianni Vattimo, *The Transparent Society*, trans. David Webb (Baltimore: Johns Hopkins University Press, 1992). See also *Beyond Interpretation: The Meaning of Hermeneutics for Philosophy*, trans. David Webb (Stanford, Calif.: Stanford University Press, 1997); and *The End of Modernity: Nihilism and Hermeneutics in Postmodern Culture*, trans. Jon R. Snyder (Baltimore: Johns Hopkins University Press, 1991).

18. In distinction to those who see media as homogenizing, Vattimo insists that hypercommunication increases cultural differences. In an online interview, media activist Richard Barbrook (*Media Freedom: the Contradictions of Media in the Age of Modernity* [London: Pluto Press, 1995]) characterizes Vattimo's view:

> The Italian thinker, Gianni Vattimo, in *The Transparent Society* argues that contemporary media will never contribute to a transparent communication and unified understanding among different tribes—but almost the obverse. That is, the society of "generalized communication" has produced an increasing pluralization of groups and identities . . . We see the proliferation of new and disorienting possibilities, new myths, hybrid tribes, multiple dialects and subcultures. Vattimo sees us as oscillating between belonging and disorientation. He finds this a promising development, something potentially positive. ("The Contradictions of Media Culture," <http://www/uoregon.edu/~uncurrent/uc4/4–barbrook.html> [March 1, 2002])

19. For a collection of essays reflecting this sensibility, see Adam Parfrey, ed., *Apocalypse Culture* (New York: Feral House, 1990). Avital Ronell extends this metaphor of addiction to include literary production; see *Crack Wars: Literature, Addiction, Mania* (Lincoln: University of Nebraska Press, 1992).

20. These authors are included in Bruce Sterling, *MirrorShades: The Cyberpunk Anthology* (New York: Bantam Books, 1986).

21. See Stuart Schneiderman, *Jacques Lacan: The Death of an Intellectual Hero* (Cambridge, Mass.: Harvard University Press, 1983), 33–37, for a discussion of Lacan's study of knots, (1973–80).

22. Ibid., 14–15.

23. Louis Althusser, *Lenin and Philosophy and Other Essays* trans. Ben Brewster (New York: Monthly Review Press, 2001).

24. Paul Virilio, *The Lost Dimension*, trans. Daniel Moshenberg (New York: Semiotext(e), (1991); Arthur Kroker and Marilouise Kroker, *Hacking the Future: Stories for the Flesh-Eating 90's*

(New York: Palgrave, 1996); Anne Balsamo, *Technologies of the Gendered Body: Reading Cyborg Women* (Durham: Duke University Press, 1996); Claudia Springer, *Electronic Eros: Bodies and Desire in the PostIndustrial Age* (Austin: University of Texas Press, 1996); Donna Haraway, *Modest Witness@Second Millennium: FemaleMan Meets Onco-mouse* (New York: Routledge, 1996); Allucquére Rosanne Stone, *The War of Desire and Technology at the Close of the Mechanical Age* (Cambridge, Mass.: MIT Press, 1991). See also Linda Singer, *Erotic Welfare: Sexual Theory and Politics in the Age of Epidemic* (New York: Routledge, 1992).

25. "The Other must not know all. This is an appropriate definition of the nontotalitarian social field" (Slavoj Žižek, *Looking Awry: An Introduction to Jacques Lacan through Popular Culture* [Cambridge, Mass.: MIT Press, 1992], 73).

26. Hayles, *How We Became Posthuman*, 1–5.

27. Jean-François Lyotard, *Discours, figure* (Paris: Klincksieck, 1971), 82: "Le réel est ce qui nous échappe."

28. Žižek, "How Real is Reality?," in *Looking Awry*, 1–66.

29. I discuss Baudrillard's *The Transparency of Evil* in chapter 3.

30. See Haraway, *Modest Witness@Second Millennium*, chapters 4 and 5: "Gene: Maps and Portraits of Life Itself," 131–172; and "Fetus: The Virtual Speculum in the New World Order," 173–212.

31. Jacques Lacan, *Écrits* (Paris: Seuil, 1966), 431: "L'Autre est le lieu où se constitue le *je* qui parle avec le *je* qui entend." For a useful listing of Lacan's terms, see the website of Jacques Siboni, "Les mathèmes de Lacan," <www.shet.ac.uk/~psysc/thesaur3.html> (March 1, 2002).

32. The Schema L is discussed in its simplest reduction in *Écrits* (1966), 248–249, but it was introduced ten years earlier, in the first version of the seminar on "The Purloined Letter," *Écrits* 1–75.

33. Lacan insists that the unconscious *speaks* from the "extimate" or alien place of the Other: "l'inconscient, c'est le discours de l'Autre" (*Écrits*, 16); "dans l'inconscient, ça parle" (*Écrits*, 437); "ça parle dans l'Autre" (*Écrits*, 689).

34. Lacan, "L'Instance de la lettre dans l'inconscient, ou la raison depuis Freud" (1957), in *Écrits*, 249–289; translation by Jan Miel, in David Lodge, ed., *Modern Criticism and Theory: A Reader* (London and New York: Longman, 1988).

35. See note 4 above. The diagrams are from Miller's 1985–86 seminar on *extimité*.

36. Throughout his work, Lacan insists on the importance of the imaginary investment of the analyst-as-site-of-knowledge by the patient: "Le support du transfert est le *sujet supposé savoir*" (*Écrits*, 308).

37. Paranoia as disbelief in the symbolic order is discussed in Jacques Lacan, *The Four Fundamental Concepts of Psycho-Analysis* (New York: W. W. Norton, 1981), 238.

38. "L'Autre n'existe pas" (Lacan, *Écrits*, 826).

39. *Das Ding* is the principal topic of Lacan's *Seminar VII* (1960), *The Ethics of Psychoanalysis* (New York: W. W. Norton, 1992).

40. See Slavoj Žižek, "Love Thy Neighbor? No, Thanks!," chapter 2 in *The Plague of Fantasies* (London: Verso, 1997), 45–85.

41. See Slavoj Žižek, "The Cartesian Subject versus the Cartesian Theater," in *Cogito and the Un-conscious* (Durham: Duke University Press, 1998), 247–274.

42. Žižek, *The Plague of Fantasies*, 8.

43. Miller, "Extimité," 122.

44. Lacan, *Écrits*, 546: "'A' est le lieu d'où peut se poser au sujet la question de son existence."

45. Žižek, *The Plague of Fantasies*, 128.

46. Lacan, *Écrits*, 53: "L'Autre peut annuler le sujet."

47. Jacques Lacan, *Annuaire et textes statutaires 1982* (Paris: École de la Cause freudienne, 1982), 83: "L'Autre manque."

AFTERWORD: IS OEDIPUS (N)ONLINE? PSYCHOANALYSIS AND NONLINEARITY

1. Freud also deals with primary process in "Creative Writers and Day-Dreaming," SE 8.

2. Freud, "Splitting of the Ego in the Process of Defence" (1938), SE 23: 275–276. See also the entry *Spaltung*/splitting in Jean Laplanche and Jean-Bertrand Pontalis, *The Language of Psychoanalysis*, trans. Donald Nicholson-Smith (New York: W. W. Norton, 1973); *Le Vocabulaire de la psychanalyse* (Paris: Presses Universitaires de France, 1967).

3. For an accessible discussion of "branes," see PBS.org online, *Nova: The Elegant Universe*, 2004 (three-part series with streaming video).

4. *Nachträglichkeit* is introduced as early as 1905, in *Three Essays on the Theory of Sexuality* (1905), SE 7: 130–243, where Freud insists that the earliest sexual experiences work unconsciously during the latency period, and become symptomatic only at puberty. See the entry *Nachträglichkeit/Après-Coup*, in Laplanche and Pontalis, *The Language of Psychoanalysis*.

5. "The Math of Non-orientable Surfaces," <http://www.math.ohio-state.edu/~fiedorow/math655/yale/math.html>, March 2, 2002.

6. Jacques Lacan, *The Four Fundamental Concepts of Psycho-Analysis* (New York: W. W. Norton, 1981), 271–272.

7. For the written directions, see <http://www.woolworks.org/patterns/klein.txt> (accessed March 12, 2002). For how to knit a Klein contraption, complete with pictures, see <http://www.memepool.com> (March 2, 2002); for a description of a version of the Klein bottle as "Fortunato's Purse," see "Projective Plane," <http://www.web.meson.org/topology/projective.html> (March 2, 2002).

8. Lacan, *Four Fundamental Concepts of Psycho-Analysis*, 156; subsequently cited within the text.

9. The same is true of the Klein bottle, which, when built in three dimensions, requires the handle to intersect the wide end. But it is a question not of a simple juncture, but of a loop, which means that inside and outside are the same surface (tracing one of the lines of the grid around will demonstrate this). We have seen that this "millennial" puzzle is an emblem of what Lacan calls "extimacy," or interior exteriority.

10. "Le Séminaire sur 'La Lettre volée,'" in Jacques Lacan, *Écrits* (Paris: Seuil, 1966), 19–76.

11. Jacques Lacan, "The Insistence of the Letter in the Unconscious," trans. Jan Miel, in David Lodge, ed., *Modern Criticism and Theory: A Reader* (London: Longman, 1988), 96. Originally in *Écrits*, 249–289.

12. <http://www.math.ohio-state.edu/~fiedorow/math655/yale/music.html> (March 2, 2002): "Moebius Strip Tease" was first presented on May 5, 1965, at Nicolas Slonimsky's Arrière-Garde Coffee House at the University of California, Los Angeles, when he was on the faculty. It is scored, originally, for two singers and a piano *non-obbligato*. The music is rotated around the head of each performer endlessly, (as the instructions specify), as the inside goes outside and the outside goes inside. "The piece is a unilateral perpetual rondo in a linearly dodecaphonic vertically consonant counterpoint," says Slonimsky.

13. Lee Smolin, "What is the Future of Cosmology?," on the PBS website "Stephen Hawking's Universe," <http://www.pbs.org/wnet/hawking/mysteries/html/smolin-1.html> (March 2, 2002).

14. Lacan's *réseau* 1–3 (*Écrits*, 60) already shows this form, portraying the "symbolic" identification as a self-perpetuating triadic looping circuit, with one position doubled:

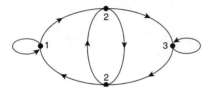

15. Freud and Breuer, *Studies on Hysteria* (1893–95), SE 2: 305:

When I have promised my patients help or improvement by means of cathartic treatment I have often been faced by this objection: "Why, you tell me yourself that my illness is probably connected with my circumstances and the events of my life. You cannot alter these in any way. How do you propose to help me then?" And I have been able to make this reply: "No doubt your fate would find it easier than I do to relieve you of your illness. But you will be able to convince yourself that much will be gained if we succeed in transforming your hysterical misery into common unhappiness."

Freud did, however, end on a more upbeat note: "With a mental life that has been restored to health you will be better armed against the unhappiness."

16. "A Theory of Everything," <http://www.virtualchaos.org> (March 2, 2002). See also Michio Kaku and Jennifer Trainer, *Beyond Einstein: The Cosmic Quest for the Theory of the Universe* (New York: Anchor Books, 1995).

17. Freud, *New Introductory Lectures on Psychoanalysis* (1933), SE 22: 182.

18. "The Human Brain," Discovery Science Channel, January 10, 2002. See also Pierce J. Howard, *The Owner's Manual for the Brain: Everyday Applications from Brain-Mind Research* (Austin: Leornian Press, 1994); Ronald Kotulak, *Inside the Brain: Revolutionary Discoveries of How the Mind Works* (Kansas City: Andrews McMeel Publishing, 1997); Ronald Restak and David Grubin, *The Secret Life of the Brain* (Washington: National Academy Press, 2001).

References

Electronic References

Internet sources are referenced in the notes.

Works by Sigmund Freud

The Standard Edition of the Complete Psychological Works of Sigmund Freud. Ed. and trans. James Strachey. London: Hogarth Press, 1955–57; New York: W. W. Norton, 1961.

"The Aetiology of Hysteria" (1896). SE 3: 191–221.

Analysis of a Phobia in a Five Year-Old Boy (1909). SE 10: 5–149.

"Analysis Terminable and Interminable" (1937). SE 23: 216–253.

"The Antithetical Meaning of Primal Words" (1910). SE 11: 155–161.

An Autobiographical Study (1925). SE 20: 7–74.

Beyond the Pleasure Principle (1920). SE 18: 7–64.

"A Case of Paranoia Running Counter to the Psychoanalytic Theory" (1915). SE 14: 261–272.

"A Childhood Recollection from *Dichtung und Wahrheit*" (1917). SE 17: 145–156.

"A Child Is Being Beaten" (1920). SE 17: 179–184.

Civilization and Its Discontents (1929). SE 21: 64–145.

"'Civilized' Sexual Morality and Modern Nervous Illness" (1908). SE 9: 181–204.

"A Connection between a Symbol and a Symptom" (1915). SE 14: 339–340.

"Creative Writers and Day-Dreaming" (1908). SE 9: 143–153.

Delusion and Dream in Jensen's "Gradiva" (1907). SE 9: 7–95.

"The Dissolution of the Oedipus Complex" (1924). SE 19: 173–179.

"A Disturbance of Memory on the Acropolis" (1936). SE 22: 239–248.

"Dostoevsky and Parricide" (1928). SE 21: 177–196.

"Dreams and Telepathy" (1922). SE 18: 197–220.

"The Dynamics of Transference" (1912). SE 12: 99–108.

"The Economic Problem of Masochism" (1923). SE 19: 159–170.

"Family Romances" (1909). SE 9: 235–244.

"Fausse reconnaissance ('déjà raconté') in Psychoanalytic Treatment" (1914). SE 13: 201–207.

"Female Sexuality" (1931). SE 21: 225–243.

"Fetishism" (1928). SE 21: 152–154.

"Five Lectures on Psychoanalysis" (1910). SE 11: 9–55.

"Formulations on the Two Principles of Mental Functioning" (1911). SE 12: 218–226.

"Fragment of an Analysis of a Case of Hysteria" (the case of Dora, 1905). SE 7: 7–122.

"From the History of an Infantile Neurosis" (the case of the Wolf Man, 1917). SE 17: 7–122.

"The Future of an Illusion" (1927). SE 21: 5–56.

"The Future Prospects of Psychoanalytic Therapy" (1910). SE 11: 141–151.

Group Psychology and the Analysis of the Ego (1921). SE 18: 69–143.

"Humour" (1928). SE 21: 161–168.

"Hypnosis" (1891). SE 1: 103–114.

"Inhibitions, Symptoms and Anxiety" (1925). SE 20: 87–172.

"Instincts and Their Vicissitudes" (1915). SE 14: 117–140.

The Interpretation of Dreams (1900). SE 4; 5: 1–625.

Introductory Lectures on Psychoanalysis (1916). SE 15: 9–239.

Jokes and Their Relation to the Unconscious (1905). SE 8: 9–236.

"The Loss of Reality in Neurosis and Psychosis" (1924). SE 19: 182–187.

"Medusa's Head" (1922). SE 18: 273–274.

"A Metapsychological Supplement to the Theory of Dreams" (1917). SE 14: 222–235.

Moses and Monotheism (1939). SE 23.

"The Moses of Michelangelo" (1914). SE 13: 211–238.

"Mourning and Melancholia" (1917). SE 14: 237–258.

"A Mythological Parallel to a Visual Obsession" (1915). SE 14: 337–338.

"Negation" (1925). SE 19: 235–239.

"Neurosis and Psychosis" (1924). SE 19: 149–153.

"A Seventeenth-Century Demonological Neurosis" (1923). SE 19: 72–105.

"Some Character-Types Met with in Psychoanalytic Work" (1916). SE 14: 311–333.

"A Special Type of Choice of Object Choice Made by Men" (1910). SE 11: 165–175.

"Splitting of the Ego in the Process of Defense" (1938). SE 23: 275–276.

Studies on Hysteria (1893–95) [with Josef Breuer]. SE 20.

"The Theme of the Three Caskets" (1913). SE 12: 291–301.

"Thoughts for the Times on War and Death" (1915). SE 14: 273–300.

Three Essays on the Theory of Sexuality (1905). SE 7: 130–243.

Totem and Taboo (1913). SE 13: 1–161.

"The Unconscious" (1915). SE 14: 166–204.

"Why War?" (1933). SE 22: 199–215.

WORKS BY JACQUES LACAN

Autres écrits. Paris: Seuil, 2001.

Écrits. Paris: Seuil, 1966.

Écrits: A Selection. Trans. Alan Sheridan. New York: W. W. Norton, 1977.

"The Insistence of the Letter in the Unconscious." Trans. Jan Miel. In David Lodge, ed., Modern Criticism and Theory: A Reader. London: Longman, 1988: 79–106. ["L'Instance de la lettre dans l'inconscient." In Lacan, Écrits, 249–289.]

Ornicar? 29 (1984): 8–25.

"Radiophonie." Scilicet 2–3 (1970), 55–99.

"Le Réel est sans loi." Ornicar? 1 (1977), 3–5.

Le Séminaire de Jacques Lacan. Ed. Jacques-Alain Miller. Paris: Seuil, 1975–.

Livre I (1953–54): Les Écrits techniques de Freud (1975).

Livre II (1954–55): Le Moi dans la théorie de Freud et dans la technique de la psychanalyse (1978).

Livre III (1955–56): Les Pychoses (1981).

Livre IV (1956–57): La Relation d'objet (1994).

Livre V (1957–58): Les Formations de l'inconscient (1994).

Livre VI (1958–59): Le Désir et son interprétation (unpublished).

Livre VII (1959–60): L'Éthique de la psychanalyse (1986).

Livre VIII (1960–61): Le Transfert (1991).

Livre IX (1961–62): L'Identification (unpublished).

Livre X (1962–63): L'Angoisse (unpublished).

Livre XI (1963–64): *Les Quatre Concepts fondamentaux de la psychanalyse* (1973).

Livre XII (1964–65): *Problèmes cruciaux pour la psychanalyse* (1973).

Livre XIII (1965–66): *L'Objet de la psychanalyse* (unpublished).

Livre XIV (1966–67): *La Logique du fantasme* (unpublished).

Livre XV (1967–68): *L'Acte psychanalytique* (unpublished).

Livre XVI (1968–69): *D'un autre à l'Autre* (unpublished).

Livre XVII (1969–70): *L'Envers de la psychanalyse* (1991).

Livre XVIII (1970–71): *D'un discours qui ne serait pas du semblant* (unpublished).

Livre XIX (1971–72): *Ou pire* (unpublished).

Livre XX (1972–73): *Encore* (1975).

Livre XXI (1973–74): *Les Non-Dupes errent* (unpublished).

Note: Portions of Seminars XXII–XXVI have appeared in *Ornicar?* 1975–79, but have not yet been published by Seuil.

"Le Séminaire sur 'La Lettre volée'," *Écrits* (1955, 1966), 19–75.

The Seminar of Jacques Lacan. Book I (1953–54): *Freud's Papers on Technique.* Ed. Jacques-Alain Miller. Trans. John Forrester. New York: W. W. Norton; Cambridge: Cambridge University Press, 1988.

The Seminar of Jacques Lacan. Book II (1954–55): *The Ego in Freud's Theory and in the Techniques of Psychoanalysis.* Ed. Jacques-Alain Miller. Trans. Sylvia Tomaselli. New York: W. W. Norton, 1991.

The Seminar of Jacques Lacan. Book III (1955–56): *The Psychoses.* Ed. Jacques-Alain Miller. Trans. Russell Grigg. New York: W. W. Norton, 1993.

The Seminar of Jacques Lacan. Book VII (1959–1960): *The Ethics of Psychoanalysis.* Ed. Jacques-Alain Miller. Trans. Alan Sheridan. New York: W. W. Norton, 1981.

The Seminar of Jacques Lacan. Book VII (1960): *The Ethics of Psychoanalysis.* Ed. Jacques-Alain Miller. Trans. Dennis Porter. New York: W. W. Norton, 1992.

The Seminar of Jacques Lacan. Book XI (1964): *The Four Fundamental Concepts of Psychoanalysis.* Ed. Jacques-Alain Miller. Trans. Alan Sheridan. New York: W. W. Norton, 1998.

The Seminar of Jacques Lacan. Book XX (1972–73): *Encore: On Feminine Sexuality, the Limits of Love and Knowledge.* Ed. Jacques-Alain Miller. Trans. Bruce Fink. New York: W. W. Norton, 1999.

Works by Other Authors

Adams, Colin C. *The Knot Book: An Elementary Introduction to the Mathematical Theory of Knots.* New York: Freeman, 1994.

Adorno, Theodor W. "Freudian Theory and the Pattern of Fascist Propaganda." In Adorno, *The Culture Industry.* London: Taylor and Francis, 2001.

Althusser, Louis. *Lenin and Philosophy and Other Essays.* Trans. Ben Brewster. New York: Monthly Review Press, 2001. [*Lénine et la philosophie.* Paris: Maspero, 1969.]

Anderson, J. W. "The Riemann Sphere." In *Hyperbolic Geometry*. Springer Undergraduate Mathematics Series. New York: Springer-Verlag, 1999: 7–16.

Arac, Jonathan. *Postmodernism and Politics*. Theory and History of Literature 28. Minneapolis: University of Minnesota Press, 1986.

Aronowitz, Stanley, et al., eds. *Technoscience and Cyberculture*. New York: Routledge, 1996.

Balsamo, Anne. *Technologies of the Gendered Body: Reading Cyborg Women*. Durham: Duke University Press, 1996.

Bao, David. *An Introduction to Riemann-Finsler Geometry*. Graduate Texts in Mathematics. New York: Springer-Verlag, 2000.

Barbrook, Richard. *Media Freedom: The Contradictions of Media in the Age of Modernity*. London: Pluto Press, 1995.

Barglow, Raymond. *The Crisis of the Self in the Age of Information*. London: Routledge, 1994.

Baudrillard, Jean. "The Ecstasy of Communication." Trans. John Johnston. In Foster, ed., 126–134.

Baudrillard, Jean. *Simulacra and Simulations*. Trans. Sheila Faria Glaser. Ann Arbor: University of Michigan Press, 1995. [*Simulations et simulacra*. Paris: Galilée, 1981.]

Baudrillard, Jean. *The Transparency of Evil: Essays on Extreme Phenomena*. Trans. J. Benedict and J. St-John Baddely. London: Verso, 1993. [*La Transparence du mal*. Paris: Galilée, 1983.]

Beckmann, John, ed. *The Virtual Dimension: Architecture, Representation, and Crash Culture*. New York: Princeton Architectural Press, 1998.

Bennett, David, ed. *Multicultural States: Rethinking Difference and Identity*. London: Routledge, 1998.

Bloom, Harold. *The Anxiety of Influence: A Theory of Poetry*. New York: Oxford University Press, 1973.

Borch-Jacobsen, Mikkel. *Lacan: The Absolute Master*. Stanford, Calif.: Stanford University Press, 1991.

Bourdieu, Pierre. *Backfire: Against the Tyranny of the Market*. Trans. Chris Turner. London: New Market Press, 2002.

Bourdieu, Pierre. *Distinction: A Social Judgement of Taste*. Trans. Richard Nice. Cambridge, Mass.: Harvard University Press, 1984.

Bourdieu, Pierre. *Outline of a Theory of Practice*. Cambridge: Cambridge University Press, 1977.

Bourdieu, Pierre. *Practical Reason: On the Theory of Action*. Trans. Randall Johnson. Stanford, Calif.: Stanford University Press, 1998.

Braidotti, Rosi. *Nomadic Subjects: Embodiment and Sexual Difference*. New York: Columbia University Press, 1994.

Brennan, Teresa. *History After Lacan*. London: Routledge, 1993.

Buchanan, Ian, ed. *A Deleuzian Century?* Durham: Duke University Press, 1999.

Buchanan, Ian, and Claire Colebrook, eds. *Deleuze and Feminist Theory*. Edinburgh: Edinburgh University Press, 2000.

Buderi, Robert. *The Invention That Changed the World: How a Small Group of Radar Pioneers Won the Second World War and Launched a Technical Revolution.* New York: Simon and Schuster, 1996.

Butler, Judith. *Bodies That Matter: On the Discursive Limits of "Sex."* London: Routledge, 1993.

Butler, Judith. *Excitable Speech: A Politics of the Performative.* London: Routledge, 1997.

Butler, Judith. *Gender Trouble: Feminism and the Subversion of Identity.* New York: Routledge, 1999.

Butler, Judith. *Subjects of Desire: Hegelian Reflections in Twentieth-Century France.* New York: Columbia University Press, 1987.

Cazdyn, E. "Uses and Abuses of the Nation: Toward a Theory of Transnational Social Exchange." *Social Text* 16 (Spring 1996), 135–159.

Childress, D. Hatcher, comp., and Albert Einstein, contrib. *The Anti-Gravity Handbook.* New York: New Adventures Press, 1993.

Cioffi, Frank. "Was Freud a Liar?" *The Listener* 91 (1974), 172–174; reprinted in *Journal of Orthomolecular Psychiatry* 5 (1975), 275–280.

Cixous, Hélène. "The Laugh of the Medusa." In Marks and de Courtivron, eds., 245–264.

Cixous, Hélène. *Veils.* Stanford, Calif.: Stanford University Press, 2001.

Cocteau, Jean. *La Machine infernale.* Paris: Grasset, 1934.

Crary, Jonathan, and Sanford Kwinter, eds. *Incorporations.* Cambridge, Mass.: Zone/MIT Press, 1990.

Crews, Frederick. *The Memory Wars: Freud's Legacy in Dispute.* New York: New York Review of Books, 1995.

Crews, Frederick. *Unauthorized Freud: Doubters Confront a Legend.* New York: Penguin, 1999.

Curd, Martin, and J. A. Cover. *Philosophy of Science: The Central Issues.* New York: W. W. Norton, 1998.

Davis, Martin. *The Universal Computer: The Road from Leibniz to Turing.* New York: W. W. Norton, 2000.

Dawkins, Richard. *The Extended Phenotype.* Oxford: Oxford University Press, 1982.

Dawkins, Richard. *The Selfish Gene.* Oxford: Oxford University Press, 1990.

Debord, Guy. *The Society of the Spectacle.* Cambridge, Mass.: Zone/MIT Press, 1995.

De Landa, Manuel. "Immanence and Transcendence in the Genesis of Form." In Buchanan, ed., 119–134.

De Landa, Manuel. *Intensive Science and Virtual Philosophy.* New York: Continuum International Publishing Group, 2002.

De Landa, Manuel. "Nonorganic Life." In Crary and Kwinter, eds., 128–167.

De Landa, Manuel. *A Thousand Years of Nonlinear History.* Cambridge, Mass.: Zone/MIT Press, 1997.

De Landa, Manuel. *War in the Age of Intelligent Machines.* Cambridge, Mass.: Zone/MIT Press, 1991.

Deleuze, Gilles. *Difference and Repetition.* Trans. Paul Patton. New York: Columbia University Press, 1994. [*Différence et répétition.* Paris: Presses Universitaires de France, 1968.]

Deleuze, Gilles. *Expressionism in Philosophy: Spinoza*. Trans. Martin Joughin. Cambridge, Mass.: Zone/MIT Press, 1997. [*Spinoza et le problème de l'expressionisme*. Paris: Minuit, 1968.]

Deleuze, Gilles, and Félix Guattari. *Anti-Oedipus*. Vol. 1 of *Capitalism and Schizophrenia*. Trans. Robert Hurley, Mark Seem, and Helen R. Lane. Minneapolis: University of Minnesota Press, 1983. [*L'Anti-Oedipe*. Paris: Seuil, 1972.]

Deleuze, Gilles, and Félix Guattari. *A Thousand Plateaus*. Vol. 2 of *Capitalism and Schizophrenia*. Trans. Brian Massumi. Minneapolis: University of Minnesota Press, 1987. [*Mille plateaux*. Paris: Minuit, 1980.]

De Man, Paul. *Blindness and Insight: Essays in the Rhetoric of Contemporary Criticism*. Oxford: Oxford University Press, 1971, 1983.

Depauli, Werner, et al. *Gödel: A Life of Logic, the Mind, and Mathematics*. New York: Perseus Books, 2000.

Derrida, Jacques. "Coming into One's Own." In Geoffrey Hartman, ed., *Psychoanalysis and the Question of the Text*. Baltimore: Johns Hopkins University Press, 1978.

Derrida, Jacques. "The Purveyor of Truth." *Yale French Studies* 52 (1975), 33–50. ["Le facteur de la vérité." *Poétique* 21 (1975), 96–147.]

Derrida, Jacques. *Writing and Difference*. Trans. Alan Bass. Chicago: University of Chicago Press, 1978. [*L'écriture et la différence*. Paris: Seuil, 1967.]

Dery, Mark. *Escape Velocity: Cyberculture at the End of the Century*. New York: Grove, 1996.

Dery, Mark. *The Pyrotechnic Insanitarium: American Culture on the Brink*. New York: Grove, 1999.

Dimien, Muriel, and Adrienne Harris, eds. *Storms in Her Head: Freud and the Construction of Hysteria*. New York: Other Press, 2001.

Drexler, K. Eric. *Nanosystems: Molecular Machinery, Manufacturing, and Computation*. New York: Wiley, 1992.

Dreyfus, Hubert L. *Mind over Machine: The Power of Human Intuition and Expertise in the Era of the Computer*. Berkeley: University of California Press, 2000.

Dreyfus, Hubert L. *What Computers Can't Do*. Cambridge, Mass.: MIT Press, 1979.

Dreyfus, Hubert L. *What Computers Still Can't Do: A Critique of Artificial Reason*. Cambridge, Mass.: MIT Press, 1992.

D'Souza T. "Elevated Nighttime Activity of Chick Pineal ILOT Channels Requires Protein Synthesis." *Biological Signals* 6 (1997), 44–62.

Dunn, Jack, and Garder R. Dozois, eds. *Nanotech*. New York: Ace Books, 1998.

Esterson, Allen. *Seductive Mirage: An Exploration of the Work of Sigmund Freud*. New York: Open Court Publishing, 1993.

Evans, Martha Noel. *Fits and Starts: A Genealogy of Hysteria in Modern France*. Ithaca: Cornell University Press, 1991.

Felman, Shoshana, ed. *Literature and Psychoanalysis: The Question of Reading, Otherwise*. Baltimore: Johns Hopkins University Press, 1982.

Fink, Bruce. *A Clinical Introduction to Lacanian Psychoanalysis: Theory and Technique.* Cambridge, Mass.: Harvard University Press, 1997.

Flapan, Erica. *When Topology Meets Chemistry: A Topological Look at Molecular Chirality.* Cambridge: Cambridge University Press, 2000.

Flieger, Jerry Aline. *The Purloined Punch Line: Freud's Comic Theory and the Postmodern Text.* Baltimore: Johns Hopkins University Press, 1990.

Forrester, John. *Dispatches from the Freud Wars: Psychoanalysis and Its Passions.* Cambridge, Mass.: Harvard University Press, 1977.

Foster, Hal, ed. *The Anti-Aesthetic: Essays on Postmodern Culture.* Port Townsend, Wash.: Bay Press, 1983.

Foucault, Michel. *Discipline and Punish: The Birth of the Prison.* Trans. Alan Sheridan. New York: Vintage, 1979. [*Surveiller et punir: La Naissance de la prison.* Paris: Gallimard, 1975.]

Foucault, Michel. *The History of Sexuality.* Trans. Robert Hurley. New York: Vintage, 1980. [*La volonté de savoir.* Paris: Gallimard, 1976.]

Foucault, Michel. *The Order of Things: An Archaeology of the Human Sciences.* New York: Vintage, 1994. [*Les Mots et les choses: Archéologie des sciences humaines.* Paris: Gallimard, 1966.]

Frow, John. *Time and Commodity Culture: Essays in Cultural Theory and Postmodernity.* Oxford: Oxford University Press, 1997.

Gallop, Jane. *Reading Lacan.* Ithaca: Cornell University Press, 1987.

Gibson, Eleanor J. *Perceiving the Affordances: Portrait of Two Psychologists.* New York: Lawrence Erlbaum and Associates, 2001.

Gibson, J. J. *The Ecological Approach to Visual Perception.* Boston: Houghton Mifflin, 1979.

Gibson, J. J. "The Theory of Affordances." In R. Shaw and J. Bransford, eds., *Perceiving, Acting, and Knowing.* New York: Lawrence Erlbaum and Associates, 1977.

Gibson, William. *Neuromancer.* New York: Ace Books, 1984.

Gleick, James. *Chaos: Making a New Science.* New York: Penguin, 1988.

Gray, Chris Hables, ed. *The Cyborg Handbook.* New York: Routledge, 1996.

Greene, Brian R. *The Elegant Universe: Superstrings, Hidden Dimensions and the Quest for Ultimate Theory.* New York: W. W. Norton, 1999.

Gribbin, John R. *Q is for Quantum: An Encyclopedia of Particle Physics.* New York: Free Press, 1999.

Grodski, Lynn, interviewer. "Approaching a Theory of Emotion," interview with Candace Pert, Ph.D. *Deep Planet Magazine,* April 2001.

Grosz, Elizabeth. "A Thousand Tiny Sexes: Feminism and Rhizomatics." In Constantin V. Boundas and Dorothea Olkowski, eds., *Gilles Deleuze and the Theater of Philosophy.* London: Routledge, 1994: 187–210.

Haraway, Donna. "A Manifesto for Cyborgs: Science, Technology and the Socialist Feminist in the 1980s." In Nicholson, ed., 190–233.

Haraway, Donna. *Modest Witness@Second Millennium: FemaleMan Meets Onco-mouse.* New York: Routledge, 1996.

Harvey, David. *The Condition of Postmodernity.* Oxford: Blackwell, 1990.

Hassan, Ihab, and Sally Hassan, eds. *Innovation/Renovation.* Madison: University of Wisconsin Press, 1983.

Hawking, Stephen. *The Illustrated Brief History of Time: Updated and Expanded.* New York: Bantam, 2000.

Hawking, Stephen. *The Universe in a Nutshell.* New York: Bantam and Doubleday, 2001.

Hayles, N. Katherine. *How We Became Posthuman: Virtual Bodies in Cybernetics, Literature, and Informatics.* Chicago: University of Chicago Press, 1999.

Heelan, Patrick A. *Quantum Mechanics and Objectivity.* The Hague: Martinus Nijhoff, 1965.

Heft, Harry. *Ecological Psychology in Context: James Gibson, Roger Barker, and the Legacy of William James's Radical Empiricism.* New York: Lawrence Erlbaum and Associates, 2001.

Henderson, David W. *Experiencing Geometry: In Euclidean, Spherical and Hyperbolic Spaces.* 2nd ed. New York: Prentice Hall, 2000.

Hjelmslev, Louis. *Language: An Introduction.* Madison: University of Wisconsin Press, 1970.

Hobson, J. Allan. *The Dream Drugstore.* Cambridge, Mass.: MIT Press, 2001.

Hobson, J. Allan. *Sleep.* New York: Freeman, 1995.

Hofstader, Douglas R. *Fluid Concepts and Creative Analogies: Computer Models of the Fundamental Mechanisms of Thought.* New York: HarperCollins, 1995.

Howard, Pierce J. *The Owner's Manual for the Brain: Everyday Applications from Brain-Mind Research.* Austin: Leornian Press, 1994.

Huyssen, Andreas. "Mapping the Postmodern." In Nicholson, ed., 234–277.

Irigaray, Luce. *This Sex Which Is Not One.* Trans. Catherine Porter. Ithaca: Cornell University Press, 1985. [*Ce sexe qui n'en est pas un.* Paris: Minuit, 1977.]

Jakobson, Roman. "Two Aspects of Language and Two Types of Aphasic Disturbances." In Jakobson and Morris Hall, *Fundamentals of Language.* 2d ed. The Hague: Mouton De Gruyter, 1980.

Jameson, Fredric. *The Political Unconscious.* Ithaca: Cornell University Press, 1981.

Jameson, Fredric. *Postmodernism; or, The Cultural Logic of Late Capitalism.* Durham: Duke University Press, 1991.

Jay, Martin. *The Downcast Eye: The Denigration of Vision in Twentieth Century French Thought.* Berkeley: University of California Press, 1993.

Jencks, Charles, ed. *The Post-Modern Reader.* London: Academy Editions, 1992.

Johnson, Steven. *Emergence: The Connected Lives of Ants, Brains, Cities, and Software.* New York: Scribner, 2001.

Kaku, Michio, and Jennifer Trainer. *Beyond Einstein: The Cosmic Quest for the Theory of the Universe.* New York: Anchor Books, 1995.

Katz, Eric, Andrew Light, and David Rothenberg, eds. *Beneath the Surface: Critical Essays in the Philosophy of Deep Ecology.* Cambridge, Mass.: MIT Press, 2000.

Kellner, Douglas, ed. *Baudrillard: A Critical Reader*. Oxford: Blackwell, 1994.

Kotulak, Ronald. *Inside the Brain: Revolutionary Discoveries of How the Mind Works*. Kansas City: Andrews McMeel Publishing, 1997.

Krause, Eugene F. *Taxicab Geometry: An Adventure in Non-Euclidean Geometry*. London: Dover, 1986.

Kristeva, Julia. *Desire in Language: A Semiotic Approach to Literature and Art*. Trans. Leon S. Roudiez et al. New York: Columbia University Press, 1980.

Kroker, Arthur, and David Cook. *The Postmodern Scene: Excremental Culture and Hyper-Aesthetics*. New York: St. Martin's Press, 1986.

Kroker, Arthur, and Marilouise Kroker. *Hacking the Future: Stories for the Flesh-Eating '90s*. New York: Palgrave, 1996.

Laplanche, Jean. *Life and Death in Psychoanalysis*. Trans. Jeffrey Mehlman. Baltimore: Johns Hopkins University Press, 1976.

Laplanche, Jean, and Jean-Bertrand Pontalis. *The Language of Psychoanalysis*. Trans. Donald Nicholson-Smith. New York: W. W. Norton, 1973. [*Le Vocabulaire de la psychanalyse*. Paris: Presses Universitaires de France, 1967.]

Lipovetsky, Gilles. *L'Ère du vide*. Paris: Gallimard, 1983.

Lodge, David, and Nigel Woods, eds. *Modern Criticism and Theory: A Reader*. London: Longman, 1988.

Loesberg, Jonathan. "Bourdieu and the Sociology of Aesthetics." *English Literary History* (ELH) 60 (1993), 1033–1056.

Lumsden, C. J., and E. O. Wilson. *Genes, Mind and Culture: The Coevolutionary Process*. Cambridge, Mass.: Harvard University Press, 1981.

Lyotard, Jean-François. *The Differend: Phrases in Dispute*. Trans. George van den Abbeele. [*Le différend*. Paris: Minuit, 1983.]

Lyotard, Jean-François. *Discours, figure*. Paris: Klincksieck, 1971.

Lyotard, Jean-François. *Économie libidinale*. Paris: Minuit, 1974.

Lyotard, Jean-François. *The Inhuman: Reflections on Time*. Trans. Geoffrey Bennington and Rachel Bowlby. Stanford.: Calif.: Stanford University Press, 1991. [*L'Inhuman: Causeries sur le temps*. Paris: Galilée, 1988.]

Lyotard, Jean-François. *The Postmodern Condition: A Report on Knowledge*. Trans. Geoffrey Bennington and Brian Massumi. Theory and History of Literature 20. Minneapolis: University of Minnesota Press, 1984.

Lyotard, Jean-François. "What Is Postmodernism?" In Lyotard, *The Postmodern Condition*. ["Réponse à la question: 'Qu'est-ce que le postmoderne?'" Critique, April 1982, 419–427.]

Mandelbrot, Benoit. *Fractal Geometry of Nature*. New York: Freeman, 1988.

Mandelbrot, Benoit. *Les Objets fractals*. Paris: Flammarion, 1995.

Marks, Elaine, and Isabelle de Courtivron, eds. *New French Feminisms: An Anthology*. New York: Schocken Books, 1981.

Marshall, Ian, and Danah Zohar. *Who's Afraid of Schrödinger's Cat? All the New Science Ideas You Need to Keep Up with the New Thinking.* New York: William Morrow, 1998.

McEvoy, J. P., Oscar Zarate, and Richard Appignanesi, eds. *Introduction to Quantum Theory.* New York: Totem Books, 2001.

Miller, Jacques-Alain. "Extimité." In Mark Bracher, et al., eds., *Lacanian Theory of Discourse: Subject, Structure, and Society.* New York: New York University Press, 1994/1997: 121–131.

Milnor, John W. *Topology from the Differentiable Viewpoint.* Princeton: Princeton University Press, 1997.

Minsky, Marvin. *The Society of Mind.* New York: Simon and Schuster, 1998.

Mitchell, Juliet, and Jacqueline Rose, eds. *Feminine Sexuality: Jacques Lacan and the École freudienne.* New York: W. W. Norton, 1983.

Moi, Toril, ed. *The Kristeva Reader.* New York: Columbia University Press, 1986.

Moritz, Elan. *Memetic Science: An Introduction.* Research Triangle, N.C.: Institute for Memetic Studies, 1990.

Nair, Rukmini Bhaya. *Technobrat: Culture in a Cybernetic Classroom.* New Delhi: HarperCollins India, 1997.

Negroponte, Nicholas. *Being Digital.* New York: Vintage, 1995.

Nicholson, Linda J., ed., *Feminism/Postmodernism.* New York: Routledge, 1990.

Ogilvy, C. Stanley. *Excursions in Geometry.* London: Dover, 1977.

Parfrey, Adam, ed. *Apocalypse Culture.* New York: Feral House, 1990.

Polchinski, Joseph Gerard. *String Theory: An Introduction to the Bosonic String.* Cambridge: Cambridge Monographs on Mathematical Physics, 1998.

Prigigone, Ilya. *From Being to Becoming: Time and Complexity in the Physical Sciences.* New York: W. H. Freeman, 1980.

Prigigone, Ilya, and D. Kondepudi. *Modern Thermodynamics: From Heat Engines to Dissipative Structures.* Chichester: Wiley, 1998.

Prigigone, Ilya, and G. Nicolis. *Exploring Complexity.* New York: Freeman, 1989.

Prigigone, Ilya, and G. Nicolis. *Self-Organization in Non-Equilibrium Systems: From Dissipative Structures to Order through Fluctuation.* New York: Wiley, 1977.

Prigigone, Ilya, and I. Stengers. *The End of Certainty: Time, Chaos and the New Laws of Nature.* New York: Free Press, 1997.

Prigigone, Ilya, and I. Stengers. *Nonequilibrium Statistical Mechanics.* New York: Wiley-Interscience, 1962.

Prigigone, Ilya, and I. Stengers. *Order Out of Chaos.* New York: Bantam, 1983.

Restak, Ronald, and David Grubin. *The Secret Life of the Brain.* Washington: National Academy Press, 2001.

Ronell, Avital. *Crack Wars: Literature, Addiction, Mania.* Lincoln: University of Nebraska Press, 1992.

Ronell, Avital. *Finitude's Score: Essays for the End of the Millennium*. Lincoln: University of Nebraska Press, 1994.

Ronell, Avital. *The Telephone Book: Technology, Schizophrenia, Electric Speech*. Lincoln: University of Nebraska Press, 1989.

Roudinesco, Élisabeth. *Jacques Lacan: Esquisse d'une vie, histoire d'un système de pensée*. Paris: Fayard, 1993.

Rucker, Rudolph B. *Geometry, Relativity, and the Fourth Dimension*. London: Dover, 1977.

Rudnytsky, Peter. *Psychoanalytic Conversations: Interviews with Clinicians, Commentators and Critics*. New York: Analytic Press, 2000.

Ryan, Patrick J. *Euclidean and Non-Euclidean Geometry*. Cambridge: Cambridge University Press, 1986.

Santner, Eric. *My Own Private Germany: Daniel Paul Schreber's Secret History of Modernity*. Princeton: Princeton University Press, 1996.

Saussure, Ferdinand de. *Course in General Linguistics*. Trans. Wade Baskin. New York: McGraw-Hill, 1966.

Schatzman, Morton. *Soul Murder: Persecution in the Family*. New York: New America Library, 1976.

Scherdtfeger, Hans. *Geometry of Complex Numbers: Circle Geometry, Moebius Transformation, Non-Euclidean Geometry*. London: Dover, 1980.

Schiller, H. I. *Information Inequality: The Deepening Social Crisis in America*. London: Routledge, 1996.

Schneiderman, Stuart. *Jacques Lacan: The Death of an Intellectual Hero*. Cambridge, Mass.: Harvard University Press, 1983.

Sellers, Susan, ed. *The Hélène Cixous Reader*. London: Routledge, 1994.

Showalter, Elaine. *Hystories: Hysterical Epidemics and Modern Media*. New York: Columbia University Press, 1997.

Siboni, Jacques. *Les Mathémes de Lacan. Anthologie des assertions entièrement transmissibles et de leurs relations dans les écrits de Jacques Lacan*. Paris: Lysimaque, 1997.

Silverman, Kaja. *World Spectators*. Stanford, Calif.: Stanford University Press, 2000.

Singer, Linda. *Erotic Welfare: Sexual Theory and Politics in the Age of Epidemic*. New York: Routledge, 1992.

Solms, Mark. "Is the Brain More Real than the Mind?" *Psychoanalytic Psychotherapy* 9 (1991), 21–35.

Solms, Mark. *A Moment of Transition: Two Neuroscientific Articles by Sigmund Freud*. London: Karnac Books, 1990.

Solms, Mark. *The Neuropsychology of Dreams: A Clinico-Anatomical Study*. Mahwah, N.J.: Lawrence Erlbaum and Associates, 1997.

Solms, Mark, and Karen Kaplan-Solms. *Clinical Studies in Neuro-Psychoanalysis: Introduction to a Depth Neuropsychology*. 2d ed. New York: Other Press, 2001.

Springer, Claudia. *Electronic Eros: Bodies and Desire in the Postindustrial Age*. Austin: University of Texas Press, 1996.

Stephenson, Neal. *Snow Crash*. New York: Bantam, 1992.

Sterling, Bruce. *Global Head*. New York: Bantam, 1994.

Sterling, Bruce, ed. *MirrorShades: The Cyberpunk Anthology*. New York: Bantam, 1986.

Stone, Allucquére Rosanne. *The War of Desire and Technology at the Close of the Mechanical Age*. Cambridge, Mass.: MIT Press, 1991.

Strathern, Paul. *Turing and the Computer*. New York: Anchor, 1999.

Teilhard de Chardin, Pierre. *Activation of Energy*. Trans. René Hague. Fort Washington, Penn.: Harvest, 1984.

Teilhard de Chardin, Pierre. *The Heart of Matter*. Trans. René Hague. Fort Washington, Penn.: Harvest, 1980.

Tomiche, Anne. "Rephrasing the Freudian Unconscious: Lyotard's Affect-Phrase." *Diacritics* 24, no. 1 (Spring 1994), 42–62.

Turkle, Sherry. *Life on the Screen: Identity in the Age of the Internet*. New York: Simon and Schuster, 1995.

Vattimo, Gianni. *Beyond Interpretation: The Meaning of Hermeneutics for Philosophy*. Trans. David Webb. Stanford, Calif.: Stanford University Press, 1997.

Vattimo, Gianni. *The End of Modernity: Nihilism and Hermeneutics in Postmodern Culture*. Trans. Jon R. Snyder. Baltimore: Johns Hopkins University Press, 1991.

Vattimo, Gianni. *The Transparent Society*. Trans. David Webb. Baltimore: Johns Hopkins University Press, 1991. [*La società trasparente*. Rome: Garzanti Libri, 2000.]

Venter, J. Craig. *Chacterization of Membrane Receptors*. Vol. 3 of *Receptor Biochemistry and Methodology*. New York: Wiley-Liss, 1984.

Virilio, Paul. *The Aesthetics of Disappearance*. New York: Semiotext(e), 1991.

Virilio, Paul. *The Information Bomb*. Trans. Chris Turner. London: Verso, 2001.

Virilio, Paul. *The Lost Dimension*. Trans. Daniel Moshenberg. New York: Semiotext(e), 1991.

Virilio, Paul. *Open Sky*. Trans. Julie Rose. London: Verso, 1997.

Wang, Hao. *Reflections on Kurt Gödel*. Cambridge, Mass.: MIT Press, 1990.

Webster, Richard. *Why Freud Was Wrong: Sin, Science, and Psychoanalysis*. New York: Lightning Source, 1996.

White, Haydn. *Metahistory: The Historical Imagination in Nineteenth-Century Europe*. Baltimore: Johns Hopkins University Press, 1973.

Wilden, Anthony. *The Language of the Self*. Baltimore: Johns Hopkins University Press, 1984.

Wright, Edmond, ed. Special issue on the work of Slavoj Žižek. *Paragraph* (July 2001) 24, no. 2.

Wright, Edmond, and Elizabeth Wright, eds. *The Žižek Reader*. Oxford: Blackwell, 1999.

Wright, Elizabeth. *Speaking Desires Can Be Dangerous: The Poetics of the Unconscious*. Oxford: Blackwell, 1999.

Zaya, Octavio, and Candice Breitz, eds. *Atlantica: Revista de las Artes. Special Bilingual Issue: Transmisiones Terminales/Terminal Transmissions*. New York and Canary Islands: Centro Atlantico de Arte Moderno, 1997.

Žižek, Slavoj. *Cogito and the Unconscious*. Durham: Duke University Press, 1998.

Žižek, Slavoj. *Looking Awry: An Introduction to Jacques Lacan through Popular Culture*. Cambridge, Mass.: MIT Press, 1992.

Žižek, Slavoj. *The Plague of Fantasies*. London: Verso, 1997.

Žižek, Slavoj. *The Sublime Object of Ideology*. London: Verso, 1989.

Žižek, Slavoj. *The Ticklish Subject: The Absent Center of Political Ontology*. London: Verso, 1999.

Zupančič, Alenka. *Ethics of the Real: Kant, Lacan*. London: Verso, 2000.

Unless otherwise noted, all computer graphics are by Roger Groce, 2004.

Page 19: Oil on canvas. From *Scenes from a Nap*. By permission of the artist.

Page 31: From the Visible Human Project Gallery, United States National Library of Medicine, National Institutes of Health <http://www.nlm.nih.gov/research/visible/visible_gallery.html> (November 13, 2003). Images provided by Michael D. Ackerman, Ph.D.

Page 43: By permission of the artist and <http://www.rebelartist.com>.

Page 78: By permission of The National Gallery, London.

Page 91: By permission of the artist.

Page 117: Watercolor on paper. By permission of the artist.

Page 119: Modeled by Roger Groce after a template at the University of Oregon Mathematics Department website <http://darkwing.uoregon.edu/~math/ma.pictures/mobiusknot> (March 2, 2002), by permission of the authors.

Page 121: Modeled by Roger Groce after an image at the University of Minnesota website <http://www.geom.umn.edu/graphics/images/medium/Special_Topics/Topology>, by permission of the authors.

Page 133: Used by professional usage agreement, November 20, 2003 <http://www.rebelartist.com>

Page 141: By permission of the photographer, Mark D. Phillips <http://www.interstellarimages.com>.

Page 157: Toned gelatin silver print. By permission of the artist.

Page 183: Modeled by Roger Groce after <http://www.geocities.com/Eureka/Plaza/4033/sierpinski_index.en.html> (March 15, 2002).

Page 185: Modeled by Roger Groce after an image at the University of Minnesota website <http://www.geom.umn.edu/apps/unifweb/html> (March 1, 2002), by permission of the authors.

Page 191: From <http://pages.infinit.net/garrick/fractals/sierpinski.html> (May 18, 2002).

Page 194: Modeled by Roger Groce after an image by Eric W. Weisstein at <http://mathworld.wolfram.com/Tetrix.html> (March 2, 2002).

Page 195: Image by Andy Burbanks, from <http://www.lboro.ac.uk/departments/ma/gallery/hyper/cube.html> (June 5, 1997).

INDEX

blot (Hitchcock), 70–73
body, 22, 25, 28–38, 40, 52, 72, 76, 88, 95,
   99, 111, 121, 152, 163–165, 179, 207,
   224–232, 244. *See also* corporeal; corpse
   in crisis, 32–36
   parts, 31, 64, 103, 137
bomb, 13, 38, 233, 239, 240
border, 4, 5, 143, 210, 233, 237, 246, 261
   borderless war, 4, 5, 143
   borderless world, 210
Borromean knot, 120, 121, 123, 203, 208,
   230
bot, 111, 185
botany, 175, 176
boundary, 13, 32, 33, 53, 54, 74, 110, 138,
   143, 160, 171, 180, 213, 219, 225, 234,
   261
Boy shape, 254, 255, 260
braid, 118, 119, 127
brain, 6, 9, 22, 28, 103, 135, 150, 153, 192,
   224, 252, 265
breaching (computer), 77, 126. *See also*
   passing
bricolage, 246
brink, 112, 123, 164, 178, 210, 251, 260,
   266
bundling, 148
butterfly effect, 191. *See also* chaos: theory
bypass, 118, 219, 256, 257

cadaver. *See* body; corpse
calling, 48, 126, 162, 163, 184, 198, 226.
   See also interpellation
camera, 14, 225, 228. *See also* surveillance
cannibalism, 74, 87, 101
ça parle, 236. *See also* Unconscious
capitalism, 7, 26, 94, 96, 97, 103, 168, 233
capture, 36, 71, 106, 135, 151, 178, 229,
   235
Cartesianism, 30, 34, 41, 185, 225, 232,
   236. *See also* dualism; *name index under*
   Descartes
case history, 25, 93, 129, 174, 179, 235
castration, 55, 61, 64, 97, 98, 108, 109,
   138, 165, 167, 218
   anxiety, 108, 138, 167
   complex, 57. *See also* Oedipus: complex
catalyst, 112
catastrophe, 29, 112, 143, 145, 164, 168,
   210, 251. *See also* apocalypse

cathexis, 9, 11, 101, 188, 197, 202, 215,
   250, 251, 263. *See also* connection; investment; linkage
causality, 4, 8, 11, 97, 138, 143, 184, 231,
   239, 250
CBS, 14, 135
cell, 15, 135, 138, 143, 149, 154, 159, 168,
   192, 207
cellular phone, 4, 15, 225
centering, 95, 133, 138
certainty, 20, 61, 65, 86, 87
chain, 38, 47, 88, 97, 103, 105, 112, 158,
   160, 200, 208, 209, 213, 218, 253
   signifying, 36, 56, 128, 195–198, 205, 214
chance, 14, 75, 76, 128, 148, 207, 231
chaos, 12, 44, 112, 121, 139, 148, 158, 185,
   188, 191, 207, 251, 264
   theory, 12, 75, 138, 154, 158, 191
chat (Internet), 4, 20, 36, 38, 41, 162, 224,
   226
   room, 40, 111
chemical reactions, 97, 103, 251. *See also*
   catalyst
Che vuoi?, 242
chiasmus, 55, 162
child, 4, 22, 58, 61, 85, 101, 108, 109, 130,
   163, 165, 173, 178, 202, 210, 218, 233,
   237, 252, 253. *See also* infant; parents
childhood, 74, 178, 237
Child Find, 4
chip, 135, 146, 233
chronic fatigue syndrome, 142
chronology, 4, 10, 124, 250. *See also* time
cipher, 130, 131, 144. *See also* code
circuit, 20, 27, 36, 40, 49, 51, 56, 58, 70,
   77, 94–96, 103–110, 113, 135, 136, 146–
   150, 164, 193, 210, 216, 218, 243, 252,
   257, 262
   directional, 148
   integrated, 149
   interrupted, 105, 147, 220
   long, 37, 58, 94, 106, 108, 252
   making and breaking, 106, 108
   short circuit, 35, 61, 64, 71, 95, 106, 107,
   147
   social, 58, 95, 110
   stable, 146, 149
   switched, 147
circuitousness, 40, 106, 108, 133, 134. *See*
   also detour

emotion, 41, 129, 136, 151, 167, 175, 219
Emperor's new clothes, 86, 204
end of analysis, 63, 214
end of the line, 34, 128, 236
end of the world, 52, 86
enemy, 6, 32, 75, 92, 153, 177, 211
energy, 10, 27, 70, 71, 94–97, 103, 108,
   111, 112, 150, 153, 154, 158, 159, 172,
   210, 251
engineering diagram, 10, 102–109, 118,
   139, 198, 205
enigma, 15, 39, 49, 61, 113, 240. See also
   code; sphinx
enjoyment, 56, 61, 64
enlightenment, 29, 30, 68, 77, 108, 131,
   150, 202, 212, 219, 226, 227, 237, 238,
   244
epidemic, 5, 29, 94. See also contagion;
   virus
episteme, 12, 60, 87, 127, 160, 171, 208
equilibrium, 138, 150, 158, 251. See also far
   from equilibrium
eroticism, 20, 63, 101, 106, 164, 165, 244
error, 9, 15, 34, 38, 87, 150, 208, 240
ethics, 4, 6, 7, 9, 23, 77, 94, 135, 166, 173,
   226, 237
Europe, 29, 118, 234, 237
Eve, 30, 129. See also Adam; Genesis; Visible
   Human Project
Eve of Destruction, 165
evil, 41, 71, 74, 75, 86, 87, 96, 142
evolution, 33, 149, 176, 207, 231, 232
ex-centric, 131, 224, 261
excess, 35, 38, 68, 71, 82, 101, 106, 137,
   164, 202, 209, 235. See also remainder
exchange, 12, 71, 88, 118, 176, 263. See also
   cloverleaf; dialogue; interaction; juncture; switch
exclusive disjunction, 94, 98
exhibitionism, 29, 164, 168, 209, 245
exile, 57, 96
existentialism, 82, 235
exogamy, 58
exoticism, 73, 136, 145, 161, 245
expansion, 5, 145, 150, 154, 161, 205, 208,
   209, 217, 219, 260
exposure, 46, 68, 94, 104, 105, 106, 246
exterior, 219, 224, 236, 237, 238
external, 13, 15, 82, 147, 224, 253, 254,
   255

externalization, 64
extimacy (extimité), 82, 217, 219, 224,
   236, 237–238, 246, 253, 254, 255, 258–
   265
extrasensory perception, 140
extraterrestrial, 14, 112, 136, 244. See also
   alien
eye, 4, 13, 14, 15, 32–36, 68, 71, 74, 77, 87,
   88, 123, 144, 231. See also opticality
   disembodied, 135
   human, 14, 15, 71
   mechanical, 136

facilitation, 11, 12, 13, 148, 174, 175. See also
   Bahnungen
family, 55, 58, 61, 63, 96, 97, 106, 118,
   166, 173, 209, 210, 213, 217, 218, 224,
   237, 263
   Oedipus, 165
   romance, 10, 22, 39, 55, 63, 92, 95, 96,
     98, 100, 103, 166, 173, 235. See also oedi-
     pal: triangle; patriarchy
fantasm, 5, 15, 23, 32, 38, 62, 64, 129, 135,
   137, 142, 168, 244
fantasy, 7, 10, 13, 25, 26, 28, 31, 35, 39,
   46, 56, 61, 62, 69, 80–82, 85, 102, 106,
   108, 118, 144, 154, 165, 168, 179, 205
   fundamental, 64
   traversing, 56, 64, 69
far from equilibrium, 150, 158, 176, 180–
   181, 197, 230, 251, 264, 266
fascination, 13, 15, 20, 31, 69, 82, 136, 137,
   167, 168, 218, 231, 244. See also fixation;
   hypnosis
fascism, 101, 218
fashion, 73, 92, 176, 206
fate, 4, 22, 33, 55, 68, 76, 164
father, 47, 61
   the Dead, 58
   devouring, 62
   oedipal, 6, 9, 37, 60, 62, 87, 93, 96, 97,
     103, 107, 108, 147, 151, 161, 166, 178,
     179, 202, 212, 219, 235–237, 252, 253
   real, 62
fear. See anxiety
feedback, 146
   loop, 73, 149
feint, 47, 64, 65
   as appearing to lie, 47
   symbolic, 47

psychoanalysis, 3. *See also* analysand; analyst; Freud; Lacan; transference
criticism of, 3–15, 92–113
and culture, 77
and cyberspace, 10, 32–38, 47–65
Deleuze and, 88–96, 98, 99, 100, 101, 102
as field, 51, 127
and fractal psyche, 184
and gender, 154, 167, 177
and knot theory, 118, 124
and millennialism, 12–54, 118, 126–130, 134, 148, 150
nonlinear, 250, 253, 265–266
and opticality, 14, 133, 190
and Otherness, 224, 230, 232, 237, 246
as precursor of new science, 12
as therapy, 126
and Žižek, 78–82
psychosis, 25, 29, 35, 38, 49, 52, 53, 55, 56, 60, 63, 65, 69, 78, 82, 83, 84, 86, 87, 94, 97, 174, 178, 233, 251. *See also* disease
psychosomatic illness, 232, 263
public, 15, 20, 22, 29, 31, 32, 47, 71, 74, 97, 138, 140, 142, 143, 159, 161, 238, 244
space, 71
pulsion, 118, 167. *See also* drive
pun, 13, 46, 87, 129, 130, 131. *See also* joke; overdetermination; wordplay
punch line, 104, 105, 106, 109, 110, 113, 131
punishment, 28
punk, 29, 229
purloined letter, 37, 84, 86, 88, 104, 260
puzzle. *See* cipher; enigma
Pygmalion, 137, 229

quadratic equation, 119, 121, 122, 125, 131, 151, 154, 172, 184, 188, 189, 193, 196, 203, 207, 218, 228, 254. *See also* algorithm; geometry; set theory
quantum theory, 139, 154, 170, 172, 175, 185, 188, 195, 234, 251, 253
quark, 159

racism, 7, 166, 168, 237
radical materialism, 140, 142, 180
radical Otherness, 95, 240

rainbow, 94, 109, 113. *See also* smooth space; striated space
Raulians, 140. *See also* alien; cloning
rave, 229
reader, 188, 192, 253. *See also* third; writer
real (Lacanian), 24, 70, 80–84, 117, 177, 179, 232–235, 239
answer of, 233, 243
automatism of, 103
effect of, 136, 230
and imaginary/symbolic, 81, 82, 86, 98, 117, 121, 142, 227, 230
little piece of the real (*peu du réel*), 59, 60, 81, 86, 88, 237
return of, 30, 41, 69, 83
reality. *See also* hyperreal
Cartesian, 20, 23
difference from Lacanian real, 232
and dream, 4, 14, 15
intersubjective, 246
material, 26, 53, 162
as socio-symbolic construct, 30, 38, 41, 48, 53, 60, 69, 75, 80, 86, 119, 136, 142, 145, 149, 162, 165
torn fabric of (psychosis), 83
virtual, 20, 35, 38, 40, 48, 53
reality TV, 4, 14, 29, 165
real numbers, 196
reason (rationality), 15, 30, 136, 143, 173, 224, 232
rebus, 11, 129, 132
receptivity, 34, 76, 77
recognition (*reconnaissance*), 34, 40, 81, 83, 108, 139, 202, 211. *See also* misrecognition
recovered memory movement, 7, 142
recursion, 37, 38, 131, 160, 185, 188, 190, 201, 202, 206, 208, 212, 263, 266
Red Shoe Diaries, 27
referee. *See* authority; subject: subject supposed to know; umpire
reference, 11, 13, 41, 51, 56, 78, 131, 145, 152, 184, 197, 208, 224, 258, 262
reflection, 22, 33, 40, 47, 73, 75, 95, 137, 158, 191, 203, 216
refraction, 4, 15, 37, 87, 88, 100, 134, 188, 203, 235, 236, 264
regression, 12, 13, 52, 62, 65, 96, 105, 203
regulation. *See* discipline; self-regulation
relational universe, 122, 123, 161, 174, 185, 188, 199, 262–266. *See also* contingency

Scylla and Charybdis, 112
seamlessness, 232
search, 10, 12, 14, 15, 24, 36, 38, 39, 40, 41, 48, 74, 80, 93, 106, 111, 134, 139, 165, 210
    engine, 10, 14, 93, 111
secondary process, 251. *See also* primary process
seduction, 35, 52, 56, 61, 70, 104, 164, 176, 180, 243, 245. *See also* eroticism
    Freud's theory of, 188
seed, 5, 128
segmented linkage, 214, 217
self, 22, 23, 50, 53, 88, 103, 172, 189, 211, 228
self-consciousness, 4, 15, 125, 224, 228
self-evidence, 209, 230, 238
self-image, 22, 30, 34, 36, 46, 50, 87, 109, 203, 211
self-organization, 103, 112, 138, 139, 148, 149, 158–160, 188, 206–208
self-perpetuation (replication), 71, 134, 213, 220
self-regulation, 149
self-similarity, 151, 189–191, 197, 203, 207, 208, 213, 216, 220. *See also* fractal
September 11, 136, 140, 141, 233
set theory, 185, 197, 263
sex, 6, 9, 15, 20, 30, 53, 63, 72, 101, 104, 143, 161, 162, 163, 164, 165, 171, 172, 175, 245
    appeal, 165
    object, 20
sexuality, 7, 30, 34, 53, 56, 58, 62, 71, 95, 100, 101, 118, 129, 158, 164, 169, 173, 179, 209, 210, 212, 232, 245, 257
shamanism, 173
shift, 146, 158, 171, 173, 184, 188, 236, 237. *See also* skew
shifter, 44
shifting, 4, 11, 12, 34, 41, 45, 47, 51, 55, 78, 84, 122, 127, 131, 134, 140, 144, 188, 201, 218, 235, 251, 263. *See also* displacement
sibling, 109, 166, 251
sidestep, 78, 256. *See also* looking awry
Sierpinski sponge, 193–194
Sierpinski triangle, 191, 209
sight, 14, 34, 56, 68, 78, 101, 135, 167, 224

sighting, 13, 138
signal, 26, 134, 144, 147, 232, 266
signification, 69, 128, 199, 202, 232
signified, 34, 202, 212, 261
signifier, 36, 38, 44, 75, 88, 96, 97, 128, 197, 201, 214, 236
Signifier of Signifiers, 236
Simone, 137, 161, 162
simulacra, 24, 52, 53, 73, 164
simulation, 48, 152, 178
Simulations, 24, 25
simultaneity, 53, 127, 136, 137, 145, 188, 193
    two places at one time, 253
single dimension, 125, 184
singularity, 138, 250. *See also* black hole
site. *See also* website
    as heraldic field, 128, 129, 132, 135, 143–145, 148, 152, 154
    as intersubjective field, 45, 57, 59, 60
    as millennial web, 118–121, 125
    millennium as, 4–13
    nonorientable, 255, 261–263
    of the Other (extimacy), 30–38, 40, 192, 196, 198, 207, 209, 227, 230, 231, 234–237, 238, 240, 244
    Oz as utopic, 95, 98, 103, 110, 111
    para-, 4, 144
    political, 101, 160, 180
siting/sighting/citing, 13, 92
skepticism, 88. *See also* belief; disbelief; paranoia
skew, 83, 122, 144. *See also* anamorphosis; projection; shifting
"Slaves Are Us," 62. *See also* sadomasochism
sleuth, 10, 12, 84, 85
slide, 31, 53, 128
slip, 127, 128, 129, 130, 161, 236, 263
slipknot, 127, 128
smooth space, 102, 110, 113, 193
social field, 23, 88, 101, 102, 123, 208, 219, 237
social network, 33, 39, 149, 150
social process, 210, 212, 240
socialization, 10, 76, 95, 100, 108, 109, 224, 263
society, 23, 36, 38, 39, 40, 51, 56, 58, 65, 91, 101, 102, 108, 109, 110, 161, 193, 198, 201, 202, 213, 219, 227, 253
    of spectacle, 226

unveiling. *See* exposure; punch line; veiling
utopia, 32, 54, 92, 94, 135, 140

vagina, 138. *See also* genitalia
valence, 125, 129, 135, 137, 165, 174, 175, 176, 184, 203
vampire, 31, 168
vanishing point. *See* perspective
vantage point, 23, 78, 80
variations on a theme, 131
vector, 10, 165, 235
veiling (*Ankleidung*), 64, 106, 142, 168, 245
velocity, 5, 145, 170, 191, 228, 230
viability, 3, 118, 123
vicissitudes, 15, 36, 63, 118, 147, 149, 154, 162, 166, 188, 209, 236
  of gender, 162
  of the subject, 36
video game, 4, 72, 164, 165
video performance, 30
viewer. *See* spectator
violence, 4, 8, 20, 30, 31, 73, 220
virginity, 96
virtual, 30, 31, 35, 36, 48, 55, 57, 60, 110, 127, 147, 165, 167, 230
  addiction, 72
  reality, 20–27, 35, 38, 40, 41, 48, 52, 53, 162
  simulacra, 52
  world, 20
virus, 4, 13, 20, 23, 28, 71, 74, 76, 92, 110, 135, 143, 153, 164, 206, 233, 240, 263
viscosity, 10, 112, 172, 191
visibility, 27, 30, 68, 70, 71, 75, 77, 80, 81, 88, 98, 202, 244
Visible Human Project, 31
vision, 9, 23, 26, 29, 33–37, 45, 59, 64, 69–81, 88, 103, 113, 121, 129, 131, 142, 145, 188, 191, 194, 196, 202, 207, 224, 238. *See also* eye; opticality
  stereoscopic, 135
visual, 14, 15, 22, 29, 34, 35, 37, 47, 64, 68, 70, 74, 78, 80, 81, 83, 87, 88, 133–138, 145, 154, 167, 190, 192, 228
  field, 15, 22, 34, 78, 80, 136
vitalism, 142, 152, 153, 159, 226, 243
voice, 38, 39, 41, 83, 86, 88, 145, 214, 225, 228, 231, 238
void, vacuum, 28, 73, 74, 82, 83, 130, 239
voyage, 36, 113

voyeurism, 30, 31, 136, 218
vulnerability, 23, 106, 143

waking experience, 11, 201, 233, 250
wandering, 40, 87. *See also* nomad
war, 4, 8, 26, 33, 48, 74, 102, 112, 135, 148, 157, 228, 239
  machine (Deleuze), 169–171
  of the sexes, 245
warp, 134, 138, 145, 161, 201, 245, 250, 266. *See also* propulsion; time
wasp. *See* orchid and wasp
Wasteland, The, 30
Watt, 131
wave-particle duality, 159
weapon, 193, 239
weather, 94, 112, 135, 142, 174, 195
web, 11, 24, 35, 36, 38, 40, 69, 110, 118, 127, 129, 132, 135, 145, 154, 192, 201, 205, 209, 227, 228, 261. *See also* net; network; node
website, 30, 38, 41, 63, 151, 190, 197
Weltanschauung, 265
Who's on First?, 44, 46, 47, 51, 56, 65
Wired, 20
wish, 10, 100, 202, 211, 232, 250
wit, 4, 11, 13, 28, 49, 61, 71, 85, 153, 159, 177, 178, 207, 236, 240, 246, 260. *See also* humor; joke
woman, 20, 26, 32, 58, 93, 104, 105, 106, 129, 138, 162–179, 209, 224, 245
wordplay, 13. *See also* joke; overdetermination; pun
words as things (Freud), 12, 27
work. *See* dream; joke
World Trade Center, 136, 140, 233
world view, 29, 184, 188, 227, 231, 258. *See also* episteme; *Weltanschauung*; zeitgeist
wormholes, 110, 266
wounding, 40, 62, 108, 211, 218
writer, 38, 78, 83, 104, 106, 180. *See also* artist
writing, 60, 74, 76, 92, 121, 131, 138, 160, 173, 175, 178, 179, 210, 218

xenophobia, 168, 234, 237, 246
x-ray, 13

Y2K, 3, 5, 6, 9, 31, 124, 154, 162, 244
yes-no rhythm. *See* fort-da